IN PURSUIT OF PLURALIST JURISPRUDENCE

The pluralist turn in jurisprudence has led to a search for new ways of thinking about law. The relationships between state law and other legal orders such as international, customary, transnational or indigenous law are particularly significant in this development. Collecting together new work by leading scholars in the field, this volume considers the basic questions about what would be an appropriate theoretical response to this shift: How precisely is it to be undertaken? Is it called for by developments in legal practice or are these adequately addressed by current legal theory? What normative challenges are raised, and what fresh promises might the pluralist turn hold? What distinctive insights can it offer for theorising about law? This book presents a rich variety of resources drawn from a number of theoretical approaches and demonstrates how they might be brought together to generate an increasingly important pluralist jurisprudence.

NICOLE ROUGHAN is the author of *Authorities: Conflicts, Cooperation and Transnational Legal Theory* (2013) and is working on a new monograph, *Officials*. She is a recipient of a 2016 Rutherford Discovery Fellowship from the Royal Society of New Zealand Te Apārangi, to undertake a major research project on Jurisprudence without Borders.

ANDREW HALPIN has published widely in areas of legal theory, including on the impact novel legal phenomena arising in a global context have had upon general theories of law. He has previously co-edited a collection of essays, *Theorising the Global Legal Order* (2009).

IN PURSUIT OF PLURALIST JURISPRUDENCE

Edited by

NICOLE ROUGHAN
National University of Singapore
ANDREW HALPIN
National University of Singapore

CAMBRIDGE
UNIVERSITY PRESS

CAMBRIDGE
UNIVERSITY PRESS

University Printing House, Cambridge CB2 8BS, United Kingdom

One Liberty Plaza, 20th Floor, New York, NY 10006, USA

477 Williamstown Road, Port Melbourne, VIC 3207, Australia

314-321, 3rd Floor, Plot 3, Splendor Forum, Jasola District Centre, New Delhi - 110025, India

79 Anson Road, #06-04/06, Singapore 079906

Cambridge University Press is part of the University of Cambridge.

It furthers the University's mission by disseminating knowledge in the pursuit of education, learning and research at the highest international levels of excellence.

www.cambridge.org
Information on this title: www.cambridge.org/9781107183964
DOI: 10.1017/9781316875056

First published 2017

A catalogue record for this publication is available from the British Library

Library of Congress Cataloging in Publication data
Names: Roughan, Nicole, editor. | Halpin, Andrew (Law teacher), editor.
Title: In pursuit of pluralist jurisprudence / edited by Nicole Roughan, National University of Singapore, Andrew Halpin, National University of Singapore.
Description: Cambridge [UK] : Cambridge University Press, 2017. | Includes bibliographical references and index.
Identifiers: LCCN 2017013048 | ISBN 9781107183964 (hardback : alk. paper)
Subjects: LCSH: Legal polycentricity. | Law–Philosophy. | Jurisprudence.
Classification: LCC K236 .I573 2017 | DDC 340.9–dc23 LC record available at https://lccn.loc.gov/2017013048

ISBN 978-1-107-18396-4 Hardback
ISBN 978-1-108-70725-1 Paperback

CONTENTS

CONTRIBUTORS

KIRSTEN ANKER
Associate Professor, Faculty of Law, McGill University

ROGER COTTERRELL
Anniversary Professor of Legal Theory, School of Law, Queen Mary University of London

MARGARET DAVIES
Matthew Flinders Distinguished Professor, Flinders Law School, Flinders University

MAKSYMILIAN DEL MAR
Reader in Legal Theory, School of Law, Queen Mary University of London

ANDREW HALPIN
Professor, Faculty of Law, National University of Singapore

MARTIN KRYGIER
Gordon Samuels Professor of Law and Social Theory, School of Law, University of New South Wales

CORMAC MAC AMHLAIGH
Senior Lecturer, Edinburgh Law School, University of Edinburgh

RALF MICHAELS
Arthur Larson Professor of Law, Duke University School of Law

JOSEPH RAZ
Thomas M. Macioce Professor of Law at Columbia Law School;

Professor (part-time) Kings College London, and Emeritus Research Professor, University of Oxford, Faculty of Law

NICOLE ROUGHAN
Associate Professor, Faculty of Law, National University of Singapore

STEFAN SCIARAFFA
Associate Professor, Department of Philosophy, McMaster University

SANNE TAEKEMA
Professor, Erasmus School of Law, Erasmus University

DETLEF VON DANIELS
Academic Coordinator of the research group, International Justice and Institutional Responsibility, Freie Berlin-Brandenburg Academy of Sciences and Humanities

NEIL WALKER
Regius Professor of Public Law and the Law of Nature and Nations, Edinburgh Law School, University of Edinburgh

ACKNOWLEDGEMENTS

This collection and its accompanying conference were made possible by the expert administrative assistance provided by Elizabeth Chua, Yvonne Lim, Wendy Wee and Kris Zhao and the conscientious research assistance of Bryan Ching, Ryan Hong and Carmen Sin. The editors are grateful for their help as well as the participation and encouragement of a number of colleagues in the Centre for Legal Theory at NUS Law.

We would also like to extend our thanks to Joe Ng at Cambridge University Press, who has been an effective and supportive publisher throughout the project. We gratefully acknowledge financial support for the research undertaken for this book from the Singapore Ministry of Education Academic Research Fund Tier 1, project number: R-241-000-129-112.

1

Introduction

NICOLE ROUGHAN AND ANDREW HALPIN

1.1 Preliminary Remarks

This book presents both advocacy and critique of a number of approaches to what is described as Pluralist Jurisprudence – theories of law moving beyond, within or without the state. Pluralist Jurisprudence, with its interest in phenomena such as customary law, international/regional law, transnational law, religious law, indigenous law and global law, takes seriously both the theoretical challenges of exploring these orders in themselves and the challenges they pose to state-centric/monist jurisprudential theories.

The objective of collecting the present contributions together in a single volume is to provide a metatheoretical interrogation of pluralist jurisprudence, its scope, its aims, its methodologies, and its distinctiveness. This objective was advanced at a conference held at the Centre for Legal Theory in the Faculty of Law, National University of Singapore, in February 2015. Most of the chapters in this book first saw light as papers delivered at that conference. In addition, the book contains a paper originally delivered by Joseph Raz as the inaugural Singapore Symposium in Legal Theory in January 2014,[1] a further chapter from Kirsten Anker commissioned for this book, and a joint reflection by the editors on the promises and pursuits of pluralist jurisprudence.

The volume does not present a united front. Instead it features scholars offering a variety of approaches to pluralist jurisprudence yielding quite different insights but willing to engage directly in foundational questions. From sociologists of law to theorists of legal reasoning, from critical theorists to scholars of liberal constitutionalism, and from conceptual analysts to theorists of the rule of law, the contributors neither assume nor take for granted the significance of

[1] We have retained the content and style of the oral presentation for its inclusion in this book.

pluralist jurisprudence. Rather, they examine whether, how and to what ends it can or should be pursued.

It is customary to use an editorial introduction to offer a frame that will illuminate the contributions and spell out their thematic connections to one another. In our view, however, the image of a frame is inapposite for an interrogation of pluralist jurisprudence. The subject matter of pluralist jurisprudence is itself contested and obscure, and the prospect of providing a clear picture bordered by a firm frame appears misguided, if not simply undeliverable. The title of the book perhaps conveys a more appropriate image. The pursuit of pluralist jurisprudence is suggestive of a chase, possibly with no quarry in sight. It suggests tracking an elusive object across terrain that may be open, or cluttered with obstacles; even, littered with the remnants of prior pursuits. The image also suggests the possibility that the pursuit itself may be fanciful, or fruitless; that it may simply fail. Nevertheless, our aim as editors, and also as contributors to this volume, is to collect the insights the authors have generously provided from a rich abundance of perspectives, and to fashion out of them a portrayal of pluralist jurisprudence that captures its qualities and potentialities, without seeking to bring it into captivity.

One obvious way to commence a more detailed setting for the interrogation of pluralist jurisprudence is by way of establishing a contrast with non-pluralist jurisprudence. But even at this preliminary point the contestability of our subject matter does not permit a sharp contrast to be made. Among the central challenges in producing a portrayal of pluralist jurisprudence are considering the precise extent to which it can be regarded as differing from non-pluralist jurisprudence, to what extent it requires new tools and methodologies, and to what extent it is called upon to deal with material that non-pluralist jurisprudence is unequipped to deal with.

The cumbersome phrase, non-pluralist jurisprudence, suggests that the problem of contestation does not commence with pluralist jurisprudence alone but is already present in its comparand. What precisely did we understand by the condition of jurisprudence before pluralist jurisprudence came along and jostled with it in a bid for special recognition? Without being committed to a definitive understanding of pre-pluralist jurisprudence, or taking a side on what might determine a significant distinction between pluralist and non-pluralist jurisprudence, it is helpful to point to a temporal point of departure from non-pluralist jurisprudence that can be noted without controversy as the impetus for contemporary interest in pluralist jurisprudence. Connected to that observation, it is also possible to note (again, uncontroversially) a key feature that has been associated with the scope of pluralist jurisprudence, and has been marked out as the basis for its distinctive recognition. In simple terms, we can take the relatively recent enthusiasm of the past couple of decades or so with the phenomena of non-state law as prompting the call for a pluralist jurisprudence; and at the same time we can regard its distinctive scope as dealing with the phenomena of non-state law in a way that traditional jurisprudence had neglected.

In these simple terms, traditional jurisprudence is municipal or state-centric jurisprudence. Even if it touches upon international law, it does so from a state-centric, Westphalian perspective of viewing international law through the agency or authority of states. It remains, in that sense, monist.[2] By contrast, pluralist jurisprudence involves the recognition of non-state law in a way that is independent of both the agency and the authority of states. In order to get the discussion started, there is some value in going along with this simple view, taking non-pluralist jurisprudence to be an established jurisprudential preoccupation with state law and in that sense to be monist in outlook; and to take that as having recently been challenged by a growing concern to recognise non-state legal phenomena, and with that recognition to acknowledge the plural bases of law beyond the state, together with their interactions, so requiring a pluralist jurisprudence.

Although this move is helpful in getting the discussion started, we shall see that the subsequent discussion soon becomes reflexive, turning in on the simplicity of this starting point. For one thing, whatever traditional jurisprudence might have been considered to be, jurisprudential thought prior to the recent awakening of interest in a pluralist jurisprudence was far from homogenous. Strong disagreements could be detected in traditional jurisprudence between and among analytical/empirical, philosophical/sociological, descriptive/normative, positivist/non-positivist approaches, and vehement oppositions which split even those approaches broadly agreeing on an appropriate intellectual emphasis (empirical, philosophical, critical) while remaining utterly at odds over the effective way of delivering it. For another thing, the mere expansion of the scope of jurisprudence to take in non-state law does not

[2] This sense of monist is wide enough to embrace both 'monist' and 'dualist' understandings of the relationship between municipal law and international law. As Cormac Mac Amhlaigh points out in Chapter 4, these conventionally used terms amount to a reordering of hierarchy between municipal and international legal orders within a non-pluralist perspective.

necessarily require a different jurisprudence, with different tools and different methodologies. Perhaps the old jurisprudence could simply be diverted to take account of the new phenomena; perhaps we are still simply dealing with questions of legality, normativity and legitimacy, which could be answered with the resources already available.

Taking these two points together, we can recognise the situation arising out of the relationship between monist and pluralist jurisprudence as being particularly complex. If traditional monist jurisprudence is fragmented into a number of competing intellectual approaches, the call for a novel pluralist jurisprudence might (opportunistically or legitimately) be directed in a partisan manner to promoting one of those previously existing approaches while criticising the inadequacies of another, as much as it might be a call for a truly original approach to be discovered. We are, accordingly, soon presented with an array of possibilities in charting the relationship between monist jurisprudence [MJ] and pluralist jurisprudence [PJ].

Some possibilities would effectively preserve a conventional MJ, of which the most straightforward would be: (1) PJ simply requires the tools and methodologies of MJ to be applied to an expanded field of phenomena. Additionally, there might be some input into the concerns of MJ, as where: (2) Dealing with the expanded field of phenomena found in PJ demonstrates the superiority of Approach_{A} from MJ over Approach_{B} from MJ. Alternatively, there might be no commerce between the two: (3) Whatever is required for an effective PJ does not touch upon the appropriateness of an effective approach to MJ.

Other possibilities would not preserve a conventional MJ. So, we might find that radical modification is called for, where: (4) Dealing with the expanded field of phenomena found in PJ requires a completely novel approach, Approach_{N}, which entails a modification of MJ due to the inadequacy or incorrectness of any of the approaches found in MJ. Here the modified MJ would sit alongside the novel PJ without being integrated within it. That amounts to a further possibility: (5) Approach_{N} adopted for PJ implies the inadequacy of any of the approaches found in MJ, and should be taken as supplanting them all in a common jurisprudence of state and non-state law.

Another possibility is that the fresh requirements of PJ exert a synthesising influence over the rival approaches within MJ: (6) Approach_{N} adopted for PJ requires a composite of the different approaches found in MJ, thus revealing their true compatibility in a common jurisprudence of state and non-state law. Alternatively, there is the possibility that: (7) There is no singular $Approach_N$ appropriate for the different phenomena found in PJ but a diversity of approaches is required by PJ, so providing no stable relationship with MJ.

This brief sketch of some of the possible relationships between monist and pluralist jurisprudence is better amplified through considering the substantive arguments of the contributions to this book, but a number of other preliminary points are worth making here, before surveying these contributions in detail.

One important point to note (which is latent in the array of different possibilities just enumerated) is that the contestability, or instability, that might be found in monist and pluralist jurisprudence can extend to the notion of pluralism itself. This involves a number of factors. First there is the potential move from a mere recognition of plurality to the adoption of pluralism. A plurality of phenomena might be fitted under a monist perspective, which dictates how exactly each of the phenomena will be regarded in accordance with the dominant understanding it imposes. (Only state law is truly law, and the great variety of other law-like phenomena must be understood as failing in different respects to fully exhibit the qualities of law.) What changes when a pluralist perspective is adopted? What seems to be deeply implicated by the pronouncement of pluralism, on top of a simple recognition of plurality, is the promotion of some degree of accommodation of diversity. Whereas a monist perspective carries with it a connotation of exclusivity (only this amounts to law in accordance with this outlook), the adoption of pluralism permits the plurality of phenomena to be approached in an expansive way so as to acquire status in whatever way suits each contender (all of these amount to law in their own different ways).

Characterising pluralism as involving a turn to liberal accommodation adds to the problems of contestability and instability, in that we now need to consider just how open the pluralist approach we adopt will be in bestowing the cherished status (of law), and on what basis or bases that status will be bestowed. The problems here are immense. It is not even as though we start with a fixed set of phenomena, whose status needs to be determined. It is not even the case that the phenomena (whichever they turn out to be) provide a stable subject for the attention of pluralism. Different aspects of the phenomena may be selected, different perceptions of the phenomena may be at stake, in liberally working through a pluralist allocation of status.

Attempting to take a theoretical interest in these matters does not reduce the problems. A unitary theory that seeks to account for the diversity of phenomena, which a liberal pluralist approach has admitted, risks diluting the credentials for obtaining the status to the point of becoming meaningless (everything is law, so having the status of law tells us nothing about anything). A less indulgent unitary theory, which restricts admission to the status (only those phenomena that satisfy these criteria in one way or another count as law), runs the risk of betraying the pluralist cause. Although less exclusive than the outright monist approach, it still sets the bar at a certain height and excludes those contenders that fail to reach it. Is the answer then to look for theories that are themselves pluralist in trying to account for the different ranges of diversities that pluralist approaches might admit?

One reason for hesitating at this extreme extension of pluralism into the theoretical realm is that it would appear to be self-defeating. If a pluralist diversity of *theories* is to be tolerated in order to account for the alternative ways in which the status of law can be bestowed, then what is to prevent a monist theory producing an exclusive bestowal of status being counted among them? Another way of expressing the danger here is that the pre-theoretical problems of contestability and instability we have recognised in taking a pluralist approach are simply resurfacing by attempting to deal with them at a higher level of theoretical pluralism. A more applied concern for avoiding ratcheting up ever-increasing levels of pluralism is that this move avoids the very practical bite of pluralist challenges. While the abstract discussions featured throughout this work situate its principal contribution in the realm of theory, it involves an area of theory which grapples with a set of challenges that, for jurists and law subjects, are real and sometimes urgent. A compelling reason to be dissatisfied with simply multiplying our theories of law, and pluralising explanations or justifications of plurality, is the disservice it represents to those who need a robust pluralist jurisprudence in order to discern the value of particular non-state legal forms against monistic legal forms that presently ignore or exclude them. Again, it is better to augment these suggestive remarks with the solid discussion of these points that can be found within the chapters that follow, which we draw attention to in the survey below.

A close consequence of admitting to contested possibilities affecting the very core of our subject matter is thus to recognise the likelihood of normative or aspirational agendas becoming interwoven with theoretical efforts to achieve clarity of understanding for that subject matter. Jurisprudence in any shape or form is notoriously difficult to insulate from normative concerns. Unsurprisingly, given the basic business of law in providing norms guiding relationships between members of a society. Move, through non-state law, beyond the society contained by a state, and it is easy to entertain grander normative ambitions for pluralist jurisprudence. These may move outwards, breaking through state barriers to encompass a cosmopolitan vision; or, unshackled from the constraints of the hierarchical submission of citizen-subjects to the law, they may move inwards to a deeper concern with a participatory status offered by non-state forms of normative ordering. And given the possibility that we have mentioned of a reflective dynamic invigorating the relationship between monist and pluralist jurisprudence, we can expect fresh enthusiasms for the normative concerns of conventional jurisprudence to be released by the theoretical investigations of pluralist jurisprudence. The normative or aspirational aspect of the pursuit of pluralist jurisprudence is a further feature that is explored in imaginative and significant ways within the chapters of this book.

In the survey of these chapters that follows we shall take the trouble to point out the particular ways they respond to the three expectations for a pluralist jurisprudence that we have mentioned above: establishing the relationship between pluralist jurisprudence and monist jurisprudence, with the respective understanding of each that follows from how that relationship is viewed; clarifying the precise role of pluralism within a pluralist jurisprudence, with the degree of accommodation or even encouragement that suggests in terms of theoretical expansiveness and practical import; and promoting a normative or aspirational agenda within a pluralist jurisprudence, with the impact that might have on working through the contested possibilities which a pluralist jurisprudence contains. That is not to suggest that other valuable features and significant controversies are not to be found in the discussions of pluralist jurisprudence these chapters contain. We shall do our best also to bring these out in our survey. Our motivation for drawing special attention to the three expectations of this introductory chapter is to set the scene for our own efforts in the final chapter to engage more fully with our contributors, and to discharge both a debt to their generous influences and a responsibility to put forward our own understanding of pluralist jurisprudence.

1.2 The Contents of This Book

The chapters by Roger Cotterrell and Maks Del Mar clearly take up the burden of the practical import of pluralist jurisprudence. In Chapter 2,

Cotterrell explicitly addresses the utility of legal theory from the viewpoint of lawyers, and in doing so draws on earlier work influenced by Gustav Radbruch to suggest a class of theoretically oriented lawyers whom he labels jurists. The responsibility of these jurists is to be concerned for the value of law as a social institution. That value is seen to be under threat from the forces of legal pluralism, which unsettle the expectations of legal orthodoxy and render monist (Western) accounts of law ineffectual. Cotterrell observes a regulatory plurality, which may or may not be perceived as a legal plurality. The task of the jurists differs from the philosophical task of getting at an essential nature of these pluralist phenomena, and from the sociological task of examining the detailed experience of claims to regulatory authority. The jurist's task is to negotiate regulatory plurality as a practical matter. Theoretical assistance to aid this task needs to focus on normative materials or doctrine, and the agencies that institutionalise it; but it also has to be combined with explicit reflection by jurists on the values law bears, importantly giving effect to aspirations for justice and security.

In the following chapter, Del Mar turns his attention to the place for a theory of legal reasoning within pluralist jurisprudence. His concern is to build on but avoid the limitations of a perspectival or hermeneutic pluralism which he associates with Neil MacCormick.[3] Despite the respect that offers to different norm-generating units, Del Mar considers that the absence of a rigorous theory of legal reasoning to determine the exact relations between those normative sources makes it vulnerable to a collapse into monism. Del Mar offers a solution to this problem by exploring the possibility of a 'relational pluralism' which permits legal reasoning to be practised in a way that maintains healthy relations between the different norm-generating units. The key to opening up this possibility is harnessing the power of the relational imagination within legal reasoning. Del Mar illustrates this potential with his own impressive collection of imaginative resources, taking in the lessons of history, a survey of cognitive devices and a study of common-law practices, before drawing on the support of recent writers (notably, Patrick Glenn) who in different ways have sought to generate 'cognitive space and time' within legal practice. This is the feature Del Mar treats as the hallmark of relational pluralism, in creating space in which otherwise conflicting

[3] For ease of terminological consistency, hermeneutic pluralism here can be equated with radical pluralism in Michaels' discussion in Chapter 5, and more generally with strong pluralism – and contrasted with weak pluralism.

norms from different norm-generating units may be maintained in a non-oppositional environment.

Although there is much that could be united in the efforts of Cotterrell and Del Mar to formulate a pluralist jurisprudence that is capable of providing practical solutions to the actual use of pluralist legal materials beyond the limitations of a monist account, it is salutary to reflect further on whether Cotterrell's understanding of the juristic task as involving the negotiation of regulatory plurality is quite so accommodating as Del Mar's insistence on the imaginative creation of cognitive space in which otherwise opposing forms of regulation could be retained. There is a possible suggestion in the former of hard negotiation, requiring the support of definite normative commitments in order to reach resolution, whereas the latter's construction of cognitive space appears to carry with it the opportunity for avoiding the need for negotiation – at least the kind of negotiation that produces losing parties – and the need for deference to other normative commitments.

If this tension exists between the approaches found in these two chapters, it is certainly a creative tension which significantly raises a basic question about the nature of the non-monist environment in which the recognised pluralism has to be encountered (whether negotiated or not) by legal practice. The straightforward, traditional monist solution of taking the environment of a sovereign state may be unworkable once the pluralism has been accepted, but quite what takes its place is a conundrum that will repeatedly surface as we explore different perspectives on pluralist jurisprudence.

Cormac Mac Amhlaigh, in Chapter 4, confronts this conundrum in his invigorating study of constitutional pluralism, which has been proposed as a way of representing the pluralist environment. Mac Amhlaigh points to the role played within this perspective by suprastate judicial bodies in asserting the credentials and terms of an authoritative and effective legal order within the normative practices that they participate in. This amounts to a self-referential transformative exercise capable of bestowing legal recognition on a plurality of such orders. Despite MacCormick's early work in this area recognising the two distinct types of radical pluralism and monist[4] pluralism covering the relationships within this

[4] What we have referred to in Section 1.1 as 'unitary' to avoid confusion with the alternative use of monist for a non-pluralist setting. MacCormick's hierarchical monist pluralism amounts to a restrictive unitary theory of pluralism (in our terms), and falls on the weak side of the strong/weak divide.

multiplication of legal orders (depending upon the absence or presence of a normative resource to manage the interactions between different orders), Mac Amhlaigh argues that the tendency within constitutional pluralism has been to assume a methodological monism, notably illustrated in the aspirations of Mattias Kumm for a unifying framework of cosmopolitan constitutionalism. Mac Amhlaigh's careful study comparing the emergence of suprastate legal orders for the EU and the ECHR, in accordance with the precepts of constitutional pluralism, leads him ineluctably to the conclusion that methodological monism fails and that the 'global disorder of constitutional pluralism' makes it necessary to pluralise constitutional pluralism itself.

Reaching a conclusion of theoretical pluralism carries with it the risks we noted above. Whether this result should be associated specifically with constitutional pluralism or be regarded as a broader manifestation of the current condition of theorising suprastate law, which Mac Amhlaigh emphasises is a work in progress, it leaves the practical import of regulatory plurality wide open, for the moment at least. A different strategy for resolving the interactions between multiple legal orders is suggested by Ralf Michaels in his efforts to advance a relational concept of law.

More accurately, Michaels' objective in Chapter 5 is to work towards a concept of *laws*. The relational nature of this concept is proposed on the assumption that a positivist account of inter-systemic recognition can be applied to an observable condition of legal pluralism. Michaels sees this as a third option to add to the prevailing trends in pluralist jurisprudence that follow MacCormick's alternatives of 'radical pluralism' (requiring extra-legal discourse) and 'monist pluralism' (requiring a higher body of law or legal values). The distinctive characteristic of Michaels' approach is to locate mutual relational recognition between pluralist legal orders in a 'rule of external recognition' found as part of each order. As a 'tertiary' rule within each system, it operates to signal a pluralist legal condition, beyond the more familiar internal Hartian rule of recognition associated with a monist conception of law. Michaels' discussion connects his relational concept of law to other recent suggestions in the literature of pluralist jurisprudence, such as Detlef von Daniels' idea of linkage rules. However, he insists on the constitutive nature of external rules of recognition. The mutuality of this constitutive aspect is seen as a strength in combatting John Griffiths's scepticism over a weak legal pluralism promoting a state-centric bias. It is also considered to amount to an admission that under conditions of global legal pluralism a concept of law(s) has to be relational, relative – and contingent.

The possibility has now emerged, here if not previously, that a situation of legal pluralism may or may not provide a ready answer to the quest to ascertain the practical import of multiple legal orders. Michaels' contingency appears to operate with regard to the expansiveness of pluralism over what gets recognised as law and to the interaction between recognised legal orders. In his view, the place where these issues become determined is found among the legal orders themselves, in rules of external recognition, giving prominence to legal officials (notably judicial officials) through whom these rules are expounded. However, there is nothing in Michaels' preliminary work on a relational concept of laws to indicate whether this contingency may play out one way in securing a stable network of interactions between legal orders, or play out another way in yielding an unstable set of conflicting interactions (there is some evidence of the latter possibility in his discussion of the relations between EU and municipal legal orders). In other words, the condition of legal pluralism may (contingently) provide resolved or unresolved answers, clear or contested outcomes, to practical issues in need of legal guidance in a pluralist setting.

Whereas Michaels' detection of the contingency of legal pluralism is limited by its focus on the actions of officials, Sanne Taekema in Chapter 6 is more expansive in her recognition of legal pluralism, as she adopts an interactionist understanding of law which amplifies the reach of any consequent contingency. Taekema's interactionist perspective is based on the recognition of two basic forms of law: enacted law (which is vertical and official) and interactional law (which is horizontal and arises out of the purposive activities of all sorts of people in legal practices). There are a number of facets to the approach she develops here, including an appeal to pragmatism, a purposive and value-laden form of instrumentalism, and a subtle inventory of different forms of law and their connections to vertical and horizontal relationships. Significantly, Taekema takes an explicitly pluralist version of interactionism to account for contemporary legal phenomena. There are many users of law, and the plural forms of law they generate pose a core challenge to any theory of law centred upon public authority. Diverse practices of subject-driven law formation and reform are expanded by the emergence of new actors, private, public and hybrid. Transnational actors as well as private and corporate individuals use law both in challenge to and in recognition of public authority. Taekema's pluralism thus embraces 'alternative interpretations and uses', and produces uncertain legal dynamics. On the other hand, there are also aspirational hints within Taekema's chapter (and its title) of the possibility of individual purposive activity being found compatible with the values of legal practice she associates with Radbruch, Fuller and Selznick.

At this point in the book, with a plethora of possible forms of law threatening to overwhelm efforts to provide a clear picture of their status and interaction, the reader might reasonably think back on the relative calm of a monist jurisprudence and reflect on what exactly it was that elevated municipal law to such prominence as to provide (if only the appearance of) a stable legal order. In Chapter 7, Joseph Raz asks the question, 'Why the State?' and offers two slants on the question. He considers why there has been a jurisprudential preoccupation with the state, and what gives the state its particular role in our social arrangements. Raz's answers to both concerns revolve around identifying the state as the most comprehensive legally based social organisation. This is evidenced by holding an extensive responsibility within its domain and enjoying freedom from external legal constraints. Raz's conclusion is that state law has met these tests until recently; that the trends associated with globalisation have significantly curtailed the freedom of states from external constraints; but, that the state is likely to remain the most comprehensive legally based social organisation in the future. Two important observations accompany Raz's reflections on these issues. He recognises that exclusive concentration on state law cannot be justified, and that the relations between state law and other legal orders require further theoretical inquiry. In addition, his analysis of the state and its law incorporates a sensitive discussion of both sovereignty and legitimacy. It is ultimately the questionable legitimacy of non-state law – in terms of earning the respect and loyalty of a global population – that prevents Raz bestowing a status on the international legal order which state law has merited.

The understanding of pluralism is taken in a different direction by Detlef von Daniels' contribution in Chapter 8. Von Daniels locates pluralism at the theoretical level. However, unlike Mac Amhlaigh's earlier resort to theoretical pluralism as a consequence of working through conflicting data, for von Daniels, pluralism is an inherent feature of theory as a self-reflective practice contemplating the richness of human experience. He illustrates this understanding of theory by means of a profound interrogation of examples from three different theoretical perspectives on law: analytical jurisprudence (Raz), legal pluralism (Tamanaha) and the philosophy of international law (the edited collection of Besson and Tasioulas). The rigorous questioning of each perspective reveals what von Daniels takes to be a 'dark side', a repressed vulnerability that leaves it open to being supplemented by an opposing theoretical tradition. In this way, von Daniels develops what he describes as a weak genealogical approach to theorising, not providing a clear taxonomy of theories nor a definitive assessment of theoretical progress, yet showing the necessary and valuable inter-relationships between theories whilst taking their own philosophical objectives seriously. In proposing that this approach should be adopted for a pluralist jurisprudence, von Daniels argues that it has two particular advantages. First, in relation to the subject matter, his genealogical approach is sensitive to the 'struggles and repressions' that have attended efforts to recognise alternative or competing forms of law. Secondly, in relation to the normative aspect of pluralist jurisprudence, it instils a theoretical self-awareness that guards against an assumed, context-insensitive self-sufficiency of theory – guarding against 'the danger of theory itself'.

Von Daniels' explicitly metatheoretical reflection is extraordinarily fertile, capable of yielding specific insights as well as offering general methodological guidance. Yet clearly, it does not itself assume the pretensions to comprehensiveness that it chides others for presuming. So, even at a metatheoretical level, it is pertinent to consider what further complementary supplements it might require. For example, as well as being context sensitive, are theorists called upon to justify the context of their theoretical investigation, or in some other way account for the purpose and value of adopting a particular contextual standpoint? Another question to consider is how far genealogical complementarity extends across all theoretical disagreements, and to what extent brute theoretical disagreement has to be acknowledged. Related to that question is the issue of where theoretical disagreement becomes the most intense. Is it possible to have genealogical complementarity at a more abstract level, while recognising outright disagreement on a more concrete or applied matter?

In Chapter 9, Stefan Sciaraffa seeks to show how different conceptions of pluralist jurisprudence from opposing positivist and non-positivist theoretical perspectives are linked to opposing views of legal reasoning, political authority, political community and, consequently, of the acceptable form of politico-moral deliberation within the reasoning of legal officials. Sciaraff uses the problem of the first recognition of customary international law as a preface to his discussion, and employs the question of the legal authority of the European Court of Human Rights for British courts to exemplify the differences between the two theoretical approaches. Despite denying that the point of his chapter is to take a side in the debate between positivism and non-positivism, Sciaraffa invests significant intellectual energy in refining a non-positivist but content-independent view of legal authority to combat Raz's well-known positivist content-independent account. Once fully expounded, the distinction between the two views critically turns on the former being open to considerations of the merits of the political authority capable of delivering the norm whose validity is itself established in a content-independent manner. Accordingly, if this non-positivist theoretical view is favoured, pluralist legal reasoning is regarded by Sciaraffa as amounting to politico-moral reasoning about political authority.

As well as illustrating a point at which theoretical disagreement might have significant practical implications, Sciaraffa's chapter reveals, as he himself insists, the connection between positivist and non-positivist disagreement within pluralist jurisprudence and 'more fundamental debates within political philosophy'. Sciaraffa's take on pluralist legal reasoning thus appears less juristic, in the narrow sense employed by Cotterrell. Yet, at the same time, his pluralism is less expansive than Del Mar's and echoes Cotterrell's in being grounded in some form of socio-political commitment. Interestingly, on this matter, Sciaraffa can also be regarded as closer to Raz's more recent work found in Chapter 7, which insists on the importance of social legitimacy for legal authority in a pluralist setting.

As for the vital connection that Sciaraffa forges between pluralist jurisprudence and political philosophy, this may be regarded as one manifestation of the importance of relating more narrowly legal theoretical concerns to a wider theoretical setting. One of the more obvious instances of this kind of relationship is that between a narrower theoretical concern with an understanding of law and a broader concern with an understanding of justice. Neil Walker laments the gap between theoretical approaches to global law and theories of global justice in Chapter 10. From a masterful survey of practical and theoretical discourse on global law and global justice, Walker points to six possible 'orientations' that we might perceive the relationship between global law and global justice as taking. The perception of orientation is regarded by Walker as relating to two different roles that academic lawyers perform in dealing with this subject matter, not merely documenting the emergence of global law but also influencing its development, so that an effective assessment of the different orientations should heed their ability to deal with the real world and to make an impact on it. From his careful scrutiny of the different options that these orientations present, Walker dismisses a primary role for those that would promote a variety of unacceptable dispositions: naïve utopianism, structural fatalism and narrowly entrenched legalism. In his view, this leaves the central debate between a 'compositive approach' and a 'compensatory approach', each of which allows for defects of state law to be remediable in a setting of global law through an aggregative, and segmented or partially ameliorative, approach, rather than by a holistic attainment of global justice.

Walker's attribution of responsibility to academic lawyers for promoting an effective relationship between global law and global justice has some similarities with Cotterrell's assignation of responsibility to jurists in Chapter 2. There are also significant contrasts to be made. There is a more practical character to the role designated by Cotterrell, with a link to values closely identified with law itself. In Walker's portrayal of the relationship between global law and global justice, the values of global justice are somehow required to meet a deficit of value in law. Walker's role for the academic promoter of a relationship between global law and global justice is not derived from meeting the vocational needs of practising lawyers, so where does it come from? His assessment of the competing orientations (which effectively shape that role) employs dual criteria, in requiring engagement with the real world and the ability to change it. Yet dual criteria notoriously create problems of priority, so even if Walker has succeeded in taking us to a more constructive arena for debate, as he claims to have done, the prospect of further disputation is significant. Put simply, the remaining question is how much of the real world should be engaged with and how much should be changed.

To make mention of the real world of law in a volume concerned with legal pluralism does, of course, itself involve a contentious subject. In Chapter 11, Margaret Davies demonstrates just how many ways there are to understand a plurality of law. Davies explores pluralities based on discursive understandings within jurisgenerative communities; those based on sociological understandings across normative domains of associative groups; and those emanating from understandings of the performative subject. Although Davies pays attention to concerns over a wholly undifferentiated use of 'law', she rejects these concerns on the ground that the open and exploratory nature of her project would be impeded by any restriction on the idea of law, however provisional. Once restrictions have been set aside, Davies produces a fascinating and sophisticated account of the varied possibilities of understanding law, delivered by moving questions from 'What is

Law?' to 'Where is Law?', and also expanding the focus of the former question to take in law's material substrata as including the human body, the earth and physical objects.

At some points Davies has clear affinities with Taekema's interactionism in Chapter 6, but unlike Taekema she has no theoretical objectives to deliver in her exploratory and speculative project, and accordingly continues well beyond any conceptual constraints imposed by Taekema's theoretical agenda. Davies herself concedes her approach in this chapter is unsuitable even for empirical studies, which require at least a provisional certainty in the concepts they employ. And she makes it clear that she is not opposed to the narrower concern of traditional legal theory with the question of what is law; legal theorising in different contexts may require particular, limited concepts of law. However, she does acknowledge conflict between some theoretical approaches – her own here being considered incompatible with an exclusive concentration on state law, or a natural-law perspective on objective morality.

In other respects, Davies shares some of von Daniels' concerns in Chapter 8 with theoretical pretensions to comprehensiveness, in denying that any theorist 'gets to see the entire elephant'; but she appears to be more sceptical than von Daniels in questioning whether the elephant exists. Possibly it is the contextual concession Davies offers to producing definite concepts of law that makes it possible to enter her vast pluralist emporium and make an actual purchase. If this is so, then the theorist's own theoretical agenda, which sets the context to investigate, provides the necessary counterpoint to Davies's plural pluralities.

The following chapter by Kirsten Anker on postcolonial jurisprudence conveniently sets a theoretical agenda which incorporates a specific form of law that makes an appearance in Davies's survey, indigenous law. Anker's chapter provides an illuminating study of the relationship legal pluralism has enjoyed with both colonial and postcolonial initiatives, moving from a supporting role in the imperial management of indigenous peoples to a critical role in promoting the independent survival of indigenous law. The emphasis of her chapter is on the problems faced by an indigenous jurisprudence in drawing on the resources of pluralism. She uses Canadian experiences as an extended case study, interwoven with pertinent discussion of the literature. The key question is how exactly a strong pluralism can assist in the 'interruption of the story of state monopoly' so as to recognise indigenous law on its own terms, in contrast to the subordinate status by incorporation that a weak pluralism would bestow. Anker is not satisfied from the range of Canadian judicial devices employed to acknowledge legal pluralism that strong legal pluralism is being embraced. She concludes that the professional role of the judge in determining '"the" correct law' is incompatible with strong pluralism. However, she also expresses doubts about the possibility of a strong sociological pluralism providing the assistance required by indigenous jurisprudence, due to its objectification of indigenous peoples and their laws. The solution Anker herself offers is to move through pluralism (having used that to set the pieces of the puzzle in place); to acknowledge with Melissaris the importance of shared experience within a community as the basis for understanding legality; and then to adopt a distinctive indigenist ontology, which is capable of reconciling different peoples. This reconciliation does not occur at the level of normative orders but from the acceptance of the primacy of an ecological reality (the 'being in place' of her title) which carries with it an inherent relatedness.

Anker's contribution is instructive in a number of ways. It is illustrative of the way in which a theoretical agenda is selective from the multiple concepts of law provided by pluralism. It is deeply informative about indigenous jurisprudence and its relationship with pluralism. It is sympathetic to the importance of social commitment to the recognition of legality that has been raised in different ways in the earlier chapters of Cotterrell, Raz and Sciaraffa. And it is provocative in its suggestion that the diverse social commitments of different peoples, conveying the potential for conflict between plural forms of law, can be reconciled through an indigenist ontology. The character of this last point remains somewhat cryptic; it is expressed in Anker's final sentence as an invitation to be members of a political community of the earth. That invitation may prove to be a particularly ambitious example of employing the aspirational to dispel the confusion of legal pluralism. As Anker's chapter points out in a number of places, what is practically at stake in the conflict between plural forms of law includes the recognition of title to land. Disputes over that kind of legal interest have not generally been displaced by discussion of ontological issues.

Chapter 13 by Martin Krygier also displays an aspirational or normative side, though one that is claimed to be relatively modest at the outset. Krygier connects legal pluralism to the value of the rule of law, and the modesty of his approach lies in the proposal that the value of the rule of law does not have to be debated (as it has been, both positively and negatively) over substantial social values whose achievement is made the task of law. Rather, the value of the rule of law can be taken in a limited way as being concerned within the restricted domain of the way power is exercised to temper the arbitrary exercise of power. The thing about modesty is that it conceals the full extent of the attributes possessed by its holder. Krygier's chapter has many qualities.

As an exercise in refining our understanding of the rule of law, Krygier neatly makes the point that his modest claim for the value of the rule of law does not have to be accepted, as any stronger claims would go through on the argument he employs for the modest value he favours. That is to say, his argument here is about the value of the rule of law, not about what value the rule of law has. The major claim that Krygier makes for advancing our understanding of the rule of law is one that he has made previously: 'the conceptual priority of *telos* over anatomy'. Krygier regards this as crucial for avoiding the trap of associating familiar anatomical features (rules or procedures) with achieving the rule of law – overlooking cases where the features are present but the rule of law is not accomplished, or ignoring cases where other anatomical features might be required in order to accomplish it. In the present chapter, this major point is amplified through an engagement with legal pluralism. Krygier develops a pluralist perspective on the rule of law informed by the work of Fuller, Moore and Galanter, so as to challenge any preoccupation with state law and state legal institutions, and to deny a privileged standing to the 'folk notions of legal folk'. This seriously expands the remit of the rule of law in pursuing the value of curbing arbitrary power.

In addition, Krygier reflects on the intellectual resources required to fully expound such an understanding of the rule of law. He observes that a sociology of the rule of law needs to be harnessed so as to explore the empirical circumstances in which arbitrary power can be exercised, and the legal means required to curb it. This resource he finds woefully lacking, with only Selznick's work regarded as an example of what is needed. The problem has been exacerbated by an unduly narrow concept of the rule of law coming from legal philosophy, underscored by paradigmatic examples from practice, and then influencing social science projects. However, Krygier does not dismiss a role for analytical jurisprudence. He calls for deep connections between jurisprudence and social science in providing an effective understanding of the rule of law. And these connections are prefaced by an earlier comment he makes on the importance of combining advocacy and analysis, a parallel to the two roles given by Walker to academic lawyers in Chapter 10.

In Krygier's own case, his advocacy is clearly engaged with arbitrary power in the variable contexts revealed by pluralism, and on behalf of its legal tempering in those settings.

We feel confident that these twelve chapters provide our readers with sufficient breadth of coverage and variety of stimulation as to invigorate their own understanding of the particular features and distinctive potential of pluralist jurisprudence, and possibly their own appreciation of how its development should be influenced. Our own reactions we save for the final chapter.

2

Do Lawyers Need a Theory of Legal Pluralism?

ROGER COTTERRELL

2.1 Introduction

The title of this chapter indicates the perspective from which the utility of legal theory is to be considered here. Theorising about law is not a self-justifying enterprise. It is necessary always to ask what theory is for, and that entails also asking *who* it is for. Much legal theory is concerned with creating analytical frameworks, clarifying the nature of phenomena, offering conceptual maps in terms of which experience can be understood, guiding further research, contributing to solving problems of practice by broadening the perspective in which they are seen and setting legal studies in wider intellectual or social contexts. But how these roles of theory are elaborated, and their relative significance, depend on the audience the theory is intended to address.

At least three broad categories of addressees should be distinguished, even though no absolute divisions exist between them. Individuals move between them and their foci of interest are inter-related. There are, first, *legal philosophers* whose focus today in the Anglo-American context is often seen as given by the concerns and outlook of philosophy as a discipline; second, social scientists, especially *legal sociologists*, whose main interest is in systematic empirical study of law as a social phenomenon in specific times and places; and third, *lawyers* who may sometimes feel the need for guidance or perspective in the practical tasks of making the law that they serve work – that is, in discovering, interpreting and applying it, negotiating the mass of legally relevant regulation and organising legal doctrine to use it to bring about practical consequences in concrete situations.

The theoretical interests of this last group are the concern of this chapter. However, most lawyers lack the time and opportunity, and arguably do not have the responsibility, to look systematically over law in general (even in their own legal system), to assess its overall condition and character, to ask generally how well law as an institution works and how it might work better. Only a few theoretically inclined lawyers assume this broader perspective. One might see their role as safeguarding the well-being of law as a practical idea; and protecting and promoting law's worth and meaningfulness as a social institution. They owe no primary allegiance to philosophy's projects of rigorous intellectual clarification, nor are they dedicated social scientists seeking disinterested explanation of the nature of the social world. Here I label these theoretically oriented lawyers *jurists*[1] and this chapter addresses their possible interests in and responsibilities with regard to legal pluralism in contemporary Western contexts.

My argument is that, because of important changes in the regulatory landscape, lawyers now need a theoretical perspective on legal pluralism and jurists should aim to provide one. Legal pluralism, as a normative project of negotiating the relations of irreducibly distinct regulatory regimes, has the potential to undermine the orthodoxies of modern juristic thought in two fundamental ways: (1) by destabilising the idea that law has any 'true', essential or timeless nature that philosophy could reveal or lawyers could assume;[2] and (2) by reviving the idea that legal authority is not revealed by applying positivist pedigree tests of validity but is to be built pragmatically through communication and compromise between different normative orders and practices. Juristic thought presently lacks the resources to deal with these emerging challenges. Confronting them demands an alliance between lawyers' practical analytical techniques and socio-legal empirical studies of regulatory practices. This chapter claims that a theoretical view of legal pluralism – centred on a minimal and flexible provisional model of law and an enlarged understanding of authority – is required to inform this alliance.

2.2 A Pluralist Landscape

Legal pluralism is a term of varied meanings. Juristically it represents a variety of possible *normative* responses to the *fact* of legal 'plurality'.[3]

1 For justification of this specific usage of the term, see R. Cotterrell, 'The Role of the Jurist: Reflections around Radbruch', *Ratio Juris*, 26 (2013), 510–22.

2 Cf. P. Zumbansen, 'Transnational Private Regulatory Governance: Ambiguities of Public Authority and Private Power', *Law and Contemporary Problems*, 76 (2013), 117–38, at 118 ('The rich accounts of legal pluralism . . . can be read as strong signals that law itself has an identity crisis, a crisis regarding its own nature and function').

3 N. Roughan, *Authorities: Conflicts, Cooperation and Transnational Legal Theory* (Oxford: Oxford University Press, 2013), p. 44.

Nowadays it is obvious that many varied kinds of laws or legal regimes regularly interact or confront each other in the same 'social space'. Indeed, legal 'plurality' usually exists in some form even in what lawyers would recognise as highly integrated legal systems. For example, relations between different traditional doctrinal fields (such as contract, torts or criminal law) are not always clear; doctrinal conflicts arise as legal reasoning develops normative ideas 'piecemeal' – as specific to a certain legal field but without any clear integration in other such fields beyond.[4] Different forms of rationality (formal, substantive, instrumental, expressive, etc.) can exist in a single legal system.[5]

Within the municipal legal systems of independent political societies (states) a deliberately maintained plurality of legal regimes or systems is commonplace. Often this is mainly geographically structured, as with federal, regional, provincial-national, state-tribal or local-central divisions of jurisdiction. In many state legal systems there exist, or historically have existed, jurisdictional divisions based on personal statuses: religious and secular, colonist and colonised, citizen and alien, noble and commoner, and many variables within these distinctions. Such types of plurality are normally well understood. Yet they rarely produce wholly unproblematic divisions of labour between jurisdictions. Often important jurisdictional disputes and enduring problems of interpretation exist. But such intra-state legal controversies are not juristically strange; they are part of the usual familiar fare presenting itself for normative processing by lawyers, judges and legislators.

Beyond such intra-state contexts, some other less traditional forms of legal plurality seem much less like juristic 'business as usual'. Relations between EU law and Member States' law, or between EU law and WTO law, are not always merely routine interpretive matters, but can often provoke debate about the fundamental nature of the legal regimes

[4] M. Davies, 'The Ethos of Pluralism', *Sydney Law Review*, 27 (2005), 87–112, at 96; M. Van Hoecke, 'Do "Legal Systems" Exist? The Concept of Law and Comparative Law' in S. Donlan and L. Urscheler (eds.), *Concepts of Law: Comparative, Jurisprudential, and Social Science Perspectives* (Farnham: Ashgate, 2014), pp. 43–57, at 53. On law's 'piecemeal' rationality, see R. Cotterrell, *The Politics of Jurisprudence: A Critical Introduction to Legal Philosophy*, 2nd edn. (Oxford: Oxford University Press, 2003), p. 5.

[5] Cf. J. Dalberg-Larsen, *The Unity of Law: An Illusion? On Legal Pluralism in Theory and Practice* (Glienicke/Berlin: Galda + Wilch Verlag, 2000), p. 105. Legal sociologists and others have also examined institutionally produced state legal plurality – that is, the situation in which different parts of the state apparatus create regulation independently and interpret state law differentially. See Dalberg-Larsen, *Unity of Law*, pp. 103–14; Davies, 'Ethos of Pluralism', 96; Roughan, *Authorities*, ch. 12. This plurality may remain unless mechanisms are available, and steps are taken, to identify it and select a final 'official' legal position.

involved. In such contexts perhaps a growing sense of juristic disquiet can be detected. The potential conflict between international law and the law of nation states long ago inspired monist-dualist theoretical debates on the location of ultimate legal authority to control such conflict. But this could remain a largely impractical concern as long as, *in actual regulatory experience*, state law wholly dominated international law. Juristically, any authority of international law could be presented (and so controlled) as merely an extension of state legal authority through treaties and the consensual establishment of international legal bodies.

However, the question of how to handle the relations of state and international legal systems operating in the same social spaces has become more acute, insofar as international law (1) has sought greater 'independent' authority less easily subsumed into state authority, for example via assertions of *ius cogens*;[6] (2) has become more prominent in the regulatory landscape by developing in many new or newly significant doctrinal fields (such as human rights, trade and finance, environment and intellectual property); and (3) now sometimes (as with international criminal law) addresses directly the citizens of particular states. Additionally, as international law has increasingly been seen as fragmented into a diversity of legal regimes whose relations are sometimes unclear, the old (usually practically insignificant) theoretical monism-dualism debates give way to (practical) monism-pluralism debates. So the idea that legal plurality has emerged as a theoretical issue for jurists (and not just a familiar commonplace) is now well established.

Beyond all this, many further dimensions of regulatory plurality are now widely recognised by legal sociologists and an increasing number of sociologically oriented lawyers. Much regulation created in networks of interaction (often transnational) – such as merchant communities,[7] corporate groups, industries, financial systems, internet developers, 'private' NGO movements,[8] religious or ethnic communities,[9] or sports

[6] E.g. A. Cassese, 'For an Enhanced Role of *Jus Cogens*' in Cassese (ed.), *Realizing Utopia: The Future of International Law* (Oxford: Oxford University Press, 2012), pp. 158–71.

[7] For a wide-ranging recent discussion, see Zumbansen, 'Transnational Private Regulatory Governance'.

[8] See e.g. K. Culver and M. Giudice, *Legality's Borders: An Essay in General Jurisprudence* (New York: Oxford University Press, 2010), pp. 75–77, discussing the Greenland Conservation Agreement as an example of transnational legality created by NGOs.

[9] For an excellent recent empirical study in a British context, see L. Tas, *Legal Pluralism in Action: Dispute Resolution and the Kurdish Peace Committee* (Farnham: Ashgate, 2014).

organisations[10] – has been shown empirically to be at least as practically powerful as much juristically recognised law, and as authoritative for those subject to it. Much is characterised by unions of primary and secondary rules, such as H. L. A. Hart associated with a legal system. Some lawyers, indeed, speak of 'transnational private law' to include at least some regulation created wholly or partly in these kinds of communal networks.[11]

But the commonest juristic stance has been to exclude much of this regulation from recognition as law. As long as lawyers can remain united in their basic assumptions about the attributes of law, such an approach remains viable. In borderline areas, fudging tactics can be used and concepts such as 'soft law' can signal the possibility of some, usually unspecified, juristic relevance in normative materials not conforming to shared assumptions about law.[12] And, whatever speculations legal philosophers may produce around the concept of law, and however much legal sociologists accumulate evidence of the landscape of 'living law' (that is, actually operative regulation), juristically it can seem dangerous to do anything other than hold the line against the unfamiliar – against new types of regulation that, once recognised, would raise numerous juristic issues about their authority, legitimacy and scope.[13]

2.3 How Lawyers Approach Legal Plurality

It would be misleading to underestimate the power of orthodox juristic techniques for dealing with legal plurality, or the determination with which they are being used today to hold the line against newly destabilising forms of plurality that threaten to escape juristic control. These techniques can be broadly summarised as four: (1) *ultimate monism* – the assumption or construction of a single overall normatively integrated regulatory structure or system to provide a unifying umbrella over

[10] A. Duval, '*Lex Sportiva*: A Playground for Transnational Law', *European Law Journal*, 19 (2013), 822–42.

[11] See e.g. G.-P. Calliess and P. Zumbansen, *Rough Consensus and Running Code: A Theory of Transnational Private Law* (Oxford: Hart, 2010).

[12] For recent discussion, see F. Terpan, 'Soft Law in the European Union: The Changing Nature of EU Law', *European Law Journal*, 21 (2015), 68–96.

[13] To the extent that legal philosophy seeks to 'legislate' any correct, essential or 'true' idea of law, this kind of context-free conceptualisation simply becomes irrelevant to the practical business of juristically managing the facts of regulatory plurality or of sociologically observing and explaining them.

plurality; (2) *hierarchical ordering* – the settling of permanent hierarchies of authority in or between regulatory regimes or systems; (3) *ad hoc resolution* – pragmatic solving of particular doctrinal conflicts without any attempt at a more general and enduring settling of relations between regulatory regimes or systems; and (4) *statist analogies* – use of juristically familiar characteristics of state law to interpret non-state forms of regulation by analogy or extension and so assess their juristic significance.

Legal scholars continue to rely on these techniques in addressing the whole range of contemporary regulatory plurality – the realm of what is now often called global legal pluralism.[14] Because they are part of the Western lawyer's normal stock in trade they are, for the most part, well-known and well understood, needing little elaboration here. Appeals to monism are used (for example, in considering relations of EU law to international law or to Member States' law) to conceptualise, integrate or articulate one system or regime from the juristic perspective of another. Appeals to hierarchy organise a vast range of codes, standards, practice rules, disciplinary norms and organisational rules in relation to the authority structures of juristic law. By this means they can be juristically assessed. Pursuit of ad hoc resolution is found, for example, in efforts to develop and rethink conflict of laws principles and practices to deal with clashes between regulatory regimes or systems as they arise.[15] State-law models of legality are widely applied;[16] and even proponents of constitutional pluralism or global administrative law, who are determined to recognise legal phenomena far removed from the limitations of state law jurisdiction, tend to appeal to sets of constitutional or public law principles and concepts that do not escape their origins in the juristic experience of Western state law.[17]

[14] See e.g. P. S. Berman 'The Evolution of Global Pluralism' in R. Cotterrell and M. Del Mar (eds.), *Authority in Transnational Legal Theory: Theorising across Disciplines* (Cheltenham: Edward Elgar, 2016), pp. 151–88; R. Michaels, 'The Re-Statement of Non-State Law: The State, Choice of Law, and the Challenge from Global Legal Pluralism', *Wayne Law Review*, 51 (2005), 1209–60.

[15] C. Joerges, 'A New Type of Conflicts Law as the Legal Paradigm of the Postnational Constellation' in C. Joerges and J. Falke (eds.), *Karl Polanyi, Globalisation and the Potential of Law in Transnational Markets* (Oxford: Hart, 2011), pp. 465–501; H. Muir Watt, 'Theorising Transnational Authority: A Private International Law Perspective' in Cotterrell and Del Mar (eds.), *Authority in Transnational Legal Theory*, pp. 325–60.

[16] Culver and Giudice, *Legality's Borders*, pp. 143–44.

[17] See e.g. N. Walker, 'The Idea of Constitutional Pluralism', *Modern Law Review*, 65 (2002), 317–59 at 342–43 (invoking 'constitutional discourse', 'citizenship' and 'sovereignty');

Insofar as these techniques continue to be effective they obviate any need for a theory of legal pluralism – that is, a theory aimed specifically at conceptualising and normatively organising legal plurality. However, they have their limits. Thus, ad hoc resolution (however practically useful in the short term) is ultimately no solution to the juristic problem of making sense of the idea of law as an organised social practice and guiding its development. Its pragmatic resolutions merely postpone addressing the task of ordering plurality in a stable, coherent manner.

Much significant new regulation arises from what lawyers typically think of as 'private' sources, within associations and organisations of civil society, or through arbitration and dispute processing in commercial networks. Of the four techniques, hierarchical ordering has been the standard juristic approach to defining relations between private and public regulation. But this has been successful only to the extent that private regulation has needed recognition or guarantee from state law or other juristically recognised public regulation. The more recent scenario has been one in which this recognition is not necessarily sought. Yet the proliferation, prominence and effectiveness of regulation produced from non-state sources in organisations, associations and communal networks are such that lawyers increasingly feel the need to take juristic account of them.

Monistic approaches seem no less unsatisfactory because monism presumes a perspective from which all legal reality can somehow be structured and integrated in an overall unity.[18] But there is no Archimedean point from which a single juristic world can be envisaged and constructed.[19] Monism presupposes an authority that can establish it; fulfilment of the juristic monistic dream in a globalised legal world must surely await the emergence of a global state.

As regards the use of statist analogies, I have suggested that this also includes the use of assumptions built out of Western experience with state law even when committed attempts are being made to recognise juristically non-state forms of regulation. But the problem here is the rootedness of this approach to legal plurality in Western juristic experience. It may be almost impossible for Western lawyers effectively to

B. Kingsbury, 'The Concept of "Law" in Global Administrative Law', *European Journal of International Law*, 20 (2009), 23–57 (emphasising attributes of 'publicness').

18 See e.g. I. Weyland, 'The Application of Kelsen's Theory of the Legal System to European Community Law: The Supremacy Puzzle Resolved', *Law and Philosophy*, 21 (2002), 1–37.

19 Cf. Walker, 'Idea of Constitutional Pluralism', 338.

survey developing global legal pluralism without imposing on it the inheritances of their own legal cultures. But global legal pluralism is not an exclusively Western phenomenon and will surely become steadily less Western-focused as it continues to develop. The question is whether juristic methods can 'bootstrap' themselves up largely from the experience of Western legal cultures to address a genuinely global plurality.[20]

The reasons why juristic techniques are no longer effectively neutralising legal pluralism as a problem are easily summarised. Much regulation that is widely seen as having juristic significance – for example, international law, transnational private law, standard-setting soft law and religious (e.g. Islamic) law, or other types of regulation often given the name 'law' – can no longer be assessed for this significance in terms of whether it can be incorporated into state law, seen as an extension of state law, or authorised or controlled by state law.[21] It appears to derive, wholly or partly, from non-state sources of authority and when it is interpreted by analogy with state law or in terms of characteristics associated with state law this often seems to distort its nature and obscure the sources of its effectiveness and legitimacy.

The experience of Western jurists has been that of municipal state legal systems, which ultimately (because of their political integration) lend themselves to explanation in terms of the overall systemic unity of ultimate monism or a hierarchical ordering that explains the structuring of authority within them. While both monism and hierarchy may be problematic juristic constructions, the idea of the modern, autonomous, centralised Westphalian state easily inspires them. However, as this idea of the state is undermined in various ways, the juristic techniques that reflect it – the quests for monism or hierarchy – lose their solid experiential foundations.

Under the pressures of globalisation, many states now seem less autonomous in their law-making authority. Their practical law-creating and law-applying sovereignty is weakened because of pressure imposed on them by more powerful states or groups of states,[22] and clearly some

20 W. Menski, 'Remembering and Applying Legal Pluralism: Law as Kite Flying' in Donlan and Urscheler (eds.), *Concepts of Law*, pp. 91–108, at 105.

21 But see Michaels, 'Re-Statement of Non-State Law', 1227–37, discussing state control of non-state law in the context of conflict of laws.

22 See e.g. G. Simpson, *Great Powers and Outlaw States: Unequal Sovereigns in the International Legal Order* (Cambridge: Cambridge University Press, 2004). In Europe, European Union commitments are one source of such pressure: see J. Clifton, 'Beyond Hollowing Out: Straitjacketing the State', *Political Quarterly*, 85 (2014), 437–44.

of this pressure is applied through law (for example, extra-territorial legal effects, extradition arrangements, bilateral treaties and subjection to obligations as convention signatories). So the sovereignty of some states extends, while that of others contracts; and the interplay of legal effects between international authorities (for example, the WTO), regional authorities (for example, the EU and NAFTA) and state authorities is so complex that monistic or hierarchical conceptions of legal authority and legal system seem to need much qualification or supplementation. Intra-state (communal or religious) authorities can also contribute to this perception, insofar as they support ambivalent responses of cultural groups to state law – sometimes mobilising it, sometimes decentring it;[23] simultaneously recognising and not recognising its normative supremacy.

Legal pluralism – taken here to mean the organisation of regulatory plurality seen as a juristic concern – can best be seen as an ecological problem, a matter of laws fighting for space in the regulatory landscape. More 'powerful' law pushes out less 'powerful' law. Different laws compete as to which should be recognised or suppressed.[24] The label 'law' is approved or refused for regulation – that is, the legal validity of regulation is decided. Claims to authority are made and are successful or unsuccessful, in the sense of whether or not they are accepted, so that authority attracts legitimacy.[25] A juristic view of legal pluralism can only be realistic[26] if it recognises and can therefore evaluate the processes and conditions in which what is legally significant is decided, and in which authority is claimed and recognised. Therefore, the remainder of this chapter focuses on these related matters: issues about what is to count as 'law' and issues of regulatory authority considered from a specifically juristic perspective. The latter issues are considered first.

[23] G. Barzilai, 'Beyond Relativism: Where is Political Power in Legal Pluralism?', *Theoretical Inquiries in Law*, 9 (2008), 395–416, at 405–06.

[24] R. Cover, 'The Supreme Court 1982 Term – Foreword: Nomos and Narrative', *Harvard Law Review*, 97 (1983), 4–68, at 40–44.

[25] In this context I treat authority as something *claimed*, and legitimacy as something *conferred* on authority claims by their acceptance by individuals (or by groups); see R. Cotterrell, 'Transnational Legal Authority: A Socio-Legal Perspective' in Cotterrell and Del Mar (eds.), *Authority in Transnational Legal Theory*, pp. 253–79. On this view, legitimacy exists, so to speak, 'in the eye of the beholder'. For further discussion see R. Cotterrell and M. Del Mar, 'Concluding Reflections: Transnational Futures of Authority' (in the same book), pp. 387–403.

[26] That is, attuned to the social and political contexts in which the jurist works.

2.4 How Should Authority Be Understood in Legal Pluralism?

Legal authority may present itself as a topic of interest for a variety of distinct theoretical reasons, and the perspectives of those viewing the topic from various philosophical, sociological or juristic standpoints may differ significantly. From a *philosophical* standpoint, the primary aim seems often to be to conceptualise it in general or universal terms so as to specify an essence that is always present whenever the concept is correctly invoked. Thus, one could distinguish generally between types of authority (for example, practical or epistemic) or bases of authority (for example, substantive or procedural) and analyze the relations between them, thereby isolating distinctive characteristics of legal authority. But such an approach could be entirely unconcerned with examining empirically how authority is understood either by those who claim it or those who accept it. A philosophically interesting concept of authority has to be plausible in relation to *some* presumed general experience but it should also be useful for assessing the correctness of assertions of authority made in practice.

By contrast, a *sociological* approach is likely to see authority as a matter of practice and experience,[27] especially the practices and experiences of those making, accepting or rejecting authority claims. It would include study of the conditions under which such claims are made and the criteria that determine what types of claims are realistically possible in particular circumstances. Therefore, a concern with actions in specific social conditions would be central. Thus, Max Weber's account of authority as legitimate domination[28] centres on identifying different types of authority claims and the particular socio-political or cultural conditions that these presuppose. Because of this focus, only provisional conceptualisations (ideal types) or working models of authority are required as a basis for empirical study of the ways in which authority is claimed.

A *juristic* approach – in the sense proposed by this chapter, of serving the well-being of law as an idea and ideal – is likely to be different again. A juristic view would be analytical (concerned to conceptualise authority) and also normatively focused and capable of judging when and whether authority is properly claimed; it would not be satisfied with sociologically recording actions and experiences – observing authority claims and

[27] Cotterrell, 'Transnational Legal Authority: A Socio-Legal Perspective'.

[28] M. Weber, *Economy and Society: An Outline of Interpretive Sociology* (Berkeley: University of California Press, 1978), vol. 2.

reactions to them. But equally, it would need to see authority as an idea that has meaning in the specific contexts of its use. Therefore, jurists faced with the challenges of legal pluralism should have only limited interest in projects of formulating essential, absolute, universal or 'true' characteristics of authority, and 'legislating' abstractly correct uses of the term without precise reference to context. A wise strategy would seem to be to keep an open mind about the variety of possible forms that legal authority might take; to adopt an exploratory approach seeking and interpreting information as to how authority claims are actually being made and received.

This approach involves sociological inquiry but surely does not entail that the jurist become a legal sociologist. Instead it suggests that juristic approaches should rely heavily on empirical studies of law and regulation and jurists should shape their evolving normative responses to authority in legal pluralism by reference to them. Insofar as this involves an ongoing accumulation of information and interpretation, juristic invocations of legal authority in conditions of regulatory plurality must, for the foreseeable future, often be provisional and tentative. They necessitate a rejection of philosophical orientations towards conceptual universalism or essentialism because these could only close off the possibility of jurisprudence becoming, through its ongoing practice, a continual learning process.

From this perspective, legal authority appears as something that takes many forms, varies greatly in jurisdictional reach, is subject to limiting pressures and requirements for accommodation, and derives from many disparate sources. In juristically familiar settings of municipal (state-focused) law, orthodox understandings of legal authority (usually involving elaborate hierarchies and divisions of jurisdiction) require little disruption. Beyond this, however, authority is a matter for negotiation, learning and gradual adjustment of juristic perceptions in interaction between regulatory regimes.

In her ground-breaking theoretical exploration of authority in conditions of legal plurality, Nicole Roughan argues that in contemporary legal pluralism distinct putative legal authorities necessarily inter-relate and limit each other's claims to authority.[29] Thus, the authority they claim has to be shared in some way, becoming 'relative'. In such conditions the overall legitimacy of this authority has to be found in normative

[29] Roughan, *Authorities.*

principles (a 'relativity condition') to govern their inter-relation. In effect, the relativity condition operates to justify the authority of any one regime or system by reference to other such regimes or systems with which it is normatively intertwined. In this specific sense, legitimate authority is 'relative authority'.

In this account, by far the most rigorous effort to date in legal philosophy to confront the problem of authority in contemporary legal plurality, Roughan seeks definitive conceptualisations not tied to specific types or contexts of authority claims. She seeks, first, to specify a universal 'test' to justify authority[30] and, second, an equally universal and essential 'relativity condition' to determine how authority can be shared and reciprocally legitimated.[31] Juristically, one could see this as an excellent specification of ideal normative conditions which jurists might envisage and aim to promote. Yet while it is surely an imaginative and necessary advance in philosophical conceptualisation, it could be criticised as failing to recognise fully the chaotic reality of global legal pluralism and the fact that jurists must work in an environment where regulatory plurality must be negotiated. In this environment no general acceptance exists for any single 'test' by which to justify authority. And jurists can hardly hope to see a universal 'relativity condition' invoked to settle the legitimacy of normative arrangements between competing authority claimants. The jurist has to balance the pursuit of conceptualisation with the observation of the varied, actually existing, shifting, often conflicting and contradictory, practices and experiences of authority.[32]

Weber's sociology emphasises that not all authority resides in rule systems, though he saw authority derived from rationally formulated rules and procedures as the dominant type in modern Western societies. Claims of authority can also be founded in charisma (the authority claims of individuals or regimes to possess special qualities justifying allegiance) or in tradition (an appeal to the familiarity of the established). It is not difficult to argue that much regulatory authority today is charismatically based (for example, in the claims to personal *expertise* of technical standard setters, adjudicators of disputes in particular fields, or learned interpreters of doctrine). As such, it often arises from what

[30] Ibid., p. 134. [31] Ibid., p. 143.

[32] Recently, Roughan has emphasised a necessary inter-dependence of philosophical and sociological approaches, presumably to address this juristic need; see N. Roughan, 'From Authority to Authorities: Bridging the Social/Normative Divide', in Cotterrell and Del Mar (eds.), *Authority in Transnational Legal Theory*, pp. 280–99.

lawyers typically see as 'private' sources (for example, in transnational communal networks centred on commerce, religion, environmental protection, sport or the promotion of technological development).

While this is sometimes set aside as epistemic[33] or theoretical[34] rather than practical authority, it could be unwise to conceptualise it out of the picture in considering legal authority. This is not only because such charismatically claimed authority is extremely widespread and powerful, given the range and scope of transnational standard-setting authorities, but also because it often competes directly with juristically familiar law, marginalising it in practice or compensating for its absence as effective regulation. To ignore it in the juristic landscape is to leave a large void in the jurist's picture of the regulatory terrain.

So, how can authority in legal pluralism be understood juristically? A philosophical approach such as Roughan's, however sensitive to the facts of plurality, seeks universal governing principles, and these may persuasively organise but will not necessarily *represent* actual regulatory experience. By contrast, a sociological approach might see legitimacy merely as a *fact*: the subjective acceptance of authority claims by those to whom they are addressed or who observe such claims being made. It would aim to study empirically the constituencies (networks, groups) over which authority is claimed and the way regulation works within them. In state legal systems, hierarchies of authority-conferring rules define what Weber characterised as legal-rational authority. Normally, jurists can leave to political theorists the task of examining democratic or other means of legitimating this. But in contemporary legal pluralism this is more problematic. Jurists trying to negotiate the 'relative' authority of competing intra-national, transnational or international regulatory regimes may need the help of sociological analyses to understand the communal networks which these regimes address, or in which they arise.

None of this solves the problem of juristically evaluating competing authority claims. Jurists have to keep in view an idea (and ideal) of law as a socially valuable practice, and seek to promote, develop and interpret that idea under the conditions that exist in the particular contexts in which they operate. The jurist's idea of law naturally reflects ongoing juristic experience and does not lend itself to definition in absolute terms,

[33] Cf. Roughan, *Authorities*, p. 20.

[34] V. Muñiz-Fraticelli, *The Structure of Pluralism: On the Authority of Associations* (Oxford: Oxford University Press, 2014), p. 170; J. Raz, *Ethics in the Public Domain: Essays in the Morality of Law and Politics* (Oxford: Oxford University Press, 1994), pp. 211–12.

or to expression as a rigorously elaborated, universally valid concept, though it may well be coloured by philosophical ideas existing in the jurist's own culture. Elsewhere I have suggested that Radbruch's hesitant, open idea of law, embodying flexible but resilient values of justice and security (or order) and adaptable to guiding social purposes and cultural assumptions of the time, gives some focus for juristic responsibilities in rapidly changing conditions.[35] I argue later that in contemporary legal pluralism this normative orientation has to be combined with an awareness of what empirical socio-legal inquiry can reveal about proliferating forms of authority, and their significance in the diverse groups or communal networks in which these forms exist.

2.5 Concepts of Law in Legal Pluralism

A relatively loose, flexible, Radbruch-inspired, juristic idea of law – worked out in practice but shaped by values understood in their cultural contexts – contrasts with dominant approaches to conceptualising law in contemporary Anglophone legal philosophy. These continue to seek some universally valid understanding of the nature of law, some ultimate 'truth' (even while recognising that conceptualisations can vary depending on their purpose),[36] or some fundamental essence of the 'legal'.[37] Certainly, some writers focus only on necessary features of 'our' – presumably their expected readers' – concept of law, or assume a particular evidentiary basis for their conceptualisation. But these limitations are usually left vague and, if mentioned at all, seem to be of little concern, hardly inhibiting very general claims about the nature of law.[38] From a practical juristic viewpoint, efforts to conceptualise law without ongoing reference to the evolving features of regulatory plurality noted earlier in this chapter can seem puzzling: one might wonder what such context-free

[35] The claims expressed in this paragraph about a specifically juristic idea of law are developed in Cotterrell, 'The Role of the Jurist' and in R. Cotterrell, 'Reading Juristic Theories in and beyond Historical Context: The Case of Lundstedt's Swedish Legal Realism' in M. Del Mar and M. Lobban (eds.), *Law, Theory and History: New Essays on a Neglected Dialogue* (Oxford: Hart, 2016), pp. 149–66.

[36] J. Raz, 'Two Views on the Nature of the Theory of Law: A Partial Comparison' in J. Coleman (ed.), *Hart's Postscript: Essays on the Postscript to The Concept of Law* (Oxford: Oxford University Press, 2001), p. 10.

[37] Cf. D. Patterson, 'Alexy on Necessity in Law and Morals', *Ratio Juris*, 25 (2012), 47–58.

[38] For full discussion see Culver and Giudice, *Legality's Borders*, pp. 80–94.

conceptualisations are for, what they can achieve; but usually no explanation is given. 'What is law?' is seen as a self-evidently important universal question.

By contrast, sociologically oriented approaches to contemporary regulatory pluralism often simply discard the what-is-law question as unhelpful.[39] Close to this position is Brian Tamanaha's view that the issue of correct conceptualisation of law in a world of vast regulatory diversity can be solved by accepting as law, for the purposes of inquiry, whatever people in a particular environment identify and treat in practice as such.[40] This approach, which turns the what-is-law question into a descriptive inquiry,[41] might seem a natural response to 'the enormity of the subject-matter' that normative plurality presents.[42] From a sociological viewpoint it might indeed be productive to prevent any drawing of sharp conceptual boundaries that could inhibit open-minded research about regulatory plurality. Andrew Halpin properly notes, however, that the 'almost universal rejection' of Tamanaha's theoretical approach results from its lacking 'any analytical or explanatory bite'.[43] It gives no analytical purchase on the idea of law;[44] yet law as an idea cannot, for juristic purposes, be discarded. Amongst many other problems with Tamanaha's conventionalism, it is not clear *which* people's views as to what is law are to count when disagreements on this matter exist in any particular place and time. Surely any empirical inquiry claiming a legal focus must make clear what specific idea of law guides the inquiry.

39 See e.g. P. S. Berman, 'The New Legal Pluralism', *Annual Review of Law and Social Science*, 5 (2009), 225–42, at 237 ('the whole debate about law versus non-law is largely irrelevant in a pluralist context because the key questions involve the normative commitments of a community and the interaction among normative orders that give rise to such commitments, not their formal status'); C. Parker, 'The Pluralization of Regulation', *Theoretical Inquiries in Law*, 9 (2008), 349–69, at 355 (noting that '[o]ne of the strengths of regulation and governance scholarship is that it is not preoccupied with what counts as "law"' in its empirical studies of how regulatory regimes interact').

40 B. Z. Tamanaha, *A General Jurisprudence of Law and Society* (Oxford: Oxford University Press, 2001), p. 166.

41 Berman, 'New Legal Pluralism', 238.

42 A. Halpin, 'The Creation and Use of Concepts of Law when Confronting Legal and Normative Plurality' in Donlan and Urscheler (eds.), *Concepts of Law*, pp. 169–92, at 181.

43 Ibid, 181; but see B. Dupret, 'The Concept of Law: A Wittgensteinian Approach with Some Ethnomethodological Specifications' in Donlan and Urscheler (eds.), *Concepts of Law*, pp. 59–74, at 63.

44 R. Cotterrell, 'Transnational Communities and the Concept of Law', *Ratio Juris*, 21 (2008), 1–18, at 8; Culver and Giudice, *Legality's Borders*, pp. 146–47.

As in considering the concept of authority, it seems that a lawyer's juristic approach to conceptualising law in legal pluralism has to occupy a position somewhere between a sociological focus on merely describing regulatory diversity and a philosophical effort to analyze and propound legal universality. If Tamanaha's 'give it up' approach to conceptualisation is discarded, one might nevertheless seek some minimal idea of law, 'as thin and formal a sense of law as possible'[45] that could have the prospect of being universally valid as a lowest common denominator of global legal pluralism. But such a conceptualisation, retaining the legal philosophical ambition of universality, would have to be so 'thin' as to embrace every known and presently unknown putative legal form. The question becomes: What analytical power can such a thin idea of law have? Is the search for the essential and the universal retained at the cost of a conceptualisation offering no guide to the jurist in the practical task of navigating regulatory plurality? And, even in such a cautious approach, certain kinds of experience of legal plurality might be too quickly ruled out. Thus, Emmanuel Melissaris, understanding 'law in terms of shared normative experiences of the participants in a community',[46] still assumes it to be an affair of rules and rule following.[47] Yet even juristically recognised law is not always a matter of rules; and standard-setting authorities that are powerfully significant in contemporary regulation and difficult for jurists to ignore are, as noted earlier, not necessarily structured around Weberian formal legal rationality. A thicker non-universalism might be much preferable to a thin universalism that is either controversial or lacks much analytical power.

A very different but no less thoughtful approach is shown in Keith Culver's and Michael Giudice's 'inter-institutional theory', inspired in some degree by Neil MacCormick's institutionalist legal philosophy. They aim to offer 'a descriptive-explanatory picture of legality as variegated combinations of legal institutions, institutions of law, and function-oriented content-independent peremptory norms and associated normative powers'.[48] Institutions of law are purpose-focused clusters of related norms;[49] legal institutions focus and deploy these but need not require

[45] E. Melissaris, 'A Sense of Law: On Shared Normative Experiences', in Donlan and Urscheler (eds.), *Concepts of Law*, pp. 109–21, at 113.

[46] E. Melissaris, *Ubiquitous Law: Legal Theory and the Space for Legal Pluralism* (Farnham: Ashgate, 2009), p. 123.

[47] Melissaris, 'Sense of Law', 109, 115, 118.

[48] Culver and Giudice, *Legality's Borders*, p. xxviii.

[49] Ibid., p. 120.

'officials' in any Hartian sense or depend on hierarchical organisation or monistic structures. So, what is envisaged as legality is a variable and often thick inter-weaving of norms and institutions seen in terms of their inter-relations. The aim is to avoid any assumption that hierarchies, systems and officials are essential aspects of legal phenomena, while recognising that these are often dominating features of the most juristically familiar types of legal regimes. The analytical focus in legal pluralism should not be on relations between different legal systems claiming to be, as in Joseph Raz's much discussed formulation, comprehensive, supreme and open (claims that do not reflect the reality of law today);[50] it should be on 'the diverse ways in which distinct institutions coordinate their normative practices and share normative powers'.[51] In some respects this approach parallels Roughan's concern with relations between authorities. The focus is on finding legality in processes of interaction and negotiation between institutional centres of diverse kinds.

How far could such a focus serve juristic needs? Culver's and Giudice's idea of legal institution suggests agencies of many different kinds in which norms are created, interpreted, organised and applied. However, in their wish to free the idea of law from any necessary tie to officials they refer to 'institutional actors' (certainly not just 'state-based actors') whose interactions can amount to 'the setting of law'.[52] The idea of officials is deliberately marginalised here because it suggests public roles within systems which officials serve. There seems much merit in trying to escape from the official, the systemic and the hierarchical as necessary features of legality. However, from a juristic point of view, the problem with Culver's and Giudice's approach may be that – in sharp contrast to Melissaris's thin universalism – it is *too rich* and thickly descriptive; embracing such complex openness and intricate diversity it gives few guides for juristically negotiating regulatory plurality as a practical matter.

2.6 A Model of Law as Institutionalized Doctrine

This juristic negotiation surely has to solve two basic problems that demand assistance from theory. The first is that of identifying the kind of normative materials (or *doctrine*) that lawyers should take into

[50] But Raz's recent effort to take account of some types and aspects of non-state law, in 'Why the State?' (2013), now Chapter 7 of this volume, relies on a seemingly looser and perhaps vaguer idea of legal system.

[51] Culver and Giudice, *Legality's Borders*, p. 58.

[52] Ibid., p. 157.

account within the pluralist landscape. In this, the role of the jurist is to make some mapping of the range of this doctrine and to recognise the extent of its authority over those it regulates. This has to be done bearing in mind that the sources of authority traditionally nurtured and stabilised in the context of state law can no longer be assumed to apply to all forms of law in global legal pluralism. What is meant here by recognising the authority of doctrine is noting how far legitimacy is actually being conferred on doctrinal claims to authority in the specific communal networks that doctrine purports to regulate or in which it arises.

The other closely related problem is that of identifying for juristic purposes the *agencies* that create, interpret, develop and enforce regulation in the many different forms it can take in global legal pluralism. The juristic need to identify these agencies arises simply because they are the authorities (the producers, controllers and managers of normative doctrine) among which legality may need to be negotiated. Beyond the familiar hierarchies of authority in state law and its extensions, this negotiation of legality will surely have to take place in the kind of interactive 'inter-institutional' processes on which Culver and Giudice focus. From a different perspective, these agencies are the diverse 'authorities' with which a shared or limited legal authority might need to be worked out in something like the manner that Roughan's conception of relative authority suggests. It could be hoped that this working out would eventually be governed, at least to some extent, in practice by a 'relativity condition' such as she prescribes. But for the moment this could only be an aspiration.

To treat these simply stated problems as juristically central in addressing global legal pluralism, a basic theoretical focus would be on (1) normative doctrine and (2) the agencies that institutionalise it. Thus, a suitable, sufficiently open, irreducibly *minimal* working model of law which has been proposed and applied elsewhere is that of 'institutionalized doctrine'.[53]

Doctrine in this model is not to be seen as necessarily limited to rules but could include principles, concepts and values. Nor must it be peremptory, as Culver and Giudice require. In global legal pluralism, doctrine can readily shade between the prescriptive and the advisory (in legal terms, 'hard' and 'soft') and can be interpreted and applied accordingly.

[53] E.g. R. Cotterrell, *Law's Community: Legal Theory in Sociological Perspective* (Oxford: Oxford University Press, 1995), pp. 37–40; R. Cotterrell, 'What is Transnational Law?' *Law & Social Inquiry*, 37 (2012), 500–24, at 506–08.

So doctrine as a category can embrace codes, guidelines, standards and protocols and there might be no reason why lawyers should avoid involvement in managing regulation that entails integrating these kinds of doctrinal elements with more juristically familiar structures of rules. As regards institutionalisation, this refers only to the idea that specific agencies of some kind exist with the task of creating, interpreting or enforcing normative doctrine. In developed state legal systems, agencies such as courts, legislatures, administrative boards and police exist to carry out each of these tasks or to combine them. In other kinds of legal regimes not all of the tasks may be fulfilled by specific agencies, or they may be fulfilled only partially. Hence, the institutionalisation of doctrine as law can be a matter of degree.

Such a thin, sketchy model is certainly not to be held out as a universal concept of law or a specification of law's essence or true nature. For juristic purposes it merely suggests where to focus the communication processes (identification, interaction, negotiation, compromise) by which legality can be developed in global legal pluralism. For legal sociologists it is a starting point from which to indicate provisionally a legal focus in empirical studies of regulation. For legal philosophers it is far too limited to contribute to their ongoing search for definitive conceptualisations and clarifications. For the future of jurisprudence – seen here as the juristic enterprise of theoretically managing the idea of law, and serving its wellbeing as a socially valuable practice[54] – the model of law as institutionalised doctrine would need to be combined with reflection by jurists on the *values* they associate with law and which they interpret in terms of their cultural experience. It would also need to be combined with socio-legal study of the *conditions* in which institutionalised doctrine develops and the *forms* it takes, as well as about the ways in which claims of *authority* are made and legitimated in the populations that today are subject to juristically significant regulation.

2.7 Conclusion

Where does this lead? It might be said that lawyers are less in need of a systematic theory than a *method* of approaching legal pluralism[55] using the resources indicated in this chapter. It has been said that, beyond

[54] R. Cotterrell, 'Why Jurisprudence is Not Legal Philosophy', *Jurisprudence*, 5 (2014), 41–55.

[55] Cf. Zumbansen, 'Transnational Private Regulatory Governance', 131–33, 137–38.

asking the what-is-law question in legal pluralism, 'we should ask who makes law, in which structures, through which agents, and for what purposes'.[56] All of these are juristic as well as socio-legal questions. So jurisprudence should be closely allied (though never reduced) to social science. Mark van Hoecke suggests that 'concepts of law should go beyond positivistic sets of rules and include the law's context',[57] but one could go further and say that, in legal pluralism, context is what actually creates juristically useful understandings of law, adding flesh to a skeletal model of institutionalised doctrine, enabling juristic identification of normative doctrine and institutionalising agencies.

Therefore, empirical sociological research on the vast range of communal networks in which regulation is created or to which it is addressed is indispensable for pluralist jurisprudence. And, crucially, this context of regulatory networks is ever *broadening* and increasingly *non-Western*. The Western heritage of juristic thought does not provide adequate resources for negotiating global legal pluralism.[58] And the universalist-essentialist tendencies in contemporary Anglophone legal philosophical thought actually pull against the flexibility which jurisprudence needs – a continual willingness to learn and pragmatically revise its ideas on the basis of diverse, evolving regulatory experience. A jurisprudence tailored to global legal pluralism has less need for rigorously developed systems of theory than for thoughtful and imaginative extensions of the lawyer's craft skills – skills of building or navigating the rationality of legal doctrine in 'piecemeal' fashion, with an awareness of the values of the cultures in which law is practised. And it should not be forgotten that the juristic role implies a commitment to aspirations for justice and security – multifaceted values[59] that in Western legal cultures find partial expression in many diverse hopes for and expectations of the rule of law.

[56] Barzilai, 'Beyond Relativism', 416.

[57] M. Van Hoecke, 'Do "Legal Systems" Exist? The Concept of Law and Comparative Law' in Donlan and Urscheler (eds.), *Concepts of Law*, pp. 43–57, at 54.

[58] On this theme see R. Cotterrell, 'Transnational Legal Authority: A Socio-Legal Perspective'.

[59] I have discussed their nature in terms of juristic responsibilities in 'The Role of the Jurist'.

3

Legal Reasoning in Pluralist Jurisprudence

The Practice of the Relational Imagination

MAKSYMILIAN DEL MAR*

> We ought to stop circumscribing the *nomos*; we ought to invite new worlds.[1]
>
> (Robert Cover)

3.1 Introduction

A history of pluralist thought about law is yet to be written.[2] When it is, an important chapter will surely need to be devoted to the work of Neil MacCormick who, perhaps more than any other legal theorist in the twentieth century, theorised about law against the backdrop of a commitment to the value of diversity (of all kinds: cultural, political, linguistic and moral).[3]

* This chapter emerged from two papers presented in Singapore and Harvard. The first presentation was for a conference on the 'The Pursuit of Pluralist Jurisprudence', at the National University of Singapore, 5–6 February 2015. The second was at a workshop on 'Contemporary Legal Thought' at Harvard Law School, as part of the Institute for Global Law and Policy Conference, 1–2 June 2015. Very warm thanks are due to: Andrew Halpin, Nicole Roughan, Justin Desautels-Stein, Christopher Tomlins, Margaret Davies, Neil Walker, Martin Krygier, Roger Cotterrell, Detlef von Daniels, Cormac Mac Amhlaigh, Ralf Michaels, Sanne Taekema and other participants in both events for very valuable comments.

1 Martha Minow, Michal Ryan, and Austin Sarat (eds.), *Narrative Violence and the Law: The Essays of Robert Cover* (Ann Arbor: University of Michigan Press, 1993), p. 172.

2 There are of course works in the history of legal pluralism, but less so in the history of pluralist legal thought. For a recent collection in the history of pluralist political thought, see Mark Bevir (ed.), *Modern Pluralism: Anglo-American Debates Since 1880* (Cambridge, Cambridge University Press, 2012).

3 This commitment is visible not only in his theoretical work, but also in his political life, e.g. MacCormick claimed that one of his proudest moments in the European Parliament was when, in the course of debates on the Convention of the Future of Europe, agreement was reached, in part as a result of his intervention, on adding to an existing clause protecting cultural diversity an extra one on protecting linguistic diversity as well.

A case can be made that a key component of MacCormick's method was the adoption of what he called a 'hermeneutic point of view', namely a view in which one seeks to understand the views of others but does not share their volitional commitments.[4] This is a third-party stance – one somewhat removed and distant, but nevertheless one actively pursuing the understanding of the positions of all parties being observed. MacCormick adopted this point of view in various contexts, but one very famous and influential example was the relationship between Member States and the European Union.[5] From the hermeneutic point of view, neither was superior to the other: they related to each other heterarchically, and not hierarchically. We can think of this as a form of 'perspectival pluralism' or 'hermeneutic pluralism': it consists in the development of a frame (what MacCormick articulated variously as 'post-sovereignty' or 'late sovereignty'),[6] which makes room for all concerned, sharing authority (as managed by subsidiarity) and thus resisting the one-winner-takes-all sovereignty games of those who insist there can only be one ultimate authority.

And yet, despite its importance and strong legacy, there are arguably some important limits to MacCormick's brand of pluralist jurisprudence. For instance, MacCormick's notorious 'move' from radical pluralism to pluralism under international law is often given as an example of the theoretical inadequacies of pluralist thought about law – the idea being

[4] This view was first developed in response to Hart's internal point of view, and appears in an appendix of his 1978 book on legal reasoning as well as in the first edition of MacCormick's book on Hart. See Neil MacCormick, *Legal Reasoning and Legal Theory* (Oxford: Clarendon Press, 1978); and Neil MacCormick, *HLA Hart* (London: Edward Arnold, 1981).

[5] Arguably, the root of this was his thought about the relations between Scotland and the United Kingdom. The earliest piece that is commonly cited as being most influential in terms of MacCormick's engagement with the European Union is the 1992 Chorley Lecture, see Neil MacCormick, 'Beyond the Sovereign State' (1993) 56 *Modern Law Review*, 1–18; the later source is Neil MacCormick, *Questioning Sovereignty: Law, State and Nation in the European Commonwealth* (Oxford: Oxford University Press, 1999). MacCormick's influence on the theory of the European Union, and on theorising sovereignty in the United Kingdom and beyond, can be seen in the following three collections: Matej Avbelj and Jan Komarek (eds.), *Constitutional Pluralism in the European Union and Beyond* (Oxford: Hart Publishing, 2012); Julie Dickson and Pavlos Eleftheriadis (eds.), *Philosophical Foundations of European Union Law* (Oxford: Oxford University Press, 2012); and Richard Rawlings, Peter Leyland, and Alison Young (eds.), *Sovereignty and the Law: Domestic, European, and International Perspectives* (Oxford: Oxford University Press, 2013).

[6] The language of 'post sovereignty' can be found in MacCormick, 'Questioning Sovereignty'; the language of 'late sovereignty' was a concession to Neil Walker's view and appears in Neil MacCormick, 'Sovereignty and After', in Hent Kalmo and Quentin Skinner (eds.), *Sovereignty in Fragments: The Past, Present and Future of a Contested Concept* (Cambridge: Cambridge University Press, 2010), pp. 151–68.

that it inevitably collapses into some form of monism or dualism.[7] These criticisms are not without some bite,[8] as I indicate in a moment, but we must set MacCormick's contribution in the overall history of pluralist jurisprudence: surely, to construct a theoretical frame in which one makes room for heterarchical co-existence, when what has preceded it or what is insisted on is either claims to supremacy or a refusal to acknowledge the existence of another relatively autonomous norm-generating unit, is a vital contribution. Nevertheless, the criticisms do point to something important, namely, the lack of further, detailed analysis by MacCormick of the relations (at the level of legal reasoning) between those heterarchically co-existing norm-generating units. Perspectival or hermeneutic pluralism, then, is an important foundation for what we might want to call 'relational pluralism', specifically an analysis of legal reasoning in its relational dimension, including a normative account of when this dimension of legal reasoning is practiced well so as to contribute to the overall improvement of the quality of relations between norm-generating units.

Studying relations in this way is much more familiar to historians than to philosophers – and, in many ways, the argument made in this chapter is designed to foster more collaboration between the two disciplines.[9] For instance, historians have long insisted on seeing any self-identifying norm-generating unit (a tradition, an institution, or a community) as the product, over time, of relations with other units. Comparative legal historians, in particular, have argued for recognising such entanglements, providing evidence of how 'all contemporary normative and legal traditions are a hybrid creation, an on-going mix of nominally native elements and new, often borrowed, features'.[10] Others have spoken of

[7] See Martin Loughlin, 'Constitutional Pluralism: An Oxymoron?' (2014) 3(1) *Global Constitutionalism*, 9-30; and Pavlos Eleftheriadis, 'Pluralism and Integrity' (2010) 23 *Ratio Juris*, 365–89.

[8] I discuss them in greater detail in Maksymilian Del Mar, 'Legality as Relative Institutionalisation: MacCormick's Diffusionism and Transnational Legal Theory' (2014) 5(2) *Transnational Legal Theory*, 177–217; and Maksymilian Del Mar, 'Imaginaries of Authority: Towards an Archaeology of Disagreement', in Roger Cotterrell and Maksymilian Del Mar (eds.), *Authority in Transnational Legal Theory* (Edward Elgar, 2016), pp. 220–251.

[9] This chapter, then, is part of an extended effort to encourage such collaboration: see Maksymilian Del Mar and Michael Lobban (eds.), *Legal Theory and Legal History: Contemporary Legal Theory, Series 2, Volume 1* (Surrey: Ashgate, 2014); and Maksymilian Del Mar and Michael Lobban (eds.), *Law in Theory and History: New Essays on a Neglected Dialogue* (Hart Publishing, 2016).

[10] Sean Donlan and Dirk Heirbaut, 'A Patchwork of Accommodations', in Sean Donlan and Dirk Heirbaut (eds.), *The Law's Many Bodies: Studies in Legal Hybridity and Jurisdictional Complexity c1600-1900* (Berlin: Duncker & Humblot, 2015), p. 7.

mutual borrowing and transplantation, and other forms of entanglement and mutual accommodation of traditions. Although the claim in this literature is often backward-looking – namely, articulating the hybrid past of current traditions or communities – it can also be understood as helping us to see how such entanglements and accommodations are an on-going practice, this being how norm-generating units continue to change and develop.

It must be stressed immediately that analyzing relational practices in this way is by no means idealistic or utopian: it is clear from the historical studies, for instance, that there have been both practices of mutual accommodation and mutual destruction of (or at least silencing or ignoring) other units. There is widespread recognition that many of the ways in which units have grown, and accumulated power, has included subsuming under their own remit other units. Arguably, this is not only in the colonial context, but also domestically where the power of civil and common law grew, in part, out of a gradual swallowing up of much of the functions of canon law.[11] Furthermore, in the studies of various kinds of imperialism[12] or certain forms of federalism, there has been recognition of what Robert Cover called 'jurispathic' practices, namely ways of killing off other norm-generating units (especially those of religious communities living under the shadow of the state).[13]

It is a fact to be lamented that little of contemporary theorising about legal reasoning connects with these historical studies of relational practices over and across time. One can put this point another way. It has been customary to theorise about legal reasoning by describing and evaluating the quality of justifications for decisions in the instant case. Theorists have, for instance, studied the role (if any) of deduction in legal justification, or the role of other kinds of justification, such as coherence or consequentialism. This focus fails to engage with these historical investigations in three ways: first, by its focus on justification; second, by its tendency to limit the analysis to the instant case or, at best, a short series of relevant cases (in a string of precedents); and third, by paying exclusive attention to sources within 'the legal system'. By contrast, and as

[11] See e.g. W. R. Jones, 'Relations of the Two Jurisdictions: Conflict and Cooperation in England during the 13th and 14th Centuries' (1970) 7 *Studies in Medieval and Renaissance History*, 79–210.

[12] See, for instance, Laura Benton and Richard Ross (eds.), *Legal Pluralism and Empires, 1500–1850* (New York: New York University Press, 2013).

[13] See Robert Cover, Narrative, Violence and the Law, ed. Martha Minow, Michael Ryan and Austin Sarat (Michigan: University of Michigan Press, 1995).

I elaborate in this chapter, studying legal reasoning in relational pluralism (in a way that allows for engagement with the earlier-mentioned historical studies) requires we broaden the inquiry to (1) imagination (and not just justification); (2) the practice of legal reasoning across time, sometimes considerable passages of time; and (3) the relational dimension of legal reasoning, namely analyzing how legal reasoning within one norm-generating unit relates with that of other norm-generating units.

There is, it must be said, change in the air: in recent years, as a result perhaps of the proliferation of international, supranational and transnational adjudicatory institutions, scholarship has turned to describe and evaluate the quality of relations between norm-generating institutions (I return to this literature later in the chapter). This has been particularly so in the context of the European Union, but there is also a growing debate as to the use of so-called foreign sources, especially in constitutional or supreme courts. This work is often highly normative, with scholars taking strong positions on how justified constitutional courts are in even citing foreign sources, or, more broadly, as to whether interactions between courts are better when they are competitive[14] or collaborative.[15] There is also an epistemological dimension to these debates: for instance, even if we just confine ourselves to public international law, does the alleged fragmentation of the international legal order mean that there are inevitable and perhaps also beneficial limits to how much cross-communication there can be between courts in different sub-systems?[16]

My purpose in this chapter is two-fold: first, to offer a conceptual framework within which we can analyze the relational dimension of legal reasoning across time; and second, to point to some relevant, existing resources that can inform any further study under that framework. The key concept I want to introduce is, as hinted previously, imagination. This I define as a set of cognitive processes that generate

[14] See Harel and Benvenisti on discordant parity: 'We are comfortable with tension. We are disposed to recommend discordant parity under which international and state norms and courts constantly compete with each other and assert their superiority over each other'. Eyal Benvenisti and Alon Harel, 'Embracing the Tension between National and International Human Rights Law: The Case for Parity', Working Paper, last accessed 19 August 2015, http://papers.ssrn.com/sol3/papers.cfm?abstract_id=2592869.

[15] See the work of Anne-Marie Slaughter; see also, recently, Timothy Endicott, 'Comity Among Authorities' (2015) 68(1) *Current Legal Problems*, 1–26.

[16] I waded into this debate myself some time ago: see Maksymilian Del Mar, 'System Values and Understanding Legal Language' (2008) 21(1) *Leiden Journal of International Law*, 29–61.

cognitive space and time.[17] There are, I suggest, modes and devices of reasoning the function of which is to enable a reasoner to stand back from the problem they are trying to resolve, to temporarily defer the solution, and thus to give the reasoner more space and time within which to consider possible or alternative solutions to the problem. I elaborate on this conception of the imagination in Part I of this chapter, including giving some examples of exercises of the imagination within common law reasoning. As I discuss, to notice instances of the imagination being exercised in this way requires that we look at the practice of legal reasoning across time.

The reason why the imagination so conceived can help us study legal reasoning in relational pluralism is that sometimes the space and time generated by such modes and devices is populated by resources from another norm-generating unit. In other words, the function of these modes and devices need not be (and, historically has not been) exclusively inward-looking. Perhaps even a stronger argument could be made – namely, that these modes and devices were devised in the course of relations with other norm-generating units: that they are inherently relational. Of course, they could still be used in ethically problematic ways: silencing another norm-generating unit, usurping their power. Equally, though, they could be used in such a way as to improve the quality of relations between norm-generating units – providing space and time for both to learn from each other, while not collapsing the differences between them and not undermining the relative autonomy of either. Further discussing this relational practice of the imagination is the task of Part II of this chapter.

3.2 The Imagination

3.2.1 Cognitive Travel

In her wonderful account of the cultural practice of philosophy (or 'theoria') in Ancient Greece, Andrea Nightingale argues that

[17] One can also speak of the imagination in another way: as an imaginary, or a reservoir of images. One can thus study the role of such images in any one thinker's thought (see Maksymilian Del Mar, 'Thinking of Images in Legal Theory', in Maksymilian Del Mar and Claudio Michelon (eds.), *The Anxiety of the Jurist: Legality, Exchange and Judgement* (Surrey: Ashgate, 2013), pp. 43–67), or in the context of a history of thought about a certain concept (see Del Mar, 'Imaginaries of Authority', 2016). This aspect of the imagination also has important application in the context of pluralist jurisprudence: arguably, we need a richer relational imaginary – a richer stock of images on the back of which we can study different kinds of relations and their qualities (e.g. think of imaginaries of friendships).

> the defining feature of *theoria* in its traditional forms is a journey to a region outside the boundaries of one's own city for the purpose of witnessing some sort of spectacle or learning about the world. *Theoria* involves 'autopsy' or seeing something for oneself: the *theoros* is an eyewitness whose experience differs radically from those who stay home and receive a mere report of the news. On the journey as well as its destination, the *theoros* encounters something foreign and different. This encounter with the unfamiliar invites the traveller to look at his own city with different eyes.[18]

It is a charming thought: the idea that the origins of philosophy are intertwined with the practice of travel to unfamiliar lands – enabling the experience of de-familiarisation – which, during the journey but perhaps especially upon one's return to one's own land, generates puzzlement and stimulates the practice of what we come to call philosophy. On this view, then, philosophical questions emerge from comparisons between the familiar and unfamiliar, generating issues about what can be seen to be common and what must remain particular.

We can move from such literal journeys to more imaginary ones, though exhibiting the same process of familiarity, travel, de-familiarisation (including wonder at otherness), return, comparison, puzzlement and thought. We might, for instance, see such cognitive travel at work (or better, at play) in our reading of literature, in thought experiments in philosophy, and in the social gymnastics of everyday discourse (which is more inventive and playful than we often give it credit).[19] We can also, or so I suggest, see it in legal reasoning.

So conceived, the imagination is composed of an enormous variety of cognitive modes and devices: various forms of displacement, detour,[20] wayfaring[21] and dislocation; the use of contradictions;[22] unexpected

[18] Andrea Nightingale, *Spectacles of Truth in Classical Greek Philosophy: Theoria in its Cultural Context* (Cambridge: Cambridge University Press, 2004), p. 68.

[19] There are important connections here between literature and everyday life, which were so aptly explored by Bakhtin; see Gary Saul Morson and Carly Emerson, *Mikhail Bakhtin: Creation of a Prosaics* (Stanford: Stanford University Press, 1990).

[20] As was made famous in contemporary thought by the anti-structure of Derrida's texts.

[21] The imagery used by Ingold is relevant here. See Tim Ingold, *Lines: A Brief History* (London: Routledge, 2007).

[22] This category is itself very broad, e.g. it can include as-if models that contradict reality, as spoken of by Vaihinger, but also for instance various forms of polarity and opposition in Greek thought. See Hans Vaihinger, *The Philosophy of 'As If': A System of the Theoretical, Practical and Religious Fictions of Mankind*, trans. Charles Kay Ogden (New York: Harcourt, Brace and Company, 1925); and G. E. R. Lloyd, *Polarity and*

juxtapositions and correlations;[23] various kinds of incongruence and incoherence;[24] counter-factuals and (impossible or unlikely) hypotheticals and other kinds of thought-experiments;[25] allegory, parable,[26] metaphor, metonymy; alliteration and other figures of repetition;[27] prediction, prophecy and other kinds of futurological cognition (figuras, utopias, dystopias); various kinds of exaggeration and creation of disproportion (comedy, of course, is linked here, as in satire, irony, caricature, sarcasm); perspective-switching and simulation – and one could go on. Arguably, in all of these, one is moving away, or distancing – creating new cognitive platforms from which to look out – thereby producing cognitive space and time. There is an attempt to construct a clearing which thought has not yet populated[28] – and thus something that can generate at least the potential for new alternatives and possibilities.

I have referred to these modes and devices as cognitive, but a fuller study would need to investigate them in multiple dimensions: for instance, material and ethical. On the material side, we can connect these modes and devices to certain material practices, for instance: the invention of footnotes, margins (and fingers pointing in them, and other

Analogy: Two Types of Argumentation in Early Greek Thought (Bristol: Bristol Classics Press, 1966).

23 Here, the literature on analogy and its connection to creativity comes to mind; e.g. Keith Holyoak and Paul Thagard, *Mental Leaps: Analogy in Creative Thought* (Cambridge, MA.: MIT Press, 1995).

24 In her big, new book on coherence (in philosophy, psychology and law) Amaya recognises (though does not develop) an important cognitive role for incoherence, e.g. in the generation of new hypotheses – see Amalia Amaya, *The Tapestry of Reason* (Oxford: Hart Publishing, 2014).

25 There is a considerable literature on the use of thought-experiments in philosophy – see e.g. Roy Sorenson, *Thought Experiments* (Oxford: Oxford University Press, 1992).

26 Parable is a particularly good example, as it includes the imagery of moving away via a parabola. On some accounts, then, the way parables work is that they allow you to move away (indeed, they transport you/whisk you away) from the text, so that you can come back to it with different eyes upon your return. This is a kind of roundabout/distracted/slow/loopy reading. Again, the notion of the thinker-as-traveler is important here.

27 Holding attention for more than we might otherwise – so slowing us down – is thus also technique of generating cognitive space and time. The emerging field of cognitive literary studies is a mine-field for these devices: see e.g. Lisa Zunshine (ed.), *The Oxford Handbook of Cognitive Literary Studies* (Oxford: Oxford University Press, 2015); and Joshua Landy, *How to Do Things with Fiction* (Oxford: Oxford University Press, 2012). One should include here specific devices in specific genres – e.g. 'red herrings', false clues in detective fiction.

28 The 'not yet' is important – the temporality of provisionality, of tentativeness, is valuable too.

marks); the use of diagrams[29] and other kinds of visualisations,[30] but also including the process of visualisation in the form of sketches and doodles;[31] the design of games (often precisely the introduction of rather arbitrary obstacles, which is also a way of slowing down, distancing, de-pragmatising space), including of course digital gaming and simulation; and the art of curating (linking, for instance, to the previously mentioned unfamiliar juxtaposition and association). There is, arguably, an ethics in this also – a relational or dialogical ethics: for example, curiosity in otherness and openness to seeing one's own limitations could be characterised as virtues (e.g. wonder and humility). Of course, one needs to be careful: there is potential here for dis-engagement, a rather mindless form of tourism that has little to do with ethics of any kind. Nevertheless, there may be scope here for building an ethics around the capacity for exercising the imagination in this way.[32]

3.2.2 *Imagination and Common Law Reasoning*

If one conceives of the imagination as broadly as I have, then this opens up some exciting avenues for analyzing legal reasoning. In what follows, I focus only on the cognitive dimension, but there are prospects here for

[29] Consider Bender and Marrinan's account of diagrams – namely, as arrays that do not impose one way of correlating their various elements, but precisely enable an exploration of different kinds of correlations. See John Bender and Michael Marrinan, *The Culture of Diagram* (Stanford: Stanford University Press, 2010).

[30] See Barbara Tversky, 'Visualising Thought' (2011) 3 *Topics in Cognitive Science*, 499–535, and references therein. Tversky also looks back much further, offering (from my perspective here) a kind of material history of the imagination, pointing to 'animals in cave paintings, maps in petroglyphs, tallies on bones, histories on columns [and arches], battles in tapestries, messages on birch bark, journeys on scrolls, stories in stained glass windows', and more recently, 'dramas in comics, diagrams in manuals, charts in magazines, graphs in journals' (ibid. at 500). Rather than seeing these material artefacts as tools for representing what the mind cannot compute or as convenient place-holders and de-complexifiers (as they may otherwise be characterised), one can see them as ways of exploring possibilities (e.g. by setting up new comparisons) and finding new ways to forage, store, travel, hunt, live, organise cities, etc.

[31] Here, Tversky's work on sketches as 'messy diagrams' is of interest: these, she says, can be 'crucial for thinking through problems, arousing and considering multiple possibilities. A common case is design, where designers typically begin with sketches that are vague and tentative. It's often not clear what the lines mean, what they refer to, even to their creators. . . . Expert designers excel both at reconfiguring ambiguous sketches and at remote associations'. See Barbara Tversky, 'The Cognitive Design of Tools of Thought' (2015) 6(1) *Review of Philosophy and Psychology*, 99–116, at 111.

[32] See e.g. Ted Cohen, *Thinking of Others* (Princeton: Princeton University Press, 2009).

something much bigger: a cognitive, material and ethical history of the legal imagination.[33] Furthermore, in this section my discussion is confined to the common law[34] – so eschewing any relational dimension (which is the focus of the second part).

I point to the following modes and devices as examples of the exercise of the imagination in common law reasoning: legal fictions, perspectival devices, and hypothetical reasoning, as well as other expressions of hesitation and doubt. These are all examples of generating cognitive space and time and, in so doing, creating resources (in this case) for future courts. These modes and devices do not bind future courts: instead, they offer resources that future courts can take up (or not), and that at their strongest, hint at possible ways forward, or provide some tentative suggestions as to whether to broaden or narrow the law's reach. One may also characterise their use as exemplifying self-limitation: the present court refrains from offering an overall solution (deferring it via a fiction, for instance) or suggests alternatives and possibilities in hypotheticals, and this self-limitation is what generates resources for the future court. One could thus call these modes and devices forms of 'resourceful restraint' (as I do at times in the following discussion). This is no mere, passive holding-back, but rather an active, curious, kind of self-limitation, for it creates resources for those future courts: it creates the space and time in which they can then act.

One (rather obvious) way to see these modes and devices is that they are often not directly relevant, or necessary, for deciding the present case. They thus include all the kinds of statements a court can make by way of *obiter dicta*. But they also include descriptions of facts that are not, in the *ratio decidendi*, seen as necessary to justify the decision – in the language sometimes deployed in this context, they are not seen by the judge as 'material' facts. The presence of these descriptions is made all the more resourceful in the common law, which allows for multiple, and also dissenting, judgments. This is resourceful because different judgments often describe the facts in different ways. The differences, which may be subtle or dramatic, include the relative degrees of detail in the description

[33] Here, one would need to look at everything from the format of legal documents (see e.g. Nils Jansen, *The Making of Legal Authority* (Oxford: Oxford University Press, 2010)), thereby connecting with the history of the book and cultural histories of typography. Within 'material artefacts' one should probably include gestures, performances, and costumes as present in rituals.

[34] This is for convenience only, it being the tradition with which I am most familiar: no claims are being made here as to the unique virtues of common law reasoning.

(and thus mentioning facts the others do not consider important) and differences of characterisation of the parties involved, but also, more rhetorically, what they emphasise (e.g. how they begin) and how they set up any narrative so as to influence the reader's sympathies. The reason this creates cognitive space and time and is resourceful for future courts is at least two-fold: first, the future court can point to a fact described, but not considered material, in the past case, and use this to distinguish the past case from the instant case (the applicability of which is otherwise based solely on the material facts said to be the same in both cases); and second, the future court can use it to change the legal significance of that past case or a string of cases, elevating a fact not previously considered to be material, and thereby changing the 'principle' for which that case or that string of cases is said to stand for. Thus, the over-description of facts allows future courts to engage in a practice of re-description of the legal significance of a past case. This is a form of resourceful restraint and equally a technique for generating cognitive space and time, for there is both modesty and utility in allowing one's decision to be re-constructed in the future.

Other kinds of strictly speaking 'unnecessary' additions to judgments include some uses of hypotheticals – the exchange between Bar and Bench often has recourse to hypothetical scenarios, and sometimes these also make it into the judgment. Sometimes, these hypotheticals play an important role in the justification of the instant case, but quite often they are presented by-the-by, illustrating a range of possible factual scenarios that are only tangentially related to the decision made in the present case. What is interesting to observe, when one looks at the life of these hypotheticals over time, is that many of them become more important for future courts than the facts (as found material) in the instant case.[35] In other words, if we do not see the present court as communicating with, offering resources to, generating cognitive space and time for, the future court – we can easily miss the value of this device.

Another, quite spectacular though also more controversial, use of the imagination in common law reasoning is the use of legal fictions. These have a notoriously bad reputation in the literature on legal reasoning,

[35] An example is the hypothetical in the contract case of *White & Carter (Councils) Ltd v. McGregor* [1962] AC 413 5; [1962] 2 WLR 17; [1961] 3 All ER 1178, which, through Lord Reid's reading of the hypothetical, becomes more important in the subsequent case law on acceptance of anticipatory breach.

but this is because[36] they are not analyzed over-time. When looked at over-time, it becomes clear that at least some legal fictions are deployed so as to avoid introducing a new rule explicitly, thereby allowing the old rule to remain valid, but simultaneously hinting at the possibility, perhaps even desirability (but without the requirement), of introducing, more explicitly, a new rule in the future. In other words, analyzed over time, the use of a legal fiction is both restrained (for it does not introduce a new rule) and resourceful (for it suggests that, sometime in the future, it may be appropriate to introduce a new rule). Legal fictions are often deployed in circumstances where the court is confronted with a tension between evidentiary difficulties and (what the present court sees as) the demands of justice: for example, a plaintiff is clearly worthy (to decide otherwise would be to allow the defendant to get away with having exploited the plaintiff) but cannot prove an element of the action.

To give a quick example, consider the requirements of proving causation in an action for damages in tort for contracting mesothelioma (a disease that one can contract after exposure to asbestos). The courts, when first confronted with this issue, employed effectively a legal fiction, treating the causation requirement as having been proved (despite the absence of evidence).[37] In time, this has developed in what may potentially be called either a new test of causation in this context (materially increasing the risk) or even a new form of liability.[38] This is, arguably, a dramatic change in the law, but the point is that it has occurred slowly over time, developed by a series of courts, and the fiction has been part of the machinery of legal reasoning that has allowed for this kind of careful, gradual, incrementalism. Put another way, legal fictions are ways of generating cognitive space and time: future courts may confine the use of the fiction to that one instance in the past case, or they may de-fictionalise the law, expressing a principle.

[36] As I have argued elsewhere: see Maksymilian Del Mar, 'Legal Fictions and Legal Change in the Common Law Tradition', in Maksymilian Del Mar and William Twining (eds.), *Legal Fictions in Theory and Practice* (Springer, 2015), pp. 225–54.

[37] See *McGhee v. National Coal Board* [1972] UKHL 7; [1973] 1 WLR 1; [1972] All ER 1008. This case involved dermatitis - the later cases involved mesothelioma.

[38] See the string of subsequent cases, including *Fairchild v. Glenhaven Funeral Services & Ors* [2003] 1 AC 32; [2002] 3 WLR 89; [2002] 3 All ER 305, *Barker v Corus (UK) Plc* [2006] 2 AC 572; [2006] 2 WLR 1027, *Sienkiewicz v. Greif (UK) Ltd* [2011] 2 AC 229; [2011] 2 WLR 523, *Employer's Liability Insurance 'Trigger' Litigation: BAI (Run Off) Ltd v. Durham & Ors* [2012] UKSC 14; [2012] 1 WLR 867; [2012] 3 All ER 1161; and now *Zurich Insurance plc UK Branch v. International Energy Group Limited* [2015] UKSC 33; [2015] 2 WLR 1471. Note here the large stretch of time (from 1972 to 2015) that one needs to take into account.

To these examples, one might add other more surface-like uses of the imagination: for instance, the kind of signalling[39] that goes in expressions of doubt[40] and hesitation[41] in judgments. Judicial expressions of doubt or hesitation include statements such as: 'It is a pity such-and-such a doctrine was not raised in argument or the pleadings', or 'I am uncomfortable about the scope being granted to this doctrine, but feel there is no other option', and so on. Of course, one can read these statements also as invitations to the legislature, but more often than not, they are hints or suggestions to future courts that other considerations might be brought to bear on a future similar case, or that something is going awry with the shape that a current rule or principle is taking. One might even think of these expressions as going beyond self-restraint, for they are almost self-undermining – they suggest that the decision being made is perhaps not the best one. Certainly, broadly speaking, they are part of the family of expressions of uncertainty in common law judgments, which are much more frequent than is usually recognised.

[39] I use the term to link up with Eisenberg, who defines signalling as 'a technique by which a court follows a precedent but puts the profession on notice that the precedent is no longer reliable. By the use of this technique, a court paves the way for overruling a doctrine it believes would otherwise have to be preserved because of justified reliance [by the parties in the present case].' See Melvin Eisenberg, *The Nature of the Common Law* (Cambridge, MA: Harvard University Press, 1988), p. 122. This is a form of restraint because the court is refraining from overruling, but it is also resourceful for it suggests to a future court that such a change might need to be introduced. Eisenberg has a fascinating discussion of one way in which such signalling may be achieved, namely by introducing what he calls 'inconsistent distinctions'. These are distinctions, 'in the form of exceptions, that seem plausible in form but are in substance either inconsistent with the announced rule, given the social propositions that support the rule, or impossible to administer in such a way that cases are treated in a consistent fashion' (ibid., p. 71). They are both law-preserving and (potentially) law-changing, for they give future courts a choice, as to whether to continue to apply the underlying rule, or to deploy (and thereby stretch) the exception (in this Janus-faced character, inconsistent distinctions resemble legal fictions).

[40] More work needs to be done on expressions of doubt in legal reasoning – for a recent example in Islamic criminal law, see I. A. Rabb, *Doubt in Islamic Law* (Cambridge: Cambridge University Press, 2015).

[41] Interestingly highlighted by Latour in his *The Making of the Law*, though he means in a different sense to the way I am using it (for example, in his case, it is not clear whether these expressions of hesitation offer any resources to future courts, for they are not published). Hesitation, for Latour, seems to signal that a decision is being made (for it is not mechanical), and thus is essential to justice being done. I am pointing to expressions of hesitation in judgments, which signal to future courts that a different approach may need to be taken. See Bruno Latour, *The Making of the Law: An Ethnography of the Conseil d'État*, trans. M. Brilman and A. Pottage (Cambridge: Cambridge University Press, 2010).

Note that all these modes and devices can be studied (as they have tended to be) from the perspective of how well they contribute to the justification of the instant case. It is clear that looking through that rubric alone, these modes and devices do not acquire a positive reputation: for instance, they begin to appear as lazy avoidances of deciding on principle (as is commonly said about fictions). It is only when we study their operation over time that we come to see their value: precisely as exercises of the imagination that generate cognitive space and time, and thereby provide resources to future courts. Note, also, that all these modes and devices sit alongside ways of deciding the current dispute: thus, fictions are both ways of deciding a present case as well as signalling a need for change in the future. In any evaluation of them, we would need to balance their contribution to the quality of the justification of the present case and their generation of resources for future courts.

3.3 The Relational Imagination

As I have analyzed them earlier, the exercises of the imagination all generated cognitive space across time and vertically – that is, to future instantiations of courts within the same norm-generating unit (the common law tradition). However, it is also possible to study those modes and devices – and others – as generating cognitive space across time and horizontally – that is, vis-à-vis other norm-generating units. In other words, the suggestion I am making in this chapter is that if we want to study legal reasoning in its relational dimension, one way of doing so is to study the practice of the relational imagination. Studying the practice of the relational imagination across time would also bring theories of legal reasoning closer to the above-mentioned historical work on the long-standing hybridity of norm-generating units.

Because an important part of any such work is acknowledging related previous efforts, in this part of the chapter, I focus on offering some resources in the contemporary literature that can profitably inform any future study of the relational imagination. I do so in two steps: first, by discussing the work of the late Patrick Glenn; and second, pointing to the related work of a number of other scholars.

3.3.1 Glenn's Cosmopolitan Legal Thought

When I began thinking about this chapter, one of my starting points was the writings of the late Patrick Glenn – one of the twentieth century's most prolific, most steadfast champions of legal diversity (past and present). Let me, then, first of all say a little about his work on forms of thought that connect with what I am calling the relational imagination.

In the last chapter of his last book, *The Cosmopolitan State*, Glenn urges us to pay attention to what he calls 'cosmopolitan forms of reasoning or cosmopolitan logics'.[42] He first defines these negatively, namely as reactions against the limits of binary forms of thinking and classical logic. According to Glenn, 'classical or binary logic (characterised for example by the laws of non-contradiction and the law of the excluded middle) is entirely incompatible with cosmopolitan perspectives'.[43] Classical or binary logic would force one to think that inconsistent texts or sources could not exist, or that one had to choose (and establish a hierarchy) between norms said to conflict, or (as in the context of private international law) between the law of the forum and the foreign law. All of these are ways of closing off the system rather than enabling co-existence or conciliation. Glenn recognises, of course, that legal reasoning has been greatly influenced by such binary logic[44] – but, he argues, if we look closely enough, we see other kinds of legal reasoning, more suited to the cosmopolitan practice of co-existence. And, furthermore, if we look around us, particularly in transnational contexts, we see that such non-binary forms of logic and thinking are on the rise.

To give us a more positive picture, then, of the alternative, Glenn points to the 'many valued turn' in logic, which has been accompanied by the development of 'new' logics.[45] This has occurred in two ways: first, logic has had to respond to certain developments in science, such as that of 'evolving lineages' and the lack of static classes in biology (this is the 'ontological' challenge), though one can add to this the attempt to capture (logically) the complexity of ordinary language;[46] second, although not new in themselves, logicians in recent decades have devised new logics to deal with age-old theoretical paradoxes that challenge the laws of classical logic. In terms of the latter, multivalent logics, which are 'degree-theoretic' rather than binary (as in the phrase, 'there is

[42] Patrick Glenn, *The Cosmopolitan State* (Oxford: Oxford University Press, 2013), p. 259.

[43] Ibid., p. 264.

[44] Though one might argue that it is scholarship about legal reasoning that has been so influenced, making us understand it as much more rigid and closed than it actually has been and is.

[45] Glenn, *The Cosmopolitan State*, p. 264.

[46] Ibid., pp. 265–66.

some truth in that' – rather than truth or falsity), and thus recognise a 'continuum of values', have become popular.[47] These 'paraconsistent' logics tolerate conflicts, and devise ways of accommodating them, that were intolerable under classical logic.[48] Here, then, we are getting closer to modes and devices for generating cognitive (and ultimately also normative) space and time – that is, a space and time in which certain cognitive operations oriented to de-complexification, singularity, univocality, non-relationality are suspended, deferred.

For Glenn, it is possible to see examples of such cosmopolitan logics at work in the law.[49] In general, the task, as he sees it, 'for a cosmopolitan, paraconsistent logic in law would thus be to acknowledge legal contradictions, to preserve existing legal diversity, and to provide cosmopolitan and practical forms of dispute resolution for the judge of the cosmopolitan state'.[50] Cosmopolitan legal thought avoids hierarchical forms of ordering, or hierarchically based resolutions of conflicts. 'The logic' here, says Glenn, 'is one that sustains diversity, avoids imposing consistency and opens up an included middle where multivalent options are available. . . . There is no single unity to be obtained, but conciliatory recognition of multiple unities'.[51] In this tradition of thought, it is 'possible to speak of contradictions or conflicts in law as being only 'apparent', and even to deny their existence altogether, which at the same time maintaining the diversity of sources of law from which the apparent contradiction or conflict derives'.[52]

It is instructive to see what Glenn counts as examples of cosmopolitan legal thought in the practice of adjudicatory institutions.[53] Within constitutional law, for instance, Glenn suggests that 'the most visible

[47] Ibid., pp. 267–68.

[48] Whether this is entirely fair to classical logic is another matter – as Glenn himself acknowledges, there were developments in logic that were compatible with classical logic, and helped solve such paradoxes, such as modal logic (and the use of possible worlds): see ibid., 268.

[49] For an example of a logician applying multivalent, paraconsistent logic to law, see Graham Priest, *In Contradiction* (Oxford: Clarendon Press, 2006). The classic author here is of course Toulmin, for whom the law is in fact a rich source of non-classical logic (memorably, logic, for Toulmin, is 'generalised jurisprudence'). See Stephen Toulmin, *The Uses of Argument* (Cambridge: Cambridge University Press, 2003). And now see the papers collected in H Patrick Glenn and Lionel Smith (eds.), *Law and the New Logics* (Cambridge: Cambridge University Press, 2017).

[50] Glenn, *The Cosmopolitan State*, p. 274. [51] Ibid., p. 275. [52] Ibid., p. 276.

[53] Glenn also points to recent legal scholarship that has called for non-classical, and non-binary modes of thought (see ibid., pp. 270–74). A recent example is Christine Bell's idea, in *On the Law of Peace*, of law as a 'holding device', advocating the 'included middle' and

application of multivalent logic' is 'now found in the widespread and related processes of 'balancing' rights in apparent conflict or 'balancing' a given right against a violative government measure'.[54] 'The essential element' here is that of 'a shift in types of reasoning from one that accords priority to rules, categories, and subsumption, to one making more use of principles, overlapping and accommodation'.[55] Under 'balancing', 'a range of valid answers' becomes 'possible and reasonable'; foreign norms are able to escape the 'binding/non-binding dichotomy' and instead conceived of in terms of 'gradated authority', and rather than speaking of conflicts between rules, the discourse is of a principle 'outweighing' another principle but without invalidating it.[56] The process of balancing (as exhibited in constitutional adjudication) is, says Glenn, 'here to stay, given the multiplication of norms and sources in the world. It is inherently cosmopolitan in its ability to bridge multiple and apparently conflicting sources, state or non-state in origin'.[57]

European adjudicatory practice is also a hot bed of examples of cosmopolitan legal thought at work. Europe confronts legal practice with 'multiple unities', each of which has distinct legitimacy, and thus with 'multiple values'.[58] 'A world of multiple values', in turn, 'appears to require a multivalent logic tolerant of what might initially appear as contradiction, and necessarily including a middle ground'.[59] Thus, for instance, the *Solange* decisions of the German Constitutional Court appear 'to have found an included middle between EU norms and the German constitution'.[60] The device of 'reserving powers', employing a presumption of the validity of EU legislation in German constitutional law, while reserving the power to invalidate them, is precisely an example of a non-monotonic resolution,[61] allowing both sides to claim victory and neither to admit defeat.[62] Glenn also discusses the most-commonly

'constructive ambiguity': see Christine Bell, *On the Law of Peace: Peace Arguments and the Lex Pacificatoria* (Oxford: Oxford University Press, 2008), p. 270, fn. 80.

[54] Glenn, *The Cosmopolitan State*, p. 281. [55] Ibid., p. 282.

[56] See ibid., pp. 282–83 and the internal references therein. [57] Ibid., p. 283.

[58] Patrick Glenn, 'Transnational Legal Thought: Plato, Europe and Beyond', in Miguel Maduro, Kaarlo Tuori, and Suvi Sankari (eds.), *Transnational Law: Rethinking European Law and Legal Thinking* (Cambridge: Cambridge University Press, 2014), pp. 61–77 at p. 69.

[59] Ibid., p. 69. [60] Ibid., p. 69.

[61] 'Resolution' may even the wrong term – it may be that some of these devices can be understood as forms of non-deciding, or avoiding have to decide (the dilemmas are left unresolved).

[62] Glenn, *The Cosmopolitan State*, p. 290.

mentioned device in this context: the margin of appreciation in the European Court of Human Rights.[63] Also within Europe, and a much-less discussed example, is the Rome Convention (now Regulation) on contractual obligations in private law, which, according to Glenn, 'does not impose a binary choice between party autonomy and the most geographically proximate state law, but allows party choice subject to "overriding mandatory" state law, with the point being that the category of "overriding mandatory" is kept "fuzzy"'.[64] Other examples include relations between states and transnational private legal regulators, where Glenn sees a 'process of mutual recognition, mutual restraint, and collaboration'[65] and Justice Simma's approach in the ICJ's *Kosovo* decision, which called for recognition of 'the possibility of degrees of non-prohibition'.[66]

These are predominantly contemporary examples, and Glenn's point in discussing them is to say that in such international, supranational and transnational contexts of adjudication we can see an ever-greater use made of cosmopolitan, multivalent, paraconsistent and fuzzy logic. There may well, then, be new modes and devices that have developed to accommodate the special needs of those contexts, but what Glenn's corpus of work also shows is that, in broad terms, such cosmopolitan legal thought has a long and rich history. Thus, perhaps the most striking examples of cosmopolitan legal thought at work appear in the context of what he called 'common laws'.

Glenn's interest in common laws was long-standing – one might surmise that this was, at least in part, because he saw within the attitudes and practices of common laws (as he described them) a neglected ethic for our pluralist age. As he conceived of it, 'the primary sense of common

[63] As he characterises it: 'By virtue of this margin or zone of discretion the Court refuses to construct a univocal or univalent interpretation of the European Convention of Human Rights, and this in order to allow multiple and varied state interpretations of it. Neither national sovereignty nor a single European standard necessarily prevails. ... A continuum or range of alternatives is opened up, which may be seen as more or less compatible with European objectives. ... In determining the breadth of the margin of appreciation in particular cases the Court relies on the presence of absence of a European consensus on the reading of a right. Where there is a Europe-wide consensus, the margin is narrow and the national law will be scrutinised closely. In the absence of such a European consensus, the margin is wide and there is an initial presumption in favour of the defendant state' (ibid., p. 290).

[64] Glenn, 'Transnational Legal Thought' at 69.

[65] Glenn, *The Cosmopolitan State*, p. 290.

[66] Glenn, 'Transnational Legal Thought' at 74, fn. 52.

law'[67] was 'that of a law that is relational or supplemental in character and that must be designated as common in order to distinguish it from particular laws'.[68] This was thus a form of law that was/is inherently relational, for it was/is the outcome of a process of incorporation and translation from multiple sources and traditions. The most obvious examples of such common laws are within Europe – where a great deal of borrowing occurred (sometimes from very different sources and traditions), all grouped together into one 'common law'.

What impressed Glenn about such 'common laws' is their 'unmistakeably cosmopolitan or multivalent' character, which was exhibited in the relations between any one common law and other laws within that jurisdiction – for example, the local (customary) laws (or, for example, canon law). Common laws yielded to local laws, and they sought to avoid conflict (while acknowledging contradiction) with other sources and traditions (incorporating and accommodating them, or finding ways of respecting them even if not applying them). Common laws involved and involve 'recognition of multiple, legitimate, legal orders and therefore of the on-going necessity of legal diversity'.[69] Sometimes, then, 'contradictory texts remain in force and there is no process of making them consistent', and sometimes – for example where there is a question of yielding to local laws – then the other law is interpreted as having a certain kind of impact on the common law, while allowing it to exist under its own interpretation.[70] This is the 'included middle' at work.[71] As Glenn put it in his book *On Common Laws*:

> Common laws were found to be relational or non-binding in character, such that they could yield to *iura propria* and co-exist with them in an on-going, dialogical manner. This was invariably done through a differentiation amongst peoples, allowing recognisable identities to be maintained while admitting commonalities in the application of law. Common laws also did not propose to abolish or abrogate other laws (being themselves non-positive in character), whole the on-going

[67] Another sense, though not the primary one for Glenn, is that of 'laws common to a territory and binding throughout it'. See Glenn, *The Cosmopolitan State*, p. 283.

[68] Ibid., p. 284.

[69] Ibid., p. 284. A quick, though more contemporary, example here is provided by the English common law courts practice of citing contradictory commonwealth authority ('but see . . .') – the foreign authority is cited (possibly allowing future courts to resort to it, should they find it more persuasive), while openly acknowledging that it takes a different route (ibid., p. 285).

[70] Ibid., p. 286. [71] Ibid., p. 286.

process of delineation amongst different laws was a large and highly visible process of decision making.[72]

What I take is important about Glenn's work is his broad canvas – past and present – and his search for, and openness to, modes and devices that I am characterising as techniques for generating cognitive space and time. His work also points to the rich history of these modes and devices, and thus once again shows us possibility for collaboration between theory and history.

3.3.2 *The Relational Imagination in Contemporary Practice*

Glenn's work is not the only one we can draw on. There is important contemporary work that may be connected to what I am calling the relational imagination. This is not the place for a full survey, but let me simply point to some resources.

The work of Mireille Delmas-Marty, for example, is important: both her *Towards a Truly Common Law*[73] and *Ordering Pluralism*[74] – to mention just two books available in English – offer a myriad of examples of what Glenn would have been happy to call 'cosmopolitan legal thought', but also much more – for example, the combination of multiple factor criteria, and then the internal variability of those criteria, is an important contribution.[75] Similarly, the work of Nico Krisch, in his *Beyond Constitutionalism*, is helpful, in particular his notions of 'bracketing of principle', the 'taking into account' of another institution's or tradition's norms, and in general what he refers to as the 'minimalism' of transnational legal reasoning.[76] Like Glenn's examples, these are techniques for generating cognitive space and time in the

[72] Patrick Glenn, *On Common Laws* (Oxford: Oxford University Press, 2005), p. 134.

[73] Mireille Delmas-Marty, *Towards a Truly Common Law: Europe as a Laboratory for Legal Pluralism*, trans. Naomi Norberg (Cambridge: Cambridge University Press, 2002).

[74] Mireille Delmas-Marty, *Ordering Pluralism*, trans. Naomi Norberg (Oxford: Hart Publishing, 2009).

[75] Delmas-Marty applies this wonderfully to the definition of 'criminal offence' under Article 6 of the ECHR by the ECtHR; see Delmas-Marty, *Towards a Truly Common Law*, pp. 102–05.

[76] Krisch takes his notion of minimalism from Cass Sunstein. As Krisch explains it, Sunstein's notion of minimalism is two-fold: 'narrow in the sense that courts restrict themselves to the circumstances of the particular case, and as shallow in the sense that they do not develop a deep theory of the law on the issue'. See Nico Krisch, *Beyond Constitutionalism: The Pluralist Structure of Postnational Law* (Oxford: Oxford University Press, 2010), p. 290. This is useful in the transnational legal context because 'Institutions with such different backgrounds will often be unable to reach a shared understanding of the 'normative

context of awareness of the quality of relations between norm-generating units.[77] The work of Paul Schiff Berman on devices of global legal pluralism is also important here,[78] as is his instructive, recent reading of Justice Ginsburg's style of reasoning.[79] As Berman puts it: 'Ginsburg often chooses a path that provides maximum play among the legal systems at issue . . . tends to reject bright-line rules that choose one legal system over another. Instead, she often seems to prefer procedural arrangements that seek accommodation and flexibility in order to ensure that multiple legal systems and a variety of norms and processes are respected.'[80]

As Berman is aware, this harks back to the work of Cover, including Cover and Aleinikoff on 'dialectical federalism'.[81] According to Cover and Aleinikoff, 'Dialectical federalism is placed in between two options: a model of hierarchical imposition of federally determined values; and a model of fragmentation, justifying value choices by the states'.[82] On the hierarchical model, 'states are left little or no room to influence the choice or shape of developing rights', while on the fragmentation model, 'states retain the major role in evolving rights subject only to some vague limits on arbitrariness and irrationality'.[83] There is, however, a third model, 'premised upon conflict and indeterminacy'. On this model,

preferences of the overall order' that could provide the basis for future convergence. Instead, agreement is more likely on a lower level of abstraction' (ibid., 291).

77 See also, on varieties and techniques of interaction between institutions in European and/or global legal pluralism: Walker's taxonomy of institutional incorporation, normative coordination, environmental overlap and sympathetic consideration, though one might want to ask whether sympathetic consideration requires, as Walker suggests it does, some search for an underlying commonality or affinity with the other institution or tradition so as to justify any sympathetic consideration. See Neil Walker, 'Beyond Boundary Disputes and Basic Grids: Mapping the Global Disorder of Normative Orders' (2008) 6 *International Journal of Constitutional Law*, 373–96 at 384; see also Ralf Michaels, 'The Re-Statement of Non-State Law' (2005) 51 *Wayne Law Review*, 1209–59; and Allan Rosas, 'The European Court of Justice in Context: Forms and Patterns of Judicial Dialogue' (2007) 1(2) *European Journal of Legal Studies*, last accessed online 16 Aug 2015, http://cadmus.eui.eu/handle/1814/7706.

78 Paul Schiff Berman, *Global Legal Pluralism: A Jurisprudence of Law Beyond Borders* (Cambridge, Cambridge University Press, 2012).

79 Paul Schiff Berman, 'Ruth Bader Ginsburg and the Interaction of Legal Systems', in Scott Dodson (ed.), *The Legacy of Ruth Bader Ginsburg* (Cambridge: Cambridge University Press, 2014), pp. 151–71.

80 Ibid., p. 151.

81 Robert Cover and TA. Aleinikoff, 'Dialectical Federalism: Habeas Corus and the Court' (1977) 86 *Yale Law Journal*, 1035–102.

82 Ibid. at 1047. 83 Ibid. at 1047.

> Values become rights when lawyers fight about their implications. This model obtains whenever jurisdictional rules link state and federal tribunals and create areas of overlap in which neither system can claim total sovereignty. Conflicts will arise where values identified by the Supreme Court are interpreted differently by the two court systems. Where the Supreme Court refuses to impose a solution, an open-ended dialogue can ensue. The 'dialectical federalism' that emerges becomes the driving force for the articulation of rights.[84]

It is, as they also characterise it, a form of 'remedial timidity'.[85] The general point, from the perspective of this chapter, is that there is much relational strength in this self-restraint. Furthermore, what is interesting is that Cover and Aleinikoff allow for the use of 'contradictory models', which, as stated earlier, is an example of the exercise of the imagination (e.g. the use of fictions, as-if thinking generally), for it is a way of generating cognitive space and time:

> *Fay v Noia* permits us both to act as if we were not committed to these uncertain constitutional values and to cherish them as indispensable. We try on both garments. And it is surprising how often both fit – how clearly each image of the process makes perfect sense so long as we suppress the other . . . But just as waves and particles are complementary, necessary, models to adequately account for the behaviour of light, so utopia and pragmatic perspectives on the criminal process may both be indispensable to a complete account of our ambivalent and contradictory social selves. If we are in such a state, it may be as foolish to give up one of our 'redundant' forums as it would be for the physicist to forgo either his wave or his particle model.[86]

Others since then have built on this work, also drawing on the U.S. federalist tradition but broadening it out to transnational. Thus, for instance, Judith Resnik's work on 'federalist discounts' is relevant here.[87] These are forms of deference and 'temporarising accommodations', which leave space for disagreement, while keeping the relations going. It is significant that these devices need to be studied over time – for example, reservations in international treaty practice might, in due course, be withdrawn, leading to the eventual commitment of a state to something that, initially, is an obstacle to becoming involved in a certain treaty.

84 Ibid. at 1048. 85 Ibid. at 1036. 86 Ibid. at 1066.

87 Judith Resnik, 'Federalism(s)' Forms and Norms: Contesting Rights, De-essentializing Jurisdictional Divides, and Temporizing Accommodations', in James Fleming and Jacob Levy (eds.), *Nomos LV: Federalism and Subsidiarity* (New York: New York University Press, 2014), pp. 363–435.

In other words, these devices can be ways of beginning conversations – initialising relations – which then grow over time. Similarly valuable in this context is the work of Robert Ahdieh on 'dialectical review', 'a hybrid pattern of judicial interaction, with values of horizontal comity operating alongside elements of vertical hierarchy'.[88] It is significant that Ahdieh moves away from the dialogical metaphor, allowing for more competition than work on 'judicial comity' typically allows for. This is significant, as it is arguably a more nuanced way of thinking relationally.

What one sees in all of this work, are modes and devices of self-restraint that need to be studied over time[89] – practices of tentative cognition,[90] which leave space and time for multiple normative traditions to contribute. Finally, let me mention that this also connects to work on comparative legal reasoning – especially the referencing of other traditions in *obiter dicta*, and indeed the use of *obiter dicta* generally[91] – as well as in the debates over the use of foreign sources.[92]

There are of course important differences in all of these approaches, and also particular problems in all of these contexts of debate. My aim in citing them is to try to think with eyes wide open, gathering all possible resources and lines of inquiry, from which we may then have to sift and to which we no doubt have to add. In particular, we may have to look in

[88] Robert Ahdieh, 'Between Dialogue and Decree: International Review of National Courts' (2004) 79 *New York University Law Review*, 2029–163 at 2034.

[89] It is, I think, no accident that the work of Alexander Bickel – especially the notions of 'mediating devices' and 'passive virtues' – is referred to often here (especially in the American literature). See for example, Cover and Aleinikoff's quotation of Bickel in 'Dialectical Federalism': 'Over time, as a problem is lived with, the Court does not work in isolation to divine the answer that is right. It has the means to elicit partial answers and reactions from the other institutions, and to try tentative answers itself' (from *The Least Dangerous Branch*, quoted at 1048, fn. 65), and they go on to talk about the passive virtues as devices for facilitating the conversation between courts and political actors. See also now the considerable literature on passive virtues.

[90] For more on tentative cognition generally, see Nicholas Rescher, *Presumption and the Practices of Tentative Cognition* (Cambridge: Cambridge University Press, 2006).

[91] Ahdieh recognises the use of dicta, and asks us to pay attention to the significant expressive, rhetoric or discursive dimension of judicial communication (see Ahdieh, 'Between Dialogue and Decree' at p. 2072). For him, 'dicta can thus be understood to have a strongly prospective orientation. It is, in some sense, a window onto the future . . . [a form of foreshadowing]' (ibid., at 2073). Statements of dicta 'warrant close attention, respect, and even deference. . .dicta may help encourage innovation' (ibid., at 2074).

[92] This debate has relatively recently attracted the attention of theorists of legal reasoning, see e.g. Stefano Bertea and Claudio Sarra, 'Foreign Precedents in Judicial Argument' (2014) 16 *European Journal of Legal Studies*, last accessed online 16 August 2015, http://www.ejls.eu/16/199UK.htm.

ever-greater detail, and again very much diachronically, at the use of modes and devices such as legal fictions, hypotheticals and constructions of perspectives (from which 'the facts' are constructed and evaluated) – in short, at all the different ways in which legal reasoning plays with facts – and consider them from the viewpoint of the quality of relations – that is, to see them as relational resources, developed and used with a view to establishing or maintaining relations with other norm-generating units. These are often modes and devices of thought that make little sense from the perspective of a theorist who thinks univocally, focusing on the identity and unity of a system, and who looks exclusively at the sources of justifications in the instance case (rather than diachronically). It is only when put in a relational context and studied over time – and thus in a context where what matters are the quality of relations across time – that these modes and devices come into their own. Outside that paradigm, they look like errors, wrinkles to be ironed out, mis-steps, or at best unnecessary detours, signs of Hercules' failing strength.

3.4 Conclusion

This collection alone is testament to the momentum currently enjoyed by pluralist thinking about law. An important dimension of pluralist jurisprudence is a theory of legal reasoning. The conceptual framework articulated in this chapter is designed to assist the further development of such a theory. It has been suggested here that such a theory must pay attention to both justification and imagination; to the exercise of both in the instant case and across time; and to the internal (intra-systemic) and the relational dimensions of reasoning. Much of this has already been recognised, if not precisely in those terms, amongst historians of legal pluralism. Thus, if there is one thing I would urge theorists enthusiastic about pluralist jurisprudence to do, it is to find ways of collaborating with and learning from history.

4

Pluralising Constitutional Pluralism

CORMAC MAC AMHLAIGH

4.1 Introduction

It is a commonplace in much contemporary political and legal thinking that global order is undergoing a transition from a 'Westphalian' era where law and politics operated, and was therefore studied, according to a neat dichotomy – domestic/international, constitutional law/public international law – to a more complex 'post-Westphalian' era where this dichotomy appears increasingly redundant. This 'post-Westphalian world' entails the demotion of the state from the centre of the political universe to one among a number of actors in a broader setting where international institutions rival states for authority and influence.[1] Sovereignty, if relevant to this worldview is of a 'late'[2] form rather than the 'high sovereignty'[3] of the Westphalian age.

Yet, even if the analytical tools of the Westphalian era, and particularly the overarching 'metaprinciple'[4] of state sovereignty, are becoming increasingly redundant as analytical frameworks to capture an emergent post-Westphalian global order, we have yet to identify an organising analytical frame which would take its place. As such, the transition from the 'Westphalian' to the 'post-Westphalian' involves the replacement of a global *order* of legal orders based on the idea of state sovereignty to a global, in Walker's memorable coining, *disorder* of legal orders.[5] Rather

[1] Nico Krisch, *Beyond Constitutionalism: The Pluralist Structure of Postnational Law* (Oxford: Oxford University Press, 2010), p. 5.

[2] Neil Walker, 'Late Sovereignty in the European Union', in Neil Walker (ed.), *Sovereignty in Transition* (Oxford: Hart Publishing, 2003).

[3] Cormac Mac Amhlaigh, 'Late Sovereignty in Post-Integration Europe: Continuity and Change in a Constitutive Concept', in Rebecca Adler-Nissen and Ulrik Pram Grad (eds.), *European Integration and Postcolonial Sovereignty Games* (London: Routledge, 2013), pp. 39–52, p. 42.

[4] Neil Walker, 'Beyond Boundary Disputes and Basic Grids: Mapping the Global Disorder of Normative Orders' (2008) 6 *International Journal of Constitutional Law*, 373–96, 376.

[5] Ibid., 376.

than one overarching meta-principle to organise the array of legal orders co-existing in the contemporary world there are a variety of competing analytical frames which attempt to organise the co-existence of multiple legal orders in particular ways.[6]

Of particular interest to law and legal theory in this context of transition from a Westphalian to a post-Westphalian globe has been the growth of self-contained regimes beyond the state[7] involving some combination of administrative, legislative or judicial functions which more closely resemble the normative orders of states than the classic model of suprastate[8] law; public international law with its attendant problems of effectiveness and enforcement[9] and its putatively 'primitive' nature.[10] The proliferation of these types of regimes – as well as the fact that their jurisdictions frequently overlap – have led to inevitable interaction and sporadic conflicts between them which, given their unusual nature, at least as compared with classic public international law, seem to resist analysis and resolution by reference to the classic monist or dualist mechanisms of mediating the relationship between state and suprastate normative orders.

6 For example, Walker identifies seven potential 'global meta-principles of legal authority'; state sovereigntist, global hierarchical, unipolar, regional, integrity, legal-field discursive and pluralist. Walker (n. 4), 386.

7 Bruno Simma and Dirk Pulkowski, 'Of Planets and the Universe: Self-contained Regimes in International Law' (2006) 17 *European Journal of International Law*, 483–529.

8 'Suprastate' in this chapter is taken to mean simply 'beyond the state'. As such, suprastate law relates to any law or legal order beyond the state regardless of its classification as public international law or otherwise. Similarly, 'state' will be used interchangeably with 'national', 'domestic' and 'municipal'.

9 See generally John Tasioulas, 'The Legitimacy of International Law', in Samantha Besson and John Tasioulas (eds.), *The Philosophy of International Law* (Oxford: Oxford University Press, 2010), pp. 97–116.

10 As asserted most famously by HLA Hart: 'In form, international law resembles . . . a [primitive] regime of primary rules, even though the content of its often elaborate rules are very unlike those of a primitive society, and many of its concepts, methods, and techniques are the same as those of modern municipal law.' HLA Hart, *The Concept of Law* (Oxford: Clarendon Press, 1994), p. 227. The debate has moved on considerably in recent years. See Jeremy Waldron, 'International Law: "A Relatively Small and Unimportant" Part of Jurisprudence?', in Luis Duarte d'Almeida, James Edwards, Andrea Dolcetti (eds.), *Reading HLA Hart's 'The Concept of Law'* (Oxford: Hart Publishing, 2013); Samantha Besson 'Theorizing the Sources of International Law', in Samantha Besson and John Tasioulas (eds.), *The Philosophy of International Law* (Oxford: Oxford University Press, 2010), pp. 163–85; Ronald Dworkin, 'A New Philosophy for International Law' (2013) 41 *Philosophy and Public Affairs*, 2–30; Andreas Paulus, 'The International Legal System as a Constitution', in Jeffrey Dunoff and Joel Tractman (eds.), *Ruling the World? Constitutionalism, International Law, and Global Governance* (Cambridge: Cambridge University Press, 2009).

The idea of constitutional pluralism has become a popular 'frame' with which to analyse and organise the global disorder of legal orders and in particular the interaction and sporadic conflicts between them.[11] Originating in the work of Neil MacCormick, and in particular his theorisation of the relationship between domestic constitutional law and the law of the European Union (EU), it has since developed and expanded beyond its traditional domicile of the relationship between EU law and national law to extend to a variety of different legal relationships globally.[12] Key to this theorisation of constitutional pluralism as a 'post-Westaphlaian' frame of law has been the role of suprastate legal officials - primarily suprastate judicial bodies and in particular their statements regarding the nature and effects of the norms of suprastate orders – which provide a measure of clarity surrounding the nature of suprastate law as a 'post-Westphalian' form of legal ordering in a context of considerable ambiguity surrounding a conception of a suprastate law distinct from the classic 'Westphalian' dichotomy.

Focusing particularly on the role of suprastate judicial actors in clarifying the nature of suprastate law through their statements surrounding its nature and effects, this chapter analyzes and critiques one feature of constitutional pluralism; namely its 'methodological monism'. This relates to the tendency in constitutional pluralist theorising to reduce the complex relationships between different legal orders to one

[11] The literature on constitutional pluralism is increasing exponentially. For some representative examples see Neil MacCormick, *Questioning Sovereignty* (Oxford: Oxford University Press, 1999), ch. 7; Neil Walker, 'The Idea of Constitutional Pluralism' (2002) 65 *Modern Law Review*, 317–59; Miguel Maduro, 'Contrapunctual Law: Europe's Constitutional Pluralism in Action', in Neil Walker (ed.), *Sovereignty in Transition* (Oxford: Hart Publishing, 2003), pp. 502–37; Mattias Kumm, 'The Jurisprudence of Constitutional Conflict: Constitutional Supremacy in Europe before and after the Constitutional Treaty' (2005) 11 *European Law Journal*, 262–307; Julo Baqeuro Cruz, 'The Legacy of the Maastricht-Urteil and the Pluralist Movement' (2008) 14 *European Law Journal*, 389–422; Krisch (n. 1); Cormac Mac Amhlaigh, 'Concepts of Law in Integration Through Law', in Daniel Augenstein (ed.), *'Integration Through Law Revisited: The Making of the European Polity* (Farnham: Ashgate, 2012); Matej Avbelj and Jan Komárek (eds.), *Constitutional Pluralism in the European Union and Beyond* (Oxford: Hart Publishing, 2012).

[12] See Krisch (n. 1); Neil Walker, 'Constitutionalism and Pluralism in Global Context', in Matej Avbelj and Jan Komárek (eds.), *Constitutional Pluralism in the European Union and Beyond* (Oxford: Hart Publishing, 2012), pp. 17–38; Mattias Kumm, 'The Cosmopolitan Turn in Constitutionalism: On the Relationship between Constitutionalism in and Beyond the State', in Jeffery Dunoff and Joel Tractman (eds.), *Ruling the World? Constitutionalism, International Law, and Global Governance* (Cambridge: Cambridge University Press, 2009), pp. 258–324.

single framework of pluralism, whether for analytical or normative purposes, in a post-Westphalian world. In particular it focuses on the problems this methodological monism poses for constitutional pluralism's explanatory ambition as well as its normative aims in understanding and managing interactions and conflicts between normative orders. Given the reliance of constitutional pluralism on the statements of (primarily suprastate) legal officials for their understanding of the nature of 'post-Westphalian' suprastate normative orders – not least for the ways in which these normative orders interact with each other along constitutional pluralist lines – the diversity of those statements in practice means that such a methodologically monist approach to regime interactions, the chapter argues, is untenable.

The challenge is mounted in a series of steps. Firstly, the methodological monist tendency in constitutional pluralism is outlined. Then, drawing primarily on MacCormick's original writings on constitutional pluralism, the relevance of reconceptualising suprastate law to constitutional pluralism is highlighted and the relationship between this reconceptualisation and the statements of suprastate legal officials is then established. The chapter then pursues the claim that the statements of suprastate legal officials differ between different suprastate legal orders by reference to an example of two suprastate legal orders which interact heavily with domestic state law: EU law and the law of the European Convention of Human Rights (ECHR). The chapter concludes that the methodological monist tendency in pluralism cannot be maintained in the light of the existence of diverse forms of suprastate law at least as evidenced by the differential claims to authority and effectiveness of suprastate normative orders by their legal officials in the emergent global (dis)order.

4.2 Constitutional Pluralism and Methodological Monism

Constitutional pluralism attempts to capture the increasingly complex global order and in particular the interactions between normative orders by establishing an analytical framework for interactions which departs from the classic 'Westphalian' account of interactions between state and suprastate law. The classic model of interaction between state law and suprastate law was dominated by the view that these forms of legal order were always necessarily in a *hierarchical* relationship to one another. As such, the relationship between domestic constitutional law and public international law was primarily understood and regulated according to the idea of dualism, presupposing the prioritisation of domestic law over public international law in a vertical or hierarchical relationship. The alternative, and rarer in practice, account of interacting legal systems – monism – operated according to this hierarchical mind-set, albeit in this case the positions were inverted such that suprastate law (essentially public international law) was hierarchical to state law;[13] a position resurrected in the context of EU law.[14] Constitutional Pluralism effectuates a shift from this Westphalian hierarchical ordering of the interaction between legal orders by collapsing the 'verticality' of traditional thinking about the relationships between legal orders to one of 'horizontality'. Constitutional pluralism encourages us to think about the relationships between state and suprastate law in a *heterarchical*[15] rather than hierarchical way; that is as operating side-by-side without the presumptive authority of one over the other.

By collapsing the interaction between legal orders from a vertical plane to a horizontal one, from a '*y* axis' to an '*x* axis', constitutional pluralism aims at providing a more nuanced and accurate account of interacting normative orders in an emergent post-Westphalian global (dis)order than the conventional hierarchical Westphalian account. Whereas this was initially aimed, in the work of Neil MacCormick, at understanding and exploring the relationships between EU law and state law, it has since been employed to explain interactions and conflicts between other legal orders up to, and including, between suprastate legal orders themselves.[16] On top of this analytical function, constitutional pluralism also has a normative function which builds on these analytical insights to either critique or endorse interactions and conflicts between normative orders by lending normative support to either their resolution or persistence. Many accounts of constitutional pluralism attempt to provide a method of resolving conflicts between interacting legal orders to ensure consistency, certainty, fairness and the values associated with the rule of law and

[13] As promoted primarily by Hans Kelsen. See Hans Kelsen, *General Theory of Law and State*, trans. Anders Wedberg (Cambridge: Harvard University Press, 1945), ch. VI.

[14] See (Case 14/64) *Costa v. Ente Nazionale per l'Energia Elettrica (ENEL)* [1964] CMLR 425. For the application of monism in the EU context see Catherine Richmond, 'Preserving the Identity Crisis: Autonomy, System and Sovereignty in European Law' (1997) 16 *Law and Philosophy*, 377–420.

[15] Walker (n. 11), 337.

[16] Such as the application of pluralism to the legal orders of the European Union and the United Nations; see Gráinne de Búrca, 'The ECJ and the International Legal Order: A Re-evaluation', in Gráinne de Búrca and Joseph Weiler (eds.), *The Worlds of European Constitutionalism* (Cambridge: Cambridge University Press, 2012), pp. 105–49.

the protection of fundamental rights in judicial decision-making involving conflicting normative orders.[17] This is usually done by fashioning a series of 'conflict principles' to be applied to regime interactions and conflicts to ensure the optimisation of these values where interactions and conflicts occur.[18] Others endorse conflicts and their *ir*resolution as per se normatively desirable. Krisch, for example, has advanced a normative defence of pluralism based on the pluralist 'virtues' of adaptation, contestation and checks and balances.[19] Unlike those normative accounts prescribing principles for the resolution of conflicts, Krisch celebrates their absence in interactions and conflicts between orders, as the absence of such conflict principles helps to attain the contestational virtues of pluralism.[20]

Notwithstanding the dual functions of constitutional pluralism, most accounts of constitutional pluralism are methodologically monist in the sense that they assume that one analytical framework of pluralism, or one set of pluralist principles or values is apt to capture, understand or legitimise the entire post-Westphalian order.[21] There are many examples which could be offered in this regard; for example, constitutional pluralism's originator, Neil MacCormick, originally sketched out two possible models of pluralism, yet still assumed that only one would be necessary to give an account of interacting legal orders in the post-Westphalian context.[22] However few constitutional pluralists rival Mattias Kumm's work on constitutional pluralism for the breadth of its ambition and its unalloyed methodological monism.[23]

17 For salient examples of this see Kumm (n. 11), Maduro (n. 11).

18 Ibid. See also Charles Sabel and Oliver Gerstenberg, 'Constitutionalising an Overlapping Consensus: The ECJ and the Emergency of a Coordinate Constitutional Order' (2010) 16 *European Law Journal*, 511–50.

19 Krisch (n. 1), ch. 3. 20 Ibid.

21 Given that normative accounts of pluralism rely on the presupposition of interacting and conflicting normative orders based on analytical accounts of pluralism, the two are inextricably linked; indeed many accounts of constitutional pluralism straddle the analytical/normative divide. However, the analytical or explanatory dimension of constitutional pluralism is necessarily 'lexically prior' to its normative dimension. The focus in this chapter is primarily on constitutional pluralism's explanatory functions, however given that its normative dimension is based on these explanatory accounts, the challenge to constitutional pluralism raised here is also relevant to normative accounts of constitutional pluralism.

22 See MacCormick (n. 11), pp. 116–17. See also the contributions to Avbelj and Komárek (n. 11) virtually all of which assume this methodological monist approach to constitutional pluralism.

23 Kumm's work on pluralism is wide-ranging. Following MacCormick, he began by looking at pluralism between municipal law and EU law; see 'Who is the Final Arbiter of Constitutionality in Europe?' (1999) 36 *Common Market Law Review*, 351–86;

Kumm argues that the transition from a Westphalian to a post-Westphalian world requires a 'Copernican turn'[24] in constitutionalism from a Westphalian 'statist paradigm'[25] regarding the relationship and interaction between state and suprastate law. This Copernican turn involves reconceptualising suprastate law in 'post-Westphalian' *constitutional* terms as well as rejecting the privileging of the 'statist paradigm' in viewing the relationship between international law and state law;[26] in other words, rejecting the state-sovereigntist paradigm as the 'metaprinciple' of global order. In the place of state sovereignty Kumm argues for a form of constitutional pluralism which he calls 'cosmopolitan constitutionalism'[27] to understand and manage interactions between orders.[28] This framework of constitutional pluralism both explains and provides normative benchmarks for interaction and conflicts between state and suprastate legal orders according to the principles of legality, subsidiarity, due process, democracy and constitutional rights protection.[29]

Most significantly from the viewpoint of methodological monism are Kumm's claims regarding the model of constitutional pluralism he advances and what it does in the context of an emergent post-Westphalian (dis)order. He claims that his paradigm of cosmopolitan constitutionalism describes the 'deep structure of public law',[30] including the 'basic structural features of international and domestic constitutional law practices in liberal constitutional democracies'.[31] 'Cosmopolitan constitutionalism', furthermore, establishes an 'integrative basic conceptual framework'[32] for a '*general theory of public law that integrates national and international law.*'[33] As such, Kumm argues, this model

'Jurisprudence' (n. 11); before moving to view pluralism in a more global context; 'The Legitimacy of International Law: A Constitutionalist Framework of Analysis' (2004) 15 *European Journal of International Law*, 907–31; 'Cosmopolitan Turn' (n. 12); 'The Moral Point of Constitutional Pluralism: Defining the Domain of Legitimate Institutional Civil Disobedience and Conscientious Objection', in Julie Dickson and Pavlos Eleftheriadis (eds.), *Philosophical Foundations of European Union Law* (Oxford: Oxford University Press, 2012), pp. 216–46; 'Rethinking Constitutional Authority: On the Structure and Limits of Constitutional Pluralism', in Matej Avbelj and Jan Komárek (eds.), *Constitutional Pluralism in the European Union and Beyond* (Oxford: Hart Publishing, 2012), pp. 39–65; 'The Cosmopolitan Turn in Constitutionalism: An Integrative Conception of Public Law' (2013) 20 *Indiana Journal*, 605–28. Here 'Cosmopolitan Turn' will be relied on in the main as a paradigm of his account of constitutional pluralism.

24 Kumm (n. 12), p. 266. 25 Ibid., p. 261. 26 Ibid., part 2. 27 Ibid., p. 272.
28 Ibid., p. 274. 29 Ibid., part 2. 30 Ibid., p. 262. 31 Ibid. 32 Ibid., p. 264.
33 Ibid., p. 264, *emphasis in original.*

of constitutional pluralism provides a '*unifying*'[34] framework for the different interactions between state and suprastate law as well as a host of other features of the post-Westphalian world including the increasing complexity of global governance, the 'functional reconceptualization' of sovereignty, as well as basic structural features of contemporary human rights practice.[35]

The remainder of this chapter demonstrates how these grand claims are unsustainable in the global context, not least by constitutional pluralism's own lights through its reliance on the statements of (particularly suprastate) legal officials as evidence of the emergence of a post-Westphalian (dis)order, the transformation of suprastate law and the relevance of constitutional pluralism to that (dis) order.

4.3 Constitutional, Not Legal, Pluralism

The idea of pluralism in law predates the current flurry of attention from lawyers and legal theorists focusing on interactions between state and suprastate law. In the 1960s and 1970s, legal anthropologists and sociologists, looking primarily at non-European, often postcolonial, states conceptualised a pluralist universe of official and unofficial legal orders which presupposed the 'coexistence within a social group of legal orders which do not belong to a single 'system'.[36] Central to these accounts of law and legal system was the debunking of the 'myth' that only formal municipal legal systems, the object of study of analytical positivism, could be classified as law and legal system properly so-called.[37]

MacCormick's influential initial exploration of constitutional pluralism in suprastate law, which has informed subsequent thinking on the topic, seemed to track these anthropological and sociological accounts of legal pluralism.[38] However, MacCormick's pluralism envisaged pluralism

[34] Ibid., *emphasis added.* [35] Ibid., p. 262.

[36] John Griffiths, 'What is Legal Pluralism?' (1986) *Journal of Legal Pluralism and Unofficial Law*, 1–55. See also Sally Eagle Merry, 'Legal Pluralism' (1988) 22 *Law and Society Review*, 869–96.

[37] Griffiths (n. 36), 4. For a critique of this charge against legal positivism, see Victor Muniz-Fraticelli, *The Structure of Pluralism* (Oxford: Oxford University Press, 2014), ch. 5.

[38] I say 'seemed' because nowhere in his writing that I could find did MacCormick explicitly refer to these writings or to these ideas advanced by legal pluralists. Krisch seems to suggest that he was inspired by these accounts but I have not found explicit evidence of this. See Nico Krisch, 'Who is Afraid of Radical Pluralism? Legal Order and Political Stability in the Postnational Space?' (2011) 24 *Ratio Juris*, 386–412, 388. Walker seems to

between 'institutional normative orders', an account of law and legal system drawing on the core tenets of analytical positivist accounts of law including the idea of legal officials, official sources and a hierarchy of norms.[39] As such, a key difference between MacCormick's (and subsequent accounts of) constitutional pluralism and previous accounts of legal pluralism was that constitutional pluralism envisaged pluralism between *official* forms of law; while simultaneously shifting the level of analysis from forms of normative order at and beneath the state level, to normative orders at and beyond the state level. Therefore, on a jurisprudential spectrum of accounts of forms of law and legal orders – from the very informal such as the 'self-regulation of a 'semi-autonomous social field'[40] to the very formal as exemplified by the analytical positivist tradition – constitutional pluralism tended strongly towards the latter form.[41]

As well as marking a break with other forms of legal pluralism, MacCormick's approach also marked a departure from conventional ways of theorising law and legal systems in analytical jurisprudence. Conventional approaches to theorising law and legal systems tended to rely on the traditional Westphalian dichotomy of municipal law/international law; the latter popularly characterised as a lesser or more 'primitive' form of law.[42] However, MacCormick eschewed this conventional Westphalian dichotomy in legal theory to conceptualise a form of law which did not recognise the boundary between the state and international levels by severing the link between law and the state.[43] All that was required for the existence of an institutional normative order for MacCormick, was a system of norms that was autonomous,

have been the first to explicitly distinguish constitutional pluralism from other forms of legal pluralism. See Walker (n. 11), 336–37.

39 MacCormick (n. 11), ch. 1; Neil MacCormick, *Institutions of Law* (Oxford: Oxford University Press, 2007).

40 Sally Falk Moore, 'Law and Social Change: The Semi-Autonomous Social Field as an Appropriate Subject of Study' (1973) 7 *Law & Society Review*, 719–46.

41 As Roughan notes, constitutional pluralism constitutes the 'low hanging fruit' in questions and puzzles thrown up by legal pluralism for jurisprudential accounts of law and legal system. Nicole Roughan, *Authorities: Conflicts, Cooperation, and Transnational Legal Theory* (Oxford: Oxford University Press, 2014), p. 69. For a broader discussion of how constitutional pluralism fits into the broader firmament of legal pluralism, see Roughan, ch. 4.

42 Hart (n. 10).

43 MacCormick, (n. 11), p. 17. See also Neil MacCormick, 'Beyond the Sovereign State' (1993) 56 *Modern Law Review*, 1–18.

involved judgment which was institutionalised and was systemic in character.[44] For MacCormick, even if states were a 'paradigmatic'[45] or 'principal'[46] example of an institutional normative order, it was but a 'species' of the 'genus'.[47] Thus, MacCormick concluded: 'law is institutional order, and state-law is simply one form of law.'[48]

As such, a particular conception of formal or official law, and particularly a reconceptualisation of the nature of suprastate law in 'constitutional' terms beyond the classic theoretical formulations of public international law as a species of 'primitive' legal order, was a crucial step in theorising interacting orders in constitutional pluralist terms. This was explicitly acknowledged by MacCormick himself in that he claimed that that certain conceptions of law (in his case law as 'institutional normative order') *admitted* a particular form of pluralism.[49] This, in turn, meant that suprastate law would interact with another institutional normative order – in particular municipal law – in a manner distinct from the conventional methods of dualism; as capable of interacting heterarchically rather than hierarchically.

4.4 Legal Officials and Constitutional Pluralism

Perhaps unsurprisingly, given the shift in MacCormick's account of pluralism in law from pluralism involving unofficial forms of law, to pluralism between official forms of law, legal officials have played a prominent role in this reconceptualisation of suprastate law. Indeed, the main catalyst for reconceptualising suprastate law beyond the Westphalian hierarchical model to a post-Westphalian heterarchical one in constitutional pluralism has been the statements of particular suprastate legal officials; namely courts and tribunals. This is clear in MacCormick's original exploration of the idea which emerged from the problematisation of the relationship between EU law and state law in the light of particular judgments from the German Federal Constitutional Court (GFCC) on the effect of EU law within the German Constitutional order,[50] but it is also true for the majority of subsequent theorising of constitutional pluralism.[51]

[44] MacCormick (n. 11), pp. 6–7. [45] Ibid., p. 1. [46] Ibid. [47] Ibid.
[48] Ibid., p. 15. [49] Ibid., p. 102.
[50] See particularly Neil MacCormick, 'The Maastricht-Urteil: Sovereignty Now' (1995) 1 *European Law Journal*, 259–66. See also MacCormick (n. 11).
[51] See references at Note 11 earlier in this chapter.

In attempting to theorise EU law in a post-Westphalian way, and particularly in an attempt to understand its relationship with other orders, MacCormick focused on the statements of the legal official par excellence of the EU legal system, the Court of Justice of the European Union (CJEU) and in particular its early decisions on the authority, nature and effects of EU law. Key to the CJEU's activities in this regard was the distinction the Court drew between EU law and conventional public international law by insisting on the autonomy and hierarchy of the former, which were not contingent upon how the law of EU Member States chose to implement it. In MacCormick's words:[52]

> The Court's initiative was a decisive one when it interpreted the juridical character of the entity brought to birth through the foundation treaties as being a distinct legal order. This was an order of a new and hitherto unique kind, one whose norms were directly applicable and directly effective [and] were to be accorded supremacy in each state over national law. These decisions necessarily imply that the foundation treaties ... amount effectively to the constitutional framework of a quite special entity, this 'European commonwealth'.

These developments, MacCormick argued, had a profound impact upon how EU law was theorised. In applying legal theory to understand EU law *qua* law, he argued that 'the [CJEU's] decisions on the juridical character of Community and Union have *particular importance*.'[53] As such, a 'post-Westphalian' conceptualisation of EU law, distinct from a 'Westphalian' understanding of EU law as public international law, was needed in the light of the statements of the EU's primary legal official. In this way, the CJEU's statements effectively 'caused' the Westphalian '*y* axis' to fall to a post-Westphalian '*x* axis' in conceptualising EU law as a particular (post-Westphalian) form of law, which had significant implications for how it interacted with other legal orders and therefore for constitutional pluralism. This reconceptualisation of suprastate law in 'post-Westphalian' terms, through the reliance on the statements of suprastate legal officials, is a key feature of most subsequent pluralist theorising of normative orders, albeit that the precise conceptions of law extrapolated from – sometimes the same – set of legal officials have differed.[54]

[52] MacCormick (n. 11), p. 97. [53] Ibid., *emphasis added.*

[54] For example, Kumm, Maduro, and Sabel and Gerstenberg in their writings on pluralism have employed a less positivist understanding of EU law in theorising the relationship between EU law and national law in pluralist terms. Kumm explicitly draws on the work

Of course, in relying on the statements of suprastate legal officials as the foundation of constitutional pluralism, constitutional pluralists are drawing on a venerable tradition of foregrounding the role of legal officials (and almost always courts) in theorising the concept of law.[55] For example, Hart famously placed legal officials at the centre of his concept of law and legal system.[56] In particular, the existence of the secondary 'rule of recognition', which established the validity of all the other norms of the system, was evidenced by its acceptance as such by the officials of the legal system.[57] Such was the centrality of legal officials to his concept of a legal system that they were included as one of two necessary conditions for the existence of a legal order.[58] Whereas the notion of legal officials was reasonably broadly construed, it was clear that with respect to the rule of recognition, it was primarily courts that Hart had in mind.[59]

In a similar vein, Raz emphasises the centrality of legal officials and particularly courts to the concept of law and the concept of a legal system. Distinguishing between norm-applying institutions and norm-creating institutions, he argues that only norm-applying institutions are necessary for the existence of a legal order.[60] These institutions are primarily concerned with 'the *authoritative* determination of normative situations in accordance with pre-existing norms',[61] of which the paradigmatic example are courts. A key feature of primary norm-applying organs in a legal order for Raz is their claim to authority; that is that their decisions and determinations of normative situations are *binding*, even where they are mistaken.[62]

Even legal theorists who distance themselves from the positivist tradition rely heavily, if not exclusively, on institutional practice, and particularly the institutional practices of courts in developing their conceptions of law. For example, Ronald Dworkin's well-known non-positivist conception of law infused with moral principles nonetheless

of non-positivists such as Ronald Dworkin and Robert Alexy in his model of pluralism, Kumm (n. 11); Maduro draws on the constitutional theoretical work of Cass Sunstein to characterise principles of pluralism in terms of 'incompletely theorized agreements', Maduro (n. 11); Sabel and Gerstenberg draw on the political theories of John Rawls (n. 18).

55 In this regard Raz attributes court-centric theories of law to a 'large number of authors - among them Holland, Gray, Salmond, Holmes, Llewelln, and Hart.' Joseph Raz, *The Authority of Law* (Oxford: Oxford University Press, 1979), p. 89.

56 Hart (n. 10). 57 Ibid., p. 115. 58 Ibid., p. 117.

59 Hanoch Sheinman, 'The Priority of Courts in the General Theory of Law' (2007) 52 *American Journal of Jurisprudence*, 229–58, 237.

60 Raz (n. 55), p. 105. 61 Ibid., p. 110. 62 Ibid., p. 108.

relies on the institutional practices of courts, and particular legal statements, to argue for the centrality of principles in any concept of law.[63]

As such, in taking the first step to a constitutional pluralist understanding of interacting legal orders, that is by positing a conception of suprastate law distinct from the conventional 'Westphalian' understanding of 'primitive' public international law, pluralists can be seen to be following in the tradition of main-stream legal theory (both positivist and non-positivist) in relying on the statements of suprastate legal officials, and particularly courts in developing particular theories of suprastate law.[64]

However, although constitutional pluralist accounts of suprastate law based on the statements of suprastate legal officials follow in the tradition of mainstream legal theory, their reliance on legal officials involves an additional function to theorising suprastate law when compared with the statements of legal officials in theorising municipal law. In municipal legal theory, a central – if not the primary – function of legal officials is to determine the validity and status of individual norms by reference to particular standards of validity within a particular legal system, or to identify the principles of the relevant legal order.[65] However, theorists of suprastate law tend to take questions of the validity of suprastate norms for granted, instead focusing primarily on the *type* of (official) law in question, that is the type of *authority* and *effectiveness* particular (suprastate) norms, and systems, enjoy. This is not to say that questions of authority and bindingness are irrelevant to the theorisation of municipal law. Instead, law's pre-emptive authority and bindingness is usually taken for granted at the state level where there is an assumption that law, properly so called, and once identified as a system, is ipso facto binding and authoritative.[66] In the suprastate legal context, however, on top of assuming questions of validity and/or principles in suprastate law from the statements of legal officials, constitutional pluralists rely on the statements of legal officials as *evidence of the transition from suprastate law as 'primitive' public international law to suprastate law as an*

[63] Ronald Dworkin, *Taking Rights Seriously* (London: Duckworth, 1978); Ronald Dworkin, *Law's Empire* (London: Duckworth, 1986).

[64] Of course MacCormick himself had a considerable stake in this 'mainstream', having been a legal theorist of note prior to examining the relationship between interacting legal orders. See for example Neil MacCormick, *Legal Reasoning and Legal Theory* (Oxford: Clarendon Press, 1979); Neil MacCormick and Ota Weinberger, *An Institutional Theory of Law* (Dordrecht: Kluwer, 1986).

[65] Hart (n. 10); Dworkin (n. 63).

[66] Raz (n. 55), ch. 2 and ch. 8.

authoritative and effective normative order, that is as 'constitutional' post-Westphalian suprastate law, capable of interacting according to a constitutional pluralist framework.

Again, MacCormick's writings on the topic are instructive in this regard. As well as foregrounding legal officials in developing his theory of law as 'institutional normative order', legal officials also have a fundamental role in allowing for a transformational reading of suprastate law beyond conventional public international law. For MacCormick, judgment was crucial to idea of normative order in that being subject to a norm was to have one's actions open to judgment as to whether one's actions conformed with a norm or not.[67] In an *institutional* normative order, this judgment is institutionalised or 'organized'.[68] Once judgment is institutionalised, MacCormick argues, there must be some rule about finality of judgment within the system which in turn leads to the systemic ordering of norms.[69] The key question of validity is entailed in MacCormick's account in that the finality of judgment within a system involves 'final authority on the question of *what counts as a binding norm* and how it bears on the case',[70] which is 'itself one which can only be pronounced with final effect by an appropriate judge or court.'[71] So far, so conventional legal theory. However, in cases of normative order whose status or authority was ambiguous or disputed, either because it was not conventionally a form of law which was considered binding like municipal law or because of its 'sui generis' nature, the question of its empowerment, authority and effects could itself be achieved, MacCormick argued, through '*institutional acts*'.[72] A clear example of this development would be where the judges of a normative order 'by their authoritative interpretation of their own powers and of other constitutional norms *transform* the character of the original empowerments involved'[73] to one of a binding and authoritative normative order akin to municipal law. As such, the question of whether the normative order was authoritative and binding itself was one to be determined by legal officials themselves (along with questions of validity). This was the case even if the determination was *transformative* of conventional understandings of the authority and bindingness of the relative order. This highlighted the 'self-referential'[74] quality of such systems.

This additional role for the statements of legal officials in theorising suprastate law can be explained by the fact that the 'post-Westphalian

[67] MacCormick (n. 11), p. 6. [68] Ibid., p. 7. [69] Ibid. [70] Ibid., p. 8. [71] Ibid.
[72] MacCormick (n. 11), p. 102, *emphasis added.* [73] Ibid., p. 103. [74] Ibid., p. 7.

world' or its emergence, is still *very much a work in progress.* If we are 'still trying to find our way through the maze, or 'mystery', of global governance'[75], then the clear and categorical statements of legal officials about the nature of suprastate normative orders in terms of their 'post-Westphalian' authority and effectiveness provide a measure of certainty, clarity and familiarity in an otherwise uncertain, unclear and unfamiliar world.

4.4.1 Municipal Legal Officials

However, it is not only with respect to the reconceptualisation of suprastate law in a post-Westphalian way that the statements of suprastate legal officials are important to constitutional pluralist theorising of the interaction of state and suprastate legal orders. If the claims of authority and effectiveness of suprastate legal actors were taken at face value vis-à-vis state law, then the 'post-Westphalian world' wouldn't look particularly post-Westphalian at all. For example, the claims of the CJEU regarding the supremacy, direct effect and *Kompetenz-Kompetenz* of EU law would have replaced Westphalian theories of hierarchical dualism, where national law was in a hierarchical relationship to suprastate law, with a Westphalian hierarchical monism, where suprastate law is in a hierarchical relationship to state law as envisaged by Kelsen in his theorisation of international law.[76] This would remain within a resolutely hierarchical mind-set, where suprastate (EU) law would take precedence over state law in cases of conflicts. However, as noted, constitutional pluralism involves a particular interpretation of a 'post-Westphalian world' whereby the emphasis shifts from hierarchical modes of interaction between orders to *heterarchical* modes. As such, the statements of legal officials with which a particular system is interacting are also relevant to conceptualising interactions in heterarchical rather than hierarchical terms. The statements of legal officials of the other interacting order (often municipal legal orders) are also central to a post-Westphalian pluralist understanding of interacting orders.

[75] Krisch (n. 1), p. 26.

[76] Kelsen (n. 13). Indeed, some authors have argued that constitutional pluralism involves the mere resurrection of monism in contemporary legal theory. See for example, Alexander Somek, 'Monism: A Tale of the Undead', in Avbelj and Komárek, *Constitutional Pluralism in the European Union and Beyond*, pp. 343–79.

In the context of interactions between suprastate law and state law, the statements of the legal officials of state law have tended to be *reactive*; that is reacting to the statements of suprastate legal officials regarding the authority and effectiveness of suprastate law; usually denying or conditioning the claims of suprastate legal officials.[77] For example, in the EU context, the statements of domestic courts, most famously but hardly exclusively the GFCC[78], tended to explicitly refute much of the authority claims of CJEU regarding the effects and status of EU law in national legal orders. These statements from domestic legal officials made clear that EU law and national law were not part of one single system with EU law at the apex, or orders interacting according to the priority of EU law, but rather distinct interacting legal orders which looked at different sources of their own validity. In MacCormick's account of the EU

[77] In this regard it is worth noting a potential shift among municipal legal officials with regard to the concept of municipal law. As noted, theories of municipal law, including those which relied on the statements of legal officials/courts, tend to assume the authority and effectiveness of the norms of these legal orders. This was usually in the absence of explicit statements from legal officials to this effect. It is interesting to speculate on whether the necessity of articulating the authority and effectiveness of municipal law by legal officials in the light of the global 'disorder of legal orders', not least EU law, would have any effect on how municipal law is conceptualised. It could be argued, for example, that the articulation of authority and effectiveness of law in this way presupposes or recognises a plurality of forms of law and legal orders in a way that conventional accounts of law and legal system may not have. Roughan's work on 'relative authority' makes an important contribution to capturing and theorising this shift. It is beyond the scope of this chapter to engage with her thesis on relative authority in any detail, however with respect to the specific case of court-based claims in the EU context, she notes the 'responsive' nature of such claims, arguing that they are examples of relative, rather than absolute, authority whereby the legitimacy of an authority lies as much in its relationship and interdependence with another authority as the substantive or procedural principles that that particular authority embodies. See Roughan (n. 41), ch. 11.

[78] The list of 'copy-cat' decisions from the apex Courts of other EU Member states is continually expanding. However, two recent intriguing additions to this list include the Czech Constitutional Court, which in its judgment Pl. US 5/12, Judgment of 31 January 2012 'Slovak Pensions' carried out the threat to defy the CJEU in a way that the GFCC only ever threated. For Comment see Robert Zbíral, 'Case Comment: A Legal Revolution or Negligible Episode? Court of Justice Decision Proclaimed *Ultra Vires*' (2012) 49 *Common Market Law Review*, 1475–92; Jan Komárek, 'Case Note: Playing with Matches: The Czech Constitutional Court Declares a Judgment of the Court of Justice of the EU *Ultra Vires*' (2012) 8 *European Constitutional Law Review*, 323–37. Also, the UK Supreme Court can now be said to have joined the ranks of 'EU constitutional pluralist courts' in the light of its decision in *R(HS2 Action Alliance Ltd) v. SS for Transport* [2014] UKSC 3. For comment see Alison Young, 'Wilkommen zum Constitutional Pluralism' UK Constitutional Law Blog (17th February 2014) (available at https://ukconstitutionallaw.org/).

context, it was the statements of municipal legal orders, and particularly their *rejection* of the authority claims of EU law vis-à-vis state law, that forced legal thinking to view interactions in constitutional pluralist terms. For MacCormick, the statements of the CJEU regarding the authority and effectiveness of EU law, alongside the *re*action by state legal officials, posed a 'profound challenge to our understanding of law and legal systems'[79] and brings us to the 'frontier of legal pluralism.'[80] The result, then, in the light of the statements of suprastate and municipal normative orders, was one of constitutional pluralism which he describes in the following terms:[81]

> [T]wo sets of constitutions, each of which is acknowledged valid, yet neither of which does, or has any compelling reason to, acknowledge the other as a source of validity. Where there is plurality of institutional normative orders, each with a functioning constitution (at least in the sense of body of higher-order norms establishing and conditioning relevant governmental powers), it is possible that each acknowledge the legitimacy of every other within its own sphere, while none asserts or acknowledges constitutional superiority over another.

In such a scenario, MacCormick concluded, 'constitutional pluralism' prevails'.[82]

4.5 Constitutional Pluralism and the Problem of Methodological Monism

The centrality of the statements of legal officials to theorising constitutional pluralism between state and suprastate legal orders poses a challenge to the 'methodological monist' tendencies of constitutional pluralists; that is, the tendency to assume that one model of constitutional pluralism can be used to explain the variety of interacting formal legal orders in the global disorder of legal orders. As noted, in the Post-Westphalian context, not only are legal officials central to the identification of law and understanding law as a system whether according to a criteria of validity or the identification of principles, but they also make further, explicit, claims to the authority and effectiveness of the norms of the system. Moreover, these claims elicit counter-claims from the legal officials of the systems at which those claims are addressed, usually municipal state legal systems. However, given that the 'post-Westphalian'

[79] MacCormick (n. 11), p. 102. [80] Ibid. [81] Ibid., p. 104. [82] Ibid.

world is very much still 'under construction', there is no fixed view of the nature, authority and effects of suprastate law as a post-Westphalian reconceptualisation of law beyond the state. As such, the global 'disorder of legal orders' is made up of a 'global disorder' of suprastate legal officials making a 'global disorder' of claims to the authority and effectiveness of different suprastate norms of different suprastate orders. These claims, in turn, provide the foundation for the understanding of these systems as post-Westphalian suprastate normative orders.

This can be illustrated by contrasting the development of EU law and the law of the European Convention of Human Rights *qua* post-Westphalian suprastate normative orders. These two legal orders entail different claims to the authority and effectiveness of their norms, different interactions with municipal law based on these claims, and therefore, it is argued, necessitate different models of constitutional pluralism to explain that interaction.[83]

The relevance of the CJEU's statements and impact on theorising EU law has already been outlined in this chapter. The key aspects of the CJEU's 'constitutionalization' of the EU Treaties were the autonomy of EU law, its authority as a form of law through the supremacy doctrine,[84] and its effects in municipal legal orders through its direct effect doctrine and its claims to its own *Kompetenz-Kompetenz*, the ability to determine the limits of EU law.[85] These statements have led both to a reconceptualisation of EU law as a form of law distinct from public international law, as well as eliciting robust counter-reactions from national courts claiming the supremacy of their municipal constitutional law and their

[83] As will be by now clear, interactions between EU law and state law are the 'paradigm case' of constitutional pluralism in post-Westphalian world and have attracted the attention of many constitutional pluralists. See for example the contributions in Avbelj and Komárek (n. 11). Pluralism between state law and ECHR law has attracted less attention but the relationship is being increasingly theorised in pluralist terms. See Nico Krisch, 'The Open Architecture of European Human Rights Law' (2008) 71 *Modern Law Review*, 183–216; Steven Greer and Luzius Wildhaber, 'Revisiting the Debate about 'constitutionalising' the European Court of Human Rights' (2013) 12 *Human Rights Law Review*, 655–87; Cormac Mac Amhlaigh, '"Even Children Lisp the Rights of Man": International Human Rights Law and National Minority Jurisdictions', in Stephen Tierney (ed.) *Nationalism and Globalisation* (Oxford: Hart Publishing, 2015), pp. 233–52.

[84] See Mac Amhlaigh (n. 11).

[85] See Cormac Mac Amhlaigh, 'The European Union's Constitutional Mosaic: Big "C" or Small "c", Is that the Question?', in Neil Walker, Jo Shaw and Stephen Tierney (eds.), *Europe's Constitutional Mosaic* (Oxford: Hart Publishing, 2011), pp. 21–47.

own *Kompetenz-Kompetenz.* This experience can be contrasted with the development of the ECHR system by its Court (ECtHR).

The ECHR's trajectory differed from that of EU law in that its evolution to a suprastate legal order occurred later, and less invasively, than that of EU law. There were a series of 'constitutionalizing' judgments from the Court in the 1970s when the key 'post-Westphalian' characteristics of the ECHR were established: the margin of appreciation doctrine, the use of the principle of proportionality and the development of particular interpretive doctrines by the Court including the 'evolutionary approach' and the use of a 'European consensus'.[86] These developments, combined with landmark high-profile judgments finding convention violations against prominent signatory states of the Convention,[87] marked a shift from Westphalian 'legal diplomacy'[88] to a more post-Westphalian 'constitutional' character – both of the norms of the convention as well as the court itself.[89] However, what is noticeable in the development of the ECHR from a Westphalian to a more post-Westphalian order is the absence of any robust claims to the authority and effectiveness of ECHR law akin to the supremacy of EU law or the *Kompetenz-Kompetenz* of the CJEU. There is a distinct absence of the idea of the 'supremacy' of the ECHR over norms of national law in the development of the ECHR system. Rather than insisting upon the supremacy of the provisions of the Convention in municipal law, their interaction was, according to the Court, to be managed by the political organs of signatory states according to their own constitutional arrangements as and when they saw fit.[90]

86 See generally Andreas Follesdal, Birgit Peters, Geir Ulfstein (eds.), *Constituting Europe: The European Court of Human Rights in a National, European and Global Context* (Cambridge: Cambridge University Press, 2013); Laurence Helfer, 'Redesigning the European Court of Human Rights: Embeddedness as a Deep Structural Principle of the European Human Rights Regime' (2008) 19 *European Journal of International Law*, 125–59.

87 Such as, for example, the Court's seminal decision in *Ireland v. the United Kingdom* (1978) 2 EHRR 25.

88 Mikael Rask Madsen, 'The Protracted Institutionalization of the Strasbourg Court: From Legal Diplomacy to Integrationist Jurisprudence', in Jonas Christoffersen and Mikael Rask Madsen (eds.), *The European Court of Human Rights between Law and Politics* (Oxford: Oxford University Press 2011), pp. 43–60, p. 44.

89 See Alec Stone Sweet, 'On the Constitutionalisation of the Convention: The European Court of Human Rights as a Constitutional Court' (2009) *Revue trimestrielle des droits de l'homme*, 923–44; Alec Stone Sweet, 'A Cosmopolitan Legal Order: Constitutional Pluralism and Rights Adjudication in Europe' (2012) 1 *Global Constitutionalism*, 53–90.

90 Of course this does not mean that the Court has not recommended changes to domestic practices deemed to be causing human rights violations. In particular, the introduction of 'pilot judgments' by the court has also led to prescriptions from the court on how to

This was in line with the Court's insistence on its 'subsidiary' role in protecting the rights contained in the Convention.[91] For the ECtHR, it was states, and not the Court, which had the primary responsibility for protecting the relevant rights within their own systems.

Furthermore, the ECtHR has never made claims regarding the effectiveness of ECHR comparable with those of the CJEU. Rather than claiming the direct effect of the norms of the ECHR, the Court found that states had autonomy as to how precisely they wished to give effect to the rights of the Convention within their domestic orders.[92] This deferential approach to the questions of the authority and effectiveness of the Convention was particularly clear in the Court's adoption of the well-known 'margin of appreciation' doctrine; a much more flexible and deferential tool to manage the interactions between ECHR law and domestic law, and the relationship between their legal officials which did not have an equivalent in EU law.[93]

Of course this more deferential approach to interactions by the ECtHR, did not avoid conflicts between ECHR law and national law. Notwithstanding the emollient tones of the Court's language on the obligations of signatory states under the treaty, this interaction takes place within the framework of the Court's exclusive jurisdiction to interpret the Convention under Article 32 ECHR[94] as well as the legal obligation of

better comply with the convention. See *Broniowski v. Poland* (2005) 40 EHRR 21; *Hutten-Czapska v. Poland* (2007) 45 EHRR 4. For discussion and analysis of this practice, see Wojciech Sadurski, 'Partnering with Strasbourg: Constitutionalisation of the European Court of Human Rights, the Accession of Central and East European States to the Council of Europe, and the Idea of Pilot Judgments' (2009) 9 *Human Rights Law Review*, 397–453. Nonetheless, even if these developments result in a more invasive scrutiny of domestic practices and recommendations for legislative change, it is still much 'softer', more dialogic than the direct effect and supremacy of EU law.

91 '[The Court] reiterates that the supervision machinery set up by the Convention is subsidiary to the national human rights protection systems.' *Salik v. Greece* (1996) 24 EHRR 323, 339.

92 See generally Helfer (n. 86).

93 The preliminary reference procedure of the EU system does not open up court dialogue in the same way. Rather, it operates to ensure the CJEU's exclusive jurisdiction in matters of EU law rather than a softening or delegation of the CJEU's jurisdiction. See generally Paul Craig and Gráinne de Búrca, *EU Law: Text, Cases and Materials* (Oxford: Oxford University Press, 2015), ch. 15.

94 Which states that 'the jurisdiction of the Court shall extend to *all matters concerning the interpretation and application of the Convention and the Protocols thereto*' (*emphasis added*). The exclusivity of its jurisdiction has been regularly emphasised by the Court. See for example *Scoppola v. Italy No 3* App No 126/05 (ECtHR, 22 May 2012) paras 53–54.; *Shamayev and others v. Georgia and Russia* ECHR 2005-III, para. 293.

signatory states to abide by its rulings under Article 46 ECHR.[95] As such, the Court has the ability to change the normative situation of both individuals and states. In light of this, national legal officials in the form of Supreme or constitutional courts have reacted to the ECtHR's decisions by making more explicit the precise nature and effect of the ECHR's norms, and, perhaps more importantly, their interpretation by the ECtHR in municipal legal orders, notwithstanding the ECtHR's views on the issue.[96] On some occasions this has led to national courts explicitly rejecting a decision or interpretation of the Convention by the ECtHR leading to a more pluralist, conflictual relationship between the two orders than the ECHR's 'soft constitutionalism' would initially suggest.[97] However the nature and tone of these reactions to the ECHR and its court by national courts is markedly different from national court reactions' to the nature and authority of EU law. Even in the most extreme forms of conflict, where domestic courts have explicitly gone against a clear judgment from the ECtHR, the reaction has not involved the rejection of the relevance of the rights and values contained in the ECHR within domestic legal orders. Rather, the conflicts have emerged from disagreements about precisely what those rights mean and how they should be protected.[98] In no instance has a domestic Court rejected the idea of the rights contained in the Convention themselves, the Court's role in interpreting them, nor found that in cases of conflict that fundamental rights protections would be subordinated in a manner similar to the threats from national courts with regard to the application of EU law.

One explanation for this difference in evolution of the relationship between ECHR law and national law, and particularly cases of conflicts between them, when compared with EU law, is the subject-matter of the relationship; the protection of fundamental rights. These rights and values

[95] 'The High Contracting Parties undertake to abide by the final judgment of the Court in any case to which they are parties.'

[96] See for example the GFCC's *Görgülü* decision, Judgment of 14 October 2004, 2 BvR 1481/04 where the GFCC stated that the Convention could not be applied in such a way that would violate the German basic law.

[97] See for example, the UK Supreme Court in *R. v. Horncastle and Others* (SC(E)) [2010] 2 AC 373 where the Court refused to follow the ECtHR's lead on the interpretation of the right to a fair trial under Article 6 of the ECHR.

[98] In refusing to follow the ECtHR in *Horncastle* (*ibid.*), the UK Supreme Court did comment that it hoped that its decision would result in a 'valuable dialogue between the domestic court and the Strasbourg court' (para. 11) within which the latter would 'take account of the reasons that have led [the UKSC] not to apply [the ECtHR's interpretation]' (para. 108).

are, according to the officials of *both* state and suprastate systems, an integral part of those systems, which creates a significant commonality between ECHR law and municipal state law and provides a basis for interaction in a less conflictual way. In this way, the 'suprapositive'[99] values of ECHR law act as a 'bridge' between the two legal orders, a common set of shared values which provide a basis of agreement between the legal officials of both systems, about which disagreement about their meaning and effects can subsequently emerge. Indeed, some courts have identified the role of the legal officials of *both* legal orders, municipal and ECHR, as '*promoting a joint European development of fundamental rights.*'[100]

As such, unlike the relationship between EU law and municipal law, the relationship between ECHR law and national law entails a common bond in the rights and values protected by the Convention itself. Although the legal officials of each system may disagree as to their meaning and effects, this has not undermined agreement on the rights themselves and their value. When compared with conflicts involving EU law, these interactions and conflicts seem of a much softer sort.

4.6 Which Pluralism?

Within the 'global disorder' of legal officials making differing claims to the authority and effectiveness of suprastate law, then, some legal orders may be best theorised as a form of municipal 'constitutional' law, others may still more closely resemble 'Westphalian' accounts of public international law and others may resemble neither, warranting a 'sui generis' conception of law. Furthermore, different concepts of law may better explain different suprastate orders based on the claims of their legal officials. As such, the global disorder of legal orders, given its emergent and uncertain state, may accommodate co-existing, yet conflicting accounts of law based on analytical positivism, interpretivism or others as yet to be theorised.[101] Indeed, in light of a global disorder of suprastate

[99] Gerald Neuman, 'Human Rights and Constitutional Rights: Harmony and Dissonance' (2003) 55 *Stanford Law Review*, 1863–900, 1868.

[100] Görgülü (n. 96), para. 62, *emphasis added.* Perhaps even more pointedly, this statement came from the GFCC, the court which had so robustly refuted the authority claims of the CJEU in respect of its application under the German constitution in its Maastricht and Lisbon decisions. 2 BvR 2134/92 and 2159/92 JZ 1993, 1100; [1994] 1 CMLR 57; BVerfGE, 2 be 2/08, Judgment of 30 June 2009.

[101] One potential move in this direction is Culver and Giudice's 'inter-institutional' account of law see Keith Culver and Michael Giudice, *Legality's Borders: An Essay in General*

authority claims, such a scenario is inevitable if the idea of a post-Westphalian conception of law as well as the idea of constitutional pluralism upon which it relies, are to make good on their explanatory claims, and as a corollary, the plausibility of their normative claims. What this tells us, then, is that the Westphalian '*y* axis' does not fall to a post-Westphalian '*x* axis' in the same way, and to the same extent, across the post-Westphalian global 'disorder of legal orders'.

At the very least, then, in light of the differential claims to authority and effectiveness of suprastate legal officials, different models of constitutional pluralism will be required to explain interactions between different types of legal orders based on the different types of claims and counter-claims of legal officials. MacCormick identified two distinct types of pluralism which have provided a template for models of constitutional pluralism more generally; radical pluralism and monist pluralism.[102] Radical pluralism entails the idea that two legal orders, such as state and suprastate, interact on a horizontal plane, each self-referentially relying on their own validity without any 'all-purpose superiority of one system over the other'.[103] Significantly, for radical pluralism, the management of the relationships between normative orders and in particular conflicts between them is not (nor should be) subject to common or shared norms between the two systems. Rather, management of interaction and conflict is a 'matter for circumspection and for political as much as legal judgment'.[104]

Monist pluralism, on the other hand, 'triangulates' the relationship between normative orders on a horizontal plane to include a third dimension. This third dimension to the relationship takes the form of a series of norms external to, or shared by, both systems which provide a normative resource for the management of interactions and conflicts. This third dimension to interacting legal orders can be another legal system or a series of principles which serve to manage the relationship and conflicts between different legal orders. An example of this type of 'monist' pluralism is MacCormick's 'pluralism under international law'

Jurisprudence (Oxford: Oxford University Press, 2010); 'Not a System but an Order: An Inter-Institutional View of European Union Law', in Julie Dickson and Pavlos Eleftheriadis (eds.), *Philosophical Foundations of European Union Law* (Oxford: Oxford University Press, 2013), pp. 54–76.

102 It should be noted that what I here call 'monist' pluralism, MacCormick called 'pluralism under international law' although he did recognise its 'monist' characteristics. MacCormick (n. 11), p. 117.

103 MacCormick (n. 11), p. 118.

104 Ibid., p. 120.

where the norms of public international law would constitute the apex of a triangular relationship between national law and EU law and provide the normative resources for the management of the conflicts between them, meaning that 'we need not run out of law (and into politics) quite as fast as suggested by radical pluralism.'[105]

In thinking about how to theorise the relationships between interacting legal orders in a post-Westphalian heterarchical rather than Westphalian hierarchical way, and in choosing between these models (and developing potential new models of pluralism), the statements of legal officials, and in particular their *diversity*, must feature prominently. As MacCormick noted in the EU context, when deciding upon the most relevant model of pluralism to capture the interactions between EU law and national law, we must be 'sensitive to the weight attached to the *sui generis* interpretation of [EU] law in the jurisprudence of the ECJ'.[106]

Notwithstanding the alternatives on offer in constitutional pluralism, the methodological monism persists in the sense that one alternative – either radical or monist or a variation thereof – is usually marshalled to explain all of the interactions between legal orders in the post-Westphalian context.[107] However, in light of the 'global disorder' of legal officials' statements and global disorder of forms of suprastate legal order, a '*global disorder of constitutional pluralism*' necessarily follows – as evidenced by the differences between the types of claims made about EU law and ECHR, the different reactions from domestic legal officials and the differences in the resulting constitutional pluralist relationship. A first step in capturing the global disorder of constitutional pluralism would be to employ different constitutional pluralist alternatives *simultaneously* to describe different relationships in a post-Westphalian disorder of legal orders. Thus, for example, in light of the robust authority claims of EU law and the invasiveness of its effects in domestic law, and the equally robust negation of these effects by domestic courts, it might be best to theorise the interaction and conflicts between EU law and domestic law in *radical* pluralist terms. The robust and seemingly categorical nature of the claims on either side seem to leave little room for an explanatory account of pluralism based on the 'triangulation' of the relationship by some overarching normative resource which could apply

[105] Ibid. [106] MacCormick (n. 11), p. 110.

[107] For example, as noted previously, Kumm sees in pluralism a 'unifying framework' Kumm (n. 12), p. 262. Similarly, Krisch argues that pluralism provides an ideal for 'postnational society' *tout court*. Krisch (n. 1), pp. 69–70.

to, and manage, conflicts between them.[108] On the other hand, it would appear that the interactions between ECHR law and national law might be better explained by reference to a monist model of pluralism. The 'softer' nature of the 'constitutionalization' of the ECHR, at least when compared with EU law, as well as the 'softer' pluralism which has emerged from national courts, calls for a more consensual or dialogic account of pluralism than is the case with EU law. As such, monist pluralism seems to fit the bill, involving the interaction of two legal orders on a horizontal plane but whose interaction is, in turn, based on a common set of 'suprapositive' values or principles which provide the basis for the resolution of conflicts between them. These values and principles provide the framework of agreement within which disagreements, conflicts and pluralism can emerge as to their precise meaning and application. Moreover, the various tools and doctrines employed by the ECHR, and particularly the 'margin of appreciation' doctrine, seem to support this 'monist' pluralist reading of the interactions between ECHR law and domestic law.

Of course, one doesn't have to agree with the characterisation of the concept of suprastate law and/or constitutional pluralism between these systems outlined here to accept the argument against methodological monism in constitutional pluralism. The methodological monism which dominates constitutional pluralist thinking cannot be reconciled with the state of affairs upon which constitutional pluralists themselves rely. It is not coherent with the assumptions that constitutional pluralists make about post-Westphalian concepts of suprastate law as well as the form and nature of interactions between suprastate law and other legal orders. If post-Westphalian accounts of suprastate law, and particularly their authority and effectiveness – that is, their 'post-Westphalian' credentials – are disproportionately determined by the statements of legal officials (at least when compared with that of municipal law) and the conceptualisation of suprastate law is determinative of the type of constitutional pluralist relationship that ensues, then the diversity of statements of suprastate legal officials and corresponding reactions by state legal officials must be encapsulated in constitutional pluralist frameworks. In order to achieve this, constitutional pluralism's methodological monism must be abandoned and a 'global disorder of constitutional pluralism' embraced.

[108] Quite a common feature of constitutional pluralist accounts of the relationship between EU law and state law. See, for example, Kumm, Maduro (n. 11), and Sabel and Gerstenberg (n. 18).

4.7 Conclusion

As a candidate 'frame' for ordering the global 'disorder of legal orders', pluralism provides a more flexible, more nuanced account of global legal ordering than some of its rivals such as the outmoded Westphalian state-sovereigntist account or some of the more rigid hierarchical accounts of global ordering such as global constitutionalism or the constitutionalisation of international law.[109] However in order to capitalize on these particular 'pluralist virtues' of explanatory accuracy and nuance in the context of the complexity of the current post-Westphalian 'unsettlement',[110] the methodological monist tendency in pluralism must be resisted. Approaches to interactions between legal orders must diversify to truly reflect the diversity itself in a global constellation of interacting normative orders as evidenced by the statements of the legal officials, both state and suprastate, engaged in constructing the realities of the post-Westphalian world. In short, we need to pluralise constitutional pluralism.

[109] Jan Klabbers, Anne Peters and Geir Ulfstein, *The Constitutionalization of International Law* (Oxford: Oxford University Press, 2009); Erika de Wet, 'The Constitutionalization of Public International Law', in Michel Rosenfeld and Andras Sajo (eds.), *The Oxford Handbook of Comparative Constitutional Law* (Oxford: Oxford University Press, 2012), pp. 1209–30; Antje Wiener, Anthony Lang, James Tully, Miguel Poiares Maduro and Mattias Kumm, 'Editorial: Global Constitutionalism: Human Rights, Democracy and the Rule of Law' (2012) 1 *Global Constitutionalism*, 1–15.

[110] Neil Walker, 'Our Constitutional Unsettlement' (2014) *Public Law*, 529–48.

5

Law and Recognition – Towards a Relational Concept of Law

RALF MICHAELS*

5.1 Introduction

Law is plural. In all but the simplest situations multiple laws overlap – national laws, subnational laws, supranational laws, non-national laws.

Our jurisprudential accounts of law have mostly not taken this in. When we speak of law, we use the singular. The plurality of laws is, at best an afterthought. This is a mistake. Plurality is built into the very reality of law.

We no longer need a concept of *law*. We need a concept of *laws*.

This chapter cannot yet provide this concept; it can serve only to develop one element. That element is recognition. Recognition is amply discussed in the context of Hart's rule of recognition, but this overlooks that recognition matters elsewhere, too. My suggestion is that we accept not one but two rules of recognition in the concept of law. One, well-known, is the rule of *internal* recognition as developed by H. L. A. Hart – the idea that a developed legal system requires its recognition as law by its officials. The other, much ignored but equally important, is the rule of *external* recognition – the idea that law is law insofar as it is recognised externally by other legal systems. The rule of internal recognition is an example of a secondary rule. The rule of external recognition is of a different type. It is a tertiary rule.[1] Hart suggested that a legal system is

* This is an attempt to explore an idea hinted at earlier: Ralf Michaels, 'Global Legal Pluralism' (2009) 5 *Annual Review of Law and Social Science*, 243–62, 254–55; Ralf Michaels, 'What is Nonstate Law? A Primer', in Michael Helfand (ed.), *Negotiating State and Non-State Law: The Challenges of Global and Local Legal Pluralism* (Cambridge: Cambridge University Press, 2015), pp. 41–58, pp. 55–58. Thanks for helpful comments are due to Matt Adler, Karen Knop, David Nelken and Nicole Roughan, as well as workshop participants at Singapore and Edinburgh.

1 For a similar use of tertiary rules, see Joel P. Trachtman, 'The Constitutions of the WTO' (2006) 17 *European Journal of International Law*, 623–46, 627; and Joel P. Trachtman, *The Future of International Law: Global Government* (Cambridge: Cambridge University

not complete unless it has, in addition to primary, also secondary rules. My suggestion is that, under conditions of legal pluralism, a legal system is not complete without such tertiary rules.

The emerging concept of laws is a positivist one in a strong sense. It assumes that the definition and the creation of law are themselves operations by the legal system. In this sense, the concept of law is autopoietic. However, in emphasising that legal systems mutually constitute each other, the concept also includes an allopoietic aspect. While the law at large is autopoietic, individual legal systems are not; they mutually constitute each other through mutual recognition. What follows is an attempt to account for this in legal theory.

5.2 Concept of Law and the Challenge from Legal Pluralism

Legal theory has long pondered questions on the nature of law; in fact, such questions may well constitute the discipline's core. It is not surprising that no consensus has emerged. Questions as to the nature of law are never just definitional or ontological questions; they carry with them ideas of legitimacy, they serve a purpose, and they are always colored by the experience of the time and place in which they are proposed.[2] If we saw, in the second half of the twentieth century, a sharp debate between positivism, natural law, and sociological definitions, then this debate mirrored a political debate over who should make relevant decisions – the legislator, society, or some transcendent entity.

These were mostly Western debates, and they played out within the Western nation state, where the idea that law was essentially the law of a state was hardly challenged. This was less clear in non-Western systems, in which state law was less effective, and in which customary and religious laws, whether or not they were recognised, played a greater role in people's lives. It was largely against these experiences that the modern

Press, 2013), p. 272, pp. 286–87. Relatedly, Thomas Schultz distinguishes two types of "relative legality" (where "relative legality" is defined through a rule of recognition: Thomas Schultz, 'Secondary Rules of Recognition and Relative Legality in Transnational Regimes' (2011) *American Journal of Jurisprudence*, 59–88, 83–84, revised in Schultz, *Transnational Legality* (Oxford: Oxford University Press, 2013), pp. 83–84

[2] See Hermann Kantorowicz, *The Definition of Law* (Cambridge: Cambridge University Press, 1958); Julie Dickson, 'Towards a Theory of European Union Legal Systems', in Julie Dickson and Pavlos Eleftheriadis (eds.), *Philosophical Foundations of European Union Law* (Oxford: Oxford University Press, 2012), pp. 25–53, pp. 26–30.

concept of legal pluralism was first developed.[3] Legal pluralism, in a definition that generalises from several definitions, describes a situation in which two or more laws (or legal systems) co-exist in (or are obeyed by) one social field (or a population or an individual).[4] In other words, three elements characterise a situation of legal pluralism.

1. Not all law is state law: some law does not emerge, directly or indirectly, from the state. Put differently, some non-state normative orders deserve to be called law.
2. There is necessarily a plurality of laws: law is not one, but many.
3. These different laws interact; there are overlaps and conflicts between laws that cannot be resolved through appeals to either hierarchy or objective delimitation.

Legal pluralism presents a dual challenge to legal theory: what counts as law, and how we account for plurality and interaction. Does this require a new concept of law?[5] Or even different concepts of law?[6]

5.2.1 *The Definition of Law – An Old Question*

Although both of these challenges are challenges to state law positivism, we can immediately see that the first question is in fact not novel for legal philosophy. Whether there is such a thing as non-state law correlates with a core concern in legal theory for millennia – the question of what

[3] I speak here of the concept of legal pluralism as it emerges especially from legal anthropology; for a recent overview, see John Griffiths, 'Legal Pluralism', in James Wright (ed.), *International Encyclopedia of the Social & Behavioral Sciences*, 2nd ed., Volume 13 (Amsterdam/Boston: Elsevier, 2015), pp. 757–61. Two other traditions of legal pluralism, developed within and for Western law, are partly different. One is the sociological idea of a law born in society, developed especially in Eugen Ehrlich, *Grundlegung der Soziologie des Rechts* (Duncker & Humblodt: Berlin, 1913), English translation 1936; and Georges Gurvitch, *Sociology of Law* (London: Kegan Paul, 1947). Another, focusing on institutions, is Santi Romano's; see Filippo Fontanelli, 'Santi Romano and L'ordinamento giuridico: The Relevance of a Forgotten Masterpiece for Contemporary International, Transnational and Global Legal Relations' (2011) 2 *Transnational Legal Theory*, 67–117.

[4] Generalised from Sally Engle Merry, 'Legal Pluralism' (1988) 22 *Law & Society Review*, 869–96, 870.

[5] Cf. Roger Cotterrell, 'Does Global Legal Pluralism Need a Concept of Law?', in Upendra Baxi, Christopher McCrudden, and Abdul Paliwala (eds.), *Law's Ethical, Global and Theoretical Contexts – Essays in Honour of William Twining* (Cambridge: Cambridge University Press, 2015), pp. 303–19.

[6] David Nelken, 'Using the Concept of Legal Culture' (2004) 29 *Australian Journal of Legal Philosophy*, 1–26, 2.

constitutes law. Saint Augustine's suggestion that bands of thieves are little kingdoms provided a precursor to our current discussions on legal pluralism. In legal theory, the idea that law does not have to be state law has a long pedigree. It exists in ideas of natural law and, more importantly for the study of legal pluralism, in ideas of customary law. In this sense, Griffith's vigorous plea that legal pluralism is a reality and that non-state legal orders exist regardless of recognition by state law was provocative, but not for legal theory.

One problem with any concept of law that goes beyond state law is that it becomes hard to draw boundaries. One may well end up where Melissaris does, suggesting that law must include clubbers queuing patiently at a bouncer's order.[7] In such expanded definition, law no longer has any distinctive value. This is one reason why proponents of legal pluralism have downplayed the importance of whether or not a normative order is called law.

If anything, it is almost too easy to accept a concept of law that is independent from the state. Simon Roberts in particular has pointed to the risks in such definitions.[8] His main argument is that the way we think of law *today* is, knowingly, or unknowingly, influenced by the reality of modern law, which is predominantly state law. As a consequence, we define non-state normative orders as law once they show a certain similarity with state law. Griffith's anti-imperialist project becomes itself imperialist: in defining non-state normative orders as 'law', we downplay their otherness, we impose a name on them that is not necessarily appropriate: 'Law, long so garrulous about itself, is now, in its contemporary enlargement, graciously embracing others in its discourse, seeking to tell those others what they are.'[9]

5.2.2 Plurality and Interaction as a New Question

In marked contrast, the second and third challenge from legal pluralism, namely the plurality of, and interaction between, legal systems, were for a long time not truly analyzed. Almost without exception, jurisprudence

[7] Emmanuel Melissaris, 'The More the Merrier? A New Take on Legal Pluralism' (2004) 13 *Social & Legal Studies*, 57–79, 75.

[8] Simon Roberts, 'Against Legal Pluralism – Some Reflections on the Contemporary Enlargement of the Legal Domain' (1998) 42 *Journal of Legal Pluralism*, 95–106; and Simon Roberts, 'After Government? On Representing Law Without the State' (2005) 68 *Modern Law Review*, 1–24.

[9] Roberts, 'Against Legal Pluralism' (n. 8), 98.

has treated law as a singular. The question goes to the nature of 'law' as though there was only one.

True, jurisprudence has long grappled with what can be called an *asymmetric* plurality of normative orders, and with friction between these orders. This concerns the seemingly eternal debate over the relation between law and morality. It also concerns discussion over relations between official law and customary law, with different hierarchies: Hart and Kelsen both viewed customary as imperfect, more primitive versions of state law; Eugen Ehrlich and Lon Fuller, by contrast, suggested that customary law (or what they call, respectively, 'living law' (Ehrlich) or 'implicit law' (Fuller)) is more real than state law.[10] However, all these debates concern the asymmetric relation between 'normal' law (state law) and other normative orders. They are not what we would need – namely, accounts for relations between laws of equal standing, or irrespective of standing.[11] A true jurisprudence of plurality is only slowly emerging.

5.2.3 *The Sequencing of the Questions*

We have, then, an old and rich jurisprudence of non-state law, and an emerging jurisprudence of plurality. But both stand in a rather unproductive order of sequencing. The common pluralist argument goes like this: first, we find that there are other normative orders than state law; then, as a consequence, we have to address the challenges arising from the ensuing pluralism. First we define what qualifies as a legal order, then we ask how that order relates to other orders. The plurality of law becomes, in this conception, a mere afterthought to the concept of law. It concerns the way in which laws operate, but not their nature itself.

This sequencing is problematic. Like the liberal view of the primacy of the individual over society, it posits that legal orders exist prior to their interaction with other laws. This seems insufficient to grasp the reality of legal pluralism with its necessarily overlapping legal orders. Such interlegality cannot be an afterthought; it is engrained into the very

10 Eugen Ehrlich, *Fundamental Principles of the Sociology of Law*, trans. W. L. Moll (Cambridge, MA: Harvard University Press, 1936); Lon L. Fuller, *Anatomy of the Law* (New York: Praeger, 1968), p. 67ff; cf. Gerald J. Postema, 'Implicit Law' (1994) 13 *Law & Philosophy*, 361–87. See also Sanne Taekema in this volume, *The Many Uses of Law. Interactional Law as a Bridge between Instrumentalism and Law's Values.*

11 Antony Allott, *The Limits of Law* (London: Butterworths, 1980), pp. 139–60.

nature of legal orders itself. A proper understanding of law today needs to grapple with this very fact. It must work interlegality into the concept of law itself.

This is what I suggest in this chapter. The three challenges from legal pluralism – non-state law, plurality and interaction – are related. In order to assess any one of them, we must consider the other ones as well. We will not get an adequate concept of law beyond the state unless we address inter-relations between legal systems at the same time. These inter-relations are not an afterthought to the concept of law; they are constitutive.

5.3 Two Types of Rules of Recognition

5.3.1 Non-State Law and the Internal Rule of Recognition

The idea of a rule of recognition was first proposed by H. L. A. Hart.[12] It emerges from his insight that legal orders do not consist merely of primary rules (commands); they require secondary rules that determine how laws are made and changed, and so forth. Amongst such secondary rules, the rule of recognition may be the most important one, because it determines what does and does not count as law.

Hart's rule of recognition rests on an internal point of view, and for this reason it may make sense to call it a rule of *internal* recognition. For Hart, the rule is a social fact; it describes the practical attitude of officials within the legal system. Other legal theories tend to place such rules within the law itself: for systems theory, secondary rules are those rules with which the legal system itself creates its own continuity and adaptability.

Hart developed his concept against the idea of state law, and it fits here best, even though it is not necessarily so confined.[13] When Hart discusses customary law, he is more ambivalent. On the one hand, custom could be viewed as a system of rules, though only primary, not secondary rules, a more primitive kind of law.[14] On the other hand, only the addition of secondary rules can 'be considered a step from the pre-legal into the legal world; since each remedy brings with it many elements that permeate law: certainly all three remedies [i.e. a rule of recognition, rules of change,

[12] See H. L. A. Hart, *The Concept of Law*, 2nd ed. (Oxford: Oxford University Press, 1994), especially at pp. 94–95, pp. 100–10 (pp. 97–107 in the 1st ed. 1964).

[13] Roberts, 'After Government?' (n. 9), 10. [14] Hart (n. 13), pp. 91–94.

and adjudication] are enough to convert the regime of primary rules into what is indisputably a legal system.'[15] This would suggest that a system of mere primary rules does not constitute law.[16]

Hart, however, suggests that so-called primitive legal systems without such secondary rules are exceedingly rare, implying that even customary law can usually qualify as a system of law.[17] Indeed, it has been argued that his criteria can be extended into non-state laws.[18] Insofar as law rests on an internal point of view, such a point of view is not confined to state law – one may even say that it is especially in non-state laws with their weaker enforcement mechanisms that an internal sense of obligation towards the law will frequently be present.[19] Insofar as Hart provides for a special role of officials, such officials need not be state officials – they could also be, as Cotterrell has pointed out, religious priests or tribal chiefs.[20] And, most importantly for this purpose, the law-making power of such priests and chiefs may well rest on a rule of recognition, too.

Thus Hart might have had a response to the first of the challenges from legal pluralism elaborated earlier: non-state orders can be law. By contrast, it appears that he would not have accepted the second and third challenge. A plurality of laws is almost completely absent from Hart's theory, and the idea of overlapping interconnected orders is absent as well.[21] More precisely: although Hart does account for the possibility of normative conflict (e.g. between law and custom), he resolves such conflicts on the basis of a priority of state law.[22] Essentially, Hart's system of law

[15] Hart (n. 13), p. 94.

[16] Thus the interpretation by Mehrdad Payandeh, 'The Concept of International Law in the Jurisprudence of H.L.A. Hart' (2011) 21 *European Journal of International Law*, 967–95, 993.

[17] Hart (n. 13) p. 291, note to p. 91. Allott forcefully emphasised the same point, based on actual experience: Allott (n. 11), pp. 49–67.

[18] See, e.g., Michael Helfand, 'The Persistence of Sovereignty and the Rise of the Legal Subject', in Michael Helfand (ed.), *Negotiating State and Non-State Law: The Challenges of Global and Local Legal Pluralism* (Cambridge: Cambridge University Press, 2015), pp. 307–32; Detlef von Daniels, 'Is Positivism a State-Centered Theory?', in Kenneth Himma (ed.), *Law, Morality, and Legal Positivism: proceedings of the 21st World Congress in Philosophy of Law and Social Philosophy*, Vol. 3 (Stuttgart: Franz Steiner Verlag, 2004), pp 19ff.

[19] See Helfand (n. 19), pp. 307, p. 321ff.

[20] Roger Cotterrell, *Law, Culture and Society* (Aldershot: Ashgate, 2006), p. 37.

[21] Jeremy Waldron, 'Legal Pluralism and the Contrast between Hart's Jurisprudence and Fuller's', in Peter Cane (ed.), *The Hart-Fuller Debate in the Twenty-First Century* (Oxford: Hart Publishing, 2010), pp. 135–55, p. 145.

[22] This aspect is underappreciated, in my view, in Helfand (n. 19), pp. 327–30.

was ordered in a pyramidal fashion, based on one rule of recognition only.[23] Even if customary law can qualify as law, the relation between state law and custom remains, for Hart, asymmetric.[24]

5.3.2 *Legal Pluralism and the Rule of External Recognition*

With all the (deserved) attention that the rule of recognition has received, one can be excused for overlooking the fact that the idea of recognition does not appear exclusively in the context of the rule of recognition. Hart must have been aware of this. Before introducing the rule of recognition, Hart discusses the importance of recognition in the relation between law and custom:

> The first [issue] is whether 'custom as such' is law or not. . . . [C]ustom is law only if it is one of a class of customs which is 'recognized' as law by a particular system. The second issue concerns the meaning of 'legal recognition'. What is it for a custom to be legally recognized?[25]

Is custom thus non-law until recognised by the state's institutions?[26] Or is custom a separate system of law that acquires normative relevance for the state the moment it is recognised, as the quote seems to suggest? There seems to be no need to resolve this issue for Hart because for him not much hinges on it. His model seems to suggest that the recognition of custom is not much different from the normal operation of the rule of recognition. Custom becomes law in one of two ways. Either, custom is treated as fact, and the law creates legal rules that mirror these facts. In this case, we can talk of deference. Or, custom is treated as law that is

[23] Cf. Nick Barber, 'The Rechtsstaat and the Rule of Law' (2003) 53 *University of Toronto Law Journal*, 443–54, 450–51. But see, for a hint of the idea of two different types of recognition (called 'original' and 'derivative') H.L.A. Hart, 'Kelsen's Doctrine of the Unity of Law,' in Hart, *Essays in Jurisprudence and Philosophy* (1983) pp. 309–43, pp. 341–342.

[24] See Waldron (n. 23), pp. 141ff. Essentially, this appears to be also the position of Joseph Raz, *Why the State* (in this volume), although he remains ambiguous. On the one hand, the state is said to have a special role vis-à-vis other normative systems based on two factors: (1) an extensive responsibility within its domain, and (2) freedom from external legal constraints. On the other hand, Raz concedes that both factors can be claimed also by non-state laws. As for extensive responsibility within its domain, Raz makes it clear that this is contingent on what the domain is, which makes it possible to think of, for example, religious law as extensively responsible within the domain of members of the religion. As for freedom from external legal constraints, see id. at n. 13.

[25] Hart (n. 13), pp. 44–45. [26] Cf. Hart (n. 13), pp. 46–48.

subordinate to state law. In this case, we can talk of delegation.[27] In either sense, the recognition that is accorded to custom is necessary to turn custom into fully fledged law. What is important for my purposes, however, is that recognition is distinct from absorption. Custom is not absorbed into the law; it is merely given relevance through recognition. We can call the recognition by a legal order of another existing order external recognition, to distinguish it from internal recognition. Internal recognition describes the relation between officials and the law. External recognition describes a relation between one law and another.

A powerful objection has been made against such a rule of external recognition from the camp of legal pluralists. The idea that custom becomes law only through an act of recognition has been virulently opposed by legal pluralists, most prominently perhaps by John Griffiths.[28] Griffiths attacked what he called legal centralism, the idea that only state law is law. Importantly, Griffith's critique extended also to scholars arguing that non-state orders could be law, as long as these scholars subordinate such non-state orders to the state and make it contingent on recognition by the state, as happened especially with religious and customary laws in colonial contexts. Such contingent acceptance of law, Griffiths suggested, creates only 'weak' legal pluralism, which is no true pluralism at all; it is a mere subcategory of legal centralism.[29] In this sense, indeed not much hinges on the distinction.

We can see how Griffith's criticism concerns both challenges from legal pluralism discussed earlier. As to the conceptual challenge, he rejects the view that all law must be state law. As to the plurality/interaction challenge, he rejects a definition of law that must ultimately be uniform: 'the very notion of "recognition" and all the doctrinal paraphernalia which it brings with it are typical reflections of the idea that "law" must ultimately depend from a single validating source.'[30]

The criterion of recognition that Griffiths rejects here is external recognition, the recognition by the state. When he suggests that '[l]egal pluralism is the fact. Legal centralism is a myth, an ideal, a claim, an illusion', we see that his rejection is both conceptual/empirical and

[27] For delegation and deference, see Ralf Michaels, 'The Re-*State*-Ment of Non-State Law: The State, Choice of Law, and the Challenge from Global Legal Pluralism' (2005) 51 *Wayne Law Review*, 1209–59, 1233–35.

[28] John Griffiths, 'What Is Legal Pluralism?' (1986) 24 *Journal of Legal Pluralism and Unofficial Law*, 1–55.

[29] Ibid., 5–8. [30] Ibid., 8.

normative. Conceptually/empirically, Griffiths suggests that legal pluralism (in the strong sense) is a fact[31] – in other words, that non-state laws exist independently of recognition. Normatively, the rejection of a requirement of external recognition is based on the rejection of an ideology, namely that of legal centralism and of the superiority of state law over non-state law.

Griffiths's emphasis that the character of law should not depend on recognition by the state has been hugely influential within the literature on legal pluralism. It has gained new support under conditions of globalisation, which brought to the mainstream a general scepticism about the central role of states. Once we realise that the normative and logical primacy of the state is not a given, we also realise that a definition of law that depends on recognition by the state is deeply suspicious. The problem has been what should come in its place. These problems, amongst others, have led even Griffiths himself to give up the emphasis on legal pluralism and to define law now as a mere dimension of continuous variation in the degree of differentiation in social control.[32]

5.3.3 *The Reciprocity of External Recognition*

The suggestion that there can be both a rule of internal and a rule of external recognition suggests that two rules of recognition can operate at the same time. In Hart's analysis, the only reason that the external recognition by courts of custom as law is effective is because the courts themselves are empowered through an internal rule of recognition. The same combination can be made to justify the effectivity of other norms than those of custom, for example EU law. For EU law to be valid in the UK, it is necessary first that Parliament was entitled to enact the 1972 European Communities Act – an application of the internal rule of recognition. And then it is necessary that this Act deferred power to EU institutions and thereby turned EU rules into valid law in the UK – an act of external recognition.[33]

[31] Ibid., 4.

[32] John Griffiths, 'The Idea of Sociology of Law and its Relation to Law and to Sociology', in Michael Freeman (ed.), *Law and Sociology* (Oxford: Oxford University Press, 2006), pp. 49–68, p. 63f. Similarly, William Twining, 'Normative and Legal Pluralism' (2010) 20 *Duke Journal of Comparative & International Law*, 473–518.

[33] Around the time this chapter was completed, the United Kingdom declared its decision to withdraw from the EU. It is worth noting that the questions discussed here play a role also as to whether this exit is governed by UK law or EU law. See, e.g., Donal Coffey,

There is a problem with this explanation, however. The suggestion that EU law becomes law only if and insofar as it is recognised by UK law appears implausible. It clashes with the self-proclaimed nature of EU law as an autonomous legal order. It clashes with the fact that the EU has several member states, each of which may defer in slightly different ways to the EU. It clashes with the fact that many officials have a practice of complying with EU law directly. And, especially, it clashes with the self-proclaimed superiority of EU law. From the perspective of EU law, it is national law that achieves its effectivity only through deference from EU law.

This problem has been discussed from the perspective of legal theory by Neil MacCormick.[34] MacCormick suggests that we should think of not one but two rules of recognition, one for UK law and one for EU law. In this sense, MacCormick responds to the definitional challenge from legal pluralism by generalising Hart's rule of recognition. A legal system remains defined internally. Indeed, he emphasises that it is internal recognition that matters:

> No state's constitution is as such validated by that of any other, nor is it validated by Community law. For each state, the internal validity of Community law in the sense mandated by the 'supremacy' doctrine results from the state's amendment of constitutional and sub-constitutional law to the extent required to give direct effect and applicability to Community law. On the other hand, the Community's legal order is neither conditional upon the validity of any particular state's constitution, nor upon the sum of the conditions that the states might impose, for that would be no Community at all. It would amount to no more than a bundle of overlapping laws to the extent that each state chose to acknowledge 'Community' laws and obligations. So relations between states inter se and between states and Community are interactive rather than hierarchical.[35]

External recognition, thus, is not necessary for a legal system's validity 'as such': 'where systems overlap, neither is necessarily a part of the ultimate reason for the validity of the other, nor do we have to presuppose some common reason for, or ground of, validity external to them both.' Hart had made a similar suggestion earlier: the mere fact that the

Brexit and Art. 50: The Key lies in Luxembourg, http://verfassungsblog.de/brexit-and-art-50-the-key-lies-in-luxembourg.

[34] Neil MacCormick, 'Beyond the Sovereign State' (1993) 56 *Modern Law Review*, 1–18.

[35] Neil MacCormick, *Questioning Sovereignty* (Oxford: Oxford University Press, 1999), pp. 117–18.

UK would pass a statute that validates Soviet law would merely create a purported validation; from the perspective of Soviet officials, the validity of Soviet law would still derive from an internal rule of recognition.[36]

However, this seems incomplete. EU law is law in an objective sense, independent of its recognition. However, it is law for UK law only if, and only because, it is recognised by UK law. Similarly, UK law is law in an objective sense, independent of its recognition. However, it is law for EU law only if, and only because, it is recognised by EU law. At least in their inter-relation, recognition therefore matters.

5.3.4 Remaining Problems

In some ways MacCormick's argument mirrors Griffiths's argument: non-state law is law independent of its recognition. In this, both Griffiths and MacCormick follow the sequencing critiqued earlier: first they define what counts as a legal system; then they analyze how the legal systems interact. Indeed, MacCormick compares EU law with custom.[37]

The rejection of a hierarchical relation between state law and other law has two important consequences. First, conflicts between systems become irresoluble, at least in a final and universal way. Once hierarchy is lost, we lose ultimate resolution. MacCormick, in his earlier article, hopes that such conflicts will be rare and can be dealt with, with the consequence that, usually, 'the systems can remain in overlapping relations without any necessary assumption of sub-or superordination of one to the other as a totality.'[38] Later he becomes less sure of this situation and suggests instead that 'international law functions as a common ground of validity both of member-state systems and of Community law, neither being therefore a sub-system of the other, but both cohering within a common legal universe governed by the norms of international law.'[39]

MacCormick calls his solution, in which international law provides the hierarchically superior umbrella organising conflicts between EU law and national law 'pluralism under international law'. He juxtaposes it with what he calls 'radical pluralism', a situation in which no such superior order exists and in which, for him consequently, 'not every legal

[36] Hart (n. 23), p. 319. [37] MacCormick (n. 36), 14–15; and MacCormick (n. 37), p. 114.
[38] Ibid, 8. [39] MacCormick (n. 37), pp. 116–17.

problem can be solved legally. The problem in principle is not that of an absence of legal answers to given problems, but of a superfluity of legal answers.'[40]

This juxtaposition between 'pluralism under international law' and 'radical pluralism' replicates Griffiths's juxtaposition, discussed earlier, between 'weak' and 'strong' legal pluralism. This means, also, that MacCormick's solution would not qualify, under Griffiths's analysis, as true pluralism in a meaningful sense – it would be a kind of legal centralism. MacCormick, by characterising his solution as one of legal monism, seems to concede as much. However, the solution of a 'pluralism under international law' may very well be just wishful thinking. In the *Kadi* case,[41] decided by the European Court of Justice not long after MacCormick developed his solution, it turned out that international law did not provide a very helpful basis to resolve conflicts between EU law and national law. The reason was, essentially, that the same problem of mutual interaction reappeared on a higher sphere: EU law and international law both claimed supremacy.[42]

A second consequence is that, on MacCormick's account, the nature of external recognition becomes unclear. If we define legal orders prior to their interaction with other legal orders, then external recognition is no longer a constitutive but an accommodating operation – an operation to regulate the inter-relations between legal systems. Remarkably, in MacCormick's later account, the recognition accorded by UK law to EU law, or that accorded by EU law to UK law, so central to the early development of his theory, have become all but irrelevant. In reality, the recognition between legal systems is now governed by a higher system, namely international law.

However, even in a system of strong legal pluralism, the rule of external recognition is weakened. As long as the rule of external recognition remains within each legal system, this creates a decentralised system: UK law determines its interactions with EU law from its own perspective; EU law determines its interactions with UK law from its

[40] Ibid., 119.

[41] European Court of Justice (Grand Chamber), *Yassin Abdullah Kadi and Al Barakaat International Finance v. Council of the European Union* joined cases C-402/05P and C-415/05P, Judgment, 3 September 2008.

[42] For good discussions, see Gráinne de Búrca, 'The EU, the European Court of Justice and the International Legal Order after Kadi' (2010) 51 *Harvard International Law Journal*, 1–49; Nico Krisch, *Beyond Constitutionalism: The Pluralist Structure of Postnational Law* (Oxford: Oxford University Press, 2010), pp. 176–87.

own perspective. Nico Krisch has called rules like this 'interface norms'.[43] For him, recognition (or 'conditional' recognition) is only one of several such interface norms–another example is a 'taking into account' norm and the European Court of Human Right's approach of equivalence. Paul Berman has listed a whole number of such techniques.[44] These remain techniques, however; they do not go to the essence of legal theory, and they do not go to the nature of law itself.

Detlef von Daniels has attempted to give a more legal-theoretical account of the phenomenon, but has thereby run into new troubles. What Krisch called interface norms is, for von Daniels, dealt with by so-called linkage rules.[45] He helpfully suggests that such rules are neither primary nor secondary rules in a Hartian sense but instead constitute a third set of rules,[46] though not of lesser importance than those others.[47] For von Daniels, such rules are not a necessary but a contingent (and indeed frequent) element of the law;[48] and indeed 'the concept of linkage rules is an indispensable component of any descriptive theory that is more than a mere interpretation of one particular practice and has overcome Kelsen's epistemological limits [of monism].'[49] However, von Daniels describes these linkage rules as 'ambiguous.' Some of them, he suggests (like Krisch) form part of the internal point of view of a particular legal system.[50] Others, however, can be viewed only from an external point, because it is not up to one legal system to determine how another legal system responds to its acts of recognition. Von Daniels suggests that linkage rules are 'Janus-faced': they concern both the treatment of foreign law and the treatment by foreign law. Here, the juxtaposition between an internal and an external point of view reflects that between strong and weak legal pluralism.[51]

5.4 The Rule of External Recognition Explored

Both problems are not just problems of theory; they are also problems of practice. The first problem, the irresolvability of conflicts, is a problem

[43] Krisch (n. 42), pp. 285–96.

[44] Paul Schiff Berman, *Global Legal Pluralism: A Jurisprudence of Law Beyond Borders* (Cambridge: Cambridge University Press, 2012), pp. 152ff.

[45] Detlef von Daniels, *The Concept of Law from a Transnational Perspective* (Burlington, VT/Farnham: Ashgate Publishing, 2010), pp. 158–66.

[46] Ibid., p. 160f. [47] Ibid., p. 156. [48] Ibid., p. 165. [49] Ibid., p. 161.

[50] Ibid., p. 164.

[51] It must remain for a different project to discuss how the concept of laws proposed here transcends the difference between an internal and an external position.

of private international law; and I want to largely ignore it here. The second problem, the unclear nature of recognition, closely parallels a problem of public international law, in particular in the definition of states. Given that states remain the most important subjects in international law, this definitional problem is quite central. And given that the recognition of a state comes with the recognition of sovereignty, and therefore lawmaking power, the requirements for being a state and the requirements for law run parallel structures (which is not to say that they need at all have the same criteria). This suggests that an excursion into the public international law of statehood could be beneficial.

5.4.1 *Recognition of States in International Law*

The definition of a state has substantive criteria and a contested formal criterion. As substantive criteria, the Montevideo Convention on the Rights and Duties of States 1933, in its Article 1, formulated four: a territory, a population, a structure of government, and the ability to enter into relations with other states.[52] These criteria are still often named, though they have become more doubtful. Of more interest for my purposes is whether these criteria alone already make a state, or whether, in addition, an act of recognition by other states or by the community of states is required.[53] Depending on the answer to this question, a declaration of recognition is either merely declaratory or actually constitutive. If recognition is merely declaratory, recognition is simply a prelude to the establishment of relations, but if it is constitutive, then the question of a duty becomes more acute.[54]

Lassa Oppenheim summed up the cleanest version of the constitutive theory: 'A State is, and becomes an International Person through recognition only and exclusively.'[55] This theory has practical and normative

[52] 165 LNTS 19.

[53] I do not here discuss the related issue of recognition of governments, especially where there is dispute as to which of several self-proclaimed governments is the legitimate one. That question bears obvious parallels to Hart's discussion of revolution and the passing of authority from Rex 1 to Rex 2, suggesting that a comparison between the recognition of governments and the rule of internal recognition would be fruitful.

[54] It is suggested that the theories are of limited help: Ian Brownlie, 'Recognition in Theory and Practice' (1982) 53 *British Yearbook of International Law*, 197–211. By contrast, it seems arguable that the practice has the advantage of highlighting elements of the theories.

[55] Lassa Oppenheim, *International Law* §§ 71, Hersch Lauterpacht (ed.), 8th ed. (London: Longmans, Green and Co Ltd, 1955), p. 125.

shortcomings, however. Practically, it could lead to what can be called limping statehood: an entity might be a state vis-à-vis some states (namely those that recognised it) and not vis-à-vis others (those that do not). Normatively, it subordinates new emerging states to the recognition of old established states – a problem of postcolonial states mirroring the problem of customary laws taken up by Griffiths.

These reasons are amongst those for which today the declaratory theory is preferred. Under this theory, expressed already in Article 3 of the Montevideo Convention, states are states independent of recognition once they fulfil substantive criteria. This has its own problems, however. First, recognition may be necessary as the best available evidence that the criteria have been met. Second, in effect a state will not be able to properly exercise its rights unless and until it has been recognised.[56] In reality, recognition still plays an important role. Without it, entities that would otherwise qualify as states find it impossible to truly act as states in the international realm.

5.4.2 *Translation to the Concept of Law*

These different approaches to statehood nicely translate to the question of what constitutes law. The declaratory theory in international law translates to the idea that we must decide first what constitutes law before we inquire into its relation with other laws. The sequencing of questions is thus that introduced in the introduction. Whether or not one law recognises another law is insofar irrelevant for the definition of law. A question is only whether there is a duty to do so arising from international law – MacCormick's 'pluralism under international law' – or not.

This makes the constitutive theory particularly interesting. Under this theory, translated into legal theory, recognition is constitutive for the identity of law as law. This resembles the idea, attacked by Griffiths, that a normative order becomes law only once it is (externally) recognised. In fact, Griffith's concerns about an ideology of (Western) state

[56] Hersch Lauterpacht, *Recognition in International Law* (Cambridge: Cambridge University Press, 1947), p. 55: '[T]he full international personality of rising communities ... cannot be automatic ... [A]s its ascertainment requires the prior determination of difficult circumstances of fact and law, there must be someone to perform that task. In the absence of a preferable solution, such as the setting up of an impartial international organ to perform that function, the latter must be fulfilled by States already existing. The valid objection is not against the fact of their discharging it, but against their carrying it out as a matter of arbitrary policy as distinguished from legal duty.'

centrality mirror closely the concerns of those who advocated against a constitutive theory in international law – the idea, namely, that it should be up to the established Western state to determine what counts or does not count as a state. This is an important concern, and I address its normative implications later in this chapter. For now, it should be pointed out that international law reminds us of something that we already know from discussions in legal pluralism: Effectively, recognition matters, even if normatively we should wish that it did not. Effectively, a state cannot operate as a state in the community of states unless it is recognised by other states. And effectively a legal system cannot operate vis-à-vis other legal systems unless it is recognized by those other legal systems.

In this context, Lauterpacht's combined theory of state recognition becomes attractive for legal theory. For Lauterpacht, recognition was 'declaratory of facts and constitutive of rights'.[57] Under this approach, the substantive criteria for a state are met independently of recognition, but for a state to actually exercise the rights arising from being a state, it needs to be recognised. This has an attractive parallel in the area of the concept of law, because it helps us put an internal recognition and a rule of external recognition in their respective places. The internal recognition is one of many ways of determining the facts necessary to determine that an order is a law. Insofar, Griffiths's criticism could be responded to in part: the definition of law as a fact would remain independent of recognition by other states. Moreover, recognition would create a law on equal footing; it would not lead to subordination. But the response is only partial: without recognition by other legal systems, such a legal system would not have an effective status externally.

5.4.3 *Assessment*

The comparison with the public international law of states has shown not just that a parallel discussion exists. It has also demonstrated additional elements that can help in a legal theory of legal pluralism.

A first such additional element is the realisation that substantive criteria and recognition are not necessarily independent from each other, nor are they necessarily sequenced. Under the constitutive theory, recognition by other states is a constitutive act, and even under the

[57] Ibid., p. 75.

declaratory theory, recognition plays a role. An entity is not a full state until it is recognised by other states.

A second such additional element is the insight that recognition need not lead to a subordinate status. Once a state is recognised, it stands on equal status with the state that has recognised it.

A third element, finally, and this may be the most important one, is that statehood is not necessarily a universal status. It is universal if an entity is recognised by all states. It is a relational status, by contrast, if the entity is recognised only by some, not all states.

These three additional elements should help get back to the legal theory debate.

5.5 Towards a Relational Concept of Law

5.5.1 *The Constitutive Role of External Recognition*

In a world of largely independent legal systems, it would be possible, but also sufficient, to define a legal order prior to its interaction with other legal systems. We could determine whether a rule of internal recognition, or some other criterion, exists, and consider that sufficient. The rare inter-relations with other legal systems could be considered no more than an afterthought. More precisely, they could be thought of as purely operational issues, dealt with through rules of private international law and other doctrines. Such rules would be independent from the concept of law: whether a certain law is applied or not would have nothing to do with whether it is or is not law.

This is very much the traditional image of law as it emerges from Western legal theory. It made sense for a concept of laws that was largely based on Western states, leaving out both the laws of suzerain states and the laws of colonies. It worked for a world in which it was possible to consider customary laws in colonies as non-laws, requiring for their elevation to the status of law recognition by the coloniser and its law. That world is no longer our world. Studies of legal pluralism in colonial and postcolonial settings provided only the first challenge to this concept. The realisation of global legal pluralism generalised the challenge and carried it into the Western world as well. This was a challenge not just to the state-based concept of law, but also to the idea that inter-relations were only an afterthought.

A concept of laws, appropriate for a situation of global legal pluralism, must take these challenges seriously. It should accept the challenge that non-state law can be law. It should reject, however, the claim that non-state law must be viewed as law irrespective of recognition. Instead, it should generalise this recognition requirement and turn it into a general requirement of law – a requirement that exists not just for non-state law, but for state law as well. A legal order, in this definition, requires not two but three kinds of rules. It requires primary rules as its content. It requires secondary rules for its operation. And it requires tertiary rules to establish its relation with other legal orders, whether they are called interface norms, linkage rules or something else.[58] In fact, the suggestion that such tertiary rules are a necessary element of legal systems should not be so provocative. For example, Julie Dickson (without using the terminology) has made a similar point to distinguish legal systems (that have such norms) from mere subsystems (that do not).[59]

At this point, von Daniels's suggestion that linkage rules are Janus-faced deserves attention again. Recall that von Daniels suggests that linkage rules are 'Janus-faced:' they concern both the way in which a legal system treats a foreign law and the way in which that foreign law treats the legal system. However, it seems wrong to think that there is some objective law that transcends relations between systems and provides the source for such linkage rules. Public international law could provide such rules if it (a) could qualify as an objective superior law, and (b) contained such rules. Thus was MacCormick's hope. But public international law does not contain such rules, so we need not even discuss whether it could qualify as an objective superior law or whether its relation to domestic laws remains one of mutual recognition, too.

Analyzed closely, von Daniels's 'Janus-faced rule' contains two different rules. System A has its own linkage rules that determine whether and how it recognises System B. System B has its own linkage rules that determine whether and how it recognises System A. Both rules can but need not overlap. Although they concern the same relation, they each concern one direction of this relation only. Only one set of these rules belongs to each system in the sense that it is created within this system

[58] Tertiary rules are not hierarchically superior to secondary rules in the way secondary rules are hierarchically superior to primary rules. Where System A and System B mutually constitute each other, System A's rule of external recognition is contingent on System A's rule of internal recognition. At the same time, System B's rule of external recognition is superior to System A's rule of internal recognition because it is necessary to create system A-vis-à-vis System B. That no ultimate hierarchy emerges is not a weakness of the theory; it is a consequence of the lack of hierarchy in global legal pluralism.

[59] Dickson (n. 3), p. 46.

Nonetheless, von Daniels is right to emphasise that both rules hang together. System A can only determine whether and how it recognises System B and insofar be constitutive for System B. It cannot determine whether and how system B recognises System A. That latter question is, however, what is constitutive of System A. In a world of inter-related laws, the nature of System A as a system of law depends on its recognition by other legal systems. But System A has no way of bringing about such recognition on its own.[60] All it can do is offer itself for such recognition, and perhaps offer reciprocal recognition as an incentive.

5.5.2 *Relativity and Relationality of Law*

The debate as MacCormick introduced it seemed to present only two possibilities to conceive of relations between legal systems. One was to develop meta-rules in a higher body of law to resolve conflicts between legal systems. The other was to resort to extra-legal means for such resolution.

This alternative permeates the debate on global legal pluralism. The first solution is endorsed by scholars like Mireille Delmas-Marty who favours an 'ordered legal pluralism' on the basis of higher principle, or proponents of a constitutional pluralism[61]. The second solution is endorsed by scholars like Maduro who advocates dialogue between legal systems (or their actors, in particular courts), and Krisch, who actually sees value in ensuing conflicts. The alternative would thus be between a legal solution (with the relevant laws found in a superior system) and a non-legal solution.

The analysis here has suggested that this alternative is incomplete. The absence of a superior legal system does not imply the absence of legal rules. Rather, such rules are found within each individual legal system. They are tertiary rules, rules of external recognition. Recognition is not the only content of such rules. Instead, tertiary rules concern the relations

[60] Nicole Roughan suggests that such mutual recognition can be negotiated. Nicole Roughan, *Authorities: Conflicts, Cooperation, and Transnational Legal Theory* (Oxford: Oxford University Press, 2013). Ch. 8–9, esp. pp. 161–63. But such negotiation is not, it appears, a legal operation. Moreover, such negotiation can fail. Ultimately, negotiation is thus not a substitute. In the related area of jurisdiction, Paul Berman once suggested the concept of jurispersuasion for this operation; although he seems to have given up on the term, it seems a useful description. Paul Schiff Berman, 'From International Law to Law and Globalization' (2005) 43 *Columbia Journal of Transnational Law*, 485–556, 533–38; cf. Michaels (n. 22), 1241–44.

[61] Matej Avbelj and Jan Komarek (eds.), *Constitutional Pluralism in the European Union and Beyond* (Oxford: Hart Publishing, 2012).

between legal systems more generally. They include the entire system of conflict of laws (which is typically a set of rules in each legal system, not a hierarchically superior set of rules).

The result is not the same as shared authority, such as proposed by Roughan.[62] External recognition does not describe the situation that legal orders negotiate which of them regulates which section of the legal realm, although this is possible. External recognition describes the prior situation that different legal orders recognise each other as laws, so as to make shared authority possible.

The constitutive role of external recognition, however, comes with a price. The price is that there no longer is an independent position from which to determine the nature of law. Instead, there are separate legal orders, each of which determines what counts as law for itself (through a rule of internal recognition) and for other orders (through a rule of external recognition).

Because such rules operate between legal systems only, they lead to a relational concept of law. The nature of law is no longer determined in an absolute fashion but only relative to other legal systems. Something can be a legal order vis-à-vis one other legal system, but not vis-à-vis another legal system. The nature of a legal system exists in relation to another legal system.

This relationality and relativity of a concept of law is the necessary consequence of global legal pluralism. We no longer have an Archimedean point from which we can determine whether something is or is not law. If we accept that the definition of law is itself the fruit of the operation of legal rules, then we have to find these rules in the law. And if laws are inter-related, then we can find these rules not merely within each legal system, but must instead look within other legal systems, too.

5.6 Objections

The concept of laws developed here needs further refinement, but it seems appropriate to address a number of possible objections. Some of these are conceptual, others are normative, and some combine both.

5.6.1 Possibility

A first objection goes against the possibility of limping status as law. The possibility that a normative order is law for one and not for another

[62] Roughan, supra n. 60.

law may appear both conceptually and normatively unattractive. It is conceptually unattractive because it holds compossible incompatible normative statements. It is normatively unattractive because it disappoints our hopes of integrity in law.

The logical problem has been addressed recently by Michael Giudice.[63] Giudice argues that a system with no ultimate hierarchy leads to logically incompatible statements, such as that EU law, at the same time, both is and is not hierarchically superior to member state law. But this is a logical impossibility only if we think of both statements as belonging to the same legal system. As it is, the claim that EU law is superior is a claim made by, and in relation to, EU law, while the claim that it is not superior is a claim made by, and in relation to, the law of a member state.[64]

Giudice would probably not accept this except in some cases. He might accept that an English court proclaiming that a contract requires consideration would not make this as a universal claim. It would be a claim only for English law, even if the court did not say this. But the situation here, he might say, is different. The Court of Justice, when it proclaims the superiority of EU law, does not express this as a statement only with regard to the EU legal order itself but instead proclaims this also vis-à-vis member state law. It proclaims to speak for both orders, just as a national court would proclaim to speak for both orders. This, then would be where the conflict lies.

But the argument of incompatibility still fails. Even if a court proclaims to speak about its relation to a foreign legal system, effectively it can only speak to that relation as a part of its own legal system. Systems theory would speak of a re-entry of the difference between two legal systems into each legal system. The Court of Justice, in speaking to the relation between EU law and UK law, speaks to this relation as a part of EU law. It speaks with regard to the rule of external recognition within EU law. The UK court, speaking to the relation between UK law and EU law, speaks to this relation as a part of UK law. It speaks with regard to the rule of external recognition within UK law. Each, then, speaks about a different rule, and within a different system. Because each is an institution only of its own legal system, they cannot reach the point above both systems at which alone such conflict would be possible.

[63] Michael Giudice, *Understanding the Nature of Law: A Case for Constructive Conceptual Analysis* (Cheltenham: Edward Elgar, 2015), pp. 144ff.

[64] For a similar argument, see H. L. A. Hart (n. 23).

The normative challenge can be developed on the basis of an argument made by Pavlos Eleftheriadis.[65] Eleftheriadis suggests that a pluralist concept of laws, as proposed here, fails to fulfil the need for integrity of the law. Instead, he suggests, different legal orders should endorse a sophisticated view of their own limits. Essentially, he suggests that if no hierarchy exists between legal systems, then no system can be the ultimate arbiter of any conflictual question. Rather, systems should, though in a decentralised way, treat each other as equal.

It may not be a sufficiently satisfactory answer that even treatment as equal may not avoid all conflicts in a decentralised system. But it seems to me that the argument itself ignores that the absence of hierarchy does not disable the possibility of an ultimate decision. Rather, the decision each order takes from its own perspective is ultimate, though only with regard to that system. If EU law decides on its priority over national law, that is an ultimate decision for EU law. If UK law decides on its own priority over EU law, that is an ultimate decision for UK law. Both systems are equal in that both can decide with ultimate force for their own context. Eleftheriadis's plea for integrity begs the question. Integrity makes sense only once we think of law as an entire whole. In a plural setting, in which no ultimate arbiter exists and in which no one coherent system is there, such a plea for integrity has no place.

5.6.2 *Contingency*

Another objection concerns contingency. One might object that recognition by other legal systems cannot be a necessary requirement because the requirement is itself contingent upon two further requirements: first, that more than one legal system exists; and second, that they interact. If either of these requirements is not met, then external recognition would not only not be necessary, it would not even be possible.

The second part of these objections is easier to respond to. A tribe in the Brazilian jungle may have its own legal order without any tertiary rules because it has never interacted with the rest of the world and therefore does not know that other legal systems exist. That does not mean, however, that no tertiary rules exist. To the extent that we know of the tribe and its system, our decision to leave it alone is its own type of recognition. The question would arise, therefore, only for a legal system

[65] Pavlos Eleftheriadis, 'Pluralism and Integrity' (2010) 23 *Ratio Juris*, 365–89.

that is as of yet unknown and would be discovered. It is not clear that legal theory must deal with theoretically possible normative orders that are, however, unknown. Once the system is discovered, however, the establishment of rules of external recognition will kick in. Before discovery, we can then say, the system was indeed complete without such external rule. But this is then only because the system did not take part in our current constellation of global legal pluralism.

The first part of the objection is, at first sight, harder to answer. Granted, if there were only one legal system in the world, the issue would not arise, but that is not the world we live in. More precisely, it would be the world we live in only if we could conceive, in a monist interpretation, of all legal systems as really only subparts of one legal system. I have assumed, for this argument here, that we have a situation of global legal pluralism however, and in this situation such monism is not plausible.

But the objection may be thought to have a stronger point. If a legal system's existence is contingent on the recognition by another legal system, then a legal system must already exist. That legal system, in turn, must have been recognised by another legal system. How then did the first legal system come into existence?

If this is a problem, it is not a problem that is specific to the idea of a rule of external recognition. The question when and how law comes into being is a general problem for any theory of law. As to the development of secondary rules, we have proposals in the literature. As to the development of tertiary rules, it makes sense to think of them as co-emergent, as can be seen in the discussion on the relation between national law and EU law.

In the end, both parts of the objection find the same response: the proposed necessity of rules of external recognition is contingent on a situation of inter-related legal systems, in other words a situation of legal pluralism. In a different situation, such rules would be unnecessary. But that does not seem to be a strong objection. It seems plausible to assume that our current situation is one of such global legal pluralism, and what we need from a concept of laws is that it is adequate for the time and place for which it is formulated.

5.6.3 *State Centrism*

A third objection, this one between conceptual and normative, emerges from Griffiths's critique of weak legal pluralism. Does the concept of relational law not re-establish legal centralism, with its preferred role for state law? After all, there is no question in the model that state law is a legal order. It remains to non-state legal systems to demonstrate that they share that characteristic.

As a pure conceptual point I think this has little strength. It is true that in most analyses the only rules of external recognition that are discussed are those formulated by the state. (The discussion in EU law and international law is a rare and partial exception.) But conceptually, other non-state laws can be expected to have such rules, too. And empirically, chances are they will be found. A good example is religious laws, which do indeed contain such rules of external recognition.[66] Christianity, famously, leaves secular matters to the state (give to Caesar what is Caesar's). Jewish law recognises state law as superior, except for religious matters (*dina d'malkuta dina*; the law of the state is the law).[67] Islamic law is less deferential; it claims superiority over state law but allows for contractual subordination under the law of a non-Islamic state.[68] Religious fundamentalism of any kind does not recognise state law as equal. We should expect that other non-state legal orders develop similar rules.

This realisation – that non-state orders also have rules of external recognition – takes away some of the normative bite of Griffiths's criticism. External recognition, under the conception proposed here, is not a one-way street. In all but the rarest cases, we will be faced with external recognition from both sides. The way to overcome the criticism of external recognition as a requirement for the quality of law is therefore not, as Griffiths had proposed, to dispense of it, but instead to universalise it.

This does not resolve a bigger normative concern that underlies Griffiths's criticism, namely the fear of hegemony and power imbalance. Even though conceptually different legal orders are put on an equal footing, effectively some such orders will remain more powerful than others. One could well criticise that a theory that emphasises the formal equality of legal systems is blind to such effective inequalities – just like international law with its emphasis on formal equality between states has been criticised as blind to the effective remaining inequality between

[66] See Ralf Michaels, 'Postsäkulare Rechtsvergleichung', in Reinhard Zimmermann (ed.), *Zukunftsfragen der Rechtsvergleichung* (Tübingen: Mohr/Siebeck 2016), pp. 39–102, 94ff.

[67] J. D. M. Lew, 'Jewish Law – Its Development and Co-Existence in the Non-Jewish World' (1976) 40 *RabelsZ*, 101–22.

[68] Mathias Rohe, 'Sharia and the Muslim Diaspora', in Peri Bearman and Rudolph Peters (eds.), *The Ashgate Research Companion to Islamic Law* (Burlington, VT/Farnham: Ashgate Publishing, 2014), p. 261ff.

states. Indeed, others have suggested that theories of legal pluralism tend to be blind to issues of power.[69] But this is a separate problem.

5.7 Conclusion

The suggested introduction of tertiary rules, and of mutual contingency of legal systems, has important implications for legal theory. It enables us to conceptualise that different legal orders are not completely separate from each other but instead are mutually constitutive. It enables us to find a concept of law that is not confined to the state and not dependent merely on the self-ascription of legal character. It enables us to think of law as one and plural at the same time. It paves the way towards a concept not of law but of laws.

[69] Gad Barzilai, 'Beyond Relativism: Where Is Political Power in Legal Pluralism?' (2008) 9 *Theoretical Inquiries in Law*, 395–416.

6

The Many Uses of Law

Interactional Law as a Bridge between Instrumentalism and Law's Values

SANNE TAEKEMA

6.1 Introduction

Law is not there for its own sake. If we agree that law is important for society, there are still numerous ways in which that claim can be made, giving rise to very different ideas of law and different ideas of its relationship to society generally. In this chapter, I focus on one particular perspective on this claim, that of legal instrumentalism. Legal instrumentalism has a bad name: it is criticised for reducing law to a policy instrument for external political or economic goals. Here, I consider whether the idea of law's instrumentality can also be interpreted differently, in a way which is not reductionist. I do this by taking a particular theoretical perspective, combining legal interactionism with pragmatist ideas. By seeing law as emerging from the interactional expectancies of people towards one another, law is conceptually based on horizontal relationships (building on the theory of Lon Fuller). In this chapter, I argue that this horizontal orientation can provide a specific version of an instrumental view of law because it pluralises law's instrumentality. Law is no longer seen as a policy instrument in the hands of authorities, but as a tool for everyone who makes use of it (making use of John Dewey's pragmatism). To substantiate such a bottom-up account of law as an instrument, I present an argument on how the purposive activities of people in legal practices shape law as an interactional phenomenon. Finally, I argue how law as a value-oriented practice relates to purposive activities and explore how law as set by official authority figures in, limits or enables, different uses ordinary people make of law, connecting horizontal and vertical dimensions of law.

The purpose of this chapter is to present and elaborate a particular theoretical perspective that is pluralist in a number of ways and can be considered a form of pluralist jurisprudence. As jurisprudence, the theory puts forward a conception of the nature of law.[1] Thus, this chapter is a contribution to debates on the concept of law. Pluralism figures in the background of this more prominently than I am able to explain within the confines of this chapter. It merits a few preliminary remarks at least. I do not consider jurisprudence to be an ahistorical enterprise: a theory of law needs to account for law as we find it in the world today. One striking feature of the present state of law is the plurality of legal orders. Although I do not wish to argue that this is necessarily a new feature of law, it seems clear that globalisation in particular leads to increased contact between legal orders and thus gives urgency to the question how legal orders relate to each other.[2] This development is reinforced by the wide variety of legal mechanisms, procedures, standards, and so on that are available today. Therefore, a central task of jurisprudence is to provide an account of law that can explain and conceptualise this given plurality. This does not necessarily lead to a pluralist jurisprudence in the sense that pluralism needs to be part of every theory; a unitary theory of law that is argued to underlie the plurality of phenomena seems possible. However, I do think that pluralism at the conceptual level is necessary as well. Most centrally, in the version of legal interactionism to which I subscribe, it is crucial that law takes different forms: interactional and enacted law, and that these forms are on an equal footing as forms of law. There is a second way in which the theory defended here is pluralist, which is particular to the substance of the theory rather than linked to the kind of jurisprudence it is. As explained later in this chapter, legal interactionism incorporates a large number of actors and the relationships between those actors, particularly in the account of law's instrumentality. Thus, a particular value of pluralist jurisprudence is that it has an eye for participation of a broader range of actors. Eventually, this may assist in democratising processes of legal change, but I fear that is too much to hope for at the moment. It may also urge legal scholars to be more open to forms and uses of law that tend to be ignored from a more traditional

[1] I do not presume to do justice to the methodological debate on jurisprudence. For a thoughtful and detailed account of these issues, see Michael Guidice, *Understanding the Nature of Law. A Case for Constructive Conceptual Explanation* (Cheltenham: Edward Elgar, 2015).

[2] Paul Schiff Berman, 'Global Legal Pluralism' (2007) 80 *Southern California Law Review*, 1155–234.

point of view, like private regulation, legal mobilisation or informal dispute resolution. I hope some of these claims may appear at least plausible by the end of this chapter.

6.2 Legal Instrumentalism

In legal theory circles, legal instrumentalism is associated with specific debates and theories. Instrumentalism is contrasted with formalism, and is often associated with the attack of Legal Realism on the formalist ideas of Christopher Columbus Langdell and others. This is an American debate with a historical flavour to it: instrumentalism was useful in supporting the progressive policies of New Deal era politics against the conservative ideas of nineteenth-century liberalism that dominated in judicial practice.[3] Detached from this history, the idea of instrumentalism is still paired with formalism: law as a means to realise external ends versus law as an autonomous system of neutral rules and procedures. Of course, both are ideal types: particular legal systems as well as particular theories of law mix elements of both. However, there is a continuing association of the idea of law as an autonomous system with formal attributes of law. Respect for the forms of law safeguards the rule of law and prevents the subordination of law to politics.[4]

In this context, legal instrumentalism takes a particular form. The system of law as a whole is regarded as an instrument, as a pliable tool in the hands of those who make the legal rules. Law is no more than a translation of policies into legal rules and procedures; law can be designed to take whatever shape is necessary to reach the goals adopted by its creators. Creating legal rules has traditionally meant legislation, but – increasingly – other forms of regulation are included. The broadening to regulation has not changed the basic idea of a central authority which determines policy and designs the rules through which to realise this. This picture of law as an instrument highlights three things: external goals, determination by a central authority, and flexible rules.

Each of these three attributes can be subjected to criticism. The idea of law as serving external goals comes under criticism from theorists who highlight the internal values of law, the most interesting for my purposes

[3] Morton Horwitz, *The Transformation of American Law, 1870–1960* (New York: Oxford University Press, 1992), pp. 6–7.

[4] Philippe Nonet and Philip Selznick, *Law and Society in Transition: Toward Responsive Law* (New York: Harper & Row, 1978).

being Gustav Radbruch,[5] Lon Fuller[6] and Philip Selznick,[7] but of whom Ronald Dworkin is the most prominent in the debate.[8] In different ways, these theorists all contend that the realm of law comes with a set of commitments, values, internal morality or master ideals, which co-determine the nature of law. Rather than contrasting instrumentalism with a formalist view of law, they draw on a substantive, value-oriented view of law's autonomy. Law is able to resist being made a vessel for external input, not primarily because of its formal structures but because of its inherent orientation towards values of legality and justice.

Theorists of legal pluralism criticise the idea that law is made by a central authority. Law can take many forms, and not all of these forms are predicated on the idea that law is posited by a central authority.[9] Customary law in particular is a form of law in which law appears as given (in more traditional settings) or evolved. However, the current debates on transnational law or the fragmentation of international law also problematise this aspect: law is seen as made by many actors.[10] Not all of these actors have public authority but they create or influence legal regimes nonetheless. Pluralism therefore challenges instrumentalism in two ways: by pointing to forms of law that are not made deliberately, and by showing that law is created by many actors.

The idea that law is flexible and can be made to fit any substantive aim is the one that comes under attack from formalist circles: the forms of law set (rule of law) limits to what law can be made to do. Because there are formal and procedural constraints, law protects citizens from sheer political power.[11] The argument here can take two forms: an analytical argument that the structure of law is such that it is not susceptible to full-blown instrumentalism and there will always be a non-instrumental core of law;[12] or a normative argument that the forms

[5] Gustav Radbruch, 'Rechtsphilosophie', in Arthur Kaufmann (ed.), *Gustav Radbruch, Gesamtausgabe, Band 2: Rechtsphilosophie II.* (Heidelberg: Müller, 1993), pp. 205–450.

[6] Lon Fuller, *The Morality of Law*, 2nd ed. (New Haven: Yale University Press, 1969).

[7] Philip Selznick, 'Sociology and Natural Law' (1961) 6 *Natural Law Forum*, 84–108.

[8] Ronald Dworkin, *Law's Empire* (Cambridge: Belknap, 1986).

[9] William Twining, *General Jurisprudence. Understanding Law from a Global Perspective* (Cambridge: Cambridge University Press, 2009), pp. 362–75.

[10] Gregory Shaffer, 'International Law and Global Public Goods in a Legal Pluralist World' (2012) 23 *European Journal of International Law*, 669–93.

[11] Brian Tamanaha, *The Perils of Pervasive Legal Instrumentalism* (Nijmegen: Wolf Legal Publishers, 2006), p. 67.

[12] This is a formalist version of Fuller's argument about internal morality. I usually interpret Fuller's morality of law in a more substantive way, but for instance Rundle's reading of

of law should be respected in order to reap the benefits of autonomous law. The latter argument sees instrumentalism as a real possibility, but one we should guard against. Tamanaha, for instance, argues that instrumentalism is pervasive in American law, which has the deplorable consequence that law is not seen as binding, but as manipulable.[13]

My argument here uses insights from all three of these strands of criticism, not to attack instrumentalism, but to investigate whether there are forms of instrumentalism which respond to these criticisms, but still see law as primarily a means to an end. My starting point for this alternative version of instrumentalism is pragmatist theory. To some, this endeavour may seem doomed: was pragmatism not one of the main instigators of the downfall of law's integrity?[14] I argue that pragmatist theory, of a certain kind, is valuable for a reassessment of instrumentalism. My main point here is that forms of pragmatism that highlight the individual's moral worth and creativity are able to give law's integrity a central role, because upholding law's values and procedures is crucial to enable an individual's uses of law. The challenge I take up here is therefore to provide an argument for a pluralised and normative instrumentalism. Although this form of instrumentalism builds on pragmatist theory, I am not so much interested in claiming that label as I am in developing an argument to reposition instrumentalism.

6.3 Interactional Law and Purposive Action

An important step in the argument for a pluralised instrumentalism is to establish what role individuals have in the context of law. This can simply start with the observation that a great variety of actors are involved in practices of law: public actors such as national or local government agencies, supranational authorities such as the European Commission, public international regulators such as the World Health Organization, private regulators such as the International Organization for Standardization (ISO), legal professionals such as lawyers and judges, enterprises, associations, and ordinary individuals. My primary focus will be on individuals, but the argument should be read as applying to groups of people as well. In Section 5, I relate the discussion to the (very large) set of actors that cannot be classified as official public actors (such as inter-, sub- and

Fuller seems to fit here. Kristen Rundle, *Forms Liberate. Reclaiming the Jurisprudence of Lon L. Fuller* (Oxford: Hart Publishing, 2012).

[13] Tamanaha (n. 11), p. 57. [14] Cf. Tamanaha (n. 11), pp. 32–33.

national governments), nor as individuals, and I consider in what way the argument applies to some of these actors as well. A focus on individuals takes a starting point opposite from the paradigm case of public national authority. Starting with individuals, we also need to be clear about the way these figure in the practice of law. Both 'the role in the context of law', or 'figuring in the practice of law' are highly vague formulations. This is unavoidable at this point. Anything more specific runs the risk of cutting off certain alternative ways of engaging with law. A first distinction that may be helpful is that between a passive and an active role of an individual. With regard to law, this means that someone can be seen as a subject of law, being governed by law's norms, or as a participant in law, doing things in and with legal practice. It is important to note that the passive and active are best regarded as two sides to someone's involvement in law rather than as separate roles. As the perpetrator of a tort, someone may be sued; but as a defendant in litigation, he may make use of legal procedure to refute the claim.

In most legal theories, the active role of individuals is neglected: the emphasis is on the system of norms (in Hart and Kelsen) or on the work of legal officials (Dworkin). In order to conceptualise the role of individuals, an interactional theory of law is more fruitful. As Wibren van der Burg and I have argued,[15] legal interactionism sees law as encompassing two basic forms, interactional law and enacted law. First developed by Lon Fuller, legal interactionism states that a large and basic part of law develops out of 'interactional expectancies'[16] and by stabilising these interactions also facilitates further interaction.[17] Interactional law can remain implicit: it is enough that the norm guides in such a way that the people involved can anticipate each other's actions and reactions. Although a completely interactional legal practice is possible, in the form of customary law, in the present world interactional law always links to enacted law. Enacted law is the law that is made by a person or body with

[15] Sanne Taekema and Wibren van der Burg, 'Towards a Fruitful Cooperation between Legal Philosophy, Legal Sociology and Doctrinal Research: How Legal Interactionism May Bridge Unproductive Oppositions', in Richard Nobles and David Schiff (eds.), *Law, Society and Community. Socio-Legal Essays in Honour of Roger Cotterrell* (Farnham: Ashgate, 2014), pp. 129–45; and Wilbren Van der Burg, *The Dynamics of Law and Morality. A Pluralist Account of Legal Interactionism* (Farnham: Ashgate, 2014).

[16] Lon Fuller, 'Human Interaction and the Law', in Kenneth I. Winston (ed.), *The Principles of Social Order. Selected essays of Lon L. Fuller* (Durham: Duke University Press, 1981) pp. 211–46, p. 219.

[17] Ibid., p. 215.

a certain competence to do so for a certain group. For interactionism, this too is a broad category, which not only includes legislation or treaties, but also the regulations of a school board, the rules of a voluntary association or the standards of a certification scheme. There are some forms of law that challenge the distinction between enacted and interactional law, most importantly contracts, to which I return later in this chapter. Crucial for the argument here is the connection between enacted law and interactional law more generally. As Fuller points out, legislation also depends on reciprocal relations between the lawgiver and the subjects of the law.[18] Fuller's principles of legality all show that a legal rule can only function if it is communicated meaningfully, which signifies that both the lawgiver and the addressees need to know what reactions to expect. Moreover, enacted law also plays a crucial role in the interactional expectancies of people towards each other, and if it does not contribute to stable patterns of interaction it will not work well.[19]

Given the forms of enacted and interactional law, a jurisprudentially relevant question is whether legal interactionism really proposes a pluralist conception of law. Both a negative and a positive answer to this question seem plausible. First, one may argue that the role of interactional expectancies is foundational: law can be seen as a practice that is made up of the actions and expectations people have. In such a view of legal interactionism, interactional law is the basic form and enacted law can be explained as a solution to some of the problems that reliance on interactional law alone encounters. According to such a view, legal interactionism is not truly pluralist, but at heart a monistic theory that recognises the possibility, and factual existence, of plural forms within the practice of law.[20] The second answer would stress the difference between enacted and interactional law and argue that there is a crucial difference between made law, declared by an authority of some kind, and interactional law, which forms spontaneously in practice. The key difference is that enacted law has an author. As said, enacted law depends on interactional expectations for its effectiveness, but this does not change the character of its form. Of the two approaches, the pluralist version of

[18] Fuller (n. 6), p. 209. [19] Taekema and Van der Burg (n. 15), p. 135.

[20] In my earlier work (especially Sanne Taekema, *The Concept of Ideals in Legal Theory* (The Hague: Kluwer Law International, 2003), pp. 229–32), I highlighted the importance of law as a practice guided by ideals, focusing on how legal ideals both provide distinctiveness to law and a bond with moral and social values. In terms of the discussion here, that view seems monistic, although I would now argue that it is best understood as a practice view that allows for pluralist forms of law.

interactionism seems better equipped to account for the phenomena of law today. Especially in light of the tensions and conflicts between different sets of norms,[21] it does not seem warranted to claim that enacted law arises out of interactional law. A more fruitful way of regarding the role of the practice of law is to see it as the social base in which all law is embedded rather than identify the practice with law itself. Different forms of law each have their place in that social practice. It is important to note, however, that it is rather difficult to distinguish interactional law from its base in practice, because it largely remains implicit in that practice. Although a distinction needs to be made theoretically, interactional law is so much part of the practice that it is not possible to separate them when considering concrete instances of interactional law.

Although the basic difference between enacted law and interactional law is the clearest form of plurality, others forms of law are best regarded as hybrid forms, rather than enacted or interactional per se. The most important category here is contract. As argued elsewhere, contracts usually deliberately lay down explicit rules for the parties, but they also depend on the accompanying interactional expectancies and sometimes are no more than an attempt to make those explicit and more stable.[22] Contracts are made by actors with the recognised competence to make rules (whether a customary or legislative recognition does not really make a difference), but their meaning is not exhausted by the terms of the contract. Often, a contract is part of a broader, interactional legal setting, or it is the starting point for further interactional expectations, which may diverge from its written form. In various jurisdictions, the interactional context of contracts is recognised by courts.[23] Thus, contracts are a third form of law, which cannot be reduced to either enacted or interactional law.

If we use a legal interactionist theory of law, individuals become central to the idea of law, because their expectations form the backbone of all legal orders. Their activities (the activities that show what expectations they have, of each other and of different lawgivers) determine what law means 'on the ground' or in daily life. Although this is a crucial point,

[21] Jan Klabbers and Touko Piiparinen (eds.), *Normative Pluralism and International Law: Exploring Global Governance* (Cambridge: Cambridge University Press, 2013).

[22] Taekema and Van der Burg (n. 15), p. 134; and Sanne Taekema, 'Private Law as an Open Legal Order: Understanding Contract and Tort as Interactional Law', *Netherlands Journal of Legal Philosophy* (2014) 43/2, 140–49, at 145–46.

[23] Taekema (n. 22), pp. 146–48.

it should not be overstated. From people's behaviour in city traffic one might doubt the reality of rules of right of way, or traffic lights. However, hardly anyone is surprised if they are fined for running a red light or not giving way. The relation individuals have to rules can be highly varied, and may be complex and even partly incoherent. Reasons for this include difference in knowledge about parts of enacted law, different attitudes to sets of rules, experiences (or lack of experience) with the administration of justice. Someone may at the same time generally support the enactment of rules by national and local government, be completely ignorant of the relevance of European and international law, think that it is okay to bend the rules on income tax, and expect business partners to give priority to their unwritten longstanding expectations rather than the contract that they made.

To make this variability manageable, a few further distinctions may be helpful. Building on Dewey, we can distinguish between habits and creative action, meaning that a large part of our activities are routine, unthinking, while some of the things we do are purposive and thought through.[24] Encountering problems is the main reason for moving from habit to purposive action, because routine no longer suffices then. The distinction is highly relevant in this context, because a habitual relation to law is primarily non-instrumental. Law is part of the background of what we do routinely. We do not think of buying groceries as making use of contracts; we do not experience the relationship with our children as following the rules of family law. Only when there is a problem in which law has a role to play does the use of law become purposive. In this chapter, I am primarily interested in the latter category: purposive action which relates to law consciously. This means that, although the basis of law is interactional, a large part of these interactions are not relevant here, because they remain implicit.

A second distinction should be made here: purposive action may be initiated by the individual in question, but may also be required because

[24] I do not use Dewey's own distinctions, but distinguish (routine) habit from purposive action to clarify the point, joining together terminology from different books. In John Dewey, 'Human Nature and Conduct', in Jo Ann Boydston (ed.), *The Middle Works, 1899–1924*, Volume 14 (Carbondale and Edwardsville: Southern Illinois University Press, 1988), p. 121, Dewey describes habit as a developmental concept: completely developed habits are routine, but new habits can be formed when a problem makes this necessary. In John Dewey, 'The Quest for Certainty', in Jo Ann Boydston (ed.), *The Later Works, 1925–1953*, Volume 4 (Carbondale and Edwardsville: Southern Illinois University Press, 1984), p. 196, Dewey uses the term purposive action to describe intelligent problem-solving.

of the actions of others, or even because of changing circumstances. In Dewey's work we encounter the work of the scientist or the school child as prime examples of purposive, problem-solving action. Legal problems are less neat: they may start with stupid mistakes, interpersonal irritations, neglect rather than curiosity. In the context of voluntary purposive action, law clearly facilitates (something that was also stressed by Fuller): it supports action or even makes certain actions possible. Many private law rights extend our possibilities because they give stability to promises and obligations. However, law may also facilitate required action. Even if legal problems are brought on by circumstance or the conduct of others, law gives means to respond to these problems. The clearest example here is procedural rights. The suspect of a crime is not just the passive subject of a legal inquiry, he can also instruct his attorney and voice his opinion. A citizen disagreeing with council building plans can lodge a complaint and argue against them. Rights can also be abused for the wrong purposes. In the Dutch city of Dordrecht, several requests for government information were received every day for years, all sent by the same person.[25] This person had a quarrel with the city about some of the houses he owned and used the law on public government information to take revenge: two civil servants were occupied full time answering these requests, because the law required a prompt response to requests for information. What the example shows is that legal rules can be part of a purposive activity, even if such activity is contrary to the purposes for which the rules were adopted. The means created by law can often be put to use in different ways, sometimes turning out to be more flexible than intended. This raises an additional important question on the link between the uses made of law by individuals and the normative substance of law. How do values and purposes of law relate to the purposive actions of individuals?

6.4 The Values of Law and Purposive Action

With regard to purposive action of individuals, I argued that the main role of law is facilitative. However, it is still an open question whether law facilitates anything and is completely flexible, or sets limits to what is facilitated. If it does facilitate any action at all, Tamanaha's criticism of instrumentalism would apply to this version of instrumentalism too.

[25] See the judgment of the Court of Appeal The Hague: Gerechtshof Den Haag 28 januari 2014 (ECLI:NL:GHDHA:2014:75).

In this vision, the legal system is prey to narrow interests of different groups who try to gain the upper hand in influencing law, one of his examples being the politicisation of the U.S. Supreme Court, which is reduced to a quarrel between conservative and liberal forces.[26] Making room for individual purposive action inevitably allows for a pluralism of purposes and activities. Law cannot facilitate purposive action without making room for determination of purpose and action by individuals themselves. However, the process of determining what to do takes place in context, not only in the context of the problem experienced, but also in the context of law. Perhaps the most crucial claim that runs through pragmatist thinking is that means and ends mutually influence each other, meaning that consideration of the means necessary to achieve a particular end will be a factor of importance for the decision whether to pursue the end.[27] The end does not justify the means: there are things we should not do even if the consequences would be valuable. Deciding on an instrument requires a broader view than simply relating it to the stated purpose it is supposed to serve. In addition, we need to consider that means can sometimes create their own ends: many technological advances enabled setting new purposes, with positive and negative examples in history. Moreover, means and ends are not fixed entities: what is regarded as an end in one context, can be the means for another end in another context. In the legal context, this dynamic is clearly visible with regard to individual rights: constitutional freedoms are an end in themselves and merit strong protection, but sometimes we are confronted with the consequences of exercising those freedoms and the need to limit them. Hate speech at first appears as protected by freedom of speech, but no longer does if we see it as a means for a despicable purpose.

If we relate the continuity of means and ends to the theoretical perspective of law as part of a value-oriented practice (which I associated earlier with Radbruch, Fuller and Selznick), we can link the idea of individual purposive action to these legal values. Elsewhere I have argued that the central values of law to be considered are justice and legality,[28] but what the values are is not central to the argument here. Individuals who use law as a means to further their own purposes need to consider the character of those means (i.e. the values implied in the legal rules).

[26] Tamanaha (n. 11), pp. 60–64.

[27] Philip Selznick, *The Moral Commonwealth: Social Theory and the Promise of Community* (Berkeley [etc.]: University of California Press, 1992), p. 328.

[28] Taekema (n. 20), pp. 187–88.

Sometimes this will lead to a reconsideration of an individual's actions, because the values of law cannot be squared with the purposes an individual may have: an unfair contractual clause may need to be reconsidered not only because the other party will not accept it, but also because it runs counter to ideas of individual justice that are part of the law (either enacted or interactional). However, there are uses of the law that are less easy to set aside, because they seem to be in line with legal values at first sight. The example of the man who quarrelled with the city council of Dordrecht can serve to make the point here. Why could this man obstruct the city council administration for so long? Because every single action (a request for government information) was completely in accordance with the law: the value of the transparency of governmental decision-making required the granting of each request. It was only when it became apparent that the man did this for the sole purpose of frustrating the administration that something could be done: eventually a court order was given to stop him. Two aspects of the role of legal values become apparent in light of such an example: the problem of one-dimensional realisation of legal values, and the importance of context. In this case, the value of transparency was at issue, which can be construed as an aspect of legality in Fuller's sense. It is, however, only one aspect of legality, which is only one of law's central values. And to complicate matters further, law also incorporates values that are not 'distinctively legal', to use Philip Selznick's phrase,[29] but involve social and moral purposes. These different values, and different dimensions of values, may conflict, and following Radbruch, I argue that law's central values go in such different directions that they can be expected to conflict.[30] When one aspect of legal values is appealed to, we should consider the consequences for other legal values, which will often make conflicting demands. Even when considering one central legal value, different dimensions conflict: the value of justice has two very different dimensions, the equal application of norms demanded by formal justice and the equitable solution of the individual case.[31] A balance needs to be struck, sometimes very pragmatically (as was done in the case mentioned:

[29] Phillip Selznick, 'The Sociology of Law', in *International Encyclopedia of the Social Sciences*, Volume 9 (New York: Macmillan and Free Press, 1968), pp. 50–59, p. 51.

[30] Radbruch, (n. 5), pp. 302–03.

[31] In German, the latter is aptly referred to as *Einzelfallgerechtigkeit*, justice in the individual case (e.g. Gabriele Britz, *Einzelfallgerechtigkeit versus Generalisierung. Verfassungsrechtliche Grenzen statistischer Diskriminierung* (Tübingen: Mohr Siebeck, 2008)), bringing out the tension with general application of norms.

the court ordered the man to restrict his requests to ten a month). The case also shows the importance of context: only when the background of the man's actions was included in the legal decision-making was there a possibility for weighing the different aspects in a responsible way. To sum up: law does not facilitate purposes indifferently, and therefore it is not completely vulnerable to being reduced to a means for any end. However, it is more difficult to guard against actions that appeal to one of law's internal values.

6.5 Instrumentality and Authority

The account so far may seem to neglect the role of legal authorities. One might say that it is fine to pay attention to the way law may facilitate purposive actions of individuals, but that this is at best a partial understanding of law, and one influenced rather heavily by a private law perspective. Although there is a natural affinity between my position and private law questions,[32] the argument is by no means limited to this type of horizontal use of law. Law generally is crucial to the actions and interactions of people because (as argued in Section 3) it manages expectations: criminal law rules (in combination with the moral norms they express) stabilise our interactions with others, because we know we can generally expect them not to hurt us. Similarly, predictability of public administration gives us a stable base to work with. In all of these areas, it is apparent that the existence of rules is not enough. The weight of public authority needs to be behind law because it is a crucial component for a stable practice. In the Netherlands, we have ample experience with the consequences of non-enforcement of enacted rules, and we see that in some contexts interactional practices arise that take the place of enacted law, while in other contexts things become chaotic.[33] However, non-enforcement of enacted law only works well if it is clear what legal officials will and will not do. Again, stable expectations are key.

Public authority thus has a role of importance to play in stabilising expectations, both of people amongst each other (i.e. horizontally), and of authorities and ordinary people towards each other (i.e. vertically).

[32] Sanne Taekema, 'Private Law as an Open Legal Order: Understanding Contract and Tort as Interactional Law' (2014) 43 *Netherlands Journal of Legal Philosophy*, 140–49.

[33] For a good discussion of the development of toleration in criminal law in the areas of euthanasia, drugs and prostitution, see Ybo Buruma, 'Dutch Tolerance: On Drugs, Prostitution and Euthanasia' (2007) 37 *Crime and Justice*, 73–113.

That vertical relationship merits further consideration, because the idea of bottom-up instrumentalism may seem less relevant in this context. Here, the idea of a plurality of uses of law is crucial. First of all, law is a means for public institutions to realise general purposes. Ideally, the processes in which these purposes are adopted and the legal forms used to achieve them are designed are democratic, so that representatives of citizens can exert influence. The realisation of these general purposes will inevitably clash with the purposive activities of individuals or groups. There are different ways in which these clashes play out and end, but in all of them procedures play a crucial role. With Jeremy Waldron, I would argue that procedural opportunities of individuals to voice arguments matter here.[34] These procedures provide space for the creative input of individuals which may lead to different interpretations and applications of the law than were first envisaged. Law's openness, through its procedures, makes it possible not only that people have a say in law, but also that they can argue that their own use of law matters and needs to be considered. Therefore, it is too easy to say that once a law has been adopted democratically, the influence of individual citizens no longer matters, and that they simply become subjects of that law. The openness of procedure (in the form of formal court proceedings or as informal mechanisms for voicing arguments) makes that influence continuous. That it is continuous does not necessarily make it large. In most contexts of interaction between official authorities and individuals, the input of individuals in decision-making will be minor, although in a few it may make a significant difference.

In the context of the vertical relationship between public authorities and individuals, a form of influence that merits particular consideration is public interest litigation. Public interest litigation can be described as action by a group of people that is unsatisfied with the pursuit or realisation of a public purpose, and uses legal procedure to further their alternative end. What defines public interest litigation is that court procedures are used to try to force a public authority to take action, rather than other forms of promoting a group's goals such as lobbying or public protest. The particular purposes of such litigation differ. Sometimes, they involve accepted legal or policy aims that have been neglected by a public body. A recent case that illustrates this well, is the case of *Urgenda*, an environmental non-governmental organisation which sued

[34] Jeremy Waldron, 'The Concept and the Rule of Law' (2008) 43 *Georgia Law Review*, 1–61, 9.

the Dutch state for not upholding its promises to implement climate change policies.[35] The court awarded the claim, citing policy documents in which the Dutch government had laid out its particular climate change objectives. In other cases, the aim is to get a public authority to choose sides in a controversial issue, think of the issue of abortion in the United States.[36] Sometimes, internal legal aims and controversy coincide: this is the case when a legal principle has clear support in enacted law, but is interpreted in a controversial way. The U.S. Supreme Court case of *Brown v. Board of Education* can serve an example: the civil rights movement successfully challenged the controversial decision of separate but equal doctrine as applied to schools.[37] With regard to this form of legal mobilisation, we can usefully link the instrumental use of law with law's internal values. Public interest litigation seems both strategically successful and normatively laudable, if it not only makes use of the procedural options of the legal system but also links its claims to internal legal values. In the case of civil rights, the link to equality and formal justice of the civil rights claim was very strong, and the separate but equal doctrine could not really be linked to the basic principles of the legal system in a coherent way. In such a case, we can also see how interactional law can at times have long lasting negative effect on legal change. Although legal values clearly point in one direction, the way law is experienced on the ground can be a conservative countering force. It then depends on individuals, and more often groups, to recognise this problem and take action, often at serious cost to themselves and others. Again, the desegregation of schools is a good example: think of the children who were the first to go to previously all-white schools.[38]

[35] District Court The Hague 24 June 2015, ECLI:NL:RBDHA:2015:7145. In English: http://deeplink.rechtspraak.nl/uitspraak?id=ECLI:NL:RBDHA:2015:7196.

[36] *Roe v. Wade*, U.S. Supreme Court 410 U.S. 113 (1973). The case established the right to abortion, but this did not silence public debate.

[37] *Brown v. Board of Education*, U.S. Supreme Court 347 U.S. 483 (1954). On the path towards the *Brown* decision, see Richard Kluger, *Simple Justice: On the History of Brown v. Board of Education and Black America's Struggle for Equality* (New York: Knopf Doubleday, 2011).

[38] Hannah Arendt wrote a highly controversial article about Little Rock, the town in which federal military forces had to escort the black students to their school, in which she claimed desegregation of schools was not a good starting point for addressing discrimination in the American South. Hannah Arendt, 'Reflections on Little Rock' (1959) 6 *Dissent*, 45–56. For recent, diverging reactions, see Maribel Morey, 'Reassessing Hannah Arendt's "Reflections on Little Rock" (1959)' (2014) 10 *Law, Culture and the Humanities*, 88–110 and Michael Burroughs, 'Hannah Arendt, "Reflections on Little Rock," and White Ignorance' (2015) 3 *Critical Philosophy of Race*, 52–78.

Tamanaha is dismissive of what he calls cause litigation in the American context,[39] but I believe that it can also be regarded as a positive aspect of the plurality of purposes that can be pursued through law. If we look at the protection of human rights, for instance in South Africa or Europe, litigation has proven to be one of the ways in which issues can be put on the agenda effectively, and sometimes lead to change.[40]

This discussion of one particular form of instrumental use of law by groups also shows that the relations between the horizontal and vertical orientations in legal practice can be complex. In addition to the typical forms of enacted law as a top-down use of law by public authorities and interactional law as horizontally stabilising individual's expectations, we can now add a bottom-up perspective on enacted law. The use of the formal structure and aims of enacted law against public authority gives ordinary individuals influence on the development of enacted law, which goes further than simply using the opportunity to voice arguments in a legal setting. It is a deliberate use of legal means in a manner more akin to top-down instrumentalism. Theoretically, however, it is continuous with the broader pragmatist and interactionist idea that law is open to the creative input of people in a non-official capacity. Law is open to alternative interpretations and uses, and does not necessarily serve the policy goals of public institutions only. Because there is procedural room for individuals, their use of the law can (at least theoretically) be the source for change. If such uses are linked to law's internal values, they may strengthen the realisation of these values. However, this is highly dependent on the context in which law operates. Pluralism of actors and purposes is a source of legal dynamics but the direction of change is uncertain.

So far, the discussion has focused on the different roles of individuals in relation to public authority. What I have left out is an investigation of a further pluralisation of the actors involved. Looking merely at individuals and groups in a society gives a highly simplified picture of law. If we want to grasp the character of law as a pluralised phenomenon, it is necessary to pay attention to other types of actors as well. The question then becomes to what extent the account given here would change, if we

[39] Tamanaha (n. 11), pp. 57–60.

[40] For this see the classic article on legal mobilisation by Burstein, who sees litigation as one form of action enabling social movements to take action, and stresses continuities between legal and political forms of protest. Paul Burstein, 'Legal Mobilization as a Social Movement Tactic: The Struggle for Equal Employment Opportunity' (1991) 96 *American Journal of Sociology*, 1201–25, 1203.

include powerful private actors such as large companies, international governmental agencies such as development banks, or technological experts?[41] At first glance, it seems that a host of actors holds the middle ground between official public institutions and individuals, and that attention for these actors may further problematise the relationship between horizontal and vertical dimensions of law. Especially in the context of transnational law, law beyond the borders of one national state but not necessarily involving public international law, the point is often made that a diverse range of actors make law.[42] Crucially, many forms of regulation involve private entities as rule-makers, entities which cannot be reduced to individuals, making regulation that is not simply contractual.[43] The traditional distinction between public, involving state actors acting in the general interest, and private, natural or legal persons acting on their own behalf, no longer holds here.[44] However, this is not particular to transnational settings. In domestic contexts, private or hybrid public-private entities also make law. Schools, sports organisations, financial supervisors, certification bodies: such organisations all make rules governing their relations with the individuals or companies in their sphere of influence. Using the lens of legal interactionism, the way many of these organisations use law may be characterised as involving both interactional and enacted law. In schools or sports associations, for instance, internal regulations, mostly enacted by a board, are

[41] In the public international law literature, this development already receives much attention: see generally Jan Klabbers, 'Setting the Scene', in Jan Klabbers, Anne Peters and Geir Ulfstein (eds.), *The Constitutionalization of International Law* (Oxford: Oxford University Press, 2009), pp. 1–44, more specifically on these actors, e.g. Larry Cata Backer, 'Private Actors and Public Governance Beyond the State: The Multinational Corporation, the Financial Stability Board and the Global Governance Order' (2011) 18 *Indiana Journal of Global Legal Studies*, 751–802; Daniel Bradlow and Megan Chapman, 'Public Participation and the Private Sector: The Role of Multilateral Development Banks in the Evolution of International Legal Standards' (2011) 4 *Erasmus Law Review*, 91–125; and Monika Ambrus et al. (eds.), *The Role of 'Experts' in International and European Decision-Making Processes. Advisors, Decision Makers or Irrelevant Actors?* (Cambridge: Cambridge University Press, 2014).

[42] Terence Halliday and Gregory Shaffer, 'Transnational Legal Orders', in Terence Halliday and Gregory Shaffer (eds.), *Transnational Legal Orders* (Cambridge: Cambridge University Press, 2015), pp. 1–67.

[43] Colin Scott, Fabrizio Cafaggi, and Linda Senden, 'The Conceptual and Constitutional Challenge of Transnational Private Regulation' (2011) 38 *Journal of Law and Society*, 1–19, 9.

[44] Cf. Peer Zumbansen, 'Neither "Public" nor "Private", "National" nor "International": Transnational Corporate Governance from a Legal Pluralist Perspective' (2011) 38 *Journal of Law and Society*, 50–75.

combined with many informal rules applying to the conduct of the individuals involved as teachers or trainers, and students or athletes. In such contexts, a mix of private, enacted and interactional law seems the best description. However, a number of private regulators seem to fulfil roles resembling public actors. The transnational example of certification bodies may illustrate the use of rules to realise social purposes. The Forest Stewardship Council (FSC), an often studied certifying body, aims to improve environmental and social sustainability of forestry,[45] and it enacts standards to be observed by the companies wishing to carry the FSC label. The FSC is not a public entity, but because it involves multiple stakeholders, including firms, NGOs, and individuals, it does not only serve particular interests. Importantly, it uses regulation to further social goals that could also be a public concern.

In the context of this chapter, the main question is how private regulators, of which many more examples could be given, relate to the forms of law distinguished in legal interactionism, and the horizontal or vertical orientation of law. It is clear that most private regulators make use of a form that most resembles enacted law. However, their relationship with those governed by the enacted rules differs from public enacted law in that there are usually contractual elements in that relationship as well. For instance, to qualify for an FSC label, a forestry company needs to contract a certifying body to check compliance. One might say that the hybridity I described in relation to contract, as a hybrid form between enacted and interactional law, multiplies: in situations where private regulators are active, there are usually multiple forms of law involved and various horizontal and vertical relationships. In contrast to contract, we can identify private regulation as a form created by an authority, other than the rule subjects themselves, which has a private background (i.e. established as an association or contractually). Compared to contract, it will usually be less clearly interactional, because the social contacts between regulator and subjects are less direct than in many contractual situations, making enacted norms more prominent. However, in practice private regulation also involves formalisation of interactional expectations, of which codes of conduct are a good example.

A second question with regard to private regulation, is how this relates to the notion of public authority. Because the rule-makers themselves are not public bodies, we may question their authority to make rules.

45 E.g. Stephen Bell and Andrew Hindmoor, 'Governance without Government. The Case of the Forest Stewardship Council' (2012) 90 *Public Administration*, 144–59.

Again, there is not one answer to this question. Some private regulators seem to be a step ahead of public rule-makers, like the FSC, pushing for sustainability, which is supported by consumer groups rather than governments. Others may serve purely commercial interests, and are authorised by a form of (collective) self-regulation. In some cases, the authority of private entities resembles public authority: schools and universities will all have their own internal regulations regardless of whether they have a public or a private legal status.[46] To those subject to their rules, the difference may not be readily apparent. However, this may in part also be due to the interactions between private and public regulation: education is one of the fields which is usually subject to at least some public rules. In this sense private regulators face challenges of multiple legal orders similar to those faced by public rule-makers: different bodies of public and private norms may apply to their rulemaking activity. Interactional law plays a less visible role than enacted rules, but this does not mean it is less important: wherever groups of people need to cooperate, their reciprocal expectations come to matter.

Thus it seems that both distinctions, between enacted and interactional law, and between public authorities and private individuals, need to be seen as providing the outer limits of a spectrum, of legal forms and of actors, respectively. Between these outer limits, various mixes and hybrid forms of law may exist.

6.6 Concluding Remarks

The overarching idea presented here is that purposive action of individuals can be the basis for a view of law's instrumentality. Instrumental use of law should not be regarded in isolation, nor should it be dismissed immediately as contrary to the idea of law. Law's instrumentality is both constrained and enabled by law's internal values. It is limited by the power of public institutions that use law as an instrument in the standard way. However, legal procedure, and the rule of law values underlying it, creates openings in the relationship between authorities and individual citizens. I have tried to sketch how a focus on purposive action can be combined with an interactional view of law, primarily because the latter's horizontal orientation not only seriously considers law as arising from

[46] Cf. Fuller (n. 6), p. 125.

social interactions but also makes it easier to see how enacted law can be related to the perspective of ordinary citizens.

The view of law that emerges can be regarded as pluralist in two ways: by providing a conception of law in which different forms of law are recognised as part of legal practice, and by recognising the range of different actors that make and use law. Although the main argument focusses on distinguishing enacted law from interactional law, hybrid forms such as contract also form part of the picture. Similarly, although the creative contributions of individuals, and the space for their actions in law, were highlighted, other actors inhabit that space as well. Thus, various actors change the shape and character of law in ways that remain obscured if we only pay attention to law as made by public authorities.

Acknowledgements

I owe thanks to a number of colleagues who commented on drafts, especially Jan Klabbers and Wibren van der Burg, my colleagues at the Erasmus School of Law Jurisprudence seminar, the researchers of the INFAR project at Erasmus University and the participants of the preparatory conference for this volume in Singapore.

7

Why the State?

JOSEPH RAZ*

7.1 The Question

I offer two questions for the price of one: Why do so many jurisprudential theories focus on the state? And what is it about the State that gives it a special place in our social arrangements? I do not mean these to address all aspects of states. They are questions about the law or legal systems of states.

We have to be open to a negative answer to the second question, thus being critical of jurisprudential theories that focus more or less exclusively on the state. That need not deny that states have their own legal systems. It could merely amount to denying them privileged status in the philosophy of law, placing them as one of various legal formations. Furthermore, once we understand the relations between state law and other kinds of law-related systems, we may well conclude that even if state law is in some ways theoretically and practically the most challenging or the most important kind of legal system, it is better understood alongside other such systems rather than through theories that focus on it to the exclusion of the others. Even if state law is in some ways the pre-eminent form of law, in the course of the inquiry, we may find that – by examining it alongside other forms of law – our understanding of state law as well as of law in general changes. That in itself could be an important outcome. It will inevitably change the way we see state law and its relations to other kinds of laws.

Current, state-focused, legal theories build their account of the law out of deliberately chosen building blocks. Just as these theories diverge in their conclusions, so their building blocks may differ; though I believe that there is much greater agreement about the building blocks than about the shape of the complete edifice. A radical inquiry into our questions may

* Earlier versions were given at the Singapore Symposium in Legal Theory 2014 and at the Legal and Political Philosophy Colloquium at NYU, 2014. I am grateful to Eyal Benvenisti, Andrew Halpin, Martin Stone, Ekow Yankah and especially to Sam Scheffler and Liam Murphy for their comments and advice.

jettison the building blocks, searching for alternatives. My search is not that radical. I will rely on many of the common ingredients of current theories, and examine possibilities of reaching different conclusions that are sustained by the same building blocks. Therefore, I start by reminding us of what we all know, namely of some of these ingredients or building blocks. I do not assume that we all agree that they are the right ones from which to start. The proof of the pudding is meant to be in the eating.

7.2 Anticipation

First, a vague indication of the direction of travel: Plato's and Aristotle's theories of law did not focus on the State. They were discussing the Polis. This is not surprising, given that at the time there were no states, in the modern sense, in Greece. What is common to jurisprudential theories generally, whether or not they are focused on the State, is that they take what they consider to be **the most comprehensive legally based social organisation of the day** as their focus. We are used to legal theory focusing, sometimes exclusively, on the State because for quite some time now the State has been, or was assumed to be, the most comprehensive law-based social organisation in the contemporary world.

Is that to say that this explains (causally) why many theorists have focused almost exclusively on state law? Is it to say that is a sufficient reason for that concentration? Both 'Yes' and 'No'. I will be hazarding various empirical statements in this paper, but I regard them all as speculative. This one is a speculation about what may be one part of the explanation for theorists' focus on state law. Once this trend is established, people keep the focus simply because that is how theory is done, and those who are interested in the theory of state law flock to do legal philosophy for that reason. Others take advantage of the fact that because state law is practically important there are more jobs and more money for those who study it, including its theory. And there may be many other factors contributing to the sought-after explanation.

More interestingly, from a theoretical point of view, a legal system that is the most comprehensive legally based organisation of its day presents more challenging theoretical puzzles. I will not enumerate them, but some will emerge in the sequel. That it is the most complex legal system is not itself theoretically interesting (though it may be related to features that are). That state law is important in the life of those subject to it forces on us practical ethical issues, and the theory of state law may help in tackling them. None of this need justify the degree of concentration on state law and the neglect of other law-like phenomena that we are witnessing. Whether this is justified remains to be seen. And I will suggest that the answer is 'No'.

But what does it mean that states are or were the most comprehensive law-based social organisation? Naturally, it is not a precise concept. Nor are we looking for a precise characterisation, if that means one that necessarily captures the law of all states and nothing but state law (when applied to the periods when state law did meet this condition). The test is meant to explain and guide people's theoretical orientation in the world they live in and it is successful if it discriminates successfully between state law and other legal structures in the central cases that actually exist during those periods.

The test I am suggesting consists in the combination of **two factors, (1) an extensive responsibility within its domain, and (2) freedom from external legal constraints.**

Even though much of legal philosophy takes state law as its starting point, writers are aware of the existence of other kinds of law, and I do not mean laws of nature, mathematics or grammar. I mean laws that are uncontroversially normative. They include international law, or the law of organisations like the European Union, but also Canon Law, Sharia law, Scottish law, the law of native nations, the rules and regulations governing the activities of voluntary associations, or those of legally recognised corporations, and more, including many very transient phenomena, like neighbourhood gangs. What does it mean that they had less extensive responsibility within their domain, and were subject to external legal constraints? That is part of what the paper is about.

7.3 Building Blocks: Practice-Based Rules

We proceed by using features that are familiar to you all. One is that the existence of rules (norms, principles, etc.), whether practice-based or not, is too basic a phenomenon to be distinctively law-related. True, laws are norms of conduct. But the existence of norms is essential for the life of any social animals of any of the advanced species. Practice-based norms of conduct are a most pervasive phenomenon; those that are laws, or belong with systems of law, are a special subclass.

However, it is helpful to remind ourselves of some characteristic features of normative practices of any kind. Both in the life of individuals and in the history of societies, people learn that certain forms of conduct are required, learn that there are reasons, addressed to them, to conduct themselves in certain ways, before they acquire the ability to understand the point or justification of those rules, and the possibility that they are not justified. People normally learn of rules and reasons largely through processes of habituation and socialisation within the groups in which the rules are practised, whether as children growing up there or as migrants into those communities. Their knowledge of the rules and their attitudes to them are both being shaped by the practices that contribute to the socialisation of people, just as those attitudes contribute to the forming and reforming of those very practices. To point to one example: as most people are born within families that live among and interact with other families, they acquire, as part of their early socialisation, knowledge, mostly implicit, of the roles, status, rights and duties that members of families have within their families, as determined by practice-based rules.

But what sort of things are we talking about when talking of 'rules'? 'Different things in different contexts', is the inevitable answer. For current purposes I do not distinguish between rules, standards, principles etc. They all refer to or express purported normative conditions, whose content when expressed reasonably explicitly[1] is expressed in normative propositions, namely propositions that non-redundantly[2] employ normative concepts, such as that someone has a right, a duty, ought to or has reason to do something, enjoys privileges or immunities, and the like. Propositions that express rules express a normative condition, which exists if they are true propositions, for example, that it is wrong to deceive people, and does not exist if they are false propositions, for example, that one has a right to deceive people.

[1] The content of practice-based rules, being determined by the practice itself, cannot be easily captured and expressed by propositions about their content. Stating such propositions may be adequate for its purpose and in its context, but it is not to be taken to be a completely explicit and exhaustive representation of the content of the rules. Perhaps such a representation is possible, but in practice it is most unlikely. Knowledge of the content of the rule exceeds people's ability to state it exhaustively and accurately, and many have no ability to state it in abstract terms, being able merely to assent or dissent to various putative examples of its application. Indeed, often the most informative way of conveying the content of the rule is by examples, real or hypothetical. These, when their informative character is undisputed, are sometimes regarded as paradigm cases. The important point is that using them to state the rule imports an implied understanding of the way one is meant to extrapolate from them to other cases.

[2] This implies the rejection of semantic reduction of normative terms. A normative expression is used redundantly when it can be replaced without change of meaning by a non-normative expression, or when the proposition's content remains the same when the expression is removed from the sentence used to express it.

They are practice-based rules for their content is fixed by a social practice.[3] Being a practice consists of patterns of behaviour that are fairly general and well-known to be general, and to be known to be so known. They include behaviour conforming to the rule, but even more crucially, behaviour expressing (sincerely or insincerely) attitudes that imply that the rule is to be taken as binding, and as providing a strong reason for action by those to whom it applies, and to be acknowledged as binding by others. I have in mind conduct such as advising people to conform, admonishing them for non-conformity, extolling conformity, or just expressing the view that the rule is binding.[4] The content of a practice identifies (and individuates) the content of a rule, and that rule is practice-based. It is not implied that the rule derives truth, validity or justification from being practice-based.

We commonly point out that the content of practice-based rules is known and known to be known. More accurately we should say that the core of the content of the rule is known and known to be known. I say the core of the rule to allow for disagreement about its content. There are two kinds of such disagreements. Sometimes people who disagree do not care whether the rule they believe in is practice-based or not. In principle they are willing to claim that that is the rule (namely a true or valid rule) even though at least in some respects it is not practice-based. We are not concerned with this kind of dispute. The other kind is where people may in principle be uncommitted as to whether the rule states a real or a merely putative normative condition (whether people really have a certain right, or whether it is merely a social rule that they have it). But they insist or deny that that is the content of the practice-based rule.

Now, the common claim is that those who share the practice know the core content of the rule based on it. This feature is important to the understanding of their functioning. It implies, among other things, that the people concerned, the people whose practice it is (and they may or may not include those to whom the rule applies) know of each other, though not necessarily in personal terms, and that knowledge is of some significance to their social attitudes, as well as their attitudes to themselves. That implies that practice-based rules are not stand-alone isolated

[3] Even so, the rule is not identical with the practice. See Joseph Raz, *Practical Reason and Norms*, 2nd ed. (Oxford: Oxford University Press, 1990).

[4] I referred to conduct expressing certain propositional attitudes rather than to the existence of those attitudes themselves to allow for the possibility of insincere expressions. Hence the cautious formulation in the text.

factors influencing people's conduct. Rather, they are embedded in a web of social relations, and our attitudes to them. The existence of norms contributes to the shaping of those social relations, as well as being affected by them, a bidirectional process that is mediated by people's attitudes.

This brings us to the second implication regarding the significance of the fact that these rules are practice-based. People's attachments to members of their families, as well as their resentments and rebellious attitudes towards their families or some of their members, are almost inevitably associated with attachments to or alienation from (or with more complex, more ambivalent, attitudes to) the institution of the family and the practices that underlie it. During their life, they will be influenced by the norms, both in conformity and in rebellious rejection, as well as when manifesting a variety of attitudes in between. And in forging their own path they will exert pressure towards changes in the norms, and the patterns of family life that they underlie.

The interaction among various factors displayed in the family example generalizes, with natural modifications, to other kinds of practice-based rules.

Furthermore, our sense of who we are and what we are like is bound up with our attitudes to our ways of life, and the norms that underlie them. So that what is often called our 'sense of identity' is constituted in part by our affirmative or resentful attitudes, our loyalty and attachment to or our alienation from the norms we have become so familiar with.

Needless to say, the combination of these factors underlies our willingness or unwillingness to conform to these norms. I do not wish to deny that incentives can affect degrees of conformity to norms. But they are additional, superimposed factors, reinforcing or counteracting the deeper, more stable attitudes we have to those norms as a result of the kind of factors I mentioned.

One final, but crucial point, before we turn to the law. Practice-based rules can be assessed normatively, their good points and their blemishes can be identified and criticised. Pressures for change and modification are sometimes motivated by (correct or incorrect) judgments about their shortcomings and ways in which they can be improved, though it is vital to remember that much change comes about independently of such evaluations. Yet, it is crucial to remember that critical assessment normally comes second to habituation and socialisation through which one comes to accept most of the practice-based rules in one's group. Both in the evolution of the species and in the development of each individual it is reasonable to assume that people are habituated into familiarity with various practice-based rules, first acquire habits and attitudes (including some of rejection) unreflectively, before they begin gradually to reflect on the meaning and merits of the practices and the rules. Moreover, it is plausible that the capacity for critical reflection is largely innate in members of some species, though in various forms and degrees. Yet its expression is learnt, and nourished by material embedded in the practice-based rules themselves.

7.4 Building Blocks: Institutions

What are law-related features? The law, we say (and I do not mean just state law), is a normative social institution. The traditional view, which is mine as well, sees the new element, additional to those present in all practice-based rules, in the institutional aspect that is essential to anything legal. The institutions I have in mind are themselves rule-governed, ultimately governed by practice-based rules that determine if not all at least the most important aspects of their constitution, powers and mode of operation. Perhaps the most elementary powers legal institutions have are enforcement and adjudicative powers, namely the powers to take measures to enforce other rules and to adjudicate disputes about their applicability.[5] Where these powers are wide-ranging and their exercise regular, the activities of these institutions inevitably affect the content of the rules that they apply, leading to, and constituting, changes in the content of these rules. But of course, there can exist legal institutions whose primary function is to amend and develop rules, and even to introduce completely new ones. For different purposes the institutions that mark the existence of law or of legal elements in the relevant social situation can be classified in various ways. What makes them institutions with legal flavour is their ability to perform actions and issue decisions and rulings that are binding even if mistaken.

Practice-based rules are generally clamped together by their subject matter. Some deal with relations within families, others with relations

[5] Readers familiar with Hart's *Concept of Law*, 2nd ed. (Oxford: Clarendon Press, 1994) may think that I am merely borrowing his distinction between primary and secondary rules, which is the basis of his distinction between pre-legal and legal normative regimes. I have criticised Hart's distinction elsewhere. Unlike his theory my observations here are not based on the character of the rules involved. There are power-conferring and right-granting rules (secondary in his terms) that are ordinary practice-based rules, and that are independent of the existence of any institutions.

among neighbours, etc. Some of these rules are logically inter-related, as, for example, the rules granting rights to some people are related to rules granting permissions to disregard these rights in some circumstances to other people. Social normative institutions bring with them another type of relations among rules and that in two steps.

First, the rules that constitute some institutions may establish relations among them, as when we have a hierarchy of courts with rights of appeal from some to others, or institutions with duties to execute the decisions of courts, or, of course, institutions whose operations are subject to review by other institutions. Second, the rules of some of the institutions that are, in some ways or to some degree, subordinated to others (allowing appeal to higher courts, or review by other institutions) recognise and accept their subordination. Some rules are under the jurisdiction of some sets of inter-related institutions, while others are not.

So, legal systems are sets of rules under the jurisdiction of an inter-related set of institutions. This is an inflationary characterisation of legal systems, as it allows for many types of inter-relationships and for rules to be part of more than one system at a time. This is at it should be. As we wish to investigate whether the focus on the state law is justified, we should keep in view a whole range of legal phenomena that may compete with the state for theoretical attention. At this stage, being inflationary and not too precise over details is an advantage. Similarly, I will not attempt to offer sufficient or necessary conditions for the sort of institutions and inter-relations that make a system. There are many kinds of systems, and all of them admit of indeterminacy about what is in and what is out of them.[6]

In this sense, both the rules of the Roman Republic and those of the University of Wales (disbanded 2011), just as the rules of the United States and of Columbia University, are legal systems. But only the last two are existing legal systems for only they are actually practised and followed by functioning normative institutions.

We need, however, to remind ourselves that once we move from mere clusters of practice-based rules to law-like institutionalised systems of rules, the connection between the rules and social practices changes. As noted, even without institutions specifically entrusted to make and change rules, and certainly with them, the rules applied and enforced by the institutions change through their activities, and not merely as a result of changes in

[6] It may be worth mentioning that whatever criteria there are for the identity of a law-like system will include the attitudes of the population, or parts of it, to these institutions.

social practices. Whether, and if so to what degree, the changed rules are or become backed by specific practices, practices of following that now changed rule, is a contingent matter. The rule is now part of the system due to the fact that the institutions are entrusted with its application and enforcement. The distinction between existing and dead systems relates more to the degree that the activities of the institutions as a whole are respected by the people to whom the rules and decisions apply, than by the degree to which the individual rules are practice-based. This is a familiar point that, as you recognise, I introduce in the way that Hart presented it.

One point some of you may remark on is that I identified law-like systems by the relations between rules, and not by relations among people, or rules and people. I believe that there is no difference of substance here, as rules apply to people and I was merely identifying the people who are relevant by reference to the rules that apply to them. This way of defining the notion of a law-like system appears to lend itself to simpler formulations, and accommodates well the desire for the notion to apply to many different ways in which people are brought together under rules. There can be law-based systems governing members of a profession, co-religionists, inhabitants of a certain territory and so on.

One pit, into which many theorists enthusiastically fall, is to characterise law-like systems by what they are good for, or what their functions are. The broad and vague characterisation that I gave helps reduce the temptation of that pit. Law-like systems may be good or bad for many reasons and in many ways, and can be used for many purposes, and fulfil many functions. Nevertheless we can discern certain human tendencies that are likely to be expressed by attitudes to such systems. One of them, noted already regarding practice-based rules, is the tendency to form attitudes of attachment or resentment towards normative arrangements. In as much as law-like systems apply to groups, united by the rules, such as members of a university, a sports club, a profession or a locality, law-like systems often become the focus of feelings of loyalty and attachment or of alienation and estrangement when people's attitudes to the relevant groups become attached to the system or the institutions that govern them. And they can be objects of resentment etc. when it is felt that they are not serving the group well in the ways they are meant (by their content) to do.

The formation of attitudes of pride, identification, loyalty and the like towards the central institutions of legal systems is now mediating between people and the law-like rules, which need no longer be practice-based. The dialectical process continues: people's attitudes and conduct are shaped by the rules, as well as influencing their content. But this time much of that process is mediated by the institutions: through their influence on the activities of institutions people's attitudes affect the content of the rules, and through people's loyalty etc. to the institutions the rules affect people's conduct and attitudes. Though mere acceptance of the institutions may be sufficient for their existence and functioning, respect towards and loyalty to them becomes vital to the smooth and efficient functioning of law-like systems.

7.5 The Most Comprehensive Legal System within Its Domain

We can now explain 'the most comprehensive law-based social organization of the day'.

I will use the term to express a complex property that can be possessed by law-based systems. I suggested that it has two components: **(1) an extensive responsibility within its domain, and (2) freedom from external legal constraints.**

The first condition is **relative to a domain**: the domain may be extensive, for example, the population of China, or all corporations throughout the world, or rather small, for example, the population of Lichtenstein or the fencing clubs of Riverdale, NY. Being relative to a domain the notion of an extensive responsibility within a domain is indifferent to the size or extent of the domain.

I use **'Responsibility'** in this context to refer to a combination of three factors: **(a) normative power** (to issue binding decrees, to change rules, enforce and apply them, to adjudicate their application etc.); **(b) coupled with duties to exercise them in certain circumstances or for certain purposes; (c) that are accepted as reason-giving by those subject to them.** In most states' legal systems there are, for example, courts with jurisdiction over certain disputes, and a duty to hear and decide complaints falling within their jurisdiction, when certain additional conditions are met.

The extent of a legal system's responsibility is a matter of degree. Some law-like systems have very limited responsibility, for example, they can be confined to adjudicating whether elections conducted within organisations that asked for their supervision were fairly conducted or not (The Electoral Reform Society in the United Kingdom), or who won a series of sporting events that they are in charge of. Others can have much more extensive responsibilities, for example, to oversee the peace, personal and property security and the fairness of all interpersonal transactions within a certain population.

Finally, a legal system's claim to normative power over people or institutions may be denied or rejected by those people or institutions. In some such cases, the strength of those supporting the claim, military, economic strength, or strength deriving from other sources, make these claims prevail in practice. Our inquiry concerns only cases in which the powers claimed are acknowledged by those subject to them to create reasons. This condition is indifferent to the grounds that lead people to accept the authorities. It does not require them even to have any grounds. They may never have contemplated why they take the decrees of the authority to be binding, or they may take them as reasons for themselves because they believe that it is in their interest to do so, or for any other reason.

What constitutes an institution making claims to have power or responsibility over people or institutions? And what constitutes an acknowledgement of its legitimacy over other institutions? As we are dealing with normative phenomena and their inter-relations, the answer is in the content of the rules governing the various institutions. A claim of responsibility is constituted by rules giving executive, adjudicative or legislative powers over other institutions or over certain people and the law-like rules that apply to them. Acknowledgement of the authority of so to speak higher institutions is expressed in rules constituting and regulating the so to speak subordinate institutions that incorporate the determinations of the higher ones as binding on the people or institutions they oversee or supervise. This allows for cases in which one institution, say, claims authority over another and the second (namely the rules that constitute and govern it) is silent regarding the claim. Absence of acknowledgement does not constitute acknowledgement.

What is the second condition, that of **independence or freedom from external legal constraints**? It denotes a normative relationship, and we have already encountered its opposite. It consists simply in not acknowledging that any institutions or rules of other law-based systems bind it. This condition itself admits of degrees. A legal system may acknowledge the normative powers of some institutions of another legal system over some aspects of its affairs, while denying it general power. Conflict of law rules are an example of such limited power granted to other legal systems. But there are many others, some of which will be mentioned later on.[7]

[7] In all its aspects the test admits of degrees, vagueness and conflicts (i.e. more than one candidate with good credentials to be the most comprehensive legal system within its domain). That, I suggest, is part of its strength. It is not meant as a definition of anything, and is not meant to provide necessary and sufficient conditions for the existence of

It will be obvious that the various ideas I brought together to explain responsibility over a domain can be combined in different ways, possibly with additional factors, to provide different configurations of the relations among institutions, and the law-like system of which they are the core. The reason for singling out the structure that I did lies in its relevance to answering the question 'Why the state?' The state, I claim, was made the focus of theories of law because it is, or was taken to be, the most extensive law-like system that is independent or free from external constraint.[8] This is a partial explanation at best, and an idealised one. It is idealised in seeking theoretically significant features of state law, whose presence, it is here conjectured, however dimly or incompletely conceived, influenced the tendency to focus on state law. It is incomplete as it is probable that other factors contribute to the focus on state law, though perhaps, unlike those other features, being the most comprehensive legal system within its domain is a necessary feature of states as we conceive them today. It is not a sufficient feature. As I mentioned, the Greek Polis was not a state. Interestingly, a close rival in today's world are some religious legal systems, and the adherents of some of them have difficulty in conceiving of them as not being the laws of states (or states in waiting).

7.6 Why the State? – The Past

I will assume that the fact that a legal system is, relative to a certain domain, the most comprehensive law-based social organisation at a given time makes it important and deserving of special theoretical attention for reasons that are obvious and require but little explanation. So if state law is in these terms the most comprehensive legal social organisation relative to its domain, namely relative to the state of which it is the law,[9] then we have a partial answer to the two questions I set out to examine (though not necessarily a justification of the almost exclusive concentration on state law that we witness in some contexts).

anything. It aims to single out for attention important features that should play a part in our understanding of various legal systems and their inter-relations.

8 The two components of 'the most comprehensive legal system within its domain' are logically independent, and arguably the presence of either of them would make legal systems that possess it worthy of theoretical attention. States, however, were perceived to have both, and quite likely do have both, subject to the points made below.

9 To be the most comprehensive law-like system within its domain it has to be, within its domain, more comprehensive than systems whose domain may be greater than its own.

But is it? There is reason to think that things are in this regard in a flux. We are in the middle of a process of change of great speed and momentum. So it is better to break up this question into two:

First: Has state law been until recently the most comprehensive legally based organisation within its domain?

If the answer is yes, then the second question comes into its own:

Second: Is it likely to remain so?

Needless to say, the degree to which states meet the test may vary over time and between states. My remarks relate to the contemporary concept of the state, and therefore to European states, which led to its development, and to all 'new' states, from say American independence, which were influenced by the European traditions. There is a strong case for an affirmative answer to the first question. The case may have been weaker in, let's say, medieval Europe, before the emergence of the contemporary concept of the state, with Church and baronial, and various other local institutions, with their laws, being at least partly independent of the state, and to a degree superior to it. The consolidation of the powers of the state and its authority since the seventeenth century proceeded along two lines of development. First, states assumed and secured power to control and regulate all other organisations within their territory. Second, they acquired an ever-expanding authority over more and more aspects of the life of those subject to them, coupled with duties to use it.

Neither process is complete. Some states acknowledge absence of jurisdiction, or limited jurisdiction, over religious organisations or over the territory and governance of native people. The United Nations and its organs enjoy extra-territorial status in various countries, etc. Perhaps more interesting, morally speaking, are the vicissitudes of claims to authority and attitudes to the scope of the state's authority over its 'ordinary' subjects and its duties towards them.

At various periods it was taken for granted that states have limited jurisdiction, and philosophers like Locke and Kant were among many theorists who advanced various accounts of what those limits should be. But of course, there were always theories and practices that assigned the state powers and duties to protect and promote the wealth and welfare of its subjects, or some of them, and/or the salvation of their immortal souls. Over the last hundred years or so, in a more secular vein, such attitudes spread, perhaps I should say: spread again, leading to views that regard the state as having responsibility to guarantee adequate education for all, to curtail unemployment, to ward off the threat of disease, to secure medical care and protection from misfortunes and deprivation from any source. Many of these duties are nowadays enshrined in international treaties, their violations exposing states to adverse international action, at least in principle. There are of course powerful reactions against those trends and in favour of what is called 'small government'. But by and large their recent history and current standing reinforces rather than casts doubt on the fact that the dominant currents, in practice as well as in theory, assign the state extremely wide powers coupled with demanding duties.

A theoretical question of some difficulty is lurking here: suppose it is true that the state is not entitled to unlimited authority within its domain. That would not establish that it does not claim to have such authority. What determines the authority that the state claims to have? The preceding suggests that the answer is to be found in the authority assigned to its institutions in its law. But what is that authority? It is not limited to the matters currently regulated by state law. Suppose that no law regulates people's use of their private property so long as that use does not amount to a criminal offence. It does not follow that tomorrow the state cannot set limits to the non-criminal use of people's property. Perhaps tomorrow it will pass a law that they are not allowed to use it in any way that has deleterious effects on the interest of third parties. Shall we assume that the limit of the state's claim to authority is set by its constitution? Some constitutions may not limit it at all, but others may, perhaps in the way that the American so-called bill of rights does. But constitutions can also be amended, and there are constitutional means of amending them. Therefore, current constitutional limits do not appear to set a limit to the state's authority. Furthermore, even if the constitution does not provide for ways of amending some of its provisions, they can be lawfully amended by its courts using creative interpretation to do so. And if the courts are not currently acknowledged to have the power to do so, who is to say that entirely lawful developments of its constitutional common law would not endow them with such powers?[10]

[10] The same is true of constitutions that explicitly prohibit the amendment of some of their provisions. They may still be changed via judicial interpretation, a major source of legal development in most countries. You may argue that this or that decision should not be made for it changes the constitution, but given that by existing law the decision is binding even if it should not have been made, there are even in these cases legal means for changing these constitutional provisions. Some commentators believe that certain recent decisions by the German Federal constitutional court exemplify this very process.

There is, therefore, a case for arguing that states' authority is, by their very nature, unlimited.[11] Furthermore, even if the state is subject to external legal control, could it not free itself from that subjugation by repealing the laws that recognise the external jurisdiction?[12] The lesson from this chain of reasoning is that if one is to deny that the state necessarily has unlimited authority one had better resort not to formal legal constraints on its authority, but to a common social understanding of what limits there are. In some respects such a test is unpromisingly vague, as well as being – like any legal test – liable to change over time. Its superiority, for our current purpose, is that it relates to the social reality underlying the legal phenomena and expressing the common understanding of their meaning by those subject to them. It is on such standards that I was relying when tracing the expanding authority of the state and its wider scope compared with other law-like systems.

This is the case for an affirmative answer to the first half of the first question, relating to the state's domestic responsibilities. The Peace of Westphalia (1648) put the seal on the state's independence from any external authority beyond it. It affirmed the principle of equality of all states, and of non-interference by any state in the affairs of any other. Or so it was generally understood. What is that independence or freedom? It denotes a normative relationship, and we have already encountered its opposite. It consists simply in not acknowledging that any institutions or rules of other law-based systems apply to the state. As was noted above, this condition itself admits of degree, and legal systems may acknowledge the normative powers of some institutions of another legal system over some aspects of its affairs, while denying it general power. Such very partial recognitions were understood to be consistent with the overall independence of states from external legal authorities.

We may wish to examine further the case for an affirmative answer to the first question later on. For now we should accept it as presumptively sufficient.

7.7 Why the State? – The Future

What about the second question? Is the state likely to remain the most comprehensive legal social organisation within its domain? Various

[11] That is the view I took in *Practical Reason and Norms* (n. 34).

[12] Needless to say, this argument can be applied to any law-like system showing that all of them can claim limitless authority.

developments give room for doubt. To examine the question we need (a) to identify the relevant developments, (b) to assess their prospects (Are they here to stay, progressing, perhaps even accelerating over time? Or, are they likely to be arrested at their current level or even reversed?), and (c) assuming, that they are going to stay with us and to develop even further, we need to interpret their significance for our question.

I can say little on the second question. The trends I will point to are, I believe, here to stay. They seem to be related to what we loosely call globalisation, by which I mean not only the growing number and power of multi-national corporations, but more broadly, developments of the means of travel and in telecommunication that make, as we say, the world smaller. Information about the conditions in far-away places is readily available, thus bringing inequalities of wealth, services and security to the vivid attention of many, as well as opening up technological possibilities of travel and migration. And of course the changes in methods of production and marketing foster much more integrated economic activities across the globe. But all this is beyond my competence to describe, let alone analyze, and I will confine myself to stating that as globalisation is likely to remain a dominant trend so will the legal changes that attend it.

But what are they? I will mention three important lines of development. First, the emergence of international organisations with independent law-making powers that are not conditional on consent by states subject to them. Second, changes in the way new international law rules emerge. Third, the extended range of agents with powers of action in international law, including individuals.

It has always been the case that in some ways international law limited the independence of states. From the point of view of our inquiry, there is no case for making much of the distinction between states that allow international law direct application within their jurisdiction and states that deny it direct application, so that it applies only if incorporated by domestic legislation or similar measures. Both recognise that they are bound by it – there are of course states that may not do so, but we will ignore them. Traditional international law theory recognises two sources of law in international law: custom and treaty.[13] Custom is binding

[13] It is common to regard Article 38 of the Statute of the ICJ as definitive of the sources of international law, which it takes to be: (a) international conventions, whether general or particular, establishing rules expressly recognised by the contesting states; (b) international custom, as evidence of a general practice accepted as law; (c) the general principles of law recognised by civilised nations; and (d) subject to the provisions of

without the consent of the state, but does not involve submission to any external organ. Treaties are like contracts. They bind because, it is said, they embody the will of the state and its consent. They do not limit its independence any more than a promise limits a person's independence.

Things are very different in contemporary international law. I will illustrate the change with three examples that exemplify the two features to which I want to draw your attention: the transformative effect of the growth of institutions difficult for members to leave, and which initiate legal developments, independent of assent of member states. First, the UN. It is a treaty-based organisation. However, unlike ordinary or traditional treaties, its founding treaty makes it a multi-purpose organisation comprehensive in membership. Opting out of it would be very isolating. Remaining in it is as free as remaining in your home country. You can emigrate (sometimes) but it is a life-changing decision. And in the case of the UN, there is no alternative to go to. The alternative is more like going to a desert island. How difficult it is for a country to leave the UN depends on its situation, but it is a very high-cost decision for any country. Furthermore: decisions of the Security Council taken under Chapter 7 of the UN Charter are binding on all member states for the purpose, and only for the purpose, of maintaining international peace and security.[14] For a long time the Security Council had a modest interpretation of its authority under Chapter 7. Recently, however, the interpretation of that power became very inflationary. Yet it has not been challenged, with the result that the Security Council now has extensive powers to override state governments over a range of issues. One significant extension is the decision to allow Chapter 7 resolutions based on the so-called responsibility to protect.[15] But perhaps the most dramatic extension of the powers of the Security Council is the most recent one:

Article 59, judicial decisions and the teachings of the most highly qualified publicists of the various nations, as subsidiary means for the determination of rules of law.

14 Article 39 states, 'The Security Council shall determine the existence of any threat to the peace, breach of the peace, or act of aggression and shall make recommendations, or decide what measures shall be taken in accordance with Articles 41 and 42, to maintain or restore international peace and security.'

15 UN Security Council Resolution 1706 (31 August 2006), calling for the deployment of UN peacekeepers to Darfur, applied the R2P principle to a particular context for the first time:

> *Recalling* also its previous resolutions . . . and 1674 (2006) on the protection of civilians in armed conflict, which reaffirms inter alia the provisions of paragraphs 138 and 139 of the 2005 United Nations World Summit outcome document. . .

in determining that the Ebola outbreak in Africa constituted a threat to international peace and security, it assumed Chapter 7 powers to interfere in the internal affairs of member states in matters affecting the Ebola outbreak.[16] Parallel reasoning could establish that *a fortiori* the economic crisis of 2008 constituted a threat to international peace and security, and the Security Council can declare so, and assume powers to regulate banking and economic affairs world-wide. I am not suggesting that it is about to do so. Only that it has removed many principled barriers to intervention in the domestic affairs of member states.

My second example is the World Trade Organization. Its importance and dominance in various aspects of international trade make membership highly prized, and exit is very costly. The WTO dispute settlement bodies as well as the general council through their interpretation of the treaties continuously develop and advance the trade law that is binding on all members.

World Summit Outcome Document, September 2005. Heads of state and government attending the 60th Session of the UN General Assembly agreed as follows:

> 138. Each individual State has the responsibility to protect its populations from genocide, war crimes, ethnic cleansing and crimes against humanity. This responsibility entails the prevention of such crimes, including their incitement, through appropriate and necessary means. We accept that responsibility and will act in accordance with it. The international community should, as appropriate, encourage and help States to exercise this responsibility and support the United Nations in establishing an early warning capability.
>
> 139. The international community, through the United Nations, also has the responsibility to use appropriate diplomatic, humanitarian and other peaceful means, in accordance with Chapters VI and VIII of the Charter, to help to protect populations from genocide, war crimes, ethnic cleansing and crimes against humanity. In this context, we are prepared to take collective action, in a timely and decisive manner, through the Security Council, in accordance with the Charter, including Chapter VII, on a case-by-case basis and in cooperation with relevant regional organizations as appropriate, should peaceful means be inadequate and national authorities are manifestly failing to protect their populations from genocide, war crimes, ethnic cleansing and crimes against humanity. We stress the need for the General Assembly to continue consideration of the responsibility to protect populations from genocide, war crimes, ethnic cleansing and crimes against humanity and its implications, bearing in mind the principles of the Charter and international law. We also intend to commit ourselves, as necessary and appropriate, to helping States build capacity to protect their populations from genocide, war crimes, ethnic cleansing and crimes against humanity and to assisting those which are under stress before crises and conflicts break out.

[16] UN Security Council Resolution 2177 (18 September 2014).

My third example relates to the emergence of regional organisations, of which the EU is the most developed. It combines the two features I mentioned: difficulty of exit, and autonomous legal development, independent of assent of member states. There are doubts whether being outside the EU is a drawback, or about the degree to which it is a drawback. But there is very little doubt that the process of leaving the Union is highly disruptive and unpredictable.

Two other developments in international law must be briefly mentioned. First, traditionally, custom was the main source of general international law, treaties binding only the countries that ratified them. And custom is established by the common practice extended over time. In recent times, there has been a marked tendency to recognise emerging customary rules, rules that emerge over a short period of time. The main route to customary standing is through multilateral treaties. A few years after the coming into effect of a multilateral treaty, its existence is taken as evidence for the emergence of a new custom. An auxiliary but important other element consists of opinions and resolutions of various international conferences, non-state bodies, academics and experts. In a way there is nothing new here, for state custom has always been legally binding. But the quantity and speed of the emergence of new rules makes a difference, as does the mode of their emergence: states that ratify treaties impose, you may say, their will on states that do not ratify them, or that enter reservations to some aspects of the treaties.

The final development to which I wanted to draw attention is the granting of standing to individuals to instigate judicial proceedings in international law. Not surprisingly one of the areas where this development is particularly important is in international human rights law. I will mention only two examples: the ability of individuals to bring human rights cases to the European Court of Human Rights, which oversees the application of the European Treaty on Human Rights, and their ability to bring various cases, not only human rights ones, before the European Court of Justice.

Various commentators affirm or deny that examples such as these and the trends that they evidence mark a fundamental change in international law. My purpose is different. There is the sheer extent of international law, the range of topics it covers and the detail in which it covers them, which continuously erode the freedom of states to regulate matters as they see fit. And this development is coupled with the erosion of the significance of consent by states to be bound by international treaties. That happens due to the fast emergence of customary rules, which are not consent-based, the fact that more of the multi-national treaties are adhered to by states in conditions that approach duress, given the cost of declining to adhere to them, and the fact that the quantity and significance of international law made by international bodies is accelerating. True, these bodies derive their authority from treaties, whose legal standing derives from being ratified by states. However, no sound normative theory of the conditions under which consent is binding will allow that the rights and obligations created by these bodies derive from the consent of those subject to them.[17]

The cumulative effect of these changes and the trends that they mark is a significant change in the standing of states. Their freedom is more limited, hemmed in by pervasive and invasive international regulations, and no longer are states free from the legal authority of bodies not under their control. These changes are part of the case for a negative answer to my second question: Will state law retain its standing as the paradigm of law, and as the focus of legal philosophy?

7.8 On the Theory of State Law

Do these trends herald the disappearance of the state, with the loss of its position as the most comprehensive law-based organisation within its domain? There is no sign of that. Most importantly, there is no single institution that appears likely to replace the state. We witness the subjection of the state to the jurisdiction of a number of specialised organisations and institutions, with no single one that rivals states in its standing and importance. Currently the only challenge often discussed comes from the European Union. Generally, regional organisations are the most likely to absorb and replace the states as we know them, and the European Union is the most developed and powerful of the regional organisations. However, the powerful centrifugal political

[17] This is of course a large and controversial subject. For my view on consent see, e.g., 'The Problem of Authority: Revisiting the Service Conception' (2006) 90 *Minnesota Law Review*, 1003–44, at 1038. I am writing about changes in the law only. A number of scholars argue that things have changed even more radically than I indicate, basing their conclusions, among other things, on the pressures forcing states or other actors to conform to international standards not set by them, even though they are not bound to do so in international law (e.g. Eyal Benvenisti, *The Law of Global Governance*, (The Hague: Hague Academy of International Law, 2014)). Needless to say, the divide between political and legal constraint is particularly hard to pinpoint regarding international law.

sentiments within most Union states must raise doubts about the prospect of the Union displacing its member states within their domain. I will come back to that.[18]

States face change but not displacement. Does that change suggest a revision of the theory of state legal systems? To answer that question requires a brief reminder of the theory of state law. As one would expect, the theory of state legal systems traces in legal terms the property that makes them special, namely being the most comprehensive legal system within their domain. It consists in a combination of two properties: Legitimacy and Sovereignty. State law and legal institutions are – or claim to be – legitimate, to have legitimate authority within their domain. They also claim to be sovereign, that is, not subject to any authority outside themselves. I will consider briefly each property and the degree to which the trends we traced present theories based on these two features with a challenge.

We expect of the law not merely that its codes, rules and regulations should be sensible and defensible, or that their implementation would be fair and sensible. We expect that its standards be produced and overseen by institutions and processes with legitimate authority. I, along with many, though not all, writers on the subject, think that such legitimacy imports a duty to obey. That is the quality we identify with the legitimacy of the law, and of the government.

That makes legitimacy special. A legitimate government not only oversees a sensible and good legal system. We all have reason to respect the good laws not only of our country, but of every country. And they may well affect what conduct is required of us. Legitimacy has an additional side to it: it is a relationship between a government and those subject to it. It places the subjects under an obligation to obey the government's legitimate laws. Legitimacy acknowledges a power in the government to impose obligations and confer rights on those subject to it, and to do so by deciding to do so. There is nothing special in the fact that the existence, fortunes and conduct of other people affect what we ought to do. If someone is standing on the road we have to walk around him rather than into him, and so on and so forth. Similarly, if France has a good legal system, I should refrain from doing anything that

[18] Looking more broadly, while the state's freedom within its domain is increasingly restricted by international regulations, international law itself is not a highly unified system. Many observers remark on its growing fragmentation. However, unifying processes are also at work and to hail or lament its fragmentation is premature.

undermines it, and on appropriate occasions I should support it. But I am not resident in France. To the residents, if their government is legitimate, it can impose obligations on them. (Governments may have jurisdiction over non-residents. I refer only to their jurisdiction over residents for illustrative purposes.) In fact, my obligations towards French law are in part dependent on those subject to French law having the obligation to obey their own law because their government is legitimate.

That is where legitimacy (of governments) comes in. It stands for the special power that governments should have over those subject to them. Legitimacy entitles those in government to affect what we (those subject to it) have a duty to do by deciding that we should have a duty to do so. That is special and problematic, not only in theory but in social life as well – we confront challenges to that ability, to the right of governments to govern, partial or thorough challenges to the legitimacy of government, all the time. I should add that while not all governments have legitimate authority, all of them claim to have legitimate authority – this is one of the defining marks of governments.[19]

Let me turn from legitimacy to sovereignty. I am using the term in a somewhat stipulative meaning: 'state sovereignty' signifies the idea that states are free from certain kinds of interference by other states and other international actors in what we call their internal affairs. The term can signify a moral doctrine, that morally states are free from certain kinds of interference in their internal affairs. But I will use it here to signify a legal claim, which may or may not be morally defensible. The explanation of sovereignty involves three main components: (a) the characterisation of types of acts or other measures that are invasive or inappropriate interference in matters relating to the sovereign state; (b) the characterisation of kinds of bodies that may not take those measures; and (c) a general international legal recognition (either in international law, or in the domestic laws of various states and other organisations) of these limits. Sovereignty can admit of degrees; it consists of recognised limits of interference in matters relating to the state by other states or

[19] There are, of course, various accounts of legitimate authority. Mine can be found in *The Morality of Freedom* (Oxford: Oxford University Press, 1986), and with some modifications in 'The Problem of Authority: Revisiting the Service Conception' (n. 17). But my argument here does not require accepting that particular account. It merely relies on the claim that necessarily state law claims to have legitimate authority.

organisations. But it is common to think that there is a basic standard of sovereignty that is enjoyed or possessed by all states.

It is said that it used to be thought that sovereign states have absolute freedom from interference by other states, and other organisations. These matters are delicate and can degenerate into verbal issues: different understandings of what counts as 'interference' would yield different scopes of sovereignty. The narrower one's conception of interference the wider is the resulting doctrine of morally justified sovereignty. Beyond asserting that sovereignty is not absolute either legally or morally, I will not inquire into its proper limits, though some of my observations bear on the issue.

It has to be admitted that the scope of either legal or moral sovereignty is far from clear. It is continuously changing with changing international conditions. Unfortunately, the topic is often neglected by normative political theorists, and many states have a vested interest in its obscurity and uncertain boundaries. For my purposes all that matters is that there is a general recognition that there is legal sovereignty, and that within some bounds it is morally defensible.

There is a trivial principle of non-intervention. It simply states that one should not intervene in correct, morally sound, actions. The doctrine of sovereignty is of a different kind. It protects states from intervention even when their actions are not morally sound (so long as they meet certain conditions set in the doctrine of sovereignty). We are accustomed to principles of this kind in individual morality. We think of them as principles protecting the autonomy of individuals. Typically, J. S. Mill concludes his statement of the Harm Principle writing: 'over himself, over his own body and mind, the individual is sovereign'.[20] Mill does not mean only that one may not coercively interfere with individuals when there is nothing wrong with their actions. The Harm Principle protects them from interference even when their actions are wrong or otherwise undesirable (so long as they do not harm others). That is why it is a principle of sovereignty.

7.9 The Relations between Sovereignty and Legitimacy

An intriguing question arises: how is legitimacy related to sovereignty? **The perfect match thesis** would have it that the limits of legitimacy are

[20] John Stuart Mill, *On Liberty*, ed. Elizabeth Rapaport (Indianapolis: Hackett, 1978), p. 9.

the limits of sovereignty, namely that states are immune from interference by other international agents in all matters that fall within the legitimate jurisdiction of their governments and in nothing else. However, this is a mistake. There is no principled reason why outside agents, say an authorised and competent international body, should not be allowed to override a decision of a government that falls within its legitimate jurisdiction. Of course, no such interference would be justified if the decision is just as it should be. But the legitimate authority of governments, their right to rule, means that their rulings are binding – that is, remain within their jurisdiction – even if mistaken. Think of courts' decisions: they are binding even when mistaken – though some of them are subject to appeal, appeal based not on lack of jurisdiction but on the fact that the decision was mistaken. In principle conditions may arise under which some external organ may have such power of appeal (overriding state-sovereignty) when governments take ill-advised decisions without exceeding their jurisdiction. Indeed, this was the situation within the British Commonwealth regarding matters over which the Judicial Committee of the Privy Council had jurisdiction, and it still has such jurisdiction regarding a few independent states. It may well exist elsewhere in international relations – perhaps where there are duties to resort to international arbitration, and such like cases.

Contrariwise, state sovereignty may well apply and prevent external intervention even when the governments of those states act beyond their legitimate authority. I am talking about the moral doctrine of state sovereignty, that is about what the legal doctrine should be.

When we think of the 'sovereignty' of individuals two considerations come to mind: First and foremost, the duty to respect their autonomy, and secondly, the fact that interference by others may be based on mistaken understanding or even on a conscious or unconscious willingness to abuse and take advantage of the person in whose affairs the outsider intervenes.

The second of these considerations applies in broadly the same way to states: history, old and recent, shows how time and time again the claimed right to intervene is abused.

The first consideration, the protection of individual autonomy, does not apply in that form, but in the relations between states it has an analogue: if you believe, as I do, that social groups should be able to develop autonomously – a difficult notion that requires distinguishing between external influences that are acceptable or even desirable and external domination that is distorting and alienating – then a measure of sovereignty is to be recognised as a condition of such autonomous development. Needless to say, this topic connects with the way what is valuable can be universal while access to the valuable and the manifestations of values vary among cultures.

These two considerations may extend sovereignty in a way that prohibits outside interference even when the government exceeds its legitimate authority.

7.10 States with Limited Sovereignty

Recalling the developments in international law canvassed earlier it is evident that they challenge previous theory and reality regarding the scope both of states' legitimate authority and of their sovereignty.

The growing scope and intrusiveness of international law challenges the extent of the state's legitimate authority, though it does so in a special way. It is common practice in international law that the primary responsibility for complying with and enforcing its provisions (when they apply to non-state agents) falls on the states. So the growing volume of international law does not curtail the range of topics that fall within the legitimate authority of states, but it requires them to use their authority in conformity with international law, and that limits their discretion in exercising their authority. This is analogous to one form of subordination of local authorities or provinces in a federal state to federal law. In some areas provinces or towns do not lose their jurisdiction to the state but they are legally bound to exercise it in conformity with superior state law.

The growth of international institutions with power over states that is not based on consent and includes law-making powers restricts the sovereignty of states.

The challenge to legal philosophers is to revive and explore theories of a limited state, one that is situated within the legal framework of international law – and here it does not matter whether international law forms a unified legal system or is fragmented beyond unity. There are plenty of similar phenomena in the legal world, though in the past they were mostly systems that are subordinated to state law, such as the law of native nations. Nowadays we need to explore in more detail the ways in which state law is limited, and the ways it is integrated within international laws and institutions.

You now have my speculative answer to my questions. State law was special in the past and is likely to remain special in the future, because it is likely to remain the most comprehensive law-based social organisation.

But exclusive concentration on state law was, it now turns out, never justified, and is even less justified today. In part, though not only, we need to rethink the relations of state-law to other legal systems, as the scope both of the authority and of the sovereignty of states has diminished and is likely to diminish still further, and the ways states integrate within the emerging international law is going to confront us with practical and theoretical problems.

7.11 Conclusion: The Individual in His State in the Future

Even though my discussion included a sprinkling of normative considerations, it belongs essentially to what we may call speculative analytical jurisprudence – speculative because it attempted to evaluate some of the dominant trends in analytical jurisprudence in light of likely developments. I will conclude with a few remarks about the promise and the dangers of these developments, remarks that also draw attention to other possible developments, and are therefore themselves speculative.

Throughout the paper, while not assuming that all states are governed by legitimate institutions, I was assuming that they could be. Similarly, while not assuming that all international bodies enjoy legitimate authority, I was assuming that international bodies can enjoy such authority. My account of authority applies to them as well.

Let us return to the empowering of individuals to address international tribunals. It opens up the possibility that at least regarding some legal areas – for example, human rights – residents of states can view state-law as just one of several legal systems that apply to them. Far from being the supreme legal system, it can come to be seen as subordinate to, accountable to the organs of some international tribunals. This can bring about a shift in allegiances. First, oppressed and discriminated against individuals and groups may feel at least as much pride in and loyalty to international bodies as to their state governments, and later this attitude may spread to many in the general population. Moreover, growing respect for human rights, coupled with the desire of rich countries to limit immigration, and the dynamics of a global economic market, may gradually improve health and living conditions across much of the globe, reinforcing the sense of respect for the international legal order that fostered such developments.

When I hear myself express these sentiments I say to myself: 'Dream on'. True, we can discern some movement in these directions. But the evidence is mixed, and much of it bears a much darker message.

In various parts of the world human rights activists, and more importantly the invocation of human rights by powerful nations, aggravated dispute, perpetuated bloodshed and made compromise impossible. And all too often the invocation of human rights blinded their advocates to the complexity of conflicts, encouraged attitudes of winner takes all, leading to the oppressed becoming oppressors. On top of that, the development of international standards all too often conflicts with local cultures and traditions that command the loyalty of local populations, a problem made worse by the fact that international organisations are disproportionately influenced by the perspectives of powerful countries, and managed and run by their citizens or members of other nationalities that converted to their culture and ideals.

The result is that international tribunals and other international organisations have largely so far failed to attract the respect and loyalty of people around the world. One of the most important facts that made state law central in life as well as in theory is that with all their faults and with all due acknowledgement of exceptions and reservations, states have engendered over their history a strong sense of identity and loyalty among their inhabitants. We are a long way from the international legal order and its institutions enjoying a similar standing. Absent respect, their legitimacy is in question, for many of the more important international institutions cannot be legitimate without their directives being accepted and respected by people generally. It is true that much of the best work in the evolving international system is done by technical bodies, whose efficiency and legitimacy does not depend on general respect and acceptance, indeed the general public is not aware of their existence, and that need not undermine their beneficial functioning. But institutions like the United Nations, or like the European Union, cannot function well, and cannot secure the benefits that their existence is meant to secure when people generally, or in the relevant regions or groups, disrespect them and are alienated from them. They must gain the respect and loyalty of people around the world if they are to secure the improvements in quality of life, and in instilling standards of mutual respect across the world, which are the promise they hold.

8

A Genealogical Perspective on Pluralist Jurisprudence

DETLEF VON DANIELS

8.1

Whenever different conceptions of something (here, the law) are proposed, the typical philosopher's inclination is to respond à la Ockham: You should never have started counting. Why did you pick three conceptions? Why not two or a dozen? Isn't it the job of the philosopher to study the timeless concept of law and not to assemble different conceptions? Pluralist-minded legal theorists often raise this question as a bogeyman of which they cannot easily dispose. Instead, I want to take the question seriously and treat it as an inescapable philosophical concern. To this end, I demonstrate through a survey of different conceptions of (transnational) law that by aiming to present itself as a self-sufficient whole or as comprehensive, each tradition reveals its systematic weaknesses that are highlighted by other traditions. The critique is genealogical in the weak sense[1] that each conception stands for a tradition in legal philosophy that upon closer inspection reveals a suppressed alternative. However, the perspective that ensues is not a strong genealogy, because it does not present a substantive explanation of the 'real' forces underlying all theories, either in form of some deconstructive logic of concepts (e.g. all concepts necessarily carry with them their *supplément*) or some realistic claims (e.g. all concepts express a will to power). Instead, the aim is to show that philosophical reflection always develops along the lines of traditions, which can be realised when adopting an outside perspective. Ultimately though, the outside perspective can be included in a genealogical account.

[1] For this use of the term see Quentin Skinner, 'A Genealogy of the Modern State', 162 *Proceedings of the British Academy* (2009), 325–70. Skinner criticises the dominant tradition of thinking about liberty in terms of 'negative liberty' by revealing the undercurrent of 'republican liberty' without buying into an overall genealogical explanation of historical developments along Foucaultian or Derriddean lines.

After a methodological reflection of different conceptions and the different levels of theory one has to take into account (Section 8.2), I show that analytical jurisprudence cannot hold on to its claim to be a general theory of universal characteristics (Section 8.3) while legal pluralism, the empirical counterpart to analytical jurisprudence, cannot avoid getting entangled in general philosophical disputes (Section 8.4). The new philosophy of international law appears at first sight to be a synthesis of the two traditions. However, on closer inspection, it reveals an open flank that allows the two others to re-assert their stance (Section 8.5). I end this chapter by arguing that the thus established genealogical perspective involves a normative component insofar as it calls for becoming self-conscious of the danger of theory itself (Section 8.6).

8.2

To begin, a reflection on the notions of 'conception' and 'transnational law' leads to the domain of analytical jurisprudence. One might think that both of these notions get a philosophical theory started on the wrong foot, because 'transnational' apparently qualifies the more general notion of 'law', and using the soft term 'conception' shirks engagement with the hard problems of conceptual analysis. So why not simply start out with a few truisms about 'the law' and then try to come up with a theory that accounts for all these features? In fact, this has become the standard pre-theoretical starting point for analytical jurisprudence.[2] Scott Shapiro cites the following truisms, among others: All legal systems have judges; courts interpret the law; every legal system has institutions for changing the law; laws always belong to legal systems; in every legal system, some person or institution has supreme authority for making certain laws.[3] Shapiro claims that his planning theory of law can account for all of these features. The basic problem with this approach, though, is that it is not evident that these are *necessary* features of law or that philosophy consists entirely in describing or accounting for these features: Ancient Athens didn't have specialised courts, Jewish law cannot be changed or amended, Roman law served as a standard of rational jurisprudence and for deciding cases without 'belonging' to a legal system, and the search

[2] The model for all subsequent legal theories that take truisms as their starting point is H. L. A. Hart, *The Concept of Law*, 2nd ed. (Oxford: Clarendon Press, 1994), 3–4.

[3] See Scott Shapiro, *Legality* (Cambridge, MA: The Belknap Press of Harvard University Press, 2011), 15.

for the highest authority in the EU is still on. One might argue that these are all 'exceptional cases' and that the 'standard case' is the law of the established nation state with full internal and external sovereignty.[4] However, according to sociologists and historians, this stage of development was only reached at the end of the nineteenth century, and some would even date it as recently as the second half of the twentieth century.[5] Previously, the sovereign nation state was either a normative ideal or an ideology that disguised the various forms of empire building taking place under the heading of the State.[6] Notwithstanding these qualifications, taking a specific historical stage as the point of reference is a legitimate premise in social theory. Whether this premise can be assumed in a conceptual analysis, however, needs further discussion.[7] Thus, the qualifier 'transnational' is not a definition of a specific area of law but merely serves to remind us that the phenomenon of law is much broader than presumed by the standard case thesis, even within the Western tradition.[8]

At this point some might also reply that even if from a historical or sociological point of view there were other phenomena called 'law', at least from the point of view of legal and political philosophy, law has always been presumed to be the law of the State or maybe the city. Thus, one could hold that in philosophy, or more specifically, in legal philosophy, there is a well-established discourse that presumes the existence of

4 For the thesis that one has to recognise 'both clear standard cases and borderline cases' see again Hart (n. 2), 4.

5 See Chris Thornhill, *A Sociology of Constitutions: Constitutions and State Legitimacy in Historical-Sociological Perspective* (Cambridge: Cambridge University Press, 2011) and for an another comparative account focusing on the development of state power up to the twentieth century, see Wolfgang Reinhard, *Geschichte der Staatsgewalt. Eine vergleichende Verfassungsgeschichte Europas von den Anfängen bis zur Gegenwart* (Berlin: Beck, 1999).

6 For an analysis of history in terms of Empires see Fred Cooper/Jane Burbank, *Empires in World History. Power and the Politics of Difference* (Princeton: Princeton University Press, 2009).

7 Raz grants that notions change over history but simply claims that the aim of philosophy is to analyse 'our' concept of law without explaining when and where our notion originated (in Ancient Athens, during the eleventh-century Gregorian Revolution or only in late-twentieth-century Oxford?) and how to cleanse 'our' understanding from contamination with illicit views of 'others'. See Joseph Raz, *Between Authority and Interpretation. On the Theory of Law and Practical Reason* (Oxford: Oxford University Press, 2009), 24–26.

8 The notion 'Western tradition' is vague. I do not use it to refer to a contemporary, late twentieth-century understanding of law but in the sense introduced by Harold Berman, *Law and Revolution. The Formation of the Western Legal Tradition* (Cambridge, MA: Harvard University Press, 1983).

law as state law. However, this argument involves a specific assumption about what constitutes philosophising or theorising about law. The assumption is that this is simply what philosophy is about: developing 'theories' about an 'object', or as Shapiro puts it, 'it analyses the nature of law and legal entities, and its objects of study include legal systems, laws, rules, rights . . . and so on.'[9]

However, further reflection shows that theorising social practices such as the law involves much more than that. Considering once again Hart's example of the evolution of a 'primitive society' into a more complex society with a legal system, it can be shown that one has to distinguish between different levels of theorising. (Note that I am using Hart's example not to talk about primary and secondary rules but to clarify ways to theorise law). The first level of theorising is the practical level of talking about law and deciding cases. Even at this level of primary or customary rules, such discourse is a theoretical activity because it calls attention to a rule (e.g. by saying 'that's the rule' or 'that's the done thing'), thereby interrupting an unquestioned social practice. The theoretical activity involved in this practice has been overshadowed by Hart's narrative of the 'defects' of 'primitive' society'.[10] Historical and anthropological studies have shown that the ability to identify something as a rule, and to distinguish between evolution and alteration, presupposes writing, and thus, a complex form of society that includes some form of reflection (theoretical or mythical).[11] Specific legal institutions such as courts and legislatures merely institutionalise this practical level of theorising in a bureaucratic way.[12] Thus the union of primary and secondary is useful to analyse aspects of legal systems but not to distinguish a pre-theoretical or pre-legal worldview from a philosophical or legal worldview. (Hart implicitly acknowledges this point as he analyses

[9] Shapiro (n. 3), 3. [10] Hart, (n. 2), 91–99.

[11] The invention of writing and the cultural changes it brought about is a complex story that has many philosophical ramifications. The founding text for all later discussions on the relation between literacy and orality is Eric A. Havelock, *Preface to Plato* (London: Basil Blackwell, 1963). Concentrating instead only on oral cultures is no way out of the quandary as James C. Scott has reminded us that oral cultures are often not pre-literal but post-literal for having myths about how they forgot to write. See James C. Scott, *The Art of not Being Governed: An Anarchist History of Upland Southeast Asia* (New Haven: Yale University Press, 2009), 222.

[12] The argument that law is a specific kind of social practice that can be institutionalised is broadly in line with Hart's analysis. For a more detailed analysis of Hart along these lines, see Detlef von Daniels, *The Concept of Law from a Transnational Perspective* (Aldershot: Ashgate, 2010), 87–128.

international law in terms of a system consisting only of primary rules. Yet he certainly would not deny that even without institutionalisation, there is much theorising going on in international law.) It is important to note that on a second level, there are different ways to theorise this complex practice: scholarly legal writings about Roman law are a part of such theorising, along with various kinds of natural law theory and analytic jurisprudence. Thus it is not only the law that constitutes a broad phenomenon – theory is broad and multifaceted as well, even if we only concentrate on the Western tradition. Whether these different theories are arranged in a hierarchy (with philosophy certainly claiming the top spot), a developmental sequence (from traditional to modern) or are in conflict (i.e. religious versus secular) need not concern us for the moment. However, we do need to draw attention to one specific kind of theory, which functions on yet another level, namely theory about theory. The paradigmatic case of this kind of theory is Marxism, for it not only provides an account of historical practices and different theories at different times, but also claims to provide a definitive explanation of the ideological function of all other theories.[13] Therefore, Marxism claims to be a theory about other theories that is not on par with them, but on a categorically different level. This is why it makes sense to say that there are three levels of theorising, the practical level, theorising about this practice and theorising about theories. Among all the pretentious claims of Marxism, I would only want to hold onto one basic insight, namely, the insight about the possibility of the historical and cultural relativity of theories, including metaphysics and moral philosophy. Note that I am not claiming that all theories are, of necessity, historically or culturally relative, but only that this question needs to be addressed.

Thus, not only is it unclear what the law – the phenomenon in question – is. It is also unclear precisely what legal philosophy is, how it should proceed, and which debates it should take up on which level. This can be demonstrated by once again using Shapiro's book as an example. He is very confident that what he is doing is philosophy. Sometimes he refers to his endeavour as legal philosophy, sometimes as analytic jurisprudence.[14] In either case, he presumes that in some way, he is following in the tradition of Plato and Hobbes; at any rate, these are two major philosophers he names. However, in reading the text, one gets

[13] Karl Marx's own more specific criticisms of Hegel are not relevant for the general point in question. Therefore it suffices to refer to the orthodox doctrine of Marxism.

[14] Shapiro (n. 3), 2.

the impression that only analytical jurisprudence is capable of grasping the nature of law, and that analytic jurisprudence only began with Hart. On the other hand, there is no reflection about what people did in the 2,500 years before Hart, what kind of fatal mistakes they made that renders their work worthless for contemporary legal philosophers, or why philosophy should be restricted to a very small circle of Hart devotees. Unlike in the natural sciences, 'scientific progress' cannot be assumed in philosophy but needs to be re-established on each occasion by arguing with predecessors and 'deviationists'.

These methodological preliminaries do not yet constitute substantive arguments. They should hardly come as news to any discipline that works in a comparative or historical way. However, the preliminaries do explain the reason I begin with a reflection on different philosophical 'conceptions' of law, and why 'law' comes with the warning: 'it could be transnational'.

8.3

Because I have used analytical jurisprudence as a counterfoil to reflect on methodology, I start by examining the conception of law that underlies analytical jurisprudence. For explicating the genealogical critique I do not try to formulate typical claims but instead refer to the views of some specific authors who I take to be representative of the tradition, as the aim of the critique is not to classify discussions but to engage in on-going discussions. Regarding the aim of analytical jurisprudence, Joseph Raz writes: 'In large measure what we study when we study the nature of law is the nature of our own self-understanding. The identification of a certain social institution as law is part of the self-consciousness, of the way we conceive and understand our society.'[15] Taking this description as a lead, we would like to understand, for instance, how WTO law influences our lives or the lives of people in developing countries, whether human rights, either in the form of constitutional law, EU law, or international law, serve to protect freedoms or undermine (legal) traditions, and last but not least, we would like to understand the effects of 'lawyer talk' and 'philosopher talk' on our life world. Thus, the question of what the law is, what it does to us, how it transforms our actions and influences our thoughts is very real and compelling. However, these questions and the examples I have

[15] Raz (n. 7), 31.

just cited are all inadmissible according to the views of analytical jurisprudence. Joseph Raz writes, 'when faced with borderline cases [e.g. international law, as Raz explains in a footnote] it is best to admit their problematic credentials, to enumerate their similarities and dissimilarities to the typical cases, and leave it at that.'[16] In a later article he briefly explains that it is an 'assumption' of analytical jurisprudence that it is only concerned with municipal legal systems. 'I think that we feel that legal systems not only happen to be the most important institutionalised system governing human society, but that that is part of their nature. We would regard an institutionalised system as a legal one only if it is necessarily in some respect the most important institutionalised system which can exist in that society.'[17] Therefore the task of legal philosophy is not to study different conceptions of law, let alone transnational law, but only to analyse the concept of law in its key instance, which is necessarily state law.[18]

One problem about this claim is that, because it is a foundational premise for analytical jurisprudence, it is rarely defended explicitly against competing views; Raz's statement that we 'feel' it this way hardly counts as an argument. One might regard foundational premises as the 'queen' of a theory, so to speak, and thus, best defended by a staggered arrangement of defensive lines. Failing to successfully defend the premise would expose a serious flaw. However, another way to think about analytical jurisprudence is as a different kind of theory, namely a constructivist theory.[19] According to this line of thought, failing to justify the foundational premise is not a flaw, but actually an inevitable feature of every theory. To follow this line of thought, the only proof of a theory is the viability of the edifice built upon its premises. An example from the area of political philosophy may help to elucidate this point. Robert Nozick starts his libertarian theory with the claim: 'People have rights.' That is a position Nozick takes for granted and simply does not want to

[16] Joseph Raz, *Practical Reasons and Norms*, 2nd ed. (Oxford: Oxford University Press, 1990), 150.

[17] Joseph Raz, *The Authority of Law. Essays on Law and Morality* (Oxford: Clarendon Press 1979), 116.

[18] Ibid., 104.

[19] For those who react with instinctive repulsion when they hear the term constructivism: W.V.O. Quine's notion of analytical hypotheses that explain the possibility of radical indeterminacy is an account of constructivism. See W. V. O. Quine, *Word and Object* (Cambridge, MA: MIT Press, 1960), 68–79. For the logical background see his *Methods of Logic* (Cambridge, MA: Harvard University Press, 1950), 211–16.

discuss. Thus, his theory is addressed only to those people who share this premise or at least understand what sharing this premise means.

Thus, pointing out that a theory has a foundational premise and questioning this premise is one possible way to criticise a theory, but it is often an unfruitful way because it does not engage the theory at its strongest point. Therefore, rather than attacking analytical jurisprudence by questioning its foundational premise, I instead point out some internal theoretical problems that result from this position. First, from a methodological point of view, it remains mysterious why the law should be the only social practice that can be analysed in this way. Money, power, religion and even war or love are social practices as well, but there are no extensive philosophical discussions on the conceptual analysis of money that aim to describe its universal nature. However, if conceptual analysis were a well-established method extending across several areas of social philosophy, this is something one would expect. Vice versa, the absence of such discussions in other areas is something that needs explaining if one employs the method as a matter of course. This observation does not rule out the possibility that describing the universal nature of law could make sense; it merely points out the kinds of arguments one would have to make if one wanted to justify this method of 'describing the nature of a social practice' and what kind of discussion one would have to engage in. When trying to describe the universal nature of a number of social practices (law, religion, family, etc.) one is inevitably led into the currents of comparative sociology, an anathema for analytical jurisprudence.[20]

Second, whenever one presumes that something has a universal nature, the metaphysical question about how it exists and how it can be conceived follows right on the heels of that presumption. When Raz describes the aim of a theory of law, he nonchalantly uses strong metaphysical language: 'Naturally, the essential properties of the law are universal characteristics of law. They are to be found in law wherever and whenever it exists. Moreover, these properties are universal properties of the law not accidentally, and not because of any prevailing economic or social circumstances, but because there is no law without them.'[21] He appears to be unaware that his 'sketchy and rather

[20] On the other hand, no sociologist would employ the method of 'conceptual analysis' to discover the 'universal nature' of marriage while assuming the 'standard case' of lifelong heterosexual relationship.

[21] Raz (n. 7), 25.

dogmatically stated remarks'[22] recall problems that already haunted Plato. A few lines from Plato might suffice to show that asserting that some entities (the good, the law, etc.) have a universal nature is only the beginning of philosophy. In Plato's late dialogue *Parmenides*, the young Socrates is questioned: '"Tell me," said Parmenides, "do you think that the abstract ideas of likeness, unity, and the rest, exist apart from individuals which partake of them?"' Of course, Socrates has to defend the theory of forms. Yet this is just the beginning, for Parmenides goes on to ask whether there are also ideas of things that 'appear laughable: of hair, mud, filth, and other things which are base and vile?' Socrates has to admit that he is undecided how to deal with those things and is consoled by Parmenides with the words: 'You are young, Socrates . . . the time will come when philosophy will have a firmer hold of you, and you will not despise even the meanest things.'[23] These are the kinds of questions that got the dispute between Plato and Aristotle started, and these questions lurk in the background and have to be addressed whenever we presume in strong metaphysical language that something has a universal nature.

A third internal theoretical problem that arises with this approach is that even if there is something that is timeless and universal such as the nature of law, the science that describes it is parochial and time-bound. We know from the philosophy of science that even the natural sciences cannot be regarded as unworldly endeavours that move steadily forward driven only by the logic of scientific discovery. Instead, the sciences are organised in paradigms and follow routes that are driven by political or economic incentives.[24] The same can be said to be true for any approach describing the nature of something. Again, this is not meant as an outright refutation of analytical jurisprudence, but instead to show the kind of reflection it would need to engage in if it wanted to uphold its claim to be a general theory about the universal features of something.

The last problem leads towards more practical considerations. Assuming there is a nature of law and assuming it can somehow be grasped and described, it still needs to be shown how this nature is realised over time

[22] Ibid., 24.

[23] Plato, Parmenides, 130a-e, transl. Mary Louise Gill and Paul Ryan (Hackett Publishing, 1996).

[24] The locus classicus is Thomas Kuhn, *The Structure of Scientific Discovery* (Chicago: University of Chicago Press, 1962). For a more radical constructivist account see Bruno Latour, *Laboratory Life* (London: Sage Publications, 1979).

(or 'how it comes to itself' as Hegel would say), and in which forms or disguises it has appeared in earlier times or in other traditions. Unlike the problems mentioned earlier, this is not a task for the future, but has, in fact, already been taken up by analytical jurisprudence. Since analytical jurisprudence has become well established in the Anglo-American legal tradition, and uses cases, examples and arguments from this tradition to make its case, it has already met the requirement to show that these concerns can be manifested in legal practice, albeit only for a single case. Here once again, Shapiro is a good example. While writing in the tradition of analytical jurisprudence and upholding its methodological claims, he argues that his planning theory of law offers a compelling interpretative methodology for U.S. law and shows that the U.S. constitution can be understood as a plan laid out by the founding fathers. Shapiro not only makes arguments about the nature of law, but also applies his general insights. However, if the American legal tradition is the only case for which the fruitfulness of this approach can be shown, the extravagant claim of having discovered universally valid insights would simply amount to an excuse for parochialism or a justification of discursive dominance.

Thus, when we consider the claims made by analytical jurisprudence and its actual practices, we see that the conception of law it promotes is driven to its own limits, so to speak. The strength of analytical jurisprudence is that it takes seriously the philosophical quest to come up with universal characterisations but for this very reason, it has an open flank. If it wants to hold on to its claim to be a philosophy in this sense, it needs to engage with the whole philosophical tradition, and if it wants to show its value, it needs to prove its relevance to different legal systems. When taking the aims of analytical jurisprudence seriously one is naturally led to inquire into the empirical realities of law.

The failure of analytical jurisprudence to come to terms with the ever-changing social reality can also be observed in Raz's recent paper 'Why the state', included in this volume. Raz explains that many jurisprudential theories have focused on state law as it is the most 'important' and 'comprehensive legal system of the day' and poses the 'more interesting theoretical puzzles.' However, when trying to come up with a *general* theory of law it is simply not relevant whether some parts of it are 'important', 'interesting' or 'comprehensive' as generality can only be tested with reference to exceptional cases. Otherwise it wouldn't be a general or conceptual theory of law but merely the general part of Western constitutional theory. Raz however develops a test to 'explain and guide people's theoretical attention' that is geared only towards 'central cases', presumably the law of Western states. According to Raz's test states are characterised by (1) an extensive responsibility within their domains, and (2) freedom from external constraints. However, in his own sketchy empirical hints Raz leaves it open to doubt that his account is true as a historical description (it suffices to mention that Church law was the first modern western legal system[25] and that the centralisation of law in nation states at home went hand in hand with the pluralisation of law through colonial regimes abroad[26]) or helpful for analysing current processes of supranational legalisation in Europe and beyond. Thus it is unclear why 'people' such as legal historians, sociologists, anthropologists, international lawyers or philosophers should employ Raz's test to guide their theoretical attention.[27]

An obvious reason why Raz might hold on to the 'importance', or 'centrality' of state law is to provide the empirical background for his notion of authority. He bolsters his theoretical claim that a state's authority is 'by its very nature' unlimited with the empirical observation that all existing legal limitations like constitutions, rights and so on could be revoked or changed over time. However, when taking a more comprehensive theoretical perspective the limits of Raz's conceptual apparatus become apparent. Raz concedes that the idea that 'authority of law is by its very nature unlimited' is not specific to state law but also applies to religious law. However, this concession is still too weak. The claim that authority is by its very nature unlimited can be seriously upheld *only* as a religious claim. Only in this area is the totally unlimited and absolute authority of a law conceivable without adding some secular disclaimer: given a territory, a domain, or the previously established practical understanding of rules (no ultra vires application).[28] To put it differently: outside of his kingdom every king is naked. It is not by chance that the

[25] According to Berman, *Law and Revolution* (n. 8) the church developed during the Gregorian revolution in the eleventh and twelfth centuries the first modern western legal system and served as a model for the secular governments of states.

[26] See Brian Z. Tamanaha, 'Understanding Legal Pluralism: Past to Present, Local to Global', 29 *Sydney Law Review* (2007), 375–411.

[27] In his conclusion, by claiming that the current challenge to legal philosophers is to explore theories of a state situated in an international framework and that the exclusive concentration on state law was never justified, Raz departs from his previous restriction of legal philosophy to a concern with state law (this chapter, at n. 18) and his current preoccupation of theoretical attention to the central case of state law.

[28] For a more detailed critique of the rule of recognition along these lines see my *The Concept of Law from a Transnational Perspective* (n. 12), 131–32.

inherent difficulty of unlimited and unqualified authority is relentlessly reflected in the law-centred Abrahamic religions. The story of the Binding of Isaac poses exactly this question and is central not only in Judaism but also in Christianity (Jesus the Lamb of God) and Islam (the pilgrimage to Mecca includes a re-enactment of the story). In the secular domain, however, the modern claim to sovereignty is a legal claim and means that a specific legal institution, the sovereign as a state-person or the State as a legal entity, is 'immediate to international law' (*völkerrechtsunmittelbar*).[29] Seen as a deontic relation, it is international law that confers rights and duties on those subject to it. The duty of non-interference may be among them.[30]

Raz misses this point as he confuses the sociological notion of a state with the legal notion. Only for this reason can he infer from the increasing dominance or power of the State (as a social system) with regard to all other social organisations (church, local communities, etc.) over the past 200 years that the legal authority of the State is 'unlimited by its very nature.' Legally, it is the other way round. By its very nature the European state is limited by the existence of other states and it is sovereign only as an entity of international law. This does not mean that violations of international law (usually through war) are unheard of in European history; these are from a legal point of view however to be seen as delicts – though may nevertheless be later on sanctified in law.[31] Thus, Raz's method of 'speculative analytical jurisprudence' does not improve his earlier analytical account but further reveals its open flank. By modifying his position and arguing that historical and political reasons give state law a key position among legal systems in general, Raz fails to realise that when based on empirical generalisation analytical jurisprudence loses its hallmark of being the only discipline to analyse the concept of law and turns into yet another social theory.

8.4

This sociological challenge to analytical jurisprudence has been brought forward most forcefully by legal pluralism, which is the second conception of law I would like to discuss. Note that I do not claim that there is a

[29] See Hans Kelsen, *Pure Theory of Law* (Berkeley: University of California Press 1967), 338.

[30] See Hans Kelsen, *General Theory of Law and State* (Cambridge, MA: Harvard University Press, 1949), 383–86.

[31] Ibid., 219–21.

necessary historical or dialectical movement from analytical jurisprudence to legal pluralism, or that the tradition of analytical jurisprudence has been refuted or 'overcome' once the phenomena and arguments I have named are taken into consideration. Instead, what I have shown is that it becomes increasingly difficult to stick to the 'pure' position of analytical jurisprudence as it aims to present itself as a self-sufficient whole but does not reflect its limits. The critique is genealogical in the sense that a reflection on the actual practice of a tradition, the way it is developed and employed, reveals an undercurrent, which as it will turn out is also not the 'real' or 'basic' fact of the matter, but instead, a theoretical position in itself. We will observe the same kind of 'switch' (the classical dialectical term would be 'Umschlag') from one tradition to another once we have further examined legal pluralism.

Legal pluralism dates back to the beginning of the twentieth century, when Eugen Ehrlich discovered the living law of the peoples in the Bukovina. Living law regulated much of social life but was conspicuously different from the official law in place at the time.[32] Ehrlich applied his insights to critique the social blindness of Hans Kelsen's pure theory of law, one of the antecedents of analytical jurisprudence. In a similar vein, Brian Tamanaha currently advocates for a version of legal pluralism by pinpointing anthropological studies and historical accounts that contradict the universalistic claims of analytical jurisprudence. Like in the previous step, I again do not name typical claims of legal pluralism but develop the argument in contestation with one proponent, Brain Tamanaha, whom I take to be representative for this line of thought.

Tamanaha began from his observation that the official state law of Micronesia only governed the actual practices of the population to a limited degree, which instead followed its own local rules.[33] At the same time, Tamanaha became aware of a weakness in the theoretical account of legal pluralism.[34] His main criticism is that there can be no single social scientific understanding of law upon which to build legal

[32] Eugen Ehrlich, *Fundamental Principles of the Sociology of Law*, trans. Walter L. Moll (Arno Press, 1975). The official history of legal pluralism is contested. From a theoretical perspective Ehrlich's debate with Hans Kelsen is most relevant. On Ehrlich as a founding father of legal pluralism see Franz von Benda-Beckmann, 'Who's Afraid of Legal Pluralism' 47 *Journal of Legal Pluralism and Unofficial Law* (2002), 37–82.

[33] Brian Tamanaha, *Understanding Law in Micronesia: An Interpretive Approach to Transplanted Law* (Amsterdam: E. J. Brill, 1993).

[34] See Brian Tamanaha, 'The Folly of the 'Social Scientific' Concept of Legal Pluralism', 20 *Journal of Law and Society* (1993), 192–217.

pluralism. Instead, he holds that a purely conventional identification of law would more fruitfully describe the phenomena studied by legal pluralism. Thus, he claims: 'A legal system exists whenever there are legal actors (conventionally identified as such) engaged in producing and reproducing a legal system through shared secondary rules, regardless of their efficacy in generating widespread conformity to the primary rules.'[35] Tamanaha's account is conventional not only regarding the identification of law but also regarding its function, as it allows us 'to question whether law satisfies any functions, and, if so, which ones and to what extent'.[36] As he does not believe in a universal concept of law, he does not regard his definition as a conceptual analysis but rather as a working definition, and uses very pragmatic criteria to identify something as law: He simply follows the fish; if something is called law, it is law and adds placatingly: '[A]s a matter of general social practice people do not lightly apply the label law.'[37] Tamanaha consolidates his position by referring to Searle's constructivist social ontology. According to Searle, all definitions are social constructions that serve a specific function and are therefore arbitrary. Thus, no definition of a concept of law can be more than a restatement of a background position.[38]

Tamanaha is at his best when he reveals the shortcomings of various definitions of law with regard to indigenous practices. He also shows that the administrative apparatus that comes along with a Western style legal system is not merely an innocuous vehicle but instead, a social reality with its own agenda – for example, when Australian courts denied Aboriginal land titles by stating that Aborigines lacked (Western) notion of sovereignty or property and hence property rights.[39] However, Tamanaha's criticism of abstract jurisprudential thinking and his keen observance of concrete phenomena on the ground are not matched by an equally strong desire to come up with abstract philosophical insights. Using a Kantian notion, one could say that Tamanaha fails to consider the possibility of reflective judgments (i.e. seeking universals for given particulars).

[35] Ibid., 148. [36] Ibid.

[37] Brian Tamanaha, 'Socio-legal Positivism and a General Jurisprudence', 21 *Oxford Journal of Legal Studies* (2001), 28. The article is a modified version of a chapter in *A General Jurisprudence of Law and Society*. The remark on social practice of using the label 'law' is added in the article.

[38] Searle is however not a radical constructivist as he does not apply this insight to his own theory or his own theoretical terms. They are for some reason 'really' true.

[39] Brian Tamanaha, 'What is "General" Jurisprudence? A Critique of Universalistic Claims by Philosophical Concepts of Law', 2 *Transnational Legal Theory* (2011), 305–08.

Tamanaha might grant the possibility of reflective judgment but would claim that in the case of the law there is no such thing as a universal concept. However, a close examination of his texts will reveal that Tamanaha frequently invokes something akin to a universal concept of law without reflecting about it any further. The underlying problem can already be detected in Tamanaha's methodological claim that it suffices to observe the usage of the word law to identify something as law. This remark is not an innocent social scientific reminder but presumes a strong nominalist position. Its pitfalls are probably best captured by Humpty Dumpty:

> When I use a word,' Humpty Dumpty said, in rather a scornful tone, 'it means just what I choose it to mean—neither more nor less.' 'The question is,' said Alice, 'whether you can make words mean so many different things.' 'The question is,' said Humpty Dumpty, 'which is to be master—that's all.

Even though Tamanaha qualifies his position to the extent that not every individual but only 'groups' of people can alter the concepts, the principal problem remains. How is the link between a specific social practice and a label established? And how can it be avoided that the same label refers to very different kinds of social practices in different linguistic communities? Two strategies are common. One can either presume that the concept of law has a universal nature, or one can assume that it is relative to our civilisation, and take it as subject of investigation, assuming as a matter of fact that it extends over the whole globe. Tamanaha rejects both strategies because he is aware of the multiplicity of legal discourses, even within the Western world. However, this still leaves the question open of how the identity of the social practice can be established.

For explaining communication among strangers or even between different cultures, it is certainly not necessary to presume the universal nature of concepts. One could also presume that law is a cluster concept of related practices. However, in this case one would still need to explain how the various practices or language games can be studied and how cultural or historical differences can be overcome. How can we know that an alien culture has a notion of law at all, whether its practices are similar to our contemporary understanding of law and whether it can be adequately grasped with our notions? These kinds of questions arise not only when dealing with indigenous cultures but also when dealing with our own Western history, especially the Medieval Age and Ancient times. Thus Tamanaha's linguistic commitments naturally lead into a different field of inquiry, the domain of historical and intercultural hermeneutics. However, Tamanaha doesn't follow this path to the end, which has repercussions for his own theory. This can be studied by observing how he deals with linguistic differences.

He concedes that notions such as *droit* or *Recht* that are usually translated as 'law' might have their own 'connotations' in the other language.[40] However, he quickly dismisses the possibility of deep cultural differences resulting from such differences. Instead he claims that problems of translation can be overcome, in principle, as evidenced by numerous cross-language interactions.[41] Both claims are revealing. While Tamanaha speaks of 'connotations' that languages other than English might attach to law, he is himself applying the distinction between substantial and accidental properties to the concept of law (connotations versus core meaning), and thus the very distinction he tried to dismiss before. Moreover, as he is unwilling to consider any other usages on their own terms but only speaks of 'connotations', he is implicitly reproducing the imperialism of a specific discourse that comes with a specific language. By way of contrast, the basic insight of philosophical hermeneutics is that understanding requires seeing oneself in the eyes of another. This only makes sense or leads to mutual understanding when the other is not conceptualised as inferior, but rather, as being as reasonable and philosophically reflective as oneself. Becoming aware of difficulties of translation and of other (philosophical) traditions is one way to enter into this kind of reflection.

This can be demonstrated with reference to the German distinction between *Recht* and *Gesetz*. Tamanaha refers to this distinction as one of the minor problems of translation, which can be dealt with so long as we approach the translation with care. However, the underlying (and false) assumption is that translation means translating word-to-word. This might suffice for a limited number of practical purposes. Yet, in all translation of cultural artefacts, translation means having to cope with a complete yet different linguistic system and a different cultural background.[42] Thus, the distinction between *Recht* and *Gesetz* does not merely add an additional concept to the 'ordinary' concept of law that can be found in all cultures, but in its various disguises, gives rise to a whole philosophical tradition. Both notions can be translated as 'law',

[40] Tamanaha (n. 30), 30. [41] Ibid.

[42] This old hermeneutic insight has been formulated as an empirical hypothesis in the twentieth century as the Sapir-Whorf Hypothesis.

but *Recht* has a linguistic resemblance to *Gerechtigkeit* (justice), similar to the Latin *ius/iustitia*. Therefore, *Recht* can refer to a whole set of written and unwritten practices, whereas *das Gesetz/die Gesetze* (the law/the laws) presupposes that it exists in written form (even if written as natural law by God). By contrast, the singular of *Recht* (*ein Recht*), is a subjective right. Of course, this is not a fixed lexical distinction but is theorised anew in each generation and by each author. Any attempt to interpret Kant's *Rechtslehre* without being aware that it starts from the notion of a *Recht* (subjective right), but does not theorise the general notion of law is doomed to fail. Similarly, it would be an expression of ignorance if all one could say about Hegel's *Rechtsphilosophie* was that this is just another cultural connotation of the word 'law'. The important point to note is not that there is an extra thing out there, *das Recht*, which is unrecognisable by English speakers, but that arbitrary linguistic conventions (no language is natural or God-given) lead to different ways of conceptualising and theorising the reality of a social world that does not exist prior to conceptualisation.

A similar story could be told for the basic notion of authority, Raz's key term. When starting the reflection on the law from the notion of *Herrschaft* (lordship) instead of authority, one is led more naturally towards the ideas of Max Weber, who saw *rationale Herrschaft* (rational lordship through legal rule) as one of several kinds of *legitime Herrschaft* (legitimate lordship.) The usual translation of 'Herrschaft' with 'power' is misleading and has contributed to the prejudice in much analytical jurisprudence that the concept of law can in all languages only be analysed in terms of authority.

Thus, as we examine Tamanaha's text, we see the very kind of abstract philosophical thinking resurfacing that he is trying to dismiss, not in the form of analytical jurisprudence, but in the form of a different philosophical tradition, one that may be roughly characterised as 'hermeneutical'.

If we focus on the practical side of Tamanaha's narrative, we can make a similar observation. He frequently recounts cases in which weak indigenous communities are suppressed or exploited by powerful political or economic actors who have the force of the official, sanctioned law on their side.[43] He implicitly makes a number of value judgments, such

[43] See Brian Tamanaha, 'The Rule of Law and Legal Pluralism in Development' in Brian Tamanaha et al. (eds.), *Legal Pluralism and Development. Scholars and Practitioners in Dialogue* (Cambridge: Cambridge University Press 2012), 34–49.

as the need to respect the autonomy of indigenous people, that natural resources should be preserved, that exploiting the lack of knowledge of weak actors is unjust, that all affected people should have a say and so on. In our times, no one would seriously question these values, quite the contrary. People would point out that these are not just desirable values but norms that are already entrenched in international law. Tamanaha is certainly aware of international law and the proliferation of human rights in particular. However, he is reluctant to grant them a special theoretical status. Instead he writes: 'A large number of particular and general phenomena are conventionally viewed as "law", including international law, customary law, canon law, the Sharia, natural law, state legal systems, the *lex mercatoria* and more.'[44] Thus we again encounter a tension between the theoretical claims made in legal pluralism (conventional identification) and its actual practice (recourse to ultimate values). In theory, it claims to overcome analytic jurisprudence's ideological focus on state legal systems by observing the whole range of legal practices in a social scientific manner. In its practice, however, legal pluralism uses a nonconventional way to identify the values with which to judge laws. There is no other way to understand Tamanaha's criticisms of exploitative or disrespectful practices of powerful actors (e.g. multinational firms or unjust governments). This methodological criticism is independent from the kind and number of universal values Tamanaha is willing to accept. As an anthropologist by vocation, he is quick to dismiss some values as parochial but still holds on that others are universal human goods, in particular the rule of law understood in a 'pre-liberal way'.[45]

Again we are facing the phenomenon that when driven to their limits, contradictions between theoretical claims and actual practice would suggest a 'switch' to a different conception. Similar to the earlier discussion, the genealogical critique is not aimed at refuting Tamanaha or disproving his findings, but instead at revealing how a different philosophical tradition is working behind his back. Even as he tries to argue the pointlessness of philosophical questioning about the nature of law, he is invoking a different kind of philosophical questioning, namely hermeneutic understanding and the quest for justice in international law. This question is not new and in recent years has been the object of

[44] Brian Z. Tamanaha, 'Law' in Stanley Katz et al. (eds.), *Oxford International Encyclopedia of Legal History* (Oxford: Oxford University Press, 2009), 17–23.

[45] Brian Tamanaha, 'The Rule of Law for Everyone?', 55 *Current Legal Problems* (2002), 119.

increased attention from international lawyers, philosophers and political theorists, so I will call it the new philosophy of international law.[46]

8.5

It goes without mentioning that international law itself is an old practice that dates back to the Roman *ius gentium*; the same is true for the philosophy of international law, ever since Hugo Grotius and Emerich de Vattel established it as an academic discipline. However, after the renaissance of political philosophy in the 1970s, it was only in the 1990s that international law gained again increasing attention. Apart from a few forerunners in the 1980s, especially Thomas Pogge, Charles Beitz and Henry Shue, philosophical discussion about international law only took off with the publication of John Rawls' *The Law of Peoples*.[47] In the past fifteen years or so, the focus has moved from moral or political theory to the field of legal philosophy. Now traditional questions of international law, such as its legitimacy, sources, adjudication, as well as relatively new areas, such as economic and environmental law, are no longer the sole domain of a small group of international lawyers, but are widely discussed by philosophers and political theorists. Because the philosophy of international law covers a wide range of topics and stretches into a variety of disciplines and legal sub-specialisations, the discussion is not restricted to a small number of philosophical treatises. Therefore it is – unlike in the previous cases – not possible to focus the discussion on one representative. Arguably, this is a specific feature of this tradition which is not just due to the relative novelty of the discussion, as if so to say its Rawls has yet to come. Instead, the diversity of topics requires a division of labour; and yet unlike in any other philosophical movement an astonishingly high like-mindedness can be observed. (One may think of the infightings among various schools of Marxism or even Maoism to acquire a sense of the unlikelihood of common ideas among philosophers.) A good collection of the various strands of the debate that shows its diversity as well as its coherence in terms of underlying principles is

[46] I have borrowed the term from Ronald Dworkin, 'A New Philosophy for International Law', 41 *Philosophy & Public Affairs* (2013), 2–30. The title shows that for him as for most legal theorists philosophy of international law appeared as a 'new' topic that had no relevance in the forty years before. In hindsight the omission of the international dimension appears to be a sign of an ideological mindset.

[47] John Rawls, *The Law of Peoples with 'The Idea of Public Reason revisited'* (Cambridge, MA: Harvard University Press, 1999).

the anthology *Philosophy of International Law* which will serve as our main point of reference in what follows.[48]

After the genealogical critique of the two previous traditions, the new philosophy of international law might seem to be in good dialectical fashion a synthesis of previous thesis and antithesis. It adopts some of the insights and concepts developed in analytical jurisprudence – for example, Raz's service conception of law,[49] but unlike analytical jurisprudence does not have a state-centred bias, but rather routinely recognises the need to reflect on the importance of other actors (e.g. NGOs, multinational corporations) and legal regimes (e.g. effects of WTO law or informal banking regulations). Like legal pluralism, it is sensitive to the adverse effects of global capitalism and unjust legal regimes on the lives of disadvantaged individuals.[50] Yet in distinction to legal pluralism, the new philosophy of international law does not describe international law and human rights law as simply one of many instances of law but instead gives reasons for their predominance and supremacy, and shows how international law and human rights serve and interact with national law and other kinds of regulations.[51] Moreover, the classical tradition of philosophy, especially Republican thinking,[52] traditional and modern social contract theory, and Kant's philosophy of history are present to a much greater extent in the new philosophy of international law than in the two previous traditions.[53] Although the discussion is broad and multifaceted, it is possible to enumerate some basic tenets.

[48] Samantha Besson and John Tasioulas (eds.), *The Philosophy of International Law* (Oxford: Oxford University Press, 2010).

[49] See Tasioulas, 'The Legitimacy of International Law' (n. 48), 97–118.

[50] See especially the contributions by Thomas Pogge who does not just develop an ideal political theory but gives numerous policy recommendations and proposed concrete changes of certain legal structures.

[51] Allen Buchanan argues that international law is only legitimate if it serves to protect human rights, while human rights are self-justifying insofar as they serve as institutions for global public deliberation. For his full account see his *Human Rights, Legitimacy, and the Use of Force* (Oxford University Press, 2010).

[52] Philip Pettit argues that the international order will be legitimate if it maximises the number of peoples living under Republican governments and protects legitimate states against domination by others. See Philip Pettit, 'International Democracy' (n. 48), 139–60.

[53] The philosophy of international law traces its history either back to the classical tradition from Grotius over Hobbes to Pufendorf or back to Immanuel Kant. Other philosophical approaches or historical times are typically not mentioned. See for this line of arguing (n. 48), 33–78.

In contrast to a traditional understanding of international law, the new philosophy no longer considers state sovereignty and state consent as the ultimate basis of international law. Instead, it stresses the role and standing of individuals in international law, sometimes to the point that it regards individuals as the ultimate concern of international law.[54] One reason for this conceptual change is that international law's claim to legitimacy is taken seriously.[55] Even though the requirements of legitimacy are discussed through a variety of theoretical approaches, there is a broad overlapping consensus concerning the underlying principles. They are either spelled out in terms of human rights[56] as a requirement to promote the common good[57] or the requirement to treat all people as equals.[58] As a consequence, states, but also other actors (e.g. multinational corporations or individuals such as warlords), can be held liable under international law. Lawyers are especially keen on showing where such principles are already at work in international law and how they could spread to other areas (e.g. environmental or economic law). Summing up the viewpoint of the philosophy of international law, one could say that its principles are well established, rules are in place, and all that is lacking is the appropriate interpretation and institutionalisation.[59] For this reason, papers about the philosophy of international law typically include references to principles or aims that should be maximised in times to come. Thus, the new philosophy of international law is future-oriented, more specifically, it is oriented towards a global future understood in a comprehensive way.

This outlook appears to stand in glaring contrast to a genealogical approach, because a genealogy moves back in time from the present to consider how specific traditions are formed and come to overshadow others. So one must ask whether a genealogical critique of the new philosophy of international law is possible at all, and whether it still

[54] This is the case if the ultimate aim of international law is to protect the human rights of individuals (but not to uphold peace, order, or promote the common good). See Buchanan, *Human Rights*.

[55] Coming up with moral standards for the evaluation of international law is the self-ascribed aim of the philosophy of international law. See (n. 48), 13.

[56] See Buchanan, *Human Rights*.

[57] Thomas Christiano argues the common good can best be promoted by democracy both on a national level and as deliberation among states.

[58] That is the basic value in Jeremy Waldron's account of self-determination.

[59] That is MNS Sellers's conclusion in his review of the Philosophy of International Law. See MNS Sellers, 'The Justice of International Law', 3 *Transnational Legal Theory* (2012), 315.

makes sense to refer to analytical jurisprudence and legal pluralism as two distinct traditions rather than subsuming them as special problems under the umbrella of the new philosophy of international law.

The very point that gets the genealogical critique off the ground is the assertion often found in the new philosophy of international law that it is a new discourse[60] and that, at last, some form of (overlapping) consensus has been reached: 'International law rests on eternal truths that are easily perceived by all good people everywhere, simply because they are human beings.'[61] Both of these claims – genuinely new discoveries and achieving a consensus among philosophers – are, indeed, novelties in the long history of philosophy. The strange point about this assertion is that the principles cited and the institutions referred to are actually quite old. The principles date back to the Age of Enlightenment and the institutions to the end of World War I (establishment of the League of Nations). Because the principles are referred to as eternal truths, we might well ask what people have been doing in the meantime and why it took humanity so long to come up with these principles or institutions. We might also wonder about the nature of the many dissenters throughout the history of philosophy, beginning with Plato: Are they not intelligent enough or are they simply evil people whose company one should shun?

At this point it makes sense to recall the three levels of theorising introduced at the beginning. What is missing in the self-description of the new philosophy of international law is not just an account of the vicissitudes of history, but above all, an explanation for why its principles have been overshadowed, forgotten, or not taken seriously for such a long time. The precariousness of a certain kind of theorising is easy to ignore when its history is simply told as a long narrative of progress, from Cicero on up to the present time.[62]

If we shift our focus to the actual evolution of theoretical discourses and try to explain why some of them are dominant at certain times, a different picture emerges. By looking at the frequency with which the term 'Human Rights' is used in a variety of sources, Samuel

[60] Besson notes that in the entry on 'Philosophy of International Law' in the *Routledge Encyclopaedia of Philosophy* nearly three-quarters of the items in the extensive bibliography were published from 2000 onwards.

[61] Sellers (n. 59), 321.

[62] In the history of ideas Quentin Skinner has most forcefully criticised attempts to write history as a systematic and progressive development. See his 'Meaning and Understanding in the History of Ideas' 8 *History and Theory* (1969), 3–53.

Moyn shows[63] that after a brief increase following World War II, human rights were practically absent in political discourse, in academia and in public discussion. The human rights discourse re-emerged rather unexpectedly in the aftermath of the Helsinki Accords, when East European intellectuals used it as an alternative to the grand ideological narratives of the times (socialist versus capitalist society). The new appeal of human rights was due to their modest character, their modest aspiration and their ecumenical language. However, Moyn also laments that with the rise of the new philosophy of international law since the 1990s, human rights have profoundly changed in character from being modest appeals to becoming comprehensive demands. As a historian, Moyn relies mostly on statistical evidence, but he fails to theorise human rights or to consider their credentials. His account is mainly useful to call our attention to the issue that a sudden increase in the popularity of a philosophical conviction, especially if it is presented as both self-evident and widely shared, actually deserves some theoretical and historical explanation.

However, in one respect, Moyn's mostly descriptive (and at times nostalgic) account can be supported by a theoretic reflection. From Moyn's narrative of the rise and inflation of the human rights discourse, one gets the sense that something is wrong with the current dominance of human rights. Although Moyn fails to specify the basis of his scepticism; is the implication that the values expressed are not worthwhile, not universal, or should they not be expressed in terms of rights? Each of these would be a possible criticism but could also be countered, because all human rights theories offer some account of the universality of human rights, their moral or political foundation, and their limits. Moyn's doubts need not be interpreted as an outright attack against human rights, but can be regarded instead as the expression of concern regarding the logic of the discourse.

From the experience of countries with constitutional rights in place and the means for constitutional review of individual cases, we know that in principle every case and every complaint can be formulated as a human rights case, and that courts could review every political or administrative decision. The limitations on constitutional courts are ultimately self-imposed or due to an implicit struggle for power on the part of different institutions. In any case, the separation of powers or constitutional provisions are not an absolute barrier, since even those legal

[63] Samuel Moyn, *The Last Utopia. Human Rights in History* (Cambridge, MA: The Belknap Press of Harvard University Press, 2010).

provisions may be subject to constitutional review. Thus, a court with jurisdiction over human rights functions like a semi-permeable membrane that stretches over all areas of society. In solidified states with a single rule of recognition in place, the scope of power of constitutional courts has often been discussed, but it is not usually a threat to the stability of the constitutional system. Even in un-solidified states, a coup d'état by a constitutional court is unheard of. However, as there is no single rule of recognition in international law or specifically in human rights law, the discourse on human rights always faces the temptation to extend its range regardless of how its limits are drawn in theory. Thus, extension of the human rights discourse is not due exclusively to an extension of human rights norms or to an overabundance of theories, but has to do instead with the logic of dealing with individual cases from this perspective. Once the language is in place, every struggle or dispute can, in principle, be reformulated as a human rights case.

The argument is only intended to explain the logic behind Moyn's complaint, but it does not support his implicit critique, for one could just as well argue that there is still a need to extend the scope of human rights into more areas, such as the trade law administered by the WTO. However, one aspect of this observation does lead back to the genealogical approach. Given that there is no single, unified rule of recognition in international law and that diverse interests, traditions and values present on a global scale may lead to very diverse interpretations, there is a need to develop an authoritative tradition that would serve as a substitute for a missing political and institutional culture, to allow us to exclude some interpretations as unreasonable and others as not. This argument may help to explain why there is greater consensus in human rights law and philosophy than one might expect if we allowed just anyone on earth to come up with his interpretation of human rights norms. (One way to get a general impression of the plethora of human rights claims would be to examine the large number of individual complaints filed with constitutional courts that are rejected outright. Especially before the German Federal Constitutional Court, every minor administrative decision has more or less been challenged as a violation of human dignity – that is, requiring a higher amount of money allocated for the buying of condoms for people living on social welfare.[64])

[64] This is an example of an actual legal claim rejected by a German administrative court and therefore could have been challenged as a violation of human dignity before the Federal

Another aspect of this argument is relevant for the genealogical perspective we are proposing here. In the case of the previous approaches, analytical jurisprudence and legal pluralism, considering their tradition could appear to be obsolete since a newer and better version of the approach would seem to supersede all earlier ones. Both analytical jurisprudence and legal pluralism might want to claim that the very notion of 'tradition' is not a relevant philosophical concept for them. This would not appear to be the case for the new philosophy of international law with human rights as its core. For this approach, it is of vital importance to establish a tradition and to conceive itself in terms of a tradition. Thus, the notion of tradition, which was invoked from the outside for analytic jurisprudence and legal pluralism, appears from within in the case of the new philosophy of international law. This might appear to represent an advantage, because the tradition is now aware of itself as a tradition, but it also has some repercussions as it might invite the two earlier traditions to launch a comeback.

From the point of view of analytical jurisprudence, developing a tradition as a constitutive part of the theory might be considered the death-knell of the theory. It smacks of an ideology (as Kelsen would say) or might prove (as Raz would say) that it is not, indeed, a general and universal theory but an interpretation of particular practice similar to a constitutional theory of a specific country. Legal pluralism, on the other hand, could apply its insights about the workings of official legal institutions that are not accompanied by a reception on the ground and inquire about the actual functions of human rights law and the human rights discourse. (Who gets to speak, how is speech changed once it is formulated in legal terms, which interests can be represented, what happens with non-represented interests, how do people talk about human rights administration outside academic or NGO settings?[65]) Thus, legal pluralism could apply its anthropological view and take the philosophy of international law as its object of investigation. These two pathways for analytical jurisprudence and legal pluralism to respond to the new philosophy of international law have yet to be explored.

Constitutional Court. See decision of 2 March 1990 by Oberverwaltungsgericht Hamburg, *Neue Juristische Wochenschrift* (1991), 941.

65 These kinds of questions are mostly taken up by anthropologists. See for the case of the European Court of Human Rights: Marie-Bénédict Dembour, *Who Believes in Human Rights? Reflections on the European Convention* (Cambridge: Cambridge University Press, 2006).

They have been mentioned here to show that a genealogical approach does not just rehearse traditions to build up a dialectical progression, but reveals their interactions by letting each theory build upon the dark side of the other. It even deconstructs the idea of a tradition itself as it shows that referring to a tradition is not necessarily a good thing, it can also be seen as a sign of sclerosis.

8.6

The final question is how to characterise the genealogical approach itself. Is it the synthesis of all conceptions above, or maybe not a conception at all but just a taxonomy of discourses? Throughout this essay I have demonstrated that taking the basic philosophical question of theories seriously while reflecting on their actual practice is a way to drive them to their tipping point. Thus the idea is precisely not to assign each theory a specific place in a well ordered universe from some vantage point: here's the place for the analytic question, here for the sociological, and here for philosophical ones. Instead, by taking each tradition in its attempt to be a self-sufficient whole seriously, it was possible to take part in the discussion and show at the same time how questions evolve out of each other. In this respect the genealogical criticism is the heir to Hegel's approach of dealing with previous philosophical positions, without claiming, however, that the traditions necessarily evolve once and for all in time, without providing one overall logic of science that describes the evolution of theories and – unfortunately – without being able to attain 'absolute knowledge' for itself.

One might think it is a cheap argument to distance oneself from Hegel's logic as everybody does so. However, the demarcation shows why a genealogical approach is an on-going practice and not a taxonomy of discourses. Any such taxonomy would have to explain its own superior point of view as Hegel did in his logic. Thus, a taxonomy would have to explain why all other theories should accept its scheme as ultimate arbiter or accept its designation of proper places in a well ordered universe of discourses. On the other hand, undermining basic assumptions by reflection on suppressed alternatives is a practice that can even be applied to the approach itself. In our discussion about the new philosophy of international law, we have seen that even the first question, 'what is law' may lose its unimpeachable role if we translate law as *Recht*.

Beyond its capacity to bring different traditions into dialogue, there are two more advantages of the genealogical approach. First, this approach is especially compatible with transnational law. As the term 'transnational' suggests, the focus in the field of transnational studies is on something that is no longer only or purely national. Thus the focus is on the occurrence of a negation of a tradition. From a historical perspective, one can easily see that law has never been national only but has always existed as a struggle between various traditions (e.g. church law versus secular law) or as a struggle between dominated and suppressed traditions (e.g. Roman law versus local law), and that philosophy took sides in the struggle (e.g. by developing the notion of state sovereignty). From a theoretical perspective, a genealogical approach is sensitive to such struggles and repressions, and traces these processes up to our current philosophical approaches. The second advantage relates to the field of normative theory and can best be introduced by way of an example.

Up to this point, one might have gained the impression that by undermining traditions a genealogical critique is only negative, and cannot be the source of a normative theory of its own. This is probably true if normative theory means giving recommendations to others. It is not true if normative theorising means the practice of becoming self-aware, including awareness of the dangers and pitfalls of theory itself. This can be explained by the example of Nazi law.

It is frequently raised as an example in the debate between positivists and natural law theory. Often the phrasing is whether Nazi law was 'really' law. Although this question is often mentioned in passing, as if it were only one problem among many, one could say that this is *the* decisive question of the post-war debate, for the underlying question is how Western civilisations could so easily fall prey to totalitarian ideologies. Yet legal philosophy has shown remarkably little interest in the actual circumstances of Nazi law or the ways people talked and theorised about the law during this period. Shapiro writes that the question of whether the Nazi regime had proper law may depend on various 'intuitions', but he does not consider that historical scholarship might actually help decide this question.[66] The challenging point when tracing the genealogy of actual legal practice and legal philosophy is that the legal practice and the legal philosophy of the Nazi era were both familiar to us to a remarkable degree, and this makes it difficult to reject them outright or take a superior outside perspective.[67] This can be shown with an

[66] Shapiro (n. 3), 17.

[67] The functioning of the legal system is of course only one aspect, and cannot explain the overall Nazi regime.

example, a typical case drawn from the state-law examination in the Nazi era. Such a case[68] might involve a 'Jewish' tenant whose lease is terminated and who then sues his 'Aryan' landlord. (There were strong tenant protection laws in place even during this time.) If the candidate solved this case by merely politicising in the best Nazi jargon, he would fail. However, a candidate who would solve the case *lege artis* in favour of the Jewish tenant would also fail. The magical way to pass the exam was to show first that one had mastered the 'fit' dimension and then, at the last possible moment, evoke the 'value' (or maybe we should say 'squeeze') dimension and interpret the law according to the 'appropriate' values.[69] Theories about those two dimensions were also developed at this time; and after the war, they were reformulated by merely changing the underlying values. This genealogical reading shows that theories that resemble Ronald Dworkin's theory of interpretation may appear in different guises at different times. This insight is not meant as a normative recommendation but rather as a call for appropriate caution when trying to sort philosophical theories according to political lines or desired outcomes. An 'interpretive' or natural law theory may be used just as effectively to justify inequitable judgments as a strictly positivist adherence to unjust laws. In the end, personal responsibility or guilt on the part of legal officials may depend very much on the ways they dealt with the specific circumstances. In this way, genealogical studies may help to raise awareness of different traditions, the importance of local circumstances and the danger of theory itself.

This kind of reflection is the best a genealogical approach can do. It draws upon insights from different approaches without concentrating on a single question (what is law), a single methodology (empirical research) or a single aim (respect for human rights). Instead, it observes the various contexts and forms in which law is practiced and reflected.

[68] It is not a real but a simplified fictitious case to explain the way the whole legal system worked. A full historical study would have to go into the details of the two exams, the different legal topics dealt in them, and detect the ideological agenda in slight changes of the wordings. For a more detailed account along these lines see Louis Pahlow, 'Ich verüble dem Verf. weniger einzelne juristische Fehler als das Versagen des Rechtsgefühls. Juristische Staatsprüfungen im Dritten Reich (1934-1945)' in Thomas Gutmann et al. (eds.), *Von den Leges Barbarorum bis zum ius barbarum des Nationalsozialismus. Festschrift für Hermann Nehlsen zum 70. Geburtstag* (Berlin: Böhlau, 2008), 399–420.

[69] The details of the sweeping transformation of the legal system are of course more complex. For the case of private law, Bernd Rüthers has shown the continuities in his classical study. *Die unbegrenzte Auslegung: zum Wandel der Privatrechtsordnung im Nationalsozialismus*, 7th ed. (Mohr Siebeck, 2012).

The benefit of opening up our perspective and allowing others to read us may be profoundly disturbing when we have to face our own enemies from the past. However, I think we have to be willing to confront this danger, as it subsists in our collective subconsciousness. The alternative would be to rely on Dolores Umbridge as our teacher for defending against the dark arts.

9

Two Conceptions of Pluralist Jurisprudence

STEFAN SCIARAFFA

As understood here, pluralist jurisprudence is the study of the legal principles and doctrines that govern disputes about the division of authoritative labour between legal systems. So construed, pluralist jurisprudence speaks to a wide range of issues, including the existence and scope of the legal authority that international customs and international legal institutions, such as the European Court of Human Rights, the WTO, the UN Security Council, have over state actors. Here, I explicate and contrast two conceptions of pluralist jurisprudence. The first is a positivist conception that distinguishes between legal and political authority, thereby drawing a clear line between pluralist jurisprudence and pluralist political philosophy. The second is a non-positivist conception that reduces questions about the legal authority of international institutions and customs to questions about whether such institutions and customs possess a distinctive form of authority – namely, political authority as characterised by the generic collectivist conception explicated in this chapter.

The core objective of this paper is to clarify what I take to be the most formidable and well-supported non-positivist and positivist conceptions of pluralist jurisprudence and to highlight three key points of contrast. First, whereas the non-positivist conception incorporates deliberations about the legitimacy and scope of political authority into legal reasoning, the positivist conception excludes such considerations. Thus, these two conceptions provide officials with very different frames for their legal reasoning about rival claims to legal authority, and accordingly, these conceptions support significantly different legal conclusions. Second, the differences between these conceptions of pluralist jurisprudence are in large part driven by a more fundamental disagreement about the nature of political community and political authority. Third, given this fundamental disagreement, these two conceptions of pluralist jurisprudence do not merely entail different approaches to legal reasoning about the existence and scope of legal authorities; they also entail different frames for legal officials' politico-moral reasoning about the legitimacy and scope of political authority. This paper's argument proceeds in a number of steps.

In Sections 9.1 and 9.2, I distinguish positivist and authority-based non-positivist pluralist jurisprudence by way of reference to an oft-noted puzzle that bedevils the doctrine of international customary law. In Section 9.3, I explicate Joseph Raz's influential authority-based defence of legal positivism and critique of non-positivism. I do so because this argument identifies a compelling account of authority and political community that supports positivist pluralist jurisprudence and impugns the authority-based non-positivist approach. In Section 9.4, I sketch an alternative to Raz's account of political authority and community that lends support to a refined version of the authority-based non-positivist theory discussed in Section 9.2.

In Section 9.5, I apply the positivist conception of pluralist jurisprudence and the refined authority-based non-positivist conception to the current debate about the existence and scope of the legal authority of the European Court of Human Rights over the British legal community. This discussion further illuminates the contrast between non-positivist and positivist pluralist legal reasoning, and it brings to the fore the key difference between authority-based non-positivist and Razian positivist politico-moral reasoning about the existence and scope of political authority.

Note that I do not seek to adjudicate here between the authority-based non-positivist and positivist conceptions of pluralist jurisprudence or between the rival conceptions of political authority and community that support these respective jurisprudential views. However, I do hope to suggest that this jurisprudential debate might very well turn on a more fundamental debate within political philosophy. In this same vein, I also hope to suggest that the jurisprudential debate between non-positivists and positivists is important (among other reasons) because it is inextricably bound to a larger debate about the nature of political authority and political community.

9.1 Contemporary Legal Positivism and Customary International Law

According to the Statute of the International Court of Justice (ICJ) and the subsequent jurisprudence of the court created by this statute, a norm has legal force as customary international law only if it meets two conditions. First, the relevant actors (states and their officials) must conform to it as a matter of practice. Second, such practice must be accompanied by an *opinio juris*, or, in other words, the practice-participants' 'belief that the practice is rendered obligatory by the existence of a rule of law requiring it.'[1]

For example, in the well-known *North Sea Cases*, the ICJ considered the question of whether a particular standard for apportioning shared continental shelf among abutting states, the equidistance principle, was legally binding as a matter of customary international law. In support of the conclusion that the equidistance principle was not a legally binding custom, the court cited (among other considerations) the lack of evidence that states followed the equidistance principle in the belief that they were 'legally compelled' to do so.

John Tasioulas characterises an oft-noted puzzle about the doctrine of customary international law (CIL) in terms of a transparency requirement that he describes as follows:

> Political legitimacy demands that exercises of political power be publicly assessable in terms of standards that appropriately constrain political decision-making. A corollary of their being assessable in this way is a transparency requirement, according to which exercises of political power must be sincerely and accurately presented and defended by their agents as the acts that they are.[2]

As Tasioulas observes, if the traditional formulation of the necessary conditions of CIL were correct, then all legally binding customs would necessarily bear the taint of an original violation of the transparency requirement.

To help see Tasioulas's point, consider first that, contra the finding of the *North Sea* court, states could have followed the equidistance principle described above with the requisite belief that this principle was legally binding. Now, consider the very first instances of states acting with this requisite *opinio juris* – that is, the belief that the equidistance principle is a legally binding custom. By definition, prior to such first-recognition,

1 *Case Concerning Military and Paramilitary Activities in and Against Nicaragua (Nicaragua v. United States of America (Merits)* [1986] ICJ Rep 14, pp. 108–09 at paras. 188–90. See also *North Sea Continental Shelf Case (Federal Republic of Germany v. Denmark and v. Netherlands)* [1969] ICJ Rep 3, paras. 76–77.

2 John Tasioulas, 'Customary International Law and the Quest for Global Justice', in Amanda Perreau Saussine and James Bernard Murphy (eds.), *The Nature of Customary Law* (Cambridge: Cambridge University Press, 2007), pp. 307–35 at p. 321.

there could be no established practice among states of conforming to the equidistance principle with the requisite *opinio juris*. Thus, per the traditional formulation of CIL, those first recognitions must have been mistaken. This point generalises. The traditional formulation of CIL implies that in order for any custom to become a legally binding norm of international law, legal officials must falsely proclaim its legal bindingness.

In order to avoid saddling the practice of CIL with unavoidable transparency requirement violations, Tasioulas and other theorists offer alternatives to the just described traditional formulation of CIL. Although differing in particular detail, these theorists employ the same basic strategy of distinguishing two aspects of CIL.[3] The first prong is the traditional formulation described earlier in this chapter. The second adds that some customary international practices are legally binding, irrespective of whether state-actors participate in those practices in the belief that they are law. So construed, CIL does not imply that first-recognisers of customary laws necessarily violate Tasioulas's transparency principle, for the second prong of CIL might license the first-recognition of a custom's legality.

Unlike Tasioulas, I am not concerned here with the implications that the traditional formulation of CIL has for the legitimacy of the practice of CIL. Rather, I rehearse Tasioulas's concerns as a preface to my argument that the contemporary legal positivist must reject dual-pronged formulations of CIL of the sort that Tasioulas proposes in favour of the traditional doctrine. Hence, the positivist must accept that legal officials' first recognition of the legal validity of any international custom is necessarily false. Moreover, as I further argue, the commitment to the traditional formulation of CIL is emblematic of a broader implication of legal positivism. Namely, legal officials' first recognition of any fundamental source of law is necessarily false.

Most contemporary legal positivists accept the core tenets of Hartian legal positivism, particularly his architectonic idea of the rule of recognition.[4] According to Hart, the keystone of any legal system is a

[3] See Tasioulas (n. 2), p. 323; and David Lefkowitz, '(Dis)Solving the Chronological Paradox in Customary International Law: A Hartian Approach' (2008) 21 *The Canadian Journal of Law and Jurisprudence*, 128–48.

[4] See Stefan Sciaraffa, 'The Questionable Presupposition Underlying Hartian Accounts of Legal Facts' (2016) 11 *Philosophy Compass*, 81–90 for a discussion of this reading of Hart and a survey of contemporary positivists who offer theories that roughly accord with Hart's positivist theory.

rule of recognition comprising criteria of validity that are, as a matter of social fact, accepted in common by the officials of that system.[5] Per the standard reading of Hart's theory, the legally valid norms of any legal system are those and only those norms recognised by the criteria of validity that the system's officials accept in common. In keeping with this account, one might hold that the British rule of recognition includes the criterion that the enactments of the Queen in Parliament are legally valid, for British legal officials accept this criterion in common.

We are now in a position to see why the positivist must reject the dual-pronged formulation of CIL in favour of the traditional account. As we have seen above, there is a great deal of evidence (including section 38 of the Statue of International Justice and subsequent case law) for the claim that the traditional prong of the CIL is accepted in common by the officials of the international legal system. However, as we have also seen, this traditional prong cannot warrant the first-recognition of any custom. Moreover, there is little evidence that the officials of the international legal system accept in common any other criterion that would warrant the first recognition of the legality of a custom. That is, there is no evidence of a criterion of validity accepted in common by international officials that would warrant the first recognition of the validity of any international custom.

This implication of legal positivism is emblematic of a larger category of similar implications. To help see this point, consider again that for the positivist, any legal system's criteria of validity are standards that the system's officials accept in common. Now, distinguish further between fundamental and derivative criteria of validity. Fundamental criteria of validity are strictly customary, whereas derivative criteria are specified by legal sources that the fundamental customary criteria specify. For example, we might imagine that the criterion 'the enactments of the Queen-in-Parliament are law' is a fundamental criterion, whereas the parliamentary enactment authorising executive agencies to establish certain legally binding rules and regulations ground a derivative criterion that recognises the validity of those rules and regulations.

As we have seen, from the positivist perspective, international legal officials must make false claims about the validity of customs at the outset of the customary practice that establishes their validity. Similarly, at the outset of any customary practice that constitutes a fundamental criterion of validity of a legal system, legal officials must make and act on

[5] H. L. A. Hart, *The Concept of Law*, 2nd ed. (Oxford: Oxford University Press, 1994), pp. 94–99, 100–10.

the basis of false claims about the classes of norms that are legally valid for their system. For example, as a matter of conceptual necessity, the first recognisers of the validity of the enactments of the Queen-in-Parliament could not have appealed to a previous official practice of recognising the validity of such norms to justify their recognition of the validity of parliamentary enactments. Thus, unless such first-recognisers could appeal to a more fundamental law, say, a royal decree or constitutional agreement between monarch and subjects establishing the validity of parliamentary enactments, the recognition of the validity of those enactments' validity could not be warranted in positivist terms.

9.2 Authority-Based Legal Non-Positivism and Novel Sources of Law

I have just argued that legal positivism implies that legal officials must systematically make false claims about the law in order to establish novel and fundamental sources of legally binding norms. By contrast, an authority-based variant of non-positivism that I sketch here readily accommodates the first-recognition of the legality of international customs and, more generally, it readily accommodates the recognition of novel and fundamental legal sources. Moreover, as I also argue, this non-positivist theory also frames the truth-conditions of such claims.

9.2.1 Authority-Based Legal Non-Positivism

John Gardner formulates his highly influential recapitulation of the defining tenet of legal positivism is as follows:

> In any legal system, whether a given norm is legally valid, and hence whether it forms part of the law of that system, depends on its sources, not its merits (where its merits, in the relevant sense, include the merits of its sources).[6]

Though pitched at a higher level of abstraction, this formulation is consistent with the Hartian legal positivist theory described earlier. That is, in keeping with Gardner's thesis, Hart's theory holds that at the most basic level, the legality of any norm depends neither on the norm's merits nor on the merits of its source.[7] Rather, for Hart, a norm's legal validity

[6] John Gardner, 'Legal Positivism: 5 ½ Myths' (2001) 46 *American Journal of Jurisprudence*, 199–227 at 201.

[7] Here I set aside the internecine dispute between exclusive and inclusive legal positivism.

fundamentally depends on its being recognised by criteria of validity that the relevant system's officials accept in common.

In contrast to Gardner's and the Hartian formulations of legal positivism, the authority-based variant of legal non-positivism holds that for any legal system, whether a norm is legally valid fundamentally depends on the merit of its sources. More specifically, it holds that a necessary condition of any norm's legal validity is the political authority of its source.

A felicitous feature of authority-based non-positivism is that it accommodates the commonplace distinction between a norm's merits and its legality, for, as is commonly acknowledged, a defining feature of any political authority is that its directives can be morally binding on its subjects despite such directives' significant moral inadequacies. To clarify this defining feature, H. L. A. Hart coined the term 'content-independence' to distinguish a subject's ordinary reasons to perform an action, say its justice or prudential concern, from the reasons of the following form: A intends for the subject to perform the action.[8]

Put in Hart's terms, authority-based non-positivism holds that all legally valid norms are substantial moral content-independent reasons. The key point for present purposes is that the considerations of political morality that ground a norm's substantial moral content-independent force are distinct from the norm's ordinary moral merits. For example, from the authority-based non-positivist perspective, considerations such as the values of democratic governance might ground the right of a majority to embody its will in law and hence, the content-independent force of the democratic assembly's enactments. Thus, the authority-based non-positivist is able to distinguish the authority-grounding merit (e.g. democratic pedigree) of a norm's source and, hence, the norm's legality from the norm's ordinary moral merits (e.g. its prudence or justice).

9.2.2 Authority-Based Non-Positivism and Customary International Law

Whereas legal positivism implies that the first recognition of the legality of any international custom must be false, authority-based non-positivism allows that such first-recognitions would be true if the recognised

[8] See H. L. A Hart, *Essays on Bentham* (Oxford: Oxford University Press, 1982), pp. 254–55; and Stefan Sciaraffa, 'On Content-Independent Reasons' (2009) 28 *Law and Philosophy*, 233–60.

customary norms are politically authoritative. In a slightly different way, authority-based non-positivism can also accommodate the traditional formulation of CIL. On this authority-based non-positivist reading, the traditional formulation of CIL is a general recognition of the political authority of any international customary practice that comprises norms that state actors have followed in the belief that they are legally valid. Crucially, the authority-based non-positivist reading of CIL does not preclude the possibility that some customary practices might have political authority, and hence, be a source of legally valid norms irrespective of whether they satisfy the *opinio juris* requirement.

A tempting objection to the authority-based non-positivist reading of CIL is that, as a matter of conceptual necessity, customary practices cannot be the intentions of any agent, and hence, they can neither be content-independent reasons nor authoritative directives. Rather than refuting the non-positivist reading of CIL, this objection calls for a more careful statement of the notion of intention that informs the idea of a content-independent reason. Namely, it is conceptually coherent to present a maxim or standard of behaviour as some agent's intention, even if there is no natural agent with that intention. In such cases, we construct an intention and the agent that bears it. For example, we might present democratically enacted legislation as the will or intention of the people. Similarly, we might hold that a community's customary practice embodies the community's intention concerning how its members ought to act.

Rather than denying the conceptual coherence of the non-positivist's claims about the authority of customs, a second objection holds that, as matters of first-order normative argument, claims about the content-independent force of a community's customs could rarely if ever by justified. To help see that this challenge can be readily met, consider first that a number of authors argue that the value of democratic governance grounds the content-independent force of democratically enacted legislation.[9] Similarly, as can be seen in the *North Sea* case, other values are plausible grounds of the content-independent force of customary practices.

As discussed earlier, the *North Sea* case features a disagreement about the appropriate formula for apportioning a stretch of continental sea shelf between a number of state-actors. Like many other disagreements

[9] See e.g., David Lefkowitz, 'A Contractualist Defense of Democratic Authority' (2005) 18 *Ratio Juris*, 346–64; and Thomas Christiano, *The Constitution of Equality* (Oxford: Oxford University Press, 2008).

about interpersonal or interstate rights and duties, this dispute has the potential to be extremely divisive and destructive. Hence, the public settlement of this dispute would be an important benefit for the international community. Note also that the realisation of any such public settlement requires a coordinated effort – namely, the convergent acceptance and observation of the terms of the public settlement by the community of state actors.

For present purposes, the key point is that insofar as a community has achieved a morally important public settlement by way of an established customary practice, and there is no alternative better feasible modality (perhaps, a representative legislative institution or a fair negotiation among the community's members) for specifying and securing the terms of that settlement, each member of the community has a reason to conform to the terms of the incipient customary settlement. The reason is that by conforming to its terms as a customary settlement, each member of the community would not only support the incipient settlement and its attendant benefits; it would also sustain the community's best feasible modality (presumably in this case, settlement by way of customary practice) for achieving and sustaining the hard won benefits of the public settlement. More pointedly, by failing to conform to the customary practice, any member of the community would disrupt that hard won settlement and the community's best feasible modality for sustaining it.

In circumstances such as those just described, a customary practice would be a substantial moral content-independent reason for each member of the relevant community, for by conforming to the customary practice, each member would thereby support and avoid disrupting the community's best feasible modality for sustaining a hard won morally important public settlement. In summary, not only would it be conceptually coherent to claim that a customary practice is a content-independent reason; such a claim might be plausible as a matter of political morality. In such circumstances, the constructed agential source of the relevant intention (e.g. the community as a whole) would satisfy a key necessary condition of political authority.

9.2.3 Authority-Based Non-Positivism and Novel Sources of Law

As I have just argued, authority-based non-positivism not only allows for the possibility that the first recognition of the validity of an international custom could be warranted; it also provides guidance as to the truth conditions of such first recognitions. From this perspective, whether a first recognition is warranted turns on the presence of considerations of political morality that would ground the substantial moral content-independent force of the norm that the custom embodies. This point generalises, for authority-based non-positivism allows for the possibility that the recognition of any novel source of law could be warranted by dint of the source's political authority. Thus, from the perspective of authority-based non-positivism, the legal validity of a norm does not fundamentally depend on whether the relevant legal system's officials accept in common some criterion of validity that recognises the norm. Rather, it fundamentally depends on the merit (i.e. the political authority) of its source.

That said, it should be noted that a source might have political authority by dint of being accepted in common by legal officials as a source of their legal system's legally valid norms. Thus, for the authority-based non-positivist, a proximate (but not fundamental) ground of a norm's legality could be that the norm belongs to a class of norms that are recognised by a criterion of validity that the relevant system's legal officials accept in common. To help see this point, recall the non-positivist claim that an international custom might be legally binding by dint of being a hard won morally important public settlement for the international community. Similarly, legal officials' common acceptance of a criterion of validity might be a hard-won, morally important public settlement for their political community. If so, that commonly accepted criterion might very well be authoritative for that political community and, hence a legally valid norm of that community's legal system that, in turn, validates the class of norms it designates as legally valid.

9.3 The Positivist's Rejoinder

In a number of places, Raz offers variations of his well-known authority-based defence of legal positivism and criticism of legal non-positivism.[10] These arguments are rich and complex, and Raz's terminology and points of emphasis vary somewhat in each statement of the argument. Here, I reconstruct this argument, and I explicate its promise to provide a compelling reason to reject authority-based non-positivism in favour of positivism.

[10] See Joseph Raz, *The Authority of Law* (Oxford: Oxford University Press, 1979); 'Authority, Law and Morality', in *Ethics in the Public Domain* (Oxford: Oxford University Press, 1994), pp. 194–221; and *Between Authority and Intepretation* (Oxford: Oxford University Press, 2009).

In the following passage, Raz draws the following connection between law and authority.

> The claims that the law makes for itself are evident from the language it adopts and from the opinions expressed by its spokesmen, i.e. by the institutions of the law. The law's claim to authority is manifested by the fact that legal institutions are officially designated as 'authorities', by the fact that they regard themselves as having the right to impose obligations on their subjects, by their claims that their subjects owe them allegiance, and that their subjects ought to obey the law as it requires to be obeyed.[11]

In short, Raz argues that the law claims authority. This thesis is the first premise of his authority-based defence of legal positivism.

At first blush, this foundational premise seems to rest on the implausible presupposition that the law is an agent capable of making claims. However, as Raz notes in the cited passage, the law's claims are made on its behalf by the institutional spokespersons, legal officials, who designate legal institutions as authorities, regard themselves as having the right to impose obligations on their subjects, claim their subjects' allegiance, and claim that their subjects ought to obey the law. Thus, for Raz, the premise that the law claims authority is a pithy formulation of the claim that legal officials claim authority for legal institutions and the directives that they issue.

Raz's service-conception of authority is the second premise of his authority-based defence of legal positivism.[12] This conception has two components. The first is a claim about the structure of relationships of authority. According to this claim, A has authority over B only if A's directives are both substantial moral content-independent reasons for B and reasons for B not to act for (at least) some of her reasons not to act as B directs. As Razian theorists often put this same point, for A to have authority over B, A's directives must exclude and replace at least some of B's reasons for not acting as A directs. The second component holds that the main justifying rationale of relationships of authority is the authority's ability to mediate between subjects and their reasons. That is, the main reason that any subject would have to accept another's authority over her is that she would do better with respect to (at least) some of her reasons by trying to follow the authority's directives (i.e. allowing them to exclude and replace those reasons) rather than trying to follow those reasons directly.[13]

[11] Raz, 'Authority, Law and Morality' (n. 10), pp. 215–16.

[12] See Raz, 'Authority, Law and Morality' (n. 10).

[13] See e.g., Raz, *The Morality of Freedom* (Oxford: Oxford University Press, 1986), p. 53.

With these first two premises in place, the thrust of Raz's defence of legal positivism comes into view. Namely, the rationale of the law is to enable its subjects to better conform to some of their reasons by following the law rather than trying to follow those reasons directly. Moreover, this rationale would be defeated if 'to establish the content of the law [the law's subjects] would have to deliberate the very considerations the law exists to pre-empt.'[14] Thus, it would be incoherent to regard legal norms as authoritative, and hence, as performing a mediating service with respect to certain reasons, while at the same time holding that legal norms must be identified by deliberating about the requirements of the reasons (e.g. the moral merits) that they serve.

Although these two premises bring the thrust of Raz's defence into view, they do not amount to a full defence of legal positivism, for as Raz acknowledges, authoritative norms need not exclude all of their subjects' reasons for not acting as directed. Thus, premises one and two alone would not preclude a version of non-positivism that tethered legal validity to the satisfaction of moral considerations not excluded or served by the law's authority. Thus, Raz's full defence of legal positivism requires two more premises.

The argument's third premise further characterises law's function as the authoritative resolution of its subjects' disputes. Raz discusses this function in a number of passages, including the following:

> This is the sense in which the laying down of law resolves the dispute about what people have to do or to avoid. The dispute is not resolved if that means reaching an agreement on the issue originally debated, namely about what is (the law apart) best or reasonable to do. The law resolves the dispute by pre-empting it.[15]

For Raz, to resolve a dispute by pre-empting it is to settle it authoritatively or, in other words, by excluding all the disputing parties' reasons for not acting in accordance with the authority's directives that resolve the dispute and replacing those reasons with the directive. Thus, Raz's third premise holds that legal officials regard their system's legally valid norms as second-order reasons (i.e. exclusionary reasons) that exclude any reason that each member of the relevant political community has for not conforming to those norms.

[14] See Raz, *Between Authority and Interpretation* (n. 10), p. 114.

[15] Raz, *Between Authority and Interpretation* (n. 10), p. 110. See also Raz, *Ethics in the Public Domain* (n. 10), p. 52.

Raz recognises that even with the addition of this third premise, his argument does not yet preclude an authority-based variant of non-positivism. As he puts it:

> The argument allows for the possibility that the identity of the authority, and the scope of its power, are determined by moral considerations: after all they are matters which depend on moral considerations.[16]

To see Raz's point, consider that if the function of law were merely to provide its subjects with the authoritative resolution of certain first-order disputes (e.g., disputes about the community's schedule of property rights or duties and benefits relating to social insurance schemes), it would not be law's function to settle who has the authority to provide the authoritative resolution of such first-order disputes. Thus, on this account, the legally valid norms would not be meant to settle the community's disputes about authority, and hence, an authority-based non-positivist could coherently claim that the legal validity of any norm depends on whether, as a matter of political morality, the norm's source has the authority to resolve the relevant political community's first order disputes.

To complete his defence of legal positivism, Raz introduces the following fourth premise:

> As I have argued elsewhere, the law is a second order co-ordinating structure. It provides not only the solution to problems of social co-ordination, but also the solution to the question when is a question a co-ordination question, and who has the public authority to solve it.[17]

Thus, Raz asserts that law's function is to provide authoritative resolutions of its subjects' first-order disputes as well as their disputes about who has the authority to implement authoritative resolutions of their disputes.

In summary, Raz argues that norms identified by way of reasoning about the political authority of such norms' sources could not, as matter of conceptual possibility, be law, for norms so identified could not perform the defining legal function of authoritatively settling their subjects' disputes about who has authority to settle their first-order disputes. Thus, Raz provides a principled reason for accepting legal positivism and rejecting non-positivism, including the authority-based variant. Namely, positivism coheres with this defining function of law, whereas non-positivism does not.

[16] Raz, *Between Authority and Interpretation* (n. 10), p. 115. [17] Ibid.

9.4 An Alternative Conception of Political Authority

As the immediately foregoing discussion makes clear, Raz's defence of legal positivism rests heavily on his characterisation of law's authoritative nature. Here, I accept Raz's thesis that the law of any community claims to authoritatively resolve the community's first-order disputes and its second-order disputes about who has the authority to resolve first-order disputes. However, I sketch an alternative to Raz's conception of law's claims to authority that readily coheres with authority-based non-positivism. To help see this alternative, consider the following passage from Raz:

> In particular, political communities are societies which decide how their own members should conduct themselves. This means that regarding political communities we recognize a distinction between standards of conduct which express the decision of the community regarding the way people should behave, the entitlements they have, etc. and views about these matters, however sound and however popular, which do not have the imprimatur of the community. By and large the law represents those standards which are considered in that community to be binding as exercising the decisions of the community.[18]

Here, Raz describes laws as 'standards of conduct which express the decision of the community regarding the way people should behave, the entitlements they have', and so on. Raz's account of law's authoritative nature demarcates between standards that are regarded as a community's decisions and those that are regarded as the decisions of individuals or smaller subgroups within the community. On this view, a standard is a community decision only if agents sufficiently powerful to enforce the community's conformity to the standard (e.g. legal officials) regard the standard as a substantial moral content-independent reason that excludes and replaces the reasons that each individual community member has for not conforming to the standard, and, accordingly, those agents enforce the standard.

Note further that in the just cited passage, Raz links the ideas of political community and community decisions. On Raz's account, a group is a political community only if it is effectively governed by a set of standards that are regarded both as reasons for each and every community member to act as directed by the standards and as reasons for each community member to exclude and replace all her reasons for

[18] Raz, *Between Authority and Interpretation* (n. 10), pp. 101–02.

not conforming to those standards. In other words, on this account a group is a political community only insofar as some set of standards are regarded as that community's decisions and, for that reason, effectively enforced. Moreover, Raz holds that an institution, custom or person has the authority that law claims only insofar as it directives actually are the substantial moral content-independent and exclusionary reasons that they are regarded to be. Thus, Raz links the idea of community decisions and political community to political authority, for political authority and the authority that law claims are one and the same.

The generic collectivist conception of political authority similarly links the ideas of community decisions, political community, and political authority (the authority that law claims). Like the Razian conception, this alternative holds that a person, custom, or institution has political authority over a community only if its directives are reasons of the sort that constitute that community's decisions. However, this alternative conception's account of the kind of reasons that constitute a community's decisions differs markedly from the Razian conception's account.

Per the Razian account, a directive is regarded as a community decision if and only if it is regarded as a moral content-independent reason for each community member to act as directed and as a reason that defeats each community member's reasons for not acting as directed by excluding and replacing those countervailing reasons. By contrast, per the alternative generic collectivist conception, a directive is regarded as a community decision if and only if it is regarded as a moral content-independent reason for each community member to act as directed and as a reason that generically defeats (as opposed to defeating specifically by way of excluding and replacing) each community member's countervailing reasons. Accordingly, we can formulate the alternative to the Razian conception of political authority as follows:

> **The Generic Collectivist Conception of Political Authority**: A has political authority over group G only if there is a non-empty set of directives such that should A issue any of them, for each member of G the directive would be a substantial moral content-independent reason to act as directed that has sufficient normative force to defeat all countervailing considerations in a broad range of circumstances and, hence, to require conformity in those circumstances.[19]

[19] I have characterised both the Razian and generic collectivist conceptions of political authority as rival statements of the necessary features of political authority. I leave open

For present purposes, the key point is that the generic collectivist account allows whereas the Razian account denies that a directive might authoritatively settle a community's disputes (and hence, be a law of that community) by dint of outweighing rather than excluding and replacing each community members' reasons (including considerations of political morality that pertain to the authority of the directives source) for not conforming to the directive. Concomitant to this difference, the Razian conception implies that by dint of regarding a directive as politically authoritative, a legal official is committed to following that directive and recognising its legal validity even if she concludes that considerations of political morality require her non-conformity, whereas this implication does not follow from the alternative collectivist conception. Thus, the generic collectivist account (unlike the Razian account) imputes no failure of coherence to the legal official who both regards her system's laws as politically authoritative and who recognises and follows as law only those norms that she concludes are politically authoritative on the basis of her politico-moral deliberations. In summary, the generic collectivist account supports authority-based non-positivist legal theory whereas the Razian account provides a basis for rejecting non-positivism.

9.5 Two Conceptions of Law and Pluralist Jurisprudence Illustrated

With the refined account of authority-based non-positivism in hand, it is possible to further clarify the distinction between the non-positivist and positivist conceptions of pluralist jurisprudence. Once again, I illustrate this distinction by way of an example drawn from the practice of pluralist jurisprudence. Specifically, I contrast the non-positivist and positivist approaches to the presently unsettled question regarding the existence and scope of the legal authority that the European Court of Human Rights has over British courts and the wider British political community. I also use this example to show that the non-positivist and positivist conceptions of pluralist jurisprudence do not merely entail different approaches to legal reasoning about the existence and scope of legal authorities; they also entail different frames for politico-moral reasoning about the legitimacy and scope of political authority.

the possibility that one of these conceptions might specify sufficient and necessary features of authority.

9.5.1 *The ECtHR and British Courts*

The European Court of Human Right (ECtHR) is a creature of a multilateral treaty, the European Convention on Human Rights (ECHR). One of the functions of the ECtHR is to adjudicate petitions from those who claim that their ECHR-rights have been violated by state signatories to the ECHR. The United Kingdom is a signatory member of this convention. Hence, it has undertaken a legally binding obligation to conform to the ECHR's terms. To this end, the UK-enacted the Human Rights Act 1998 (HRA).

The HRA prohibits British officials from violating the rights enumerated in the ECHR unless bound by a statutory duty that requires them to do so. It also vests British courts with the power and duty to interpret British legislation in a way that accords with the ECHR if possible. Also, Section 2 of the HRA requires British courts to 'take account' of the ECtHR's decisions. In light of Section 2 and other considerations, a key unsettled question queries the extent to which the decisions of the ECtHR are legally binding for British courts.

One answer to this question is embodied by the now embattled *Ullah* principle. In the eponymous 2004 case, the House of Lords held that British courts 'should, in the absence of some special circumstances, follow any clear and constant jurisprudence of the Strasbourg court'.[20] Recently, British courts have questioned the *Ullah* principle, holding that ECtHR precedents need not be followed in a variety of situations. To name just one, British courts have held that any ECtHR decision that is inconsistent with some fundamental substantive or procedural aspect of British law need not be followed.[21] In summary, at the moment, there is no settled doctrine specifying the scope of the ECtHR's legal authority over British courts.

9.5.2 *Authority-Based Legal Non-Positivism and the ECtHR's Legal Authority*

For the authority-based non-positivist, a key question is whether the ECtHR's rulings are substantial moral content-independent reasons for British courts and other members of the British political community that would defeat all countervailing considerations (e.g. the countervailing

[20] *R (Ullah) v. Special Adjudicator* [2004] 2 AC 323; [2004] UKHL 26.

[21] See e.g., Manchester City Council v Pinnock, [2010] 3 WLR 1441; [2010] UKSC 45.

directives of the British apex courts and ordinary considerations of political morality such as the injustice or inefficiency that the ECtHR's rulings might embody) across a broad range of circumstances. If so, per this non-positivist theory, this would be because the ECtHR has both political authority and legal authority over the British courts and those other members.

Earlier I discussed the possibility that a customary practice or the enactments of a democratic legislature would be substantial moral content-independent reasons insofar as these institutions were the relevant political community's best modality for publicly settling potentially divisive and destructive disputes. In a similar vein, the authority-based non-positivist might argue that insofar as the ECtHR is the best modality for the British political community and courts to settle their disputes about the requirements of the ECHR, then the ECtHR would have collectivist political and legal authority over that public. That is, they would be moral content-independent reasons for British courts and the other members of the British political community that would be sufficiently weighty to defeat the countervailing directives of the British apex courts and ordinary considerations of political morality such as the injustice or inefficiency that the ECtHR's rulings might embody.

In support of the ECtHR's legal and political authority to settle such disputes, an authority-based non-positivist jurist might cite the importance of achieving a common public settlement of these disputes for all state signatories to the Convention and note that the ECtHR is the only existing institution capable of doing so. To put this same idea in slightly different terms, this non-positivist jurist might cite the importance of forging a unified European political community with respect to these issues.

To name just one countervailing consideration, an authority-based non-positivist jurist arguing against the ECtHR's legal and political authority could argue that British courts have a firmer grasp of the distinctive way that the British legal system protects the right of the British community. This consideration could be marshalled wholesale against the ECtHR's claim to moral and legal authority. Alternatively, in keeping with some recent opinions of British courts, it might be offered as a reason to limit the ECtHR's jurisdiction to issues that do not concern fundamental aspects of British substantive and procedural law.[22] So, for example, a jurist might

[22] See id.

argue that the importance of forging a pan-European human rights settlement supports the ECtHR's authority, but the British Court's understanding of how the British system protects those rights requires limiting the ECtHR's authority to cases that do not concern these particular features of the British system. In summary, for the authority-based non-positivist, the foregoing line of argument would support either a denial of the ECtHR's political and legal authority vis-à-vis British courts, or a key limitation on the scope of its authority.

Note also that authority-based non-positivist plural jurisprudence countenances a denial of the ECtHR's political and legal authority accompanied by a recognition of its quasi-legal authority. To see this point, consider that there might be no clearly defined practical domain in which the ECtHR's directives are content-independent reasons that would defeat the countervailing directives of British courts. Hence, there might be no clearly defined domain in which the ECtHR has political and legal authority over British courts. However, it might also be that the best modality for authoritatively settling the contours of the British public's civil and political rights (e.g. the modality that reflects the appropriate balance of values such as deliberative competence and the importance of forging a common European political community) is an institutional framework in which British courts and ECtHR engage in a kind of dialogue.[23]

For example, a modality of dispute resolution in which the ECtHR and British courts reciprocally acknowledged the content-independent force of one another's directives might do better with respect to the values of deliberative competence and forging a European identity described earlier than would a modality of resolving disputes by way of the plenary or circumscribed legal authority of the ECtHR discussed previously. If so, the ECtHR would not be authoritative vis-à-vis British courts; however, it would have a kind of quasi-authority, for the scope of the British courts' moral and legal authority with respect to the British political community would turn on their giving due recognition to the content-independent force of the ECtHR's rulings in their deliberative procedures.

[23] See id. See also Nicole Roughan, *Authorities: Conflicts, Cooperation and Transnational Legal Theory* (Oxford: Oxford University Press, 2013) for a careful discussion of the various ways that political authority over a single public might be shared by numerous political institutions.

9.5.3 *Positivism and Reasoning about the ECtHR's Legal Authority*

As a matter of positivist pluralist jurisprudential theory, the criterion of legal validity that British officials accept in common could directly refer to the rulings of the ECtHR court and, hence, ground its legal authority directly. However, this would be an implausible characterisation of current British legal practice. With greater empirical plausibly, the positivist might claim that British officials accept in common the validity of certain norms that in turn validate the legal authority of the ECtHR's authority or at least frame the general parameters of its scope. For example, a positivist might cite the British Parliament's enactment of the 1998 Human Rights Act, particularly Section 2 that requires British courts to take the ECtHR's jurisprudence into account, and the fact that the HRA was enacted pursuant to the UK's obligations under the ECHR. On this basis, such a pro-European positivist might then argue that the commonly accepted doctrines of parliamentary supremacy and *pacta sunt servanda* require British courts to recognise the authority of the ECtHR's decisions as stipulated by the HRA and the ECHR treaty.[24]

A crucial point for present purposes is that the provision of the HRA that holds that British courts must 'take into account' the rulings of the ECtHR does not rule out any of the three constructions of the ECtHR's authority over British courts discussed previously. This point generalises the issue. The language of statutes and treaties that create new governing bodies are likely to leave unsettled questions about the existence and scope of those institutions' legal authority. Moreover, in many cases, the positivist would consider the indeterminate language of such statutes and treaties to be the only legal reasons relevant to such pluralist jurisprudential questions. Thus, from the positivist perspective, oftentimes pluralist jurisprudential questions such as those addressed by the *Ullah* court will lack a determinate legal answer.

9.5.4 *Two Conceptions of Pluralist Politico-Moral Reasoning*

In sum, I have now discussed two kinds of cases in which, from the positivist perspective, legal officials make decisions about the scope and existence of legal authority that are not necessitated by the relevant set of

[24] See discussion in the last paragraph of Section 2.3 for suggestions as to why these commonly accepted legal doctrines might also be germane to non-positivist pluralist legal reasoning about the ECtHR's legal authority.

legal reasons. First, as discussed in Section 1, positivist legal reasons cannot warrant the first recognition of fundamental legal authorities. Second, as discussed in Section 5.3, positivist legal reasons often leave undetermined the precise scope of novel and derivative legal authorities. By contrast, as discussed in Sections 2 and 5.2, the authority-based non-positivist perspective suggests relatively determinate truth conditions for both the first-recognition of fundamental legal authorities and the specification of the precise limits of novel legal authorities. Thus, positivist and authority-based non-positivist pluralist jurisprudence offer significantly different accounts of legal reasoning about the scope and existence of legal authority. As I now argue, they also offer different accounts of the nature of legal officials' politico-moral reasoning about the norms they should take to be the authoritative bases of their legal decision-making.

Consider the following question that a legal official might pose:

> As a matter of political morality, to what extent, if any, do considerations of political morality require that I accept that this institution's norms have the authority that law claims (i.e. political authority)?

As we have seen, for the authority-based non-positivist, legal officials determine the scope and extent of norms' legal authority by answering this politico-moral question about the scope and extent of their political authority. By contrast, the positivist keeps these questions separate, for the positivist holds that the existence and scope of any such institution's legal authority turns on the contents of the criteria of validity that the relevant system's officials accept in common rather than considerations of political morality.

That said, positivist legal theory does not deny the cogency of the politico-moral question. More pointedly, positivism allows that the consideration of political morality that positivism excludes from legal reasoning might require legal officials to reach decisions that go beyond or perhaps even conflict with legal requirements. For example, positivist pluralist jurisprudence allows that considerations of political morality should guide legal officials' decisions within the interstices of indeterminate legal reasons (e.g. the indeterminate language of the HRA discussed above). To name a second example drawn from earlier discussion, positivist pluralist jurisprudence allows that considerations of political morality might sometimes require officials to proclaim falsely the legal validity of the norms issued by some novel and fundamental source and to act as if those claims were true.

In summary, positivists and non-positivists agree that legal officials might assess whether an institution's norms have the authority that law claims, and positivism does not rule out the possibility that legal officials might be morally required to heed the conclusions of politico-moral deliberations that conflict with positivist legal requirements, deliberations. However, and this is the key point of this section, these camps adhere to very different conceptions of the politico-moral reasoning required to determine whether, as matter of political morality, a norm or some class of norms has the authority that law claims.

For the Razian positivist, the politico-moral question is whether an institution's directives are both substantial moral content-independent reasons and reasons that defeat the reasons that any member of the relevant community has not to conform by excluding and replacing those countervailing reasons. By contrast, for the authority-based non-positivist, the question is whether the institution's directives defeat all such countervailing reasons, be it by dint of the directives' first-order substantial moral content-independent force or (should the directives also be exclusionary reasons) their exclusionary force. Thus, to establish that an institution possesses Razian authority one must establish that its directives are both exclusionary reasons and substantial moral content-independent reasons, whereas to establish such an institution's generic collectivist authority, one need only establish that its directives are substantial moral content-independent reasons.

The justificatory burden borne by these respective accounts differs significantly, for the grounds of the substantial moral content-independent force of an institution's directives are not necessarily also grounds of its exclusionary force. Moreover, many accept Raz's famed claim that normally, an institution's directives are content-independent and exclusionary reasons for its subjects only when the 'alleged subject is likely better to comply with reasons which apply to him . . . if he accepts the directives of the alleged authority as authoritatively binding and tries to follow them, rather than by trying to follow the reasons which apply to him directly.'[25]

By contrast, the apologist for generic collectivist authority does not bear the burden of showing that this particular condition obtains. Rather, she need only establish that they are first-order substantial moral content-independent reasons. Hence, for example, the defender of an

[25] Raz (n. 13), p. 53.

institution's generic collectivist authority can appeal to the institution's democratic pedigree or its unique ability to secure highly beneficial forms of social coordination as grounds of the content-independent force of the content-independent directives, without need to establish further that such directives are also exclusionary reasons.

To see that the foregoing point ramifies, consider that the positivist and non-positivist could agree that legal officials shape political communities by joining together in recognising that certain institutions are sources of norms that have the authority that law claims. For example, legal officials might maintain the extant structure of their political community by continuing to accept in common and, accordingly, continuing to enforce the same sources of legal authority (e.g. the enactments of parliament). Or, they might alter the structure of their political community by recognising and enforcing novel sources of authoritative norms (e.g. the rulings of the ECtHR) and specifying their limits. Moreover, legal officials might forge new political communities by joining with the officials of other legal systems in recognising and enforcing the directives of novel authorities vis-à-vis an expanded political community (e.g. joining with the officials of other state signatories of the ECHR in recognising and enforcing the authority of the ECtHR's rulings). In short, neither the positivist nor the non-positivist denies that legal officials should engage in such political community-shaping efforts in accordance with the conclusions of their politico-moral reasoning. However, as I have just explained, the Razian positivist and the authority-based non-positivist offer significantly different accounts of the considerations that are germane to such politico-moral deliberations.

9.6 Conclusion

In summary, I have contrasted two authority-based conceptions of pluralist jurisprudence – one positivist and the other non-positivist. I have argued that the fundamental disagreement between these conceptions concerns the nature of the authoritative resolutions that the law claims to provide. According to this argument, the positivist's exclusionary-reason based conception of the authority that law claims (i.e. political authority) leads to the conclusion that the only legal reasons relevant to pluralist legal reasoning are the criteria of validity that the officials of the relevant legal system accept in common and the norms that those criteria recognise as legally valid. By contrast, the generic collectivist conception of the authority that law claims (i.e. political authority) supports the authority-based non-positivist's reduction of pluralist legal reasoning to politico-moral reasoning about political authority (as set out in the generic collectivist conception), or so I have argued.

In a similar vein, I have argued that concomitant to the positivist and non-positivist disagreement about pluralist jurisprudence is a further disagreement about the politico-moral considerations that should inform legal officials' political community-shaping efforts. Furthermore, I hope to have shown that the debate between positivist and non-positivist pluralist jurisprudence turns on the resolution of debates about the nature of political authority and political community. If so, one reason why this jurisprudential debate is important is that it joins with and addresses yet more fundamental debates within political philosophy.

10

The Gap between Global Law and Global Justice

A Preliminary Analysis

NEIL WALKER

10.1 Between Global Law and Global Justice

Today, we hear more and more, both in academic discourse and in the more practical vernaculars of transnational lawyering and transnational politics, about something called Global Law as well as something called Global Justice. These terms are expanded upon in this chapter, but let us start from the shorthand idea of Global Law as 'any practical endorsement of or commitment to the universal or global-in-general warrant of some laws or of some dimension of law'[1], and of Global Justice as any conception of just institutional arrangements and outcomes that treats the planet as a whole as the ultimate basis of assessment. What is meant by each of these terms is much contested, but there is no doubting their increased prominence in legal, moral and political discourse. Yet we hear much less of the *relationship between* these key ideas, and what we do hear is often poorly developed and inadequately engaged with the complexity of the issues involved. The two concepts, and the discussion and engagement of the two concepts, often seem remote from one another.

There are a number of reasons for this 'gap', both objective and cultural. In objective terms, 'law' and 'justice' – 'global' or otherwise – are quite different types of concepts, and, relatedly, they also have quite different empirical referents. Conceptually, Global Law is a (externally) descriptive and (internally) interpretive term, whereas Global Justice is an essentially (and highly contested) normative and evaluative term. It follows that the two terms occupy quite different places on the fact/value spectrum. Global Law treats an existing legal-institutional pattern

[1] Neil Walker, *Intimations of Public Law* (Cambridge: Cambridge University Press, 2015), p. 18.

as its reference point and tends towards the factual end of the continuum, even if – as we shall see – the various developing strains of Global Law allow considerable interpretive license and the introduction of value preferences. For its part, Global Justice tends towards the value-centred end of the continuum, even if – as we shall also see – many conceptions of justice are constrained or tempered by practical considerations. In empirical terms, there is a practice-aspiration spectrum to match the fact-value spectrum. While Global Law involves endorsement of or commitment to some existing or, at least, arguably emergent form of legal practice, Global Justice typically speaks to a goal as yet not fully attained or standard as yet not fully realised.

As they are made manifest in particular contexts these objective differences are overlaid by a tendency to cultural distancing. For we may observe a pattern of non-communication or miscommunication between the epistemic and practice communities concerned with the understanding and development of global and transnational law on the one hand, and of global or transnational ethics on the other.[2] It is tempting, indeed, to view this deficit in terms of one fundamental division between a single Global Law community whose focus is the 'real world' of institutional design, doctrinal detail and prudential possibilities and constraints, and a single Global Justice community whose focus is 'blue sky' moral thinking and ideal theory, with each community contributing to a cycle of mutual indifference and ignorance. Yet that would be a caricature. On either side there are in fact diverse epistemic and practice communities with quite different knowledge-constitutive interests and deep perspectives, some of which share a certain affinity with such communities on the other side. And so the differences between the two constituencies considered as a whole are both more wide-ranging and subtler than the caricatured version allows.

A first perspective that *does* set many members of the Global Law constituency apart is a kind of *institutional pragmatism*, a professionally 'compartmentalised'[3] concern with client-based or other forms of applied legal 'service'.[4] This can lead to a blindness to, impatience with, or even

[2] For a thoughtful and wide-ranging analysis, see Steven Ratner, 'Ethics and International Law: Integrating the Global Justice Project(s)' (2013) 5 *International Law Theory*, 1–34; and now also his *The Thin Justice of International Law* (Oxford: Oxford University Press, 2015).

[3] Walker, *Intimations of Public Law* (n. 1), p. 192.

[4] See Neil Walker, 'The Jurist in a Global Age', in Rob Van Gestel, Hans-W. Micklitz and Edward Rubin (eds.), *Methodology in the New Legal World* (Cambridge:

a learned detachment from wider questions regarding the causes, manifestations and consequences of global justice and injustice. Yet alongside – and against – this kind of entrenched legalism we also find an *unanchored idealism*. This is a perspective that affects members of Global Law and Global Justice constituencies alike. On the Global Law side, it involves a juris-centric view of the world – one in which law is seen as a deep and (relatively) autonomous steering mechanism for other global social and economic forces. But this is matched by a version of normative political theory on the part of theorists and activists more centrally concerned with Global Justice which consciously puts institutional and other standing political and economic constraints to one side in imagining and drafting just arrangements and outcomes. In either case, whether the author's creative license is law-coded or not, such an uncompromising normative approach courts the danger of a naïve or hubristic utopianism. In turn, however, this unanchored idealism can be contrasted with a third and final general perspective, namely one of *radical critique*. Again, this can affect both the Global Law constituency and the wider circles of those concerned with Global Justice. Here law tends to be seen as the instrument of larger social and economic forces tending towards global *injustice*, and both the quality of Global Law and the prospects of Global Justice are viewed less generously. As in the case of the other two perspectives, the critical approach harbours an extreme and pathological tendency – namely, an attitude of structural fatalism that cannot countenance any amelioration of global injustice through law.

What this summary of the key perspectives within and across the relevant epistemic and practice communities points to is a whole series of blockages – and associated 'gaps' in mutual understanding and sympathy – between Global Law-thinking and Global Justice-thinking. The Global Law constituency may be insufficiently curious about the Global Justice implications of their commitments and conservatively indifferent to or dismissive of the unrealistic ambition of some members of the justice constituency. Alternatively, they may be either unduly naïve, or unduly fatalistic, when considering what difference law can make to justice. The Global Justice constituency, for their part, may neglect the significance of law either as a means to deliver justice or as

Cambridge University Press, 2017); available at *Edinburgh School of Law Research Paper2015/13*
http://papers.ssrn.com/sol3/papers.cfm?abstract_id=2580114.

an impediment to its delivery. Alternatively, they may be unduly cynical about the interests or values that law is capable of representing.

In light of these concerns, by engaging in a preliminary analysis of the wider set of claims of Global Law, the wider set of claims of Global Justice, and, crucially, the ways in which the relationship between these two wider sets of claims are or might be understood, this chapter may serve a number of useful purposes. To begin, and most basically, it provides a resource for mutual awareness and information and, hopefully, for mutual engagement across positions that have too often been marked by mutual neglect. In the second place, if we focus in particular on the prominent pragmatic perspective within the Global Law constituency, here obliviousness or indifference towards the possible Global Justice implications of particular positions and practices within Global Law emphatically does not mean that there are no such implications. One advantage of a fuller analysis of Global Law is to make this clear – to reveal the often merely implicit and underdetermined justice-relevant assumptions that lie behind or are necessarily presupposed by the expanse of actual and emergent global law practices.

In the third place, an emphasis on the range of such positions, and their inherent diversity, also shows that the 'gap' – in terms of practical achievements and possibilities – between Global Law and Global Justice is not one large and general gap but many particular ones, depending on which of the emergent versions of Global Law or conceptions of Global Justice are in play and their multiple connections and disconnections. And if we step back from the complex detail of this picture, we may, as we shall see, discern the outline of a number of different and contending overall orientations towards justice inscribed in the practice of Global Law, (whether or not these orientations are consciously *subscribed to* by the sponsors of particular Global Law practices) which, if considered in the round, inevitably generate and realise a multi-faceted or hybrid conception of Global Justice. What is more, as our final section sketches, this hybrid conception remains unsettled, with considerable continuing scope for flexible development in which the various different overall orientations towards Global Justice are given greater or lesser emphasis.

Fourthly and finally, a closer analysis of these diverse forms and unsettled properties of Global Law also underlines how well placed the global juristic community, including its significant academic component, is to intervene in the very construction and reconstruction of Global Law. That is to say, it demonstrates the extent to which the Global Law constituency are active players rather than simply passive spectators and chroniclers in the development of Global Law, and, therefore, well positioned to reflect and act upon a more considered understanding of the highly fluid and contentious relationship between Global Law and Global Justice.

10.2 The Variety of Global Law

In other work, I have sought at length to uncover a deeper commonality beneath the variety that is present in the increasingly popular semantic surface of 'global law' (and its functional equivalents).[5] It is in so doing that I arrived at an understanding of Global Law as a distinct and significant sub-set of transnational law; namely, as previewed earlier, Global Law embraces 'any practical endorsement of or commitment to the universal or otherwise global-in-general warrant of some laws or some dimension of law'. The emphasis on a universal or at least global-in-general warrant is intended to convey the idea of a jurisdictionally unbound law; that is to say, it involves a claim to legal jurisdiction that knows no direct or indirect (e.g. through citizenship) territorial limits but is instead, within its own material remit, planetary in its extension. The 'globality' of Global Law so conceived, therefore, does not depend upon source or pedigree, but upon intended destination. Global Law may be produced at the *global institutional level* (e.g. the UN) or in *global conventions of rule formation* (e.g. general international law), but it may equally be posited at the national or other *locally site-specific* level (through notions such as 'universal jurisdiction') or, more commonly, as we shall see, it may be found in the *cross-site acknowledgment, development and circulation* of a shared body of doctrine or general legal world-view.[6] The 'producers' of Global Law are equally diverse, including legislators, administrators, judges, innovative practitioners and a broader category of framer-jurists that reaches into the academy.[7] With this open-ended understanding of its origins and authors, we can point to a large number of contemporary trends as the aggregate sum of Global Law.

If we are to appreciate what lies behind the diverse contexts of production and full range of Global Law we must emphasise that while, under the terms of our definition, Global Law is concerned with patterns of common normativity conceived of in universal or at least global-in-general terms, it is a common normativity predicated upon underlying

[5] Walker, *Intimations of Public Law* (n. 1), ch. 1. [6] Ibid., pp. 19–21. [7] Ibid., ch. 2.

difference. Whether explicitly so-called or implicitly conceived, Global Law involves various different ways of imagining – and in turn *imaging* – the practice of law on a global scale as somehow 'containing' and shaping a deeper world of legal variety. Global Law, therefore, never operates in isolation, but always 'acts upon' other and more localised and particular law. We may group these different approaches to the practice of global law, depending upon how they treat that underlying world of legal variety, into either *convergence-promoting* approaches or *divergence-accommodating* approaches.[8]

The convergence-promoting approaches cover both *structural* and *formal* extensions of public international law beyond its traditional image as a merely 'transactional' law between states. These candidates for global law are exemplified, respectively, by a UN-centred institutional hierarchy sharpened through a non-consent based and so globally pervasive use-of-force capacity, and by a reconceptualisation of international law as a formally integrated, state-consent-independent world legal system complete with general principles, obligations *erga omnes, ius cogens* and so on. In both of these cases the prevailing juridical image is one of a *pyramid* flowing from a high point of global-wide normativity. Also within the convergence-accommodating basket we find a wide range of *abstract-normative approaches*, from general doctrinal approaches such as the promotion of global human rights as a kind of fundamental law with (all) persons rather than states as ultimate legal subjects, to pre-positive or proto-positive framing ideas – such as, the cosmopolitan framing principles (e.g. accountability, participation, public reason, subsidiarity, human rights protection), identified by Mattias Kumm,[9] Rafael Domingo[10] and others, or Klaus Gunther's universal code of legality,[11] or various recent formulations of a global rule of law.[12] Here the defining image is of the container,

[8] Ibid., ch. 3.

[9] See e.g. Mattias Kumm, 'The Cosmopolitan Turn in Constitutionalism: On the Relationship between Constitutionalism in and beyond the State', in Jeffrey Dunoff and Joel Trachtmann (eds.), *Ruling the World?* (Cambridge: Cambridge University Press, 2009), pp. 258–324.

[10] Rafael Domingo, *The New Global Law* (Cambridge: Cambridge University Press, 2010).

[11] Klaus Gunther, 'Legal Pluralism or Uniform Concept of Law? Globalisation as a Problem of Legal Theory' (2008) 5 *NoFo - Journal of Extreme Legal Positivism*, 5–21.

[12] See e.g. Gianluigi Palombella, 'The (re)Constitution of the Public', in Cormac MacAmhlaigh, Claudio Michelon and Neil Walker (eds.), *After Public Law* (Oxford: Oxford University Press, 2013), pp. 286–310.

either the over-container or *umbrella* of abstract doctrine or principle or the under-container or *vessel* of pre-positive common code.

As to the divergence-accommodating perspective, this includes *laterally coordinate approaches*, such as the emergence of a new global 'law of conflicts'[13] through broader non-state centred inter-jurisdictional choice-of-law processes and mechanisms in what is conventionally called 'private international law', as well as the plethora of new transnational constitutional and other legal pluralisms.[14] The image here is of links in a vertical *chain* formed out of thin principles of mutual accommodation between different legal orders, although for the radical pluralists it is disputable whether the connecting mechanism has 'legal' in its DNA at all.[15] Another divergence-accommodating approach focuses on those *functionally specific regimes* concerned with thematically circumscribed public goods in which the entire world is the relevant community of risk or fate, as is gradually and unevenly emergent in areas such as climate change, migration and nuclear non-proliferation. The image here is of the *segment* – the slice or section which presupposes a global whole but, rather than looking for a common legal theme across the whole, is concerned with the demarcation and extraction of only one part of that whole. In addition, there is a further divergence-accommodating approach to Global Law, which involves mergers of existing specialist legal fields into new hybrids or composite fields. Examples include the so-called new law of peace[16] or the new humanity's law,[17] both of which, at

[13] See e.g., Christian Joerges, 'The Idea of a Three-Dimensional Conflicts Law as Constitutional Form', in Christian Joerges and Ernst-Ulrich Petersmann (eds.), *Constitutionalism, Multilevel Trade Governance and International Economic Law* (Oxford: Hart Publishing, 2011), pp. 413–55; see more broadly, Horatia Muir Watt, 'Private International Law Beyond the Schism' (2011) 2 *Transnational Legal Theory*, 347–427; Colin Scott, Fabrizio Cafaggi and Linda Senden, 'The Conceptual and Constitutional Challenge of Transnational Private Regulation' (2011) 38 *Journal of Law and Society*, 1–19; Jacco Bonhoff and Anne Meuwese, 'The Meta-Regulation of Transnational Private Regulation' (2011) 38 *Journal of Law and Society*, 138–62; Peer Zumbansen, 'Transnational Legal Pluralism' (2010) 1 *Transnational Legal Theory*, 141–89; Alex Mills, *The Confluence of Public and Private International Law: Justice, Pluralism and Subsidiarity in the International Constitutional Ordering of Private Law* (Cambridge: Cambridge University Press, 2009); see also Walker, *Intimations of Public Law* (n. 1), pp. 107–14.

[14] See e.g. Walker, *Intimations of Public Law* (n. 1), pp. 114–18.

[15] See e.g. Nico Krisch, 'Who is Afraid of Radical Pluralism? Legal Order and Political Stability in the Postnational Space' (2011) 24 *Ratio Juris*, 386–412.

[16] Christine Bell, *On The Law of Peace: Peace Agreements and the Lex Pacificatoria* (Oxford: Oxford University Press, 2008).

[17] Ruti Teitel, *Humanity's Law* (Oxford: Oxford University Press, 2011).

least as imagined by their academic sponsors, involve a fresh mix of international criminal law, human rights law and other cognate elements to provide a novel conception of Global Justice in the area of conflict resolution. A further example is offered by the new global 'law of recognition',[18] vastly extended from the traditional state-centred international law of recognition to cover the dignitarian and participation dimensions of recognition for all active contemporary global constituencies, women, racial and religious minorities and so on, previously denied them. Again, in all these areas, what is striking is the movement beyond the boundaries of international law as inter-state law, and indeed constitutional law as intra-polity law, in search of a warrant that is genuinely global in its justificatory claim and in its jurisdictional reach. The image here is one of law as *flow*, as once separate tributaries merging into a wider but still clearly embanked global legal river. In all cases, moreover, as in the mobilisation of Global Law generally, those who coin or develop the terms are seeking not simply to make an 'academic' proposal, but to capture and reinforce what they already understand as an incipient trend in legal doctrine and practice.

A final group of global approaches to law also suggests a fluid movement, though in this case the idea of a common historical *thread* is key. Here, we turn to notions like global constitutional law or Global Administrative Law,[19] or the renewal of the concept of *ius gentium*,[20] or the widely revived interest in the *ius commune*. Rather than new hybrids, however, these are merely adaptations of a venerable legal discourse to the new global stage. These tend, moreover, to be highly open-ended, capable of being either convergence-promoting or divergence-accommodating, and so overlapping heavily with the approaches already mentioned. For example, global constitutionalism can focus on the convergence-sponsoring 'global constitution' of the United Nations, but equally, it can fix on the thin inter-systemic, divergence – accommodating links of constitutional pluralism – concerned particularly but not exclusively with relations between the EU and

[18] Emmanuelle Tourme-Jouannet, 'International Law of Recognition' (2013) 24 *European Journal of International Law*, 667–90.

[19] See, for example, the signature article by Benedict Kingsbury, Nico Krisch and Richard B. Stewart, 'The Emergence of Global Administrative Law' (2005) 68 *Law and Contemporary Problems*, 15–61.

[20] See e.g. Jeremy Waldron, 'Foreign Law and the Modern *Ius Gentium*' (2005) 119 *Harvard Law Review*, 129–47; and Jeremy Waldron, '*Partly Laws Common to All Mankind*': *Foreign Law in American Courts* (New Haven: Yale University Press, 2012), chs. 3–5.

national constitutions, or on Gunther Teubner's functionally segmented 'societal constitutionalism'.[21] Here, under such a broad sign, the idea of Global Law reaches its limit of open texture, the common language as much a cue for disputation as the trace of a common code. It remains remarkable, however, that a common term of trade and a common ambition in this context of disputation remains the potentially *global* warrant of the law or dimension of law under consideration.

A number of points stand out from this catalogue of the forms of Global Law as particularly significant for present purposes. First, far from being straightforwardly rival candidate meta-principles, these different conceptions of Global Law, with their various images of pyramid, umbrella, vessel, chain, segment, flow and thread, stand in a complex relationship. This is as much about complementarity as conflict. In all spheres of social and economic life, globalisation, with its unprecedented compression of time and space, creates and amplifies both new territorially unbounded commonalities and new territorially unbounded differences in respect of interests, identities and values. Law is no exception. Each of the Global Law models is a response to the ways in which transnational law, by introducing regimes and patterns of law that are non-state-centred or non-state-contained unleashes and places in dynamic tension new forms of legal commonality and difference. Both divergence-accommodating approaches and convergence-promoting approaches, as already noted, set out in their different ways to contain and re-order 'unruly' elements in the transnational mix. They do so whether by focusing on difference and particularity and so either connecting or delimiting the transnational fragments (as in divergence-accommodating approaches), or by focusing on new forms of general normative leverage and so either fashioning hierarchies or denoting commonalities (as in convergence-promoting approaches). In the weaving of these various normative patterns, they may supplement one another. Equally, however, for example, as in the case of relationship between the new legal cosmopolitanism of shared universal principles and the new constitutional pluralism, or between the vision of a single, overarching international legal order and that of globally segmented and fragmented regimes, they may challenge and provoke each other in a relationship of productive tension.[22]

[21] See e.g. Gunther Teubner, *Constitutional Fragments* (Oxford: Oxford University Press, 2012).

[22] Walker, *Intimations of Public Law* (n. 1), ch. 4.

Secondly, and connected to the unsettled quality of global law, as already noted, the 'insider' legal experts associated with Global Law have a prominent role in its production and reproduction. And in particular, the scholarly community – as the key map makers and symbolic entrepreneurs of the legal world – are heavily implicated in the naming, framing and suggestive (re)shaping of globally resonant legal doctrines and practices emerging within judicial, legislative and administrative communities. In some cases, as our definition suggests, the model of Global Law in question is more about 'commitment' than 'endorsement', projection than refinement, novel construction than reconstruction, and in these areas the scholarly community is particularly to the fore. In other cases, for example the structural and formal models, it is much more a question of the incremental extension and retailoring of well-established existing doctrine and practice, but even here the scholarly community is much involved in the work of persuasive adaptation. Generally speaking, moreover, there is a much greater interaction and even continuity of personnel within the broad guild of 'global law-craft'[23] between practitioners and scholars than one finds in the typical national context, which is itself both a reflection and a reinforcing cause of Global Law's fluid character. Global Law is never entirely 'academic' in the sense of being either a matter of pure normative speculation or of disinterested description; it always has an element of 'practical' engagement, even if this may be at some level of abstraction from recognised doctrine (hence the reference to 'some dimension of law' as well as to 'some laws'), but it remains in a process of fluid and, of course, normatively contested becoming – of intimation rather than final resolution.

Some might see this intermingling of the academic and the institutional as a confusion – and illegitimate collapsing – of theory and doctrine. Yet it is important to understand the deep reasons (beyond the occupational sociology of a thickly networked global 'law-craft') why they are so intimately connected in the making of global law. Global Law in all of its variants is about articulating and responding to questions about the basis of legal authority in a world in which the 'box matrix' of mutually exclusive instances of state sovereignty no longer provides a sufficient or even dominant meta-authoritative principle. Global Law tries to find new if typically less pervasive meta-principles to reframe and refashion existing and emergent doctrinal and institutional

[23] Ibid., p. 59.

tendencies in ways that are appropriate to the planetary interdependence of law and legal purposes. Hence the need for creative interpretation and refinement of fluid trends, and the inevitable degree of competition and disharmony in that process. Hence, too, the fact that a concern with Global Justice is already built into the reflexive development of Global Law. For in responding to the decline of a historically dominant meta-principle of legal authority Global Law tends gradually – and notwithstanding the underlying cultural and discursive 'gap' between Global Law and Global Justice and the continuing influence of institutional pragmatism – to look more explicitly to general ethical principles and purposes in search of a legitimate grounding for its authority.

10.3 The Variety of Global Justice

Let us now turn directly to Global Justice. Previously, we defined Global Justice as any conception of justice that treats the planet as a whole as the ultimate unit of assessment. Global conceptions of justice are as disparate as global practices and projections of law. These conceptions vary across different dimensions, four of which are particularly significant.

First, conceptions of global justice vary in terms of the *relevant constituencies* of justice. Do we think of the collective subject of *global* justice in terms of a *single* planetary constituency (i.e. the planet as a whole) as the only grouping, or at the least the only ultimately relevant grouping? Or, in stark contrast, do we merely count and aggregate the justice claims of a *plurality* of justice constituencies – whether territorial or functionally demarcated communities? Or if we do not concede everything to such an aggregative approach, can we imagine instead a mixed or *compound* structure of Global Justice? That is to say, can we envisage alongside such discrete communities a supplementary overall planetary constituency – constructed by reference to certain common normative characteristics and/or by the justice-relevant 'externalities' and interdependencies of territorially and functionally discrete communities?

Second, of even deeper significance and so requiring somewhat more extended treatment, global conceptions of justice, including the choice to be made on the singular/compound/plural spectrum, vary in terms of the conception of *morally relevant global interconnectedness*.[24] We can order

[24] For extended discussion, see Neil Walker, 'Human Rights and Global Public Goods: The Sound of One Hand Clapping?' (2016) 23 *Indiana Journal of Global Legal Studies*, 249–65.

these variants progressively, from thinner to thicker expectations of joint action and conceptions of underlying connectedness. First, there is a model of *concurrent interests*. Second, there is a model of *mutual responsibility*. Third, there is a model of *common concern*.

The *concurrent-interests* model concentrates on those areas where, regardless of cultural and ethical differences, we are manifestly interdependent in certain key domains of social life. In these domains, the globe has become a community of palpably common risk and interwoven life-chances. The emphasis here is upon clear and often urgent areas of interdependent prospect and predicament between states and peoples; where both the common harm or benefit over matters where our interests coincide, and the fact that we have been and remain in a position to act to cause or prevent such harm or secure such benefit to one another, is undeniable and unavoidable.[25] The most obvious candidate objects for inclusion within this approach are those global concerns, such as free trade, climate change, nuclear safety, security and pandemic disease – which most closely approximate to the classical (economic) public goods model of 'non-excludability' of access (to the problem and its solution) and 'non-rivalness' in consumption' (i.e. non-exhaustible benefits, or at least significant economies of scale).[26]

The *mutual-responsibility* model reaches beyond the manifest interdependence of the concurrent-interests model to find a deeper seam of causation and associated obligation. The guiding premise here, perhaps most forcefully portrayed and most extensively developed today in the work of Thomas Pogge,[27] is that the very arrangement of the world into sovereign states and their peoples (with the international resource, borrowing, treaty and arms privileges consecrated by that state-sovereigntist arrangement) and the institutional configuration of state-centred international law and politics that reflects this, is no neutral framework or international 'state of nature'. Rather, it is a background structure with significant and uneven effects on the global distribution of benefits and burdens. In particular, the historical embedding and perpetuation of these arrangements in ways that systematically favour some

[25] This remains the most common framework for thinking about questions of global justice both within the political classes and in the academy. See e.g. Kimberly Hutchings, *Global Ethics: An Introduction* (Cambridge: Polity, 2010), ch. 1.

[26] See Paul A. Samuelson, 'The Pure Theory of Public Expenditure' (1954) 36 *Review of Economics and Statistics*, 387–89.

[27] See in particular Thomas Pogge, *World Poverty and Human Rights*, 2nd ed. (Cambridge: Polity, 2008).

parts of the globe over others, specifically those that have been prominent in the original design and continuing refinement of the system, accounts for many of the world's deep inequalities, including the catastrophe of global poverty. It follows from this deeper investigation of the causal dynamics of the world order that those states and their citizens who are responsible for inequalities and other distributive injustices are under a duty to correct or mitigate the harm that we have caused, which require a level of compensatory common action much greater than under the concurrent-interests model.

Finally, *the common concern* model argues for a deeper framework of mutual commitment and obligation just in view of our common humanity.[28] In other words, it is not the proximity of our actions and action-effects and the greater or lesser interdependence due to that proximity that leads us to take responsibility for each other, or at least to recognise manifest concurrent-interests and the associated entanglement of predicaments and prospects, but a deeper affinity and solidarity as members of the same species.

All three models become increasingly salient under conditions of globalisation. Our manifest interdependence in the face of climate change, pandemic disease, global insecurity and so on increases. So too does recognition of the deeper dynamics of the interdependence of our life-chances, as also, partly on account of this denser web of interconnections, does a cosmopolitan awareness of our common human condition. Yet the solutions and responses suggested are different. As noted previously, the economic public goods approach clearly belongs to the first model – concurrent interests – with its emphasis on manifest interdependence. In general terms, the second and third models, with their thicker sense of common ties, are more likely to generate notions of global economic redistribution and social reform, and also of enhanced global institutional capacity, which go beyond those we associate with classical public goods.

This does not mean that the different approaches need be mutually exclusive. It is perfectly possible to subscribe to the concurrent interests, mutual responsibility and common concern models together (to varying degrees and in varying combinations), and most who subscribe to the public goods model would make at least some concession to the other

[28] See e.g. Peter Singer, *One World: The Ethics of Globalization*, 2nd ed. (New Haven: Yale University Press, 2004); Peter Unger, *Living High and Letting Die: Our Illusion of Innocence* (Oxford: Oxford University Press, 1996).

two. For example, this may be through recognition of the moral jeopardy of untrammeled state sovereignty and a concern to mitigate its effects through doctrines of humanitarian intervention and basic rights protection under the mutual responsibility model;[29] or through acknowledgement of at least minimum standards of species-wide humanitarian assistance[30] under the common concern model. Yet for all that, important differences remain. The stress upon one rather than the other approaches tends to reveal distinct and in some measure rival mentalities of global governance. And the mentality of global governance associated with the concurrent interests approach is undoubtedly a presumptively modest one. It involves no deep interrogation of the underlying state system, and assumes that much public provision should remain state-based and state-justified. It assumes the global political sphere to be supplementary, and one that that is both truncated in terms of its consideration of common ends and the search for a deliberated international consensus, and fragmented in form. Truncated, because its emphasis is largely on areas of close interdependence and already apparent manifest common cause. Fragmented, because it tends to deal with the public goods associated with each of these areas discretely.[31]

Moving on from the key question of the morally relevant quality of global interconnectedness, we may briefly introduce two final dimension of variation. In the third place, then, global conceptions of justice also vary in terms of the *extension (both scope and concreteness) of the subject-matter* of justice. Is justice restricted to certain *limited* areas of interpersonal or communal life and/or to certain circumscribed aspects of these areas, or is it an *open-ended* and more broadly penetrative concept dealing with the widest and deepest social and economic

[29] See e.g. Ronald Dworkin, '*A New Philosophy for International Law*' (2013) 41 *Philosophy & Public Affairs*, 2–30.

[30] See e.g. Thomas Nagel, 'The Problem of Global Justice' (2005) 33 *Philosophy & Public Affairs*, 113–47; see also John Rawls, *The Law of Peoples* (Harvard: Harvard University Press, 1997).

[31] The precise mode of treatment under the concurrent interests approach will differ depending upon whether we are dealing with single shot, aggregate or weakest link public goods, but for any of these sub-types our current transnational institutional infrastructure seems weakly equipped, and vulnerable to capture by strong ideological or epistemic interests. See e.g. Gregory Schaffer, 'International Law and Global Public Goods in a Pluralist World' (2012) 23 *European Journal of International Law*, 669–93; Nico Krisch, 'The Decay of Consent: International Law in an Age of Global Public Goods' (2014) 108 *American Journal of International Law*, 1–40.

effects of the global interdependencies of populations upon the life-chances of these populations?[32]

Fourth and finally, global conceptions of justice vary in terms of *the basic structure of justice* as it relates to its subject-matter(s)? Do we think of global *justice*, however far it might extend, as one integrated test or standard for all justice-relevant matters or as the combination of a series of discrete tests or standards? In other words, is global justice an *aggregate* or composite of environmental, economic, health educational, legal-procedural justice, or does it operate as a single *holistic* measure?

10.4 Regarding the Gap: Orientations towards Global Justice

With these fuller descriptions and categorisations in place, we can now identify, in crude terms, six separate possible understandings of the overall orientation of Global Law towards Global Justice. For reasons that will immediately become obvious, we may call these the six orientations the six 'Cs'. Global Law can be regarded as in some significant sense *constitutive* of Global Justice, or as *(partially) compositive of* Global Justice, or as *collateral* to the achievement of Global Justice, or as *compensatory* for its relative absence, or as only *contingently* related to its achievement, or as *culpable* in its failure. These different orientations vary in accordance with a number of factors. They vary, in terms of their content, according to the general quality of the relationship posited between Global Law and Global Justice, with the previous list arranged in order from more to less affirmative. The positions also vary, in terms of their explanatory input, in accordance with the kind and degree of autonomy, integrity and influence they ascribe to (Global) Law on the one hand, which depends upon which combination from the menu of convergence-promoting and divergence-accommodating conceptions of Global Law is favoured; and also in accordance with the kind of good that they consider Global Justice to be. This, as we have already seen, differs according to whether Global Justice is regarded as singular, compound or plural in terms of its constituencies (who are the collective subjects of Global Justice?), thin or thickly connective (through what forms of association are these collective subjects appropriately identified?) limited or open-ended in extent (what is the range of Global

[32] On the relationship between the political and the economic dimensions of the argument for global justice, see e.g. Charles R. Beitz, 'Cosmopolitanism and Global Justice' (2005) 9 *The Journal of Ethics*, 11–27.

Justice?), and aggregative or holistic (should the matters within the range of global justice be viewed discretely or as one?) Let us now briefly examine each of these candidate relationships in turn.

10.4.1 *Constitutive*

According to this view, there is something in the deep structure of law that, while always imperfectly realised in practice, is well adapted to the needs of justice in general and Global Justice in particular, and indeed, provides the framing conditions for justice, including Global Justice. Law, from this perspective, is not merely derivative of any particular political or economic set of forces, but is seen as in important respects an autonomous force of practical reason – a distinct forum of principle and an important and indispensable means of fashioning the justice-relevant elements of global social order. Law also has integrity; its various features fit together regardless of the context of application. It follows that law on a global scale is cut from the same cloth as law on a local scale, and also that the various normative dimensions of law so conceived work together as a consistent whole. This law-constitutive conception of Global Justice, in line with its equal regard for all levels of law and all levels of justice, tends to be of a compound form that accords great significance to the various internally integrated parts as well as to the global community as an integrated whole. Additionally, the idea of Global Justice, according to the constitutive ambition, must be thickly connective and holistic, although also necessarily abstract and limited in social penetration. Law cannot specify the detail of Global Justice in it many particulars, but influences through setting out the basic criteria or principles in accordance with which a just arrangement of global society can be organised and against which it can be tested.

Global Law so understood as a constitutive project is likely to follow the convergence-promoting 'umbrella' or 'vessel' models, in so doing also building on the formal and structural forms of common normativity we increasingly find in the existing 'pyramid' of international law. Many rights-based visions of Global Justice, for example, follow this approach, as do abstract normative approaches emphasising the development of a cosmopolitan rule of law within and across different regions. A particularly distinctive feature of these cosmopolitan approaches[33]

[33] See e.g. Kumm, 'The Cosmopolitan Turn in Constitutionalism' (n. 9); Domingo, *The New Global Law* (n. 10).

is the fusion of substantive and procedural principles; their consideration that just law, understood as a law that is respectful and protective of autonomy and well-being on a global scale, is as much about respecting and ensuring the 'responsible autonomy' of certain collective decision-making contexts as it is about ensuring substantively just and autonomy-regarding outcomes for the individuals who inhabit these contexts. Global Law, then, is 'constitutive' not only in certifying certain general standards of just treatment, typically in the context of rights-protection, but also in its procedurally focused stipulation of the need to identify the right sites and combination of sites of justice-relevant decision-making within the whole, which will cover a range from the local to the global taking account of subsidiarity-sensitive considerations of democracy and efficiency, and also of proper mechanisms of accountability and due process within these decision-making sites. The balance of process and substance, however, also limits the substantive range and extension of Global Justice under this model of Global Law. Global Law, in short, cannot be committed to a radical form of global economic equalisation through the international transfer of resources because the collective-autonomy respecting aspects of subsidiarity would militate against any such non-consensual transfer.[34]

10.4.2 Compositive

In this perspective, law's contribution to Global Justice is cumulative, aggregative, and both derivative of and instrumental to various independently conceived transnational political projects rather than constitutive, integrative and autonomous. Global Law can contribute in various disparate ways in the composition of Global Justice, but it neither has any overall framing influence as a steering mechanism nor does it speak with one coherent voice to all the objects of Global Justice, which themselves are seen as disparate and aggregative rather than as comprising a holistic unity. Instead, Global Law's influence, while real, is piecemeal. It may be that law influences particular spheres of Global Justice, contributing to

[34] On the optimal relationship between authorities located at different sites and levels in the global order, see Kumm, 'The Cosmopolitan Turn in Constitutionalism' (n. 9); see also Nico Krisch, *Beyond Constitutionalism: The Pluralist Structure of Postnational Law* (Oxford: Oxford University Press, 2011); Nicole Roughan, *Authorities: Conflicts, Co-operation and Transnational Legal Theory* (Oxford: Oxford University Press, 2013).

global public goods (sometimes in the language of 'sectoral'[35] or 'societal constitutionalism'[36]) in areas such as nuclear disarmament, mitigation of climate change, global public health or global internet freedom, but it does so in different ways and through diverse normative principles or orientations.

Global Law, understood as a compositive process, is likely to be of the functionally specific variety, and so follow the 'segmented' model, or of the hybrid variety model, disparate areas of existing doctrine 'flowing' together in expanded but still subject-specific streams of global jurisprudence. Under this compositive orientation, law's contribution and achievement with regard to Global Justice is incomplete and uneven across sectors, with thicker patterns of interconnectedness based on ethics of common concerns and mutual responsibility developing in some sectors and a more limited conception of concurrent interests dominating in others.

10.4.3 Collateral

From this viewpoint, Global Law's contribution to Global Justice is auxiliary rather than central. Justice is largely a local community good. There is no significant global constituency as the collective subject of Global Justice. Rather, Global Justice is a pluralistic affair and an aggregate calculation. It is the sum of the goods of all the states in the international system, moderated only to take account of certain limited externalities and special humanitarian duties. This is Global Law firmly under the concurrent interests model of thin global connectedness, adapted to the kind of restricted conception of purposes set out within John Rawls's 'law of peoples'.[37] States remain sovereign, with very limited responsibilities to non-state citizens on the one hand, and significant claims to be protected from the interference of other states or state coalitions on the other. Many state-centred theorists uninterested in or sceptical of the very idea of a globally expansive law take this view, although often their approach can descend into 'nostalgia' for a lost world or 'denial' of the erosion of state sovereignty, rather than a

[35] Anne Peters, 'Membership in the Global Constitutional Community', in Jan Klabbers, Anne Peters and Geir Ulfstein (eds.), *The Constitutionalization of International Law* (Oxford: Oxford University Press, 2009), pp. 153–262.

[36] See e.g. Teubner, *Constitutional Fragments* (n. 21).

[37] Rawls, *The Law of Peoples* (n. 30).

developed case for its defence or re-assertion.[38] From this perspective, Global Law would have little traction, except on the 'chain' model as a set of pluralist 'interface'[39] norms necessary to accommodate difference, and under a transactional understanding of the purposes of UN and other treaty-based law, with scant conception of global reach beyond the always provisional consent of individual states.

10.4.4 Compensatory

On the compensatory view, Global Law is the platform from which some of the justice deficits associated with a traditionally state-centred world order can be mitigated. It shares with the collateral view, therefore, a sense of the challenged primacy of the state-centred approach, but unlike the collateral view, rather than seeking to shore up the state-centred perspective it seeks to develop the compensatory role of the global level. It takes a more expansive view of the proper scope of reference of the idea of Global Justice and of the extent of state-sponsored global injustice or indifference to questions of Global Justice. It also adopts a more robustly critical perspective as to the limited but non-negligible capacity of law, under a modestly developed ethic of mutual responsibility or common concern, to help compensate for these losses and deficits.[40]

Global Administrative Law is a case in point. The focus here is on forms of global administration (e.g. public/private, informally public, purely private, treaty sub-delegated) which escape the pedigree either of the state or formally constituted international bodies, but which nevertheless possess significant collective authority in areas as diverse as forestry, the internet, sport and banking regulation. The idea is to apply certain accountability, due process and public reason-giving principles from the national administrative law tradition, not as a replacement for 'lost' democratic authority, but in partial mitigation of its absence. Other compensatory examples would include the replication or adaptation of the familiar template of constitutional design (with, e.g., accompanying

[38] See Walker, *Intimations of Public Law* (n. 1), ch. 6; see also Mattias Kumm, 'The Best of Times and the Worst of Times: Between Constitutional Triumphalism and Nostalgia', in Petra Dobner and Martin Loughlin (eds.), *The Twilight of Constitutionalism?* (Oxford: Oxford University Press, 2010), pp. 201–19.

[39] Krisch, *Beyond Constitutionalism* (n. 34), ch. 8.

[40] On 'compensatory constitutionalism', see, for example, see Anne Peters, 'Compensatory Constitutionalism: The Function and Potential of Fundamental International Norms and Structures' (2006) 19 *Leiden Journal of International Law*, 579–610.

accountability, separation of powers, rights protection principles) as a connecting 'thread' in the framing of international regimes, or the thin 'pyramid' of rules of formal integrity (*ius cogens,* etc.,) in general international law as a partial corrective to impunity in the case of the new wave of transnational non-state-based 'new wars'.[41] Global Law, on this view, is internally conflicted from the perspective of Global Justice. It is only 'relatively autonomous' of national and international political forces, including many forces that have contributed to global injustice, yet still capable of contributing to Global Justice, especially to the extent that this is conceived of in a sectorally disaggregated fashion. In particular, drawing on the resources of past 'threads' or new hybrid 'flows', or the thin force of *opinio juris* in the cumulative higher order 'pyramidal' principles of general international law, it can exert some degree of influence beyond and against the instrumentality of justice-insensitive international legal and political forces.

10.4.5 Contingent

The contingent approach understands the relationship between Global Law and Global Justice as possessing no necessary properties. Rather, it is an 'irrelation'. This is not simply, as in the other models, because there is a perception of a significant standing 'gap' between aspiration and achievement, itself in some measure a consequence of the diversity of Global Law and the element of internal rivalry or trade-off between its different images of the legal world and its relationship to Global Justice. More than that, the contingent approach, whether or not it doubts the moral coherence of the very idea of Global Justice, it does not perceive any quality in law that relates in any systematic way to the achievement or otherwise of Global Justice On this view, law in its various globally expansive articulations is heteronomous rather than autonomous, influenced rather than influencing, miscellaneous rather than integrated in character. Global Law, here, is reduced to an archipelago of entrenched legalisms. It is the fragmentally instrumental product of a deep diversity of institutional decisions and influences by political, administrative and judicial bodies and juristic sources. What is more, the contextually narrow or compartmentalised nature of much legal decision-making at the point of delivery encourages myopia at the 'throughput' stage to

[41] Mary Kaldor, *New and Old Wars: Organised Violence in a Global Era*, 3rd ed. (Cambridge: Polity Press, 2012).

reinforce diversity at the 'input' stage. Global given its myriad manifestations and micro-contexts of application, is simply incapable of connecting to Global Justice in any patterned way.

10.4.6 Culpable

From this last and most critical standpoint, Global Law is viewed as an active agent of global injustice. In particular, Global Law reflects the hegemony of certain Western-centred conceptions of political authority and economic organisation. Partly, this is the 'original sin' of the international system, with Western powers creating an international political and economic framework that favoured their own interests. Partly, it is about the continuing influence of certain legal ideas that simultaneously protect the sovereign privileges of Western powers and legitimate other forms of transnational authority in which powerful Western players continue to have undue influence. On this 'postcolonial' imperialist view, the problem is avowedly not the loss of the state-centred system, but the continuity of its founding principles in a world of increasing political, military and economic interdependences. Global Law, here, is mainly heteronomous and with little self-standing integrity,[42] an instrumental set of 'rules of the powerful', with a deep-rooted systemic bias.[43] Global Justice, for its part, is often from this perspective seen as singular, based upon a thick ethic of mutual responsibility, extensive in scope, and holistic – especially in its full incorporation of an economic dimension of distributive justice alongside other more common features of commutative justice or justice in political and administrative relations between individuals and public authorities.[44]

10.5 Re-Orienting Global Law

The legal academy, we should recall, has a dual role with regard to Global Law, and, in turn, with regard to Global Justice. In a manner more

[42] Although, see Koskenniemi, a leading critical figure in international law, on the importance of 'chastened formalism' in the development of international relations through law today, Martti. Koskenniemi, 'The Fate of Public International Law; Between Technique and Politics' (2007) 70 *Modern Law Review*, 1–30.

[43] See Walker, *Intimations of Public Law* (n, 1) on radical scepticism about global law both within and beyond the legal constituency.

[44] See e.g. Pogge, *World Poverty and Human Rights* (n. 27); Singer, *One World: The Ethics of Globalization* (n. 28).

pronounced that in other more settled domains of legal authority, scholars are not only observers and documenters of the growing body of Global Law but also participants in its growth. Yet while we are never mere spectators before a world over which we have no influence, some of the orientations set out above seem to possess more 'real world' traction than others. The capacity to make a difference, in other words, is variable across the different orientations.

To begin, the 'constitutive' orientation on the one hand and the 'culpable' orientation on the other, tend towards the 'pure' alternatives of unanchored idealism and radical critique, with a further tendency towards the extremes of naïve utopianism and structural fatalism respectively. The roles associated with these opposite stances are better understood as those of regulative ideal (in the case of the constitutive orientation) and deep sceptic (in the case of the culpable orientation) challenging and moderating other orientations, rather than as orientations possessing a strongly independent shaping influence.

For its part, the 'collateral' approach increasingly suffers from the excessive realism of a state-centred institutional conservatism. The 'contingent' approach too, in its refusal to look beyond the diverse legal-institutional facts, is unduly cynical in its refusal to countenance the (even moderate) influence of law in projecting ideals of Global Justice. Yet these orientations, both products of an institutional pragmatism with a tendency towards an entrenched and compartmentalised legalism, while far from dominant, continue to have moderating or diluting influence on other orientations.

That leaves the 'compositive' and the 'compensatory' orientations competing for prominence today. Both have a critically constructive view of the role of Global Law. Both tend to treat Global Justice as open-ended and socially penetrative, to take the overall global constituency seriously, and to subscribe to conceptions of global connectedness that go beyond mere concurrent state interests. Yet both also tend to view Global Justice as an aggregate good rather than a holistic good – a perspective that allows and invites Global Law, at least in some of its variants, to make a discernible contribution to Global Justice, even if Global Justice is held to a high critical standard.

Alongside these similarities, significant differences remain between these orientations. In the final analysis, a compensatory approach remains more critical of the existing role of law than a compositive approach. The compensatory approach is also less confident about law's capacity to engage and resolve injustice, which is a function of either (or both) a more ambitious conception of Global Justice or a more sceptical understanding of law's overall contribution as a societal steering mechanism. Yet these compositive and compensatory positions stand today in close juxtaposition – as fluid points on a spectrum rather than categorical alternatives. When all is said and done, they are where the debate, not least amongst jurists, about the place of Global Law in the pursuit of Global Justice can find its most productive point of departure today, and where the perils and pitfalls of naïve utopianism, structural fatalism and narrowly entrenched legalism can most readily be kept at bay.

11

Plural Pluralities of Law

MARGARET DAVIES

Law's plurality can be understood in a variety of ways. It can be seen geographically, with different spaces and scales being associated with types of law beyond and within the nation state.[1] It can be understood discursively, with 'jurisgenerative' communities creating a multitude of readings and understandings of law.[2] It can be understood sociologically, with layers of formal and informal law making up the normative domain for particular associative groups.[3] It can even be understood from the position of the performative subject who creates law in their everyday interpretations and actions.[4] The plurality of law can refer to the inherent plurality of the singular system of state law, or it can refer to the existence of a plurality of legal systems. Legal pluralism is a plurality of pluralities, generated in part by paying attention to the bottom-up and material conditions of law production. In trying to unravel some of these complexities, this chapter also adds to them by radically expanding the meaning and reach of law so that its material substrata consist not only of the social and discursive domains, but also the human body, the earth, and the world of objects.

11.1 Law Has No Limits

I begin by briefly considering, and then putting to one side, the concern – often raised in discussions of legal pluralism – that it risks sliding into an

1 Boaventura de Sousa Santos, 'Law: A Map of Misreading – Toward a Postmodern Conception of Law' (1987) 14 *Journal of Law and Society*, 279–302.
2 Robert Cover, 'Nomos and Narrative' (1983) 97 *Harvard Law Review*, 4–68.
3 Sally Falk Moore, 'Law and Social Change: The Semi-Autonomous Social Field as an Appropriate Subject of Study' (1973) 7 *Law and Society Review*, 719–46.
4 Martha-Marie Kleinhans and Roderick Macdonald, 'What is a Critical Legal Pluralism?' (1997) 12 *Canadian Journal of Law and Society/Revue Canadienne de droit et societe*, 25–46; Desmond Manderson 'Beyond the Provincial: Space, Aesthetics, and Modernist Legal Theory' (1996) 20 *Melbourne University Law Review*, 1048–71.

undifferentiated mélange of various types of normativities. In this context, Sally Engle Merry's question is frequently quoted – 'Where do we stop speaking of law and find ourselves simply describing social life? Is it useful to call all these forms of ordering law?'[5] Once we have moved beyond the limits of a single state-defined system of law as the model and exclusive case of law, many normative environments intrude into the analysis of legal plurality. These 'laws' include not only the indigenous legal orders of colonised societies which have been suppressed but not destroyed by the colonial state. They also include religious forms of law, some of which have a decidedly state-like appearance (and even in one case a quasi-state recognition in the international legal order). They include 'semi-autonomous social fields',[6] multiple scales of law (global, national, local),[7] and the intersectional, hybrid, dynamics that arise when systems with different origins come into contact with each other or when people subjected to different systems try to make sense of them.[8] 'Law' in such contexts may be difficult to pin down: it may be as mobile as the subjects guided by it and recreated in new forms for different circumstances. But where, as Merry asks, does law stop? Do we lose the meaning of 'law' if we allow too many things to count?

The issue has generated some debate around the use of the term 'law'. Boaventura de Sousa Santos asks, essentially, why we should *not* regard 'rule systems', 'private governments', and so forth as 'law'?[9] He points out that the choice to label something 'law' or not is a political choice which in the past has been exercised in such a way as to value a core meaning of law – associated with the state – and to devalue or exclude senses of law regarded as marginal or 'primitive' (so-called). In response to Santos, however, Brian Tamanaha says that 'to view law in this manner is

[5] Sally Engle Merry, 'Legal Pluralism' (1988) 22 *Law and Society Review*, 869–96.

[6] Sally Falk Moore, 'Law and Social Change: The Semi-Autonomous Social Field as an Appropriate Subject of Study' (1973) 7 *Law and Society Review*, 719–46.

[7] Boaventura de Sousa Santos, 'Law: A Map of Misreading. Toward a Postmodern Conception of Law' (1987) 14 *Journal of Law and Society*, 279–302.

[8] Werner Zips, '"Global Fire": Repatriation and Reparations from a Rastafari (Re)Migrant's Perspective', in Franz von Benda-Beckman, Keebet von Benda-Beckman, and Anne Griffiths (eds.) *Mobile People, Mobile Law: Expanding Legal Relations in a Contracting World* (Aldershot: Ashgate, 2005); Anne Griffiths, 'Reconfiguring Law: An Ethnographic Perspective from Botswana' (1998) 23 *Law and Social Enquiry*, 587–616.

[9] Boaventura de Sousa Santos, *Toward a New Legal Common Sense*, 2nd ed. (London: Butterworths, 2002), p. 91. Santos compares law to medicine, where there are many forms, including many which are not officially recognised. But the term 'medicine' is singularised or essentialised so that its core form is Western medicine.

confusing, counter-intuitive, and hinders a more acute analysis of the many different forms of social regulation involved'.[10]

Not only can we think of the term 'law' as having a variety of referents, we can also think of the methods for identifying and understanding law to be multiple. Sociologists Monika Büscher and John Urry speak of 'mobile methods', or methodological approaches to the social fact of mobility and flux. How, they ask, can research methods respond to movement, to mobility and to fluidity in social interactions, rather than simplifying the facts of social life to that which is immobile, static and structured? A 'mobile method' is one in which researchers in a sense travel with the moving object, 'immersing themselves in the fleeting, multi-sensory, distributed, mobile and multiple, yet local, practical and ordered making of social and material realities'.[11] For law and legal pluralism in particular, such a method might involve zooming in and out of local to transnational spaces, or tracking citizens and subjects as they move between them.[12] Or it might involve following legal actors in their localised engagements with and performances of a variegated domestic law. A mobile method takes methodological notice of flux and tries to carve it up using non-obvious parameters, which might cut across accepted lines of scholarly engagement.[13]

It may be, of course, that the research object does not appear to move a great deal, but methodological plurality may nonetheless characterise the scholarly *looking*. In speaking of the 'broad church' of legal philosophy (including jurisprudence and legal theory), Julie Dickson writes:[14]

> Explanations of the same phenomena may start in different places, and explain different things in different ways – ways that are apposite to the existing knowledge base and familiar points of reference and

[10] Brian Tamanaha, 'Understanding Legal Pluralism: Past to Present, Local to Global' (2008) 30 *Sydney Law Review*, 375–411, 394. See also comments by Tamanaha, *A General Jurisprudence of Law and Society* (Oxford: Oxford University Press, 2001), pp. 172–75.

[11] Monika Büscher and John Urry, 'Mobile Methods and the Empirical' (2009) 12 *European Journal of Social Theory*, 99–116.

[12] See, in particular, Benda-Beckman et al, *Mobile People, Mobile Law* (n. 8).

[13] In this context, Büscher and Urry refer to the work of quantum theorist Karen Barad, and her idea that knowledge involves a cut in the flux of material movement. Büscher and Urry, 'Mobile Methods and the Empirical' (n. 11), 109–10. See Barad, *Meeting the Universe Halfway: Quantum Physics and the Entanglement of Matter and Meaning* (Durham: Duke University Press, 2007).

[14] Julie Dickson, 'Ours is a Broad Church: Indirectly Evaluative Legal Philosophy as a Facet of Jurisprudenctial inquiry' (2015) 6 *Jurisprudence*, 207–30.

> understanding of the relevant audience. This may result in explanations of the same phenomena varying significantly in content and structure. . . .
>
> Law should be thought of as a complex, multi-faceted phenomenon, and various (as well as various combinations) of those facets can be illuminated by theoretical shafts of light striking different parts of it from different directions and in different combination.

To add to Dickson's points about the plurality of audiences, perspectives, and illuminations (and to mix the metaphor badly) I would also say that no one theorist gets to see the entire elephant – and indeed, arguably, that there is no such thing.

Adopting a 'mobile method' for identifying law does raise conceptual questions – especially for those whose preference is for analytical certainty in the idea of law. For many reasons, which will become apparent in the course of this chapter, I do not accept that any such limitation can be sustained conceptually. There *is* no definition of law that will work for all times and in all places.[15] At the same time, limitations in the idea of law *can* be sustained in a practical sense, by acts of inclusion and exclusion, or by practicing a kind of border control in the idea of law. There is, and will always be, conceptual instability between law and non-law for the simple reason that law is a human construct and does not have pre-given conceptual edges. Its edges are constantly being created and re-created (*by whom* is an important question, to which I return).

There is therefore much sense in accepting provisional concepts of law for the purposes of socio-legal and sociological analysis.[16] Adopting a limited concept or understanding of law, or of a normative domain, for the purposes of allowing an empirical analysis to be undertaken is in most instances, essential. Some commentators have adopted a kind of procedural approach for identifying law – law may be a different thing in different locations or for different people, but the observer will be able to identify it with a context-specific question or set of observations. Brian Tamanaha's approach is probably the best known – it does not offer a concept or a social scientific definition but rather a simple adaptable description: law is 'whatever [is] accepted as legal by the social actors' in a particular context. It follows that: 'Legal pluralism exists whenever social

[15] Tamanaha, 'Understanding Legal Pluralism' (n. 10), 392.

[16] Roger Cotterrell, 'Review of Emmanuel Melissaris Ubiquitous Law: Legal Theory and the Space for Legal Pluralism' (2009) 19 (10) *Law and Politics Book Review*, 774–79; see generally Tamanaha, *General Jurisprudence* (n. 10), ch. 7.

actors identify more than one source of "law" within a social arena.'[17] Such provisionality does not always sit well with philosophy, which has tended to prefer universal and constant definitions. The approach offered by Emmanuel Melissaris, though equally context-dependent, is perhaps more committed to the desire to find a basic *concept* of law.[18] Melissaris proposes a 'thin' concept of law based on the 'shared normative experiences' of participants in a community.[19] Law is 'ubiquitous' because people everywhere inevitably experience law, and it is also plural and open-ended because communities and individuals have varying normative commitments. Law is conceptualised and somewhat limited by Melissaris, but its content is a matter of empirical investigation.

But what if even these rather adaptable approaches to identifying law still limit it unnecessarily? What if, for instance, a community is divided or in conflict about what its law is? What if the identification of law is gendered in some way (interpreted and even identified differently by people of various genders) or understood quite differently by differently located persons in the community? What if law has a materiality and partly arises from the relations between human bodies in particular locations? What if law is just as much a matter of neural pathways as it is of conceptual categories and practical behaviours? And what if law is not actually a 'thing' at all, and cannot be described?[20] My main reason for putting aside concerns based on the need to limit law in some way is essentially methodological. The presumption that law *must* be differentiated from non-law, even provisionally, establishes a boundary around the idea of law and may inhibit an expansive and open-ended enquiry about the multiple forms of law. This is a deliberately exploratory approach and is not intended to foreclose more analytically oriented enquiries, especially where a sensitivity to conceptual and de facto plurality is maintained.[21] There is no reason why different forms of legal

[17] Tamanaha, 'Understanding Legal Pluralism' (n. 10), 396.

[18] See comments by Cotterrell, 'Review' (n. 16), 777–78.

[19] Emmanuel Melissaris, *Ubiquitous Law: Legal Theory and the Space for Legal Pluralism* (Aldershot: Ashgate, 2009).

[20] Desmond Manderson comments in relation to mainstream (as opposed to critical) legal pluralism that 'There is a shared imaginary here: an understanding of law as comprised of overlapping *objects* in space. The problem of such an approach is exactly what one would expect: reification. . . . Legal pluralism multiplies legal systems but it does not doubt their objective and defined content.' 'Beyond the Provincial: Space, Aesthetics, and Modernist Legal Theory' (n. 4), p. 1060.

[21] As illustrated by many of the other contributions to this volume. See also Nicole Roughan, 'From Authority to Authorities: Bridging the Social/Normative Divide', forthcoming in

theorising should not co-exist.[22] In particular contexts and for particular purposes it may well be preferable or even crucial to adopt provisional and limited definitions of law and its adjacent concepts. All of Western state-based legality may itself be based on such a provisional understanding (albeit a very widespread and long-lasting one). But it is equally important for theory of law not to assume that provisional concepts of law, and especially not dominant concepts, exhaust the possibilities for how law may be understood.

Therefore, even as a theorist rather than a sociologist, I prefer to adopt not only a provisional approach to the *content* of law, but also to its concept, definition, location and status (as real or not, as material or ideal, as fact or norm, as known or made, etc.). Indeed, Melissaris may be promoting such a view when he says that his *prima facie* sense of law is 'defeasible and temporary'.[23] Rather than regard theory-construction as an exercise in finding a general form or even a general identifying process to suit a diversity of circumstances, I prefer to think of it, in the style of Deleuze and Guattari, as a form of experimentation.[24] Concepts are unsatisfactory approximations of a complex world and cannot be fixed or regarded as entities with their own reality, because they always exclude the non-conceptual elements of their object.[25] Theory develops by testing and modifying previous theory, but it can also be inhibited by what N. Katherine Hayles has termed the 'Platonic backhand'[26] – which

Maksymilian del Mar and Roger Cotterrell (eds.) *Transnational Authority: Theorising Across Disciplines* (Edward Elgar, 2016). Roughan points to the mutual reliance of the normative and the social in accounts of authority, locating this mutuality in the transnational sphere where authorities are plural, and often overlapping. The account allows Roughan to deal with a somewhat limited abstract notion in a complex environment.

22 But this is also not to suggest that all theoretical approaches are compatible: see Dickson, 'Ours is a Broad Church' (n. 14), 214. For instance, my approach is incompatible with the view that the concept of law is necessarily limited to a state, as well as the view that there is 'natural' law in the form of objective moral standards.

23 Melissaris, *Ubiquitous Law* (n. 19), p. 109.

24 Giles Deleuze and Felix Guattari, *What is Philosophy?*, trans. G Burchill and H Tomlinson (London: Verso, 1994).

25 Theodor Adorno, *Negative Dialectics*, trans. E. B. Ashton (New York: Continuum, 1973). See generally Nicholas Gane, 'Concepts and the New Empiricism' (2009) 12 *European Journal of Social Theory*, 83–97.

26 N. Katherine Hayles, *How We Became Posthuman: Virtual Bodies in Cybernetics, Literature, and Informatics* (Chicago: Chicago University Press, 1999), p. 12. Bourdieu also speaks of a 'theorisation effect' – 'forced synchronization of the successive, fictitious totalization, neutralization of functions, substitution of the system of products for the system of principles'. Pierre Bourdieu, *The Logic of Practice* (Cambridge: Polity, 1990), p. 86.

is essentially treating the results of an induction as prior to the facts from which they were drawn:

> The Platonic backhand works by inferring from the world's noisy multiplicity a simplified abstraction. So far, so good: this is what theorizing should do. The problem comes when the move circles around to constitute the abstraction as the original form from which the world's multiplicity derives. The complexity appears as a 'fuzzing up' of an essential reality rather than as a manifestation of the world's holistic nature.

While it is perfectly reasonable to infer a concept of law from one or a variety of empirical contexts, it is problematic to then regard this as some original or basic form of law.[27] Any inferences and any provisional definitions need to be regarded as what they are – partial, open to revision and highly dependent on their mobile place in the 'noisy multiplicity' around us. Things that do not quite fit within the definition we have constructed can be then regarded as a signal of the *contingency* of the definition and its status as an effect of power, rather than as a 'fuzzing up', a penumbra, a non-core case, or an incomplete case of a category which is falsely taken to be original or basic.

An empirical study needs more conceptual certainty (however provisional) than the position I am adopting. Moreover, my approach is not of much relevance to those whose task is to understand state law or other systematic forms of law. However, engaging in a study of social norms, or the state, or normative systems in general are not my objectives. Rather, my interest is in experimenting with the extremely expansive possibilities for understanding law once we remove any presumptions about what law is. 'Law' is a term with a range of different referents, none of which I would want to rule out of bounds for a broadly conceived legal theory and which, as a group, are also not necessarily exhaustive of the possible objects of legal theory.[28] That may seem impossibly vague (and I agree that it is), but theory is revealed in its own performance and some aspects of my orientation to law are narrowed in the course of the chapter.

27 Tamahana seems to observe such a move by Hart, who started his analysis in a conventionalist style to identify how the term 'law' is used, but then switched to a more essentialist analysis by taking this form of law as basic or essential. Tamanaha, *General Jurisprudence* (n. 10), p. 136.

28 I use the term 'legal theory' in a very broad sense, to refer to all forms of theory which touch upon law as a practice, concept, symbol, narrative or imagined entity. This includes subcategories known as feminist legal theory, socio-legal theory, analytical jurisprudence, critical race theory, critical legal theory, law and geography, law and humanities and legal philosophy.

Some of these parameters include, for instance, attention to the locatedness of law, its generation by legal subjects, its performativity and its materiality.

11.2 Law Becomes *What* It Is, *Where* It Is

'Before rules were facts: in the beginning was not a Word, but a Doing'.[29]

For some decades, legal geographers have been asking a disruptive question of legal theory. Instead of 'what is law?' the question they have posed is 'where is law?'[30] On the one hand, 'where' may seem to imply a 'what': how can we look for something if we do not know what it is we are looking for? On the other hand, it feels unsettling for a legal theorist to be asked 'where?' instead of 'what?' Some legal theory, in particular in the tradition of analytical jurisprudence, has tended to presume that the concept of law is un-located – by definition it is general, abstract, an ideational thing, but not a physical thing with its own place.

Law might easily be seen as leaving a trace or an imprint on a location – for instance in property boundaries – and in such instances it can even constitute its own enforcement, for instance where a boundary is made virtually impenetrable.[31] Law might equally easily be seen as delimiting action in time and space – for instance how fast a car is permitted to travel or how many laying hens can be fitted into a 'free range' space – but it is not normally regarded as itself physically visible. Only its effect is visible. Even though we might regard parliament and the courts as the places where law is created, we would not necessarily say that it resides or *is* there. We might broadly say that Australian commonwealth law is 'in' Australia and European law is 'in' Europe, but these observations do not satisfy the specific question 'where is law?' To suggest that law has a place

[29] Karl Llewellyn, 'Some Realism about Realism – Responding to Dean Pound' (1931) 44 *Harvard Law Review*, 1222–64, 1222.

[30] David Delaney, Richard Ford and Nicholas Blomley, 'Preface: Where is Law?', in Blomley, Delaney and Ford (eds.) *The Legal Geographies Reader* (Oxford: Blackwell, 2001).

[31] There is now a significant literature about boundaries in legal theory. See, for instance, Sarah Blandy and David Sibley, 'Law, Boundaries, and the Production of Space' (2010) 19 *Social and Legal Studies*, 275–84, as well as the articles contained in this special edition of *SLS*; see also Zenon Bańkowski, and Maksymilian Del Mar, 'Images of Borders and the Politics and Legality of Identity', in Richard Nobles and David Schiff (eds.) *Law, Society and Community: Socio-Legal Essays in Honour of Roger Cotterrell* (Aldershot: Ashgate, 2014), pp. 61–77; David Delaney, *The Spatial, the Legal, and the Pragmatics of World-Making: Nomospheric Investigations* (Abingdon: Routledge, 2010), pp. 21–22.

is troubling, because – although it defines space – it is regarded itself as outside particular locations and outside the physical world altogether.

The question 'where is law?' seems to require that we can point to it, like a literal reversal of Wittgenstein's famous sign-post.[32] Rather than say 'a rule stands there like a sign-post' we might say 'the sign-post (or other physical object) which stands there is a rule'. If we could say that the sign post *is* the rule, rather than communicating or reflecting the rule, we might be closer to a legal geographical situation of law *in* place.[33] Of course, Wittgenstein's signpost did not interpret itself – 'where is it said which way I am to follow it; whether in the direction of its finger or (e.g.) in the opposite one?'[34] Reflecting on this question brings us closer to locating law in fact, not as a static thing in a place, but rather as enmeshed in a network of performances of human (and potentially other) agents. The sign in itself is readable in the sense that it can be variously interpreted, but its interpretations narrow because of the surrounding conventions, made and replicated in discourse and practice. Law becomes *what* it is, *where* it is – in physical locations, in bodies, in things, and in the ways that it is created and performed by recipients and purveyors of law.

There is a solid tradition, although not the philosophically dominant one in the legal theory of the Anglosphere, of regarding law as material. It is one of the points of departure for the famous dispute between Eugen Ehrlich and Hans Kelsen about facts and norms.[35] More than a century ago, Ehrlich located 'living' law in the factual social relationships between people in any given community, and contrasted this with official state law – a mere bureaucratic and static manifestation of law.[36] In response, Kelsen argued that Ehrlich had muddled the empirical and the normative, is and ought, and that sociology of law had to be kept separate from a pure theory of law. Empirical facts cannot be used in explanation of the

[32] Ludwig Wittgenstein, *Philosophical Investigations*, trans. GEM Anscombe (Oxford: Basil Blackwell, 1958), p. 85.

[33] The relationship between law and space is described by the editors of *The Legal Geographies Reader* as mutual or co-constitutive: see Delaney, Ford and Blomley 'Preface: Where is Law?'(n. 30), xviii.

[34] Ibid.

[35] See generally Bart van Klink, 'Facts and Norms: The unfinished Business between Eugen Ehrlich and Hans Kelsen', in Marc Hertogh (ed.) *Living Law: Reconsidering Eugen Ehrlich* (Oxford: Hart Publishing, 2009), pp. 127–55.

[36] Eugen Ehrlich, *Fundamental Principles of the Sociology of Law*, trans. Walter Moll (New York: Russell and Russell, 1962). See generally David Nelken, 'Law in Action or Living Law: Back to the Beginning in Sociology of Law' (1984) 4 *Legal Studies*, 157–74.

normative quality of law – they are just facts, observable regularities, and do not explain the existence of the *ought*. (And indeed the separation of is and ought is sometimes taken as a self-evident truth by legal theorists, including some pluralists.[37])

Later, in *The Pure Theory of Law*, Kelsen observed that law existed in 'natural' space, but instantly separated this from the domain of legal meaning:[38]

> [L]aw – or what is customarily so called – seems at least partly to be rooted in nature and to have a 'natural' existence. For if you analyse any body of facts interpreted as 'legal' or somehow tied up with law . . . two elements are distinguishable: one, an act or series of acts – a happening occurring at a certain time and in a certain place, perceived by our senses: an external manifestation of human conduct; two, the legal meaning of this act, that is, the meaning conferred upon the act by the law.

It is not (in my view) necessary to enter into the debate about facts and norms to perceive that this passage at the very least, and contrary to Kelsen's intention, suggests the *inseparability* of law and matter. Although Kelsen's neo-Kantian intellectual agenda demanded such a separation be made conceptually, from another angle it is equally arguable that, in fact, law is *never* separated from its materiality and cannot be so separated. Kelsen says that 'two elements are distinguishable', but are they? In what way are they distinguishable? Law always takes a physical form: in words, in actions, in some 'external manifestation'. Legislation and cases have physicality, as do courtroom performances, including the words spoken by judges and lawyers in courts, and by other people in more everyday situations. Because our intellectual habits enforce a separation of ideal and material, mind and body, it can be difficult to see the normative and the factual together and we assume that the law sits behind or above its physical expression. Nonetheless, the fact that they always *are* together is important. It means not only that is and ought are not separate, because an 'ought' is always expressed in (and yes, often

[37] Melissaris, *Ubiquitous Law* (n. 19), p. 115.

[38] Hans Kelsen, *The Pure Theory of Law* (Berkeley: University of California Press, 1967), p. 2. As Iain Stewart explains 'The neo-Kantians, as they came to be called, distinguished between two kinds of science: the natural sciences (*Naturwissenschaften*) and the sciences of mind (*Geisteswissenschaften*) or culture (*Kulturwissenschaften*). . . . [T]he former were to be concerned with material facts, the latter with meanings; or the former with regularities, the latter with individual events. In terms of separating 'is' and 'ought', the former were to be concerned with material facts, the latter with values.' Iain Stewart, 'The Critical Legal Science of Hans Kelsen, (1990) 17 *Journal of Law and Society*, 273–308; see also Bart van Klink 'Facts and Norms' (n. 35), 129–30.

derived from) an 'is',[39] but also that fact and norm co-exist dynamically. Although Llewellyn placed the fact 'before' the rule – at any given moment neither is prior and any conceptual separation is the result of an intellectual tradition, not a necessary point of departure for theory. It is this necessary co-existence of law and fact that sociology of law draws upon so powerfully, in particular in the form of legal pluralism. Pluralism pays theoretical attention to the materiality of law, its locatedness in specific contexts, and the complex relationships which form it into various systems and normative commitments.

I have moved away slightly from questions about the geographical locatedness of law, but the point of these reflections has been to emphasise that law cannot be isolated from the material conditions in which is it expressed, and that in fact it equally arises from those conditions. Law always has a place and a time, and a materiality to support it.[40] Thinking about law in this way promotes an image of it as distributed across space and throughout the material networks that make up our social lives. Such an image of law is intrinsically plural. It is plural because law is understood, conceptualised and experienced differently in different locations and by different people as individuals or in groups. It may be crystallised in different formats – for instance as state law,

39 Another argument against the separation of is and ought is simply to observe the gravitational pull of things being a particular way. A pattern of behaviour tends to be followed – gender is not just an observable set of behaviours, it is normative (and not because it is 'natural'). While a description of a thing does not imply that it *must* be that way, there is nonetheless a norm – normality – suggested by commonality. This is essentially the view of the foundation of customs and laws as understood by early jurists. As Sir John Davies said 'by often iteration and multiplication of the act it becometh a *Custome*; and being continued without interruption time out of mind, it obtaineth the force of a *Law*' Irish Reports, quoted in J. G. A. Pocock, *The Ancient Constitution and the Feudal Law* (New York: Norton, 1957), p. 33. Carolyn Merchant says 'A statement's normative function lies in the use itself as description. The norms may be tacit assumptions hidden within the descriptions in such a way as to act as invisible restraints or moral ought-nots. The writer or culture may not be conscious of the ethical import yet may act in accordance with its dictates.' *The Death of Nature: Women, Ecology, and the Scientific Revolution* (San Francisco: Harper and Rowe, 1980), p. 4. There are many examples, one of the clearest in recent years being debate over what marriage 'is'.

40 Is it possible to think of an entirely immaterial law? The abstract thing is only what remains once all of the material conditions are removed but what, then, is left? This is not a question that I can answer here, but in thinking of ideal and material as inseparable (though without negating the existence of the ideal) I have taken some inspiration from theories of embodied mind and in particular what Malafouris calls 'Material engagement theory'. See Lambros Malafouris, *How Things Shape the Mind* (Cambridge, MA: MIT Press, 2013).

customary law, religious law or semi-autonomous social fields – but it exceeds the edges of such delineations not only because of the difficulty of capturing what is 'in' and what is 'out' but because law is an effect (and also often the cause) of a dynamic set of relationships.

This distributed 'all over'[41] image of law is too vague (deliberately so) to be understood as a concept, or even a provisional description of law. Both its form and its content are completely mobile and it cannot support any clear differentiation of law from non-law. Nonetheless, as a picture of law, it does have an intellectual heritage (beyond geography), and in the next three sections, I try to unpick some of the threads which compose my view of law as materially located and performed. These threads do not exhaust the possibilities for understanding law's pluralism – they are merely some of the critical points of departure for a multidimensional conceptualisation of law.

11.3 Subjects Constitute the Law

> 'Law is . . . only realized through the actions of particular human beings who exist in several discourses.'[42]

Legal philosophy has often regarded the knowing subject as significant in the construction of law though, in the tradition of legal positivism and its variants, it is legal insiders whose knowledge constitutes the law. Two well-known examples come from the work of H. L. A. Hart and Ronald Dworkin. Hart's 'rule of recognition' which was at the basis of a legal system was recognised and acknowledged by legal officials.[43] In Hart's universe, legal experts were essentially responsible for constituting and understanding law. And while Dworkin paid attention to the broad community values that inform interpretations of law, he entrusted its 'best' knowledge or interpretation to an idealised philosopher-judge, who is in a sense the ultimate legal insider.[44]

Despite the very limited identities of the legal elites whose subjective intentions or knowledge constitute law in such state-based legal theory, the thought that underpins them is important. It is that law (whatever it is)

[41] Austin Sarat '". . .The Law is All Over": Power, Resistance, and the Legal Consciousness of the Welfare Poor' (1990) 2 *Yale Journal of Law and the Humanities*, 343–79.

[42] Manderson, 'Beyond the Provincial' (n. 4), 1064.

[43] H. L. A. Hart, *The Concept of Law* 2nd ed. (Oxford: Oxford University Press, 1994).

[44] Ronald Dworkin, *Law's Empire* (London: Fontana, 1986).

is created, understood, applied and reproduced, at least in part by human agents with their own distinct perspectives. This is not to suggest that law is always necessarily the product of an act of will,[45] but rather that law is produced within networks of meaning-producers – normally though not necessarily exclusively, human agents. State-based legal theory has tended to limit the relevant perspective to a specific type – the legal expert, as reduced to an impersonal subject or ideal form by the legal philosopher. By contrast to these self-determining images of law as produced and known by legal experts, several forms of socio-legal and critical theory, including some types of legal pluralism, have located the subject who knows and constructs the law much more broadly – in the population at large.[46] And rather than relying on an impersonalised and de-located subject, one who is essentially a mirror image of a singular law, they have drawn on empirical evidence, stories and experiences of marginalisation in order to illustrate diversity in the social constitution of law.

Expanding the set of subjects who know and constitute the law in their engagements with it can lead theory in several connected directions. In particular, it leads first towards a more layered understanding of the plural and hybrid legalities outwardly evident in any social field, and secondly towards the multiple and entangled perspectives of legal subjects within these complex normative environments. I consider these two dimensions in this section, before turning in the next to a further extension of these points, which is to think about law as located in an interdependent and performative corporeality of humans bodies in physical locations that bridges the material-semiotic divide of fact and norm.

In many of its twentieth century iterations legal pluralism tended to focus on the co-existence of essentially different legal orders in a single geographical space. The plurality involved was a plurality of legal systems, which (in time) came to be understood as overlapping, inter-meshed, and combined in different ways. These different normative orders can be described from the outside as sets of rules and relations that operate in a given space. However, looking at this plurality from the

[45] As argued by Hans Kelsen. See eg *General Theory of Norms* (Oxford: Oxford University Press, 1991), p. 27.

[46] See in particular Kleinhans and MacDonald 'What is a *Critical* Legal Pluralism?' (n. 4); Kirsten Anker, *Declarations of Interdependence: A Legal Pluralist Approach to Indigenous Rights* (Aldershot: Ashgate, 2014); Melissaris, *Ubiquitous Law* (n. 19).

point of view of legal actors gives rise to a more complex pluralism,[47] one which can appreciate the plasticity of normativity when it is not seen as a mandatory form of order but rather as a resource to be used by those with specific problems or disputes.

This fluidity of normative engagement is illustrated, for instance, in the work of Anne Griffiths in Botswana.[48] Looking at disputes about the division of property after divorce she analyses the layers of custom, locatedness in family and community, and formal law which make up the normative surrounds of any dispute. Starting with the person and their particular situation illustrates a fluidity in subjects' engagement with law, that cannot be regarded as a simple application of rules to a factual situation. Rather, the 'rules exhibit a plasticity that is molded by the different contexts in which people apply and manipulate them.'[49] Moreover, the study illustrates very clearly in an African context the ways that the social normativity associated with gender cannot be simply separated from any formal set of rules or customs. The 'situatedness' of the legal actor includes their location as a social actor. And therefore, compared to a pluralism that simply looks at different systems of law, 'the type of pluralism that these disputes characterise is of a more fluid order, based on links made between legal and social identities drawn from numerous sources configured by networks in varying ways'.[50] Although this particular study is confined to a particular locality, it is easy to see that where people are globally mobile the opportunities (and the need) to engage with a multitude of intersecting normative orders is considerably expanded.

A second theme arising from thinking about plurality and locatedness at the level of the human legal actor is associated with knowledge and interpretation of law(s), understood not so much through observed engagement with normative plurality, but as perceived and constructed by subjects. Even where only 'one' legal system is in play, its normative substructure is extremely diverse, because it is produced by complex and situated persons in their multiple, reiterative, cultural engagements. Legal agents have different cultural backgrounds, different locations in relation

[47] See generally Benda-Beckman et al., *Mobile people, Mobile Law* (n. 8).

[48] Anne Griffiths 'Reconfiguring Law' (n. 8). See also von Benda-Beckman et al. *Mobile People, Mobile Law* (n. 8), in particular Franz von Benda Beckman, Keebet von Benda-Beckman, and Anne Griffiths 'Mobile People, Mobile Law: An Introduction'; 'Nina Glick-Schiller 'Transborder Citizenship: An Outcome of legal Pluralism' and Werner Zips '"Global Fire": Repatriation and Reparations from a Rastafari (Re)Migrant's Perspective'.

[49] Ibid., 613. [50] Griffiths 'Reconfiguring Law' (n. 8), 598.

to cultural forms of power, and varying forms of legal consciousness. The result is a fractured and often inconsistent normative environment which is nonetheless integral to all forms of separated law, such as state law. These matters have been famously explored by Robert Cover, who pointed out that formal law is just one small part of the *nomos* or normative universe which we inhabit.[51] Norm construction in the *nomos* – juris-genesis – is the product of communities and their underlying narratives, and therefore law cannot be understood separately from the narratives and stories which shape a community. Because of the sheer quantity and diversity of norms generated in this way, there is a surplus of law and one role of the state is to filter it, or kill some of it off – thus Cover said that courts are 'jurispathic'.[52]

In different ways, legal consciousness studies and critical legal pluralism have also made the case for paying attention to the subject-centred, bottom up, perspective in theorising and understanding law. Patricia Ewick and Susan Silbey's work in legal consciousness aimed to understand how 'what [people] ... think and do coalesces into a recognizable, durable phenomena and institution we recognize as the law'.[53] Legal consciousness is not only about people's varying interpretation of law, but also about how they make law in their own lives: law and consciousness of law are not separate, but rather different aspects of the plane of meaning through which law becomes a thing – consciousness of law in all its diversity *is* law, from which basis (maybe, and in certain situations) a singular form is extracted.

Similarly, critical legal pluralism has insisted that law is generated by subjects who have their own diversity and plurality – their group allegiances, their own specific histories, and their socio-cultural locatedness.[54] As Kirsten Anker has described it, in critical pluralism

[51] Cover, 'Nomos and Narrative' (n. 2). Some useful updates and extensions of Cover's work include Judith Resnik, 'Living their Legal Commitments: Paideic Communities, Courts and Robert Cover' (2005) 17 *Yale Journal of Law and the Humanities*, 17–53; Robert Post, 'Who's Afraid of Jurispathic Courts: Violence and Public Reason in *Nomos and Narrative*' (2005) 17 *Yale Journal of Law and the Humanities*, 9–16; Aviam Soifer, 'Covered Bridges' (2005) 17 *Yale Journal of Law and the Humanities*, 55–80.

[52] Cover 'Nomos and Narrative' (n. 2), 40. Of course, as Robert Post notes, 'The state is not uniquely jurispathic; every *nomos* exists by virtue of its exclusion and denial of competing *nomoi*. Jurispathology is in this sense built into the very sociology of human meaning.'

[53] Silbey, describing her work with Ewick. 'After Legal Consciousness' (2005) 1 *Annual Review of Law and Social Science*, 323–68.

[54] Kleinhans and MacDonald, 'What is a *Critical* Legal Pluralism?' (n. 4); Manderson 'Beyond the Provincial' (n. 4); Margaret Davies, 'Legal Pluralism', in Peter Cane and

'there is not a clash of two distinct systems in a social field, but a permanent interplay of ideas and principles in peoples' minds, gleaned from innumerable sources, that resolves into "the law" for any one person in any one situation.'[55] This is not to say that law is purely subjective, though it has a subjective element. Rather, law and legal plurality is a process, formed by everyday relations and in everyday perception: law is, after all, entirely constituted in human relations, and therefore knowledge and understanding of law is not separate from the 'law itself'.[56] Law can have no separate existence, nor can normative systems be separated except contingently and for essentially instrumental purposes. Understanding law to be produced by persons who are both many in number and in themselves plurally situated,[57] means that law is always becoming, and can never be objectified. Indeed law as object is equally of the subject – subjects of law and law as an object are constantly in dialogue.

11.4 Law Is Performed and Lived

Persons are not only their mental processes and are not only situated in discourse and in a web of abstract norms. Legal subjects are also their corporeal presence. Therefore, we can also situate the human in law at the level of bodily relations between persons and, as I indicate in the last section of this chapter, at the level of human interaction with the physical world. Returning to the discussion of Kelsen (earlier in this chapter), law is always emergent through the conduct of human bodies – a number of such bodies in fact – located in particular material contexts and performing particular actions. As I have indicated, we are habituated to cognitively dissociate body from mind and to build theoretical systems which presume that ideas and concepts can be understood on their own without reference to their

Herbert Kritzer (eds.) *The Oxford Handbook of Empirical Legal Research* (Oxford: Oxford University Press, 2010); Anker, *Declarations of Interdependence* (n. 46).

55 Anker, *Declarations of Interdependence* (n. 46), p. 187.

56 Kleinhans and Macdonald, 'What is a *Critical* Legal Pluralism?' (n. 4), 39–40.

57 As Deleuze and Guattari say at the beginning of *A Thousand Plateaus*, 'The two of us wrote Anti-Oedipus together. Since each of us was several, there was already quite a crowd.' Gilles Deleuze and Felix Guattari, *A Thousand Plateaus: Capitalism and Schizophrenia*, trans. Brian Massumi, (Minneapolis: University of Minnesota Press, 1987), p. 3. A more grounded consideration of multiple and fragmented identity is found in critical race theory and feminist thought, in particular in theorists of multiple consciousness. See, in particular, Deborah King, 'Multiple Jeopardy, Multiple Consciousness: The Context of a Black Feminist Ideology' (1988) 14 *Signs*, 42–72; Mari Matsuda, 'When the First Quail Calls: Multiple Consciousness as Jurisprudential Method' (1989) 11 *Women's Rights Law Reporter*, 7–10.

materiality. Law becomes de-physicalised and reified. But we cannot observe or experience mind and body separately any more than we can observe or experience law in any pure form. Law, the body, the world, and language are always together and their effects are co-emergent.

The point that law is always materially constructed is not explicitly developed in critical legal pluralism but is nonetheless implied, because of the emphasis on situated and multiple identities. Critical pluralism has tended to foreground discourse, myth and the subject's knowledge of law, and has not considered in detail the physical dimensions of any process of law-creation. However, a subject-oriented pluralism is not antithetical to an approach that emphasises the physicality of the relations which in combination give rise to legal effects and embodied legal subjectivities. On the contrary, critical pluralism leads precisely in this direction. It suggests the substantial nature of the relations in which subjects and their law are situated. What happens to law, then, when we seriously regard the subjects who know, perceive and narrate law as not only characterised by their abstract cognitive or mental capacities and their location in discourse, but also as corporeal bodies? I would like to mention briefly first, the issue of physicality in social inter-relationship and, second, the dynamics of legal performance.

The culture-nature and mind-body distinctions are gendered, and so it is not surprising that it is feminist theorists who have been at the forefront of challenging them in various ways.[58] In feminist thought, material social life, the life of inter-connected bodies in specific locations and formations, is often counter-posed to the abstract individualism of traditional liberalism, with its emphasis on disembodied forms of the person and abstract ideational constructions. In a legal context, the mismatch of the abstract individual and 'real life' has often been revealed by the falsification of legal doctrine by empirical means. Simply put, law based upon abstract individuals has tended to reify (particular types of) male lives, and has not represented the material differences experienced by women and other marginalised groups in lived circumstances.[59] Historical and social

[58] For an early but still relevant description of the modalities of challenging the mind-body distinction in feminism see Elizabeth Grosz, *Volatile Bodies: Toward a Corporeal Feminism* (Bloomington: Indiana University Press, 1993), pp. 13–19.

[59] As Judith Grbich put it 'legal reasoning transforms the embodied imaginings from male lives into the "objective" form of doctrine which passes for the "normative"': 'The Body in Legal Theory' (1992) 11 *University of Tasmania Law Review*, 26–58.

considerations are excluded from the interpretation of legal doctrine with its reflection of a narrow segment of privileged masculinity.

But embodied existence is not only a point of departure for critique of law. It is also the inspiration for finding alternative normative forms in everyday life, where this is understood as a network or web of entangled relationships. Imagining law to be produced through the micro-processes of daily life is essentially to see it as produced through praxis and performance. Understanding practical and performative actions in this way means that we do not see them as simply applications of a rule where the action is determined by or reflective of an abstract doctrine or concept. Rather, performances in time and space produce normative facts for that particular context: they underpin and ultimately contribute to the production of rules and doctrines but also to counter-hegemonic norms with subcultural presence and pre-figurative potential.[60] This is not to say that there are never instances of rules simply being created and then followed, but these instances also need to be seen within the context in which they are themselves made as the effect of accumulated socio-legal actions. It is certainly true that parliament can create a rule which people then follow. But the conditions of possibility for a parliamentary performance, or a judicial decision, or any 'legal' act, are the repeated micro-actions and attitudes of a large number of social actors in everyday life as well as those who participate in the state with a 'formal' role. These are part of the texture of law and indeed arguably its very substance.

Thinking of performativity in this way as the material substance and basis for law is to revitalise a much older tradition in the understanding of law which emphasised custom. Like performativity, the core mechanism of custom is repetition. Custom, or usage, was long recognised within common law as the foundation for law.[61] When formalised and understood as reducible to justiciable rules, it also undoubtedly takes on an inherently conservative or static dimension, emphasising sameness

[60] See generally Margaret Davies, 'The Law Becomes Us: Prefiguring Judgment' (2012) 20 *Feminist Legal Studies*, 167–81; for an extended elaboration of performativity in a legal context see Nicholas Blomley, 'Performing Property: Making the World' (2013) 26 *Canadian Journal of Law and Jurisprudence*, 23–48. Although Blomley is specifically theorising property as performance, there is no reason that his arguments cannot be extended generally to law. See also Sara Ramshaw, *Justice as Improvisation: The Law of the Extempore* (Abingdon: Routledge, 2013).

[61] See e.g. Sir John Fortescue, *On the Laws and Governance of England*, ed. Shelley Lockwood (Cambridge: Cambridge University Press, 1997), pp. 24–27.

rather than difference.[62] However, regarded more broadly as the reiterative practices and attitudes which go into the everyday normativity of law construction, performance can be reconstructive, resistive, or essentially conservative. Performance always implies a singular action or event, a particular movement at a particular time and place. Performance therefore implies some degree of novelty, even though it also necessarily refers to a precedent (understood as either a previous practice, an existing norm, or in a more formal legal sense as a prior decision on a similar set of facts).[63] Seeing law as performance emphasises its materiality, and also its living and dynamic nature, rather than a code or set of doctrines, law emerges in intricately networked actions and relationships.

11.5 The Place of Objects

Having gone this far in thinking about a pluralistic materialism in law, it is impossible to stop at human beings relating and networking in social contexts. There is, after all, the physical environment to consider. Human subjects in Western thought are in many ways constructed as different, separate and exceptional compared to the world of objects. For Descartes, even animals were mere mechanical objects. As Plumwood comments, '[c]onsciousness now divides the universe completely in a total cleavage between the thinking being and mindless nature, and between the thinking substance and "its" body, which becomes the division between consciousness and clockwork.'[64] Thus the physical world has been written out of much Western theory, with its emphasis on human meanings, generated by human consciousness.

Increasingly, in response to improved understanding of Indigenous cosmologies but also from concern about unchecked environmental

[62] Sir John Davies, for instance, said 'a Custome doth never become a Law to bind the people, until it hath been tried and approved time out of mind': Irish Reports (1612), quoted in J. G. A. Pocock, *The Ancient Constitution and the Feudal Law* (New York: Norton, 1957), p. 33.

[63] Derrida's use of the word 'iteration' as a term of art to capture this oscillation between same and other, generality and particularity, is well discussed in literature about performance, especially in relation to law. See Jacques Derrida, *Limited Inc* (Evanston: Northwestern University Press, 1988), p. 53; Margaret Davies, *Delimiting the Law: 'Postmodernism' and the Politics of Law* (London: Pluto Press, 1996), pp. 111–13; Ramshaw, *Justice as Improvisation* (n. 60), ch. 3.

[64] Val Plumwood, *Feminism and the Mastery of Nature* (London: Routledge, 1993), p. 116.

destruction,[65] Western theory is beginning to challenge, and make efforts to imagine a way out of, its narcissism. It is true that the critique of the mind-body and nature-culture distinctions has been prominent for decades in feminist, environmental, and Indigenous philosophies – the first two of which draw on older, but somewhat submerged, traditions within Western philosophy, such as the monism of Spinoza.[66] But recently a renewed scholarly interest in rethinking the relationship of human beings to the physical world has been evident and a 'new materialism' has emerged in areas of social philosophy and the humanities.[67] This work challenges the mind-body and nature culture distinctions as well as the resistant assumption that the physical world is primarily passive stuff available for human extraction and exploitation. Its key theoretical shift is away from the dualistic separations of modernism (matter and meaning, the physical and the discursive, body and mind, etc.) towards a view of their entanglement and co-emergence.

Imagining objects and matter generally as an integral and interacting part of social life is probably the defining feature of new materialism. In one sense, this seems obvious – it is trivial to say that we are surrounded by things, that we rely on them, that they shape our conditions for existence and so forth. But the point is to more fully embed this physicality in Western ontology, to embed the human *in* the world rather than see ourselves as separate from it, and to understand that objects and

[65] These are not the only drivers of theoretical change, but they are arguably the most significant because they come from outside the realm of theoretical introspection – another driver has been that during the 1980s and 1990s theory became too focused on the cultural, discursive and contingent at the expense of attention to the real and the material. This concern may generate essentially a swing back to the 'real', the 'material' and the ontological and perpetuate the founding dichotomies rather than challenge them.

[66] See, e.g., Grosz, *Volatile Bodies* (n. 58), pp. 10–13; Susan James, Genevieve Lloyd, and Moira Gatens, 'The Power of Spinoza: Feminist Conjunctions. Susan Lloyd interviews Genevieve Lloyd and Moira Gatens' (2000) 15 *Hypatia*, 40–58.

[67] The most developed theoretical elaboration of new materialism that I am aware of connects quantum physics to social theory. See Karen Barad, *Meeting the Universe Halfway: Quantum Physics and the Entanglement of Matter and Meaning* (Durham: Duke University Press, 2007). See also Jane Bennett, *Vibrant Matter: A Political Ecology of Things* (Durham: Duke University Press, 2010); Tim Ingold, 'Toward an Ecology of Materials' (2012) 41 *Annual Review of Anthropology*, 427–42; Bill Brown, 'Thing Theory' (2001) 28 *Critical Inquiry*, 1–22; Rick Dolphijn and Iris van der Tuin, *New Materialisms: Interviews and Cartographies* (Ann Arbor: Open Humanities Press, 2012). In legal theory, see Andreas Phillipopoulos-Mihalopoulos, 'Atmospheres of Law: Senses, Affects, Landscapes' (2013) 7 *Emotion, Space, and Society*, 35–44; Philippopoulos-Mihalopoulos 'Critical Autopoeisis and the Materiality of Law' (2014) 27 *International Journal of the Semiotics of Law*, 389–418.

things have a kind of agency in their positions in these networks. This is not an intentional agency in the sense that objects can think, exercise reason, and make decisions. Rather, it is an agency based on the reactive and interactive effects of things (living and non-living) in human and non-human networks. It reminds us, moreover, that the human body is also matter – flesh and bones are bio-chemical formations and, as such, have an unavoidable interdependence with the physical matter beyond the human body.[68] Again, the point seems extremely obvious and trivial, but the challenge is to make it integral to theory – which has tended to be obsessed with ideas and abstractions.

Such thinking holds the promise of paradigm change, towards theory that does not counter-pose extractive human society against increasingly scarce natural resources. It asks us to think nature and culture together, and to understand that we are all ecologically connected. There is an inescapable ethical dimension to this shift,[69] away from the view that human beings dominate nature, towards the value of interconnection and mutual reliance. This shift in position for social thinking poses significant challenges for law, which in the West has been entirely conceptualised as an abstract product of human society. Legal scholarship can become more attentive to law's material surrounds and more explicitly relational in orientation. Such relationality cannot be abstracted from context – as I have indicated above, it needs to be understood as geographically located, attentive to subjective aspects of meaning, but nonetheless based in observable, performed, relations between human beings. All of these dimensions of understanding law are intrinsically pluralistic as they cannot give rise to a single description or concept of law. Moreover, the production of theory itself, as an 'embodied imagining'[70] that is experimental and contingent, means finding ourselves as theorists in these localities.

[68] Carol Bacchi and Chris Beasley have coined the term 'social flesh' to describe the interdependence and the 'mutual reliance' of human bodies: 'Envisaging a New Politics for an Ethical Future: Beyond Trust, Care and Generosity – Toward an Ethic of "Social Flesh"' (2007) 8 *Feminist Theory*, 279–98. See also Bennett, *Vibrant Matter* (n. 67).

[69] Anna Grear speaks of a new 'juridical imaginary' based on this ethics, which would view humans as part of nature, and be more open to nature-culture interactions as norm-generating. See Grear, 'Toward New Legal Futures? In Search of Renewing Foundations', in Anna Grear and Evadne Grant (eds.) *Thought, Law, Rights and Action in an Age of Environmental Crisis* (Cheltenham: Edward Elgar, 2015), pp. 283–313.

[70] Grbich, 'The Body in Legal Theory' (n. 59).

Paying attention to physical and ecological relationships, however, also means situating law in relation to the material interconnectedness of all life systems. We should not delude ourselves that this fundamental view of law as part of the world is anything new – it has been the foundation of indigenous knowledges and ways of being for many tens of thousands of years. It is new for the West, however, with its distinctive responsibility for human exceptionalism and its techno-industrial-capitalist consequences. Law can no longer be regarded as a separate human sphere and any singularity it might have retained as a result of its primarily human dimension (which always seems to allow for some abstraction or reduction of life's complexity) is no longer tenable.

11.6 Conclusion

A theoretical narrative that starts with the presumption that its object must be defined and limited in some way is obviously going to look very different from one which endeavours not to draw boundaries, but is explicitly open and exploratory. Neither approach is 'right' in some absolute philosophical sense, and clearly each method will lead in a different direction. The fact that I have taken the more speculative pathway does not mean, however, that I reject the traditional question of legal theory, 'what is law?'[71] I simply do not regard it as the only theoretical question or even the fundamental one. As I have discussed, the legal geographical question 'where is law?' is equally interesting and provocative. Moreover, as I hope to have shown, answers to the 'what is law?' question can be conditional, inessential, culturally specific, embedded in a narrative form, and open ended.

[71] Among critical theorists, Costas Douzinas and Adam Geary have argued that 'once the question [about law] has been posed as a "what is" one, the answer will necessarily give a series of predicates for the word "law", a definition of its essence, which will then be sought out in all legal phenomena. As a result, a limited number of institutions, practices and actors will be included and considered relevant to jurisprudential inquiry and a large number of questions will go unanswered', *Critical Jurisprudence: The Political Philosophy of Justice* (Oxford: Hart Publishing, 2005), p. 10.

12

Postcolonial Jurisprudence and the Pluralist Turn: From Making Space to Being in Place

KIRSTEN ANKER*

12.1 Introduction

Legal pluralism as a field of study has gone hand in hand with colonial politics, promoted in furtherance of an imperial apparatus to manage Indigenous peoples, as well as invoked in challenges to colonial orders *by* Indigenous peoples. Plural legal phenomena and institutional arrangements clearly predated nineteenth-century European imperialism and extended beyond its geographical reach.[1] However, many of the tools and outlooks of the discipline were developed in the context of European colonisation in Asia and Africa by intellectual forerunners to the self-labelled legal pluralists who emerged in the 1970s.[2] Often funded by colonial administrations, these researchers vaunted their methods as providing a firm scientific basis for the imposition of centralised colonial law, the codification of local 'customary law' and, later, the transition to self-rule.[3] Thus a first wave of 'classic' legal pluralist studies developed in the context of the co-existence of, and complex interactions between, formal law and state institutions, religious law, customary obligations and traditional dispute resolution in postcolonial societies where 'legal pluralism was an obvious and

* Many thanks to Nicole Roughan, Genevieve Painter and Bradley Por for their careful reading and useful feedback. Any errors remain my own.

1 Lauren Benton and Richard Ross (eds.), *Legal Pluralism and Empires: 1500–1850* (New York: New York University Press, 2013); Lauren Benton, 'Historical Perspectives on Legal Pluralism' (2011) 3 *Hague Journal on the Rule of Law*, 57–69; Patrick Glenn, *Legal Traditions of the World* (Oxford: Oxford University Press, 2010).

2 Such as early-twentieth-century British social anthropologist Bronislaw Malinowski. Note, though, that other precursors can be located in European sociology, American legal realism, and studies of mixed jurisdictions: Ralf Michaels, 'Global Legal Pluralism' (2009) 5 *Annual Review of Law & Social Science*, 243–62, 245.

3 Stephan Feuchtwang, 'The Discipline and its Sponsors', in Talal Asad (ed.), *Anthropology and the Colonial Encounter* (New York: Humanities Press, 1973), pp. 71–100, p. 92.

unambiguous fact of life'.[4] Once researchers turned their attention to the multiple sources of normativity in Western and industrial nations, and then to transnational, supranational and international law,[5] the foci of legal pluralist studies expanded beyond colonial settings. Nonetheless, in the past twenty-five years, the growing global Indigenist movement has once more brought the colonial context to the fore in questioning the primacy of state sovereignty and the premise that the state is the principal form of political association.[6] Legal pluralism in turn has become a more prevalent part of an anti-colonial or aspiring postcolonial discourse in settler colonies, as well as in Indigenist theory.[7]

Even though none of the settler colonies are postcolonial in either a temporal or political sense, and although colonialism is emphatically not 'finished business',[8] the postcolonial label is adopted by those critiquing the effects of colonialism and seeking to move beyond them. However, given the origins of postcolonial theory in European discourse, some authors assert a distinctly Indigenous postcolonial theory.[9] According to Sákéj Henderson, postcolonial Indigenous legal consciousness is the

[4] Sally Engel Merry, 'Legal Pluralism' (1988) 22 *Law & Society Review*, 869–96, 874.

[5] Michaels, 'Global Legal Pluralism' (n. 2).

[6] James Anaya, 'Indigenous Law and its Contribution to Global Pluralism' (2007) 6 *Indigenous Law Journal*, 3–12, 8–9; Gavin Anderson, 'Postcolonial Legality and Legitimacy: The Challenge of Indigenous Peoples', in Chris Thornhill and Samantha Ashenden (eds.), *Legality and Legitimacy: Normative and Sociological Approaches* (Baden-Baden: Nomos Verlagsgesellschaft, 2010), pp. 235–55.

[7] Lester-Irabinna Rigney, 'Internationalisation of an Indigenous Anticolonial Cultural Critique of Research Methodologies: A Guide to Indigenist Research Methodologies and its Principles' (1999) 14 *Wicazo Sa Review*, 109–21; Kiera Ladner, 'Take 35: Reconciling Constitutional Orders', in Annis May Timpson (ed.), *First Nations, First Thoughts: The Impact of Indigenous Thought in Canada* (Vancouver: University of British Columbia Press, 2009), pp. 279–300; John Borrows, *Recovering Canada: The Resurgence of Indigenous Law* (Toronto: University of Toronto Press, 2002).

[8] Linda Tuhiwai Smith, *Decolonizing Methodologies: Research and Indigenous Peoples* (Dunedin, NZ: Otago University Press, 1999), p. 98; see also Brenda Gunn, 'Protecting Indigenous Peoples' Lands: Making Room for the Application of Indigenous Peoples' Laws within the Canadian Legal System' (2007) 6 *Indigenous Law Journal*, 31–69. Note the distinction drawn by Marie Battiste between postcolonial literary theory and postcolonial Indigenous thought: 'Introduction: Unfolding the Lessons of Colonization', in Marie Battiste (ed.), *Reclaiming Indigenous Voice and Vision* (Vancouver: University of British Columbia Press, 2003), xix; and between Indigenous movements and postcolonial humanism: Malreddy Pavan Kumar, '(An)other Way of Being Human: "Indigenous" Alternatives to Postcolonial Humanism' (2011) 32 *Third World Quarterly*, 1557–72.

[9] Battiste, 'Introduction' (n. 8), xix. See generally Haifa Alfaisal, 'Indigenous Epistemology and the Decolonisation of Postcolonialism' (2011) 19 *Studies in Social and Political Thought*, 24–40.

'the attempt to unfold the law of colonisation and its adjudicative legacy ... to create an equitable society that never has been and yet must be.'[10] As I demonstrate in this chapter, the language and methodologies of legal pluralism offer a way to critique state dominance and assert the survival of Indigenous law, to think through the processes with which the mainstream system attempts to recognise, accommodate or 'make space for' Indigenous law, and to articulate a jurisprudence grounded in Indigenous thought and practice. Nevertheless, Indigenist, postcolonial engagement with pluralist discourse and methods raises a number or challenges for pluralist jurisprudence.

In Canada, whence the concrete illustrations in this chapter are drawn, much of the reflection around legal pluralism has as its touchstone the constitutional provision (s.35) in which 'Aboriginal and treaty rights are... recognized and affirmed',[11] and, in particular, the courts' understanding of Aboriginal rights as deriving historically from 'intersocietal' norms and of s.35 as requiring the reconciliation of Indigenous and non-Indigenous perspectives on law.[12] Multiple critiques of current forms of recognition under s.35 have been made, many of which share an underlying dissatisfaction with the treatment of Indigenous law as 'culture' or as (fixed historical) social fact to be proved in evidence, as well as with the dominant and authoritative role played by a predominantly non-Indigenous judiciary in determining its content. For judges, and many others, the presumptive 'real law' is state law, and any suggestion of plural legal orders threatens the rule of law: when push comes to shove, there cannot be 'one system of law for the Aboriginals and one for the non-Aboriginals' lest the rule of law be replaced by chaos.[13] Even when a more 'highly textured' understanding of the rule of law is adopted – as including, for instance, the 'reconciliation of Aboriginal

[10] Sákéj Henderson, 'Postcolonial Indigenous Consciousness' (2002) 1 *Indigenous Law Journal*, 1–56, 3.

[11] *Constitution Act, 1982*, being Schedule B to the *Canada Act 1982* (UK), 1982, c 11, s.35.

[12] The entities to be reconciled shift throughout the case law: at times, it is the 'fact' of Crown sovereignty with fact of Indigenous pre-existence, at others, it is Aboriginal and non-Aboriginal perspective on rights, or different legal cultures. See Mark Walters, 'The Jurisprudence of Reconciliation: Aboriginal Rights in Canada', in Will Kymlicka and Bashir Bashir (eds.), *The Politics of Reconciliation in Multi-Cultural Societies* (Oxford: Oxford University Press, 2008), pp. 165–91.

[13] *Platinex Inc. v. Kitchenuhmaykoosib Inninuwug* [2008] OJ No. 1014 (OntSC), per Smith J, [44]; see generally Ryan Newell, 'Only One Law: Indigenous Land Disputes and the Contested Nature of the Rule of Law' (2012) 11 *Indigenous Law Journal*, 41–72.

and non-Aboriginal interests through negotiations'[14] – the gestures towards Indigenous law are largely empty. Critics, in response, urge us to 'take Indigenous law seriously' *as law.*[15]

Resistance to the state's monopoly over the label 'real law' (or simply unmodified 'law') is, of course, a thread running throughout the social scientific tradition of legal pluralism. Even state recognition of 'other' law is rejected as the sine qua non of legal plurality, and was famously dismissed by John Griffiths as a 'weak' or juristic version of legal pluralism, because it subsumes diverse legal orders into one source of legitimacy as law.[16] Yet the persistence of calls for state recognition as a tool of decolonisation raises the question of whether it is possible to accommodate stronger versions of legal pluralism – ones that recognise Indigenous law as law in its own right – within or alongside state institutions.[17] It requires us to ask about the congruence of the empirical project in which plurality in law is understood to be a ubiquitous fact of life and the normative or political one which urges that state law change and 'become' pluralist in order to decolonise itself.

Taking Indigenous law seriously poses challenges not just, as most pluralist jurisprudence does, to a singular view of the rule of law,[18] but also to several defining dichotomies in the disciplinary pursuits of pluralist jurisprudence: juristic versus sociological preoccupations, normative versus empirical projects, law versus fact. At first blush, the call to take Indigenous law as law runs contrary to the sociological emphasis on plurality in law – and thus law itself – as a fact. For Griffiths, this claim was important in countering the cogency of the juristic approach, in which the criteria for what counts as law is driven by the ideology and self-interest of the state.[19] However, while postcolonial jurisprudence claims Indigenous law as a reality, it rejects the fact-based approach, because empirical ethnographic or sociological techniques that render

[14] *Henco Industries v. Haudenosaune Six Nations Confederacy Council* [2006] 82 O.R. (3d) 721, 2006 CanLII 41649 (ON CA), per Laskin JA.

[15] Hadley Friedland and Val Napoleon, 'Gathering the Threads: Developing a Methodology for Researching and Rebuilding Indigenous Legal Traditions' (2015) 1 *Lakehead Law Journal*, 16–44, 17.

[16] John Griffiths, 'What is Legal Pluralism?' (1988) 18 *Journal of Legal Pluralism & Unofficial Law*, 1–55, 5.

[17] Note the analogous debate on religious law: see e.g. Russel Sandberg (ed.), *Religion and Legal Pluralism* (London: Routledge, 2016).

[18] Gordon Woodman, 'Legal Pluralism and the Search for Justice' (1996) 40 *Journal of African Law*, 152–67, 160.

[19] Griffiths, 'What is Legal Pluralism?' (n. 16), 3–4.

Indigenous peoples and their laws as objects of factual knowledge are seen as stripping them of their normative significance and engaging in a colonial power-play.

But this raises the question of what it means for law to be law and not mere fact. On the one hand, the call to take law as law may, in H. L. A. Hart's distinction, ask us to adopt the 'internal perspective' – even the juristic ideology – of a participant, rather than the external perspective of an observer, and thus to be aware of the distinctions between describing, practicing or justifying law. On the other hand, Indigenous claims challenge both the prevailing internal perspective of jurists and the external one of sociologists as being parochial, and invite us both to engage with other perspectives, and with the languages and forms in which other laws live. Furthermore, they show that empirical claims – to the existence of law, for instance – are entangled with normative claims for justice.

Engaging with Indigenous law in a strong way thus brings us to consider what Emmanuel Melissaris has called the meta-theoretical and meta-jurisprudential aspect of legal pluralism.[20] That is, to contemplate the possibility of multiple legal orders or forms of law is to put into question previously unexamined theoretical assumptions about the characteristics of law and its associated ontologies and epistemologies, and to ask jurisprudential questions about which normative order should prevail. Melissaris argues for an inter-perspectival, critical dialog as an appropriate methodology for legal pluralist theory.[21] For those of us trained in a Western legal tradition, a critical dialog with Indigenous jurisprudences invites us to ask about, for example, the ways in which our ideas about law privilege concepts rather than practice, explicit rules rather than implicit knowledge, or spaces of territory and empire rather than places of belonging. As becomes clear, it is not sufficient for legal theory to 'make space' for alternative understandings of law by simply stepping aside. Instead, pluralist jurisprudence has to engage with these other legal theories and jurisprudences, which are always particular and located in place and time. Thus, in order to contemplate the kinds of questions raised earlier, this chapter focuses on Canada, and on a few specific Indigenous traditions in those northern parts of Turtle Island.

[20] Emmanuel Melissaris, *Ubiquitous Law: Legal Theory and the Space for Legal Pluralism* (Farnam, Surrey: Ashgate, 2009), p. 25.

[21] Ibid., pp. 71–77.

But intellectual inquiry is not sufficient to experience the 'lawness' of law; the internal perspective is not just a matter of how rules are understood, but the ways in which they are felt to bind us. In the literature I review in the last part of this chapter, a growing articulation of a 'grounded jurisprudence' amongst Indigenous scholars points to law's inevitable relation to specific places and their ecologies and argues that law should come 'from' our experiences of interdependence with the land. Therefore, while many of the approaches within Indigenist jurisprudence that focus on cross-cultural understanding resonate with that of Melissaris, grounded jurisprudence provides a different way of framing conflicting normativites by posing the problem of law's actual – physical – foundation. It brings into view a version of pluralism that is not about multiple overlapping or nested *spaces*, but – perhaps counter-intuitively – about the singularity of life in particular *places* and the living of forms of relationships that make it possible.

12.2 Pluralist Themes in Postcolonial Critiques

In Canada, as in Australasia and the rest of the Americas, the pluralist turn in jurisprudence has been invigorated by increasingly voluble claims by Indigenous peoples for recognition of their rights, their laws and their sovereignty as self-determining peoples, and by accompanying critiques of a colonial legal and political order that has alternatively both ignored and attempted to suppress Indigenous ones. In Iris Marion Young's words, the postcolonial project has institutional and interpretive dimensions. The first dimension relates to the construction of systems of governance that can meet demands for Indigenous self-determination; the second dimension involves rereading the history of modern nation-states from the view point of Indigenous peoples as actors.[22] This practice of rereading – which Young draws from Homi Bhabha's exhortation to hybridise colonial history so that it is more than the 'noisy command of colonialist authority or the silent repression of native traditions'[23] – demonstrates a number of affinities between pluralist and postcolonial jurisprudence that I will elaborate on in what follows.

[22] Iris Marion Young, 'Hybrid Democracies: Iroquois Federalism and the Postcolonial Project', in Duncan Ivison and Paul Patton (eds.), *Political Theory and the Rights of Indigenous Peoples* (Cambridge: Cambridge University Press, 2000), pp. 238–39.

[23] Homi Bhabha, *The Location of Culture* (Milton Park, Oxon: Routledge, 1994), p. 111.

Interrupting the single story. As a practice of empire, settler-colonialism involved taking land from its original occupants for the permanent settlement of people from the home country, and its exploitation for colonial benefit. Settler-colonialism was justified according to first a theological, then a political, theory of Indigenous peoples as infidel and uncivilised savages, and enacted by the subjugation of local peoples to an imported or reconstituted legal and political order, an erasure or reduction of existing entitlements to land and practices of self-government, and attempts to eliminate or culturally assimilate the peoples that it colonised.[24] Just as the first move in the pluralist stratagem is to deny the conceptual and effective monopoly of state law and acknowledge the possibility of, and justification for, other laws, in an anti-colonial politics, the interruption of this single story of state sovereignty asserts the incompleteness of colonial assimilation and dispossession. As Bhabha writes, to perform this strategy is to 'estrange the basis of [colonial] authority.'[25] In the face of the history of policies that attempted to suppress Indigenous legal and political institutions and eradicate language and culture through compulsory residential schooling, Indigenous peoples announce 'we are here'. This 'survivance'[26] gets articulated through the language of nationhood, sovereignty and law, and has manifested in armed resistance, blockades and protests, in the refusal of treaties, and in participation in outlawed ceremonies.[27] It is striking how many texts on Indigenous law or justice begin with the emphatic assertion that Indigenous laws exist and have always existed. Val Napoleon and Hadley Friedland note that having to explicitly identify this starting point is discomforting but necessary because the 'myth of Indigenous peoples as lawless' is still often presumed

24 Robert Williams, *The American Indian in Western Legal Thought: The Discourses of Conquest* (New York: Oxford University Press, 1990); Patrick Wolfe, *Settler Colonialism and the Transformation of Anthropology: The Politics and Poetics of an Ethnographic Event* (London: Cassel, 1999); Stuart Banner, *How the Indians Lost their Land: Law and Power on the Frontier* (Cambridge, MA: Belknap Press, 2005); Antony Anghie, *Imperialism, Sovereignty and the Making of International Law* (Cambridge: Cambridge University Press, 2004).

25 Bhabha, *The Location of Culture* (n. 23), p. 162.

26 Gerald Vizenor revived this English term that implies survival and resistance, but also a secondary sense of succession: 'Aesthetics of Survivance: Literary Theory and Practice', in Gerald Vizenor (ed.), *Survivance: Narratives of Native Presence* (Lincoln: University of Nebraska Press, 2008), pp. 1–23.

27 Tracey Lindberg, *Critical Indigenous Legal Theory* (PhD Thesis, University of Ottawa, 2007), p. 8.

as common sense.[28] Legal pluralism as a discursive resource for postcolonial jurisprudence begins with the threshold shift to the bare fact of another law and an interruption of the story of state monopoly.

Unpacking ethnocentrism The assumption in both international[29] and domestic Canadian law[30] that Indigenous legal orders did not exist was rationalised by political theories – such as those of Hobbes, Locke and Rousseau – that posited Indigenous peoples as living in a (lawless) state of nature and frequently constructed ideas of European law and government in opposition to that void.[31] Consequently, identifying ways in which these postulates were built into self-justificatory theories for colonial powers and embedded in legal doctrine has been claimed as a key task within a postcolonial legal consciousness,[32] one in keeping with the anti-ethnocentrism of legal pluralist theory regarding the definition of law.[33] If law is uniquely associated with the state, and law is 'the singular characteristic of a civilized society',[34] then the statist understanding of law perpetrates an ethnocentric judgment on non-state societies that renders them lawless by definitional fiat.[35]

The antidote has been to insist that, as a point of equal dignity, 'all societies have law'. However, at least as far back as the Gluckman-Bohannan

[28] Val Napoleon and Hadley Friedland, 'Indigenous Legal Traditions: Roots to Renaissance', in Markus Dubber and Tatjana Hörnle (eds.), *Oxford Handbook of Criminal Law* (Oxford: Oxford University Press, 2014), pp. 225–47, p. 227.

[29] Anghie, *Imperialism, Sovereignty and the Making of International Law* (n. 24), p. 34, pp. 52–61.

[30] Grace Li Xiu Woo, *Ghost Dancing with Colonialism* (Vancouver: University of British Columbia Press, 2011), ch. 5.

[31] James (Sákéj) Youngblood Henderson, 'The Context of the State of Nature', in Marie Battiste (ed.), *Reclaiming Indigenous Voice and Vision* (Vancouver: University of British Columbia Press, 2003), pp. 11–38; Peter Fitzpatrick, *The Mythology of Modern Law* (London: Routledge, 1992); Barbara Arneil, *John Locke and America: The Defence of English Colonialism* (Oxford: Clarendon Press, 1996).

[32] Henderson, 'Postcolonial Indigenous Consciousness' (n. 10); Dale Turner, *This is Not a Peace Pipe: Towards a Critical Indigenous Philosophy* (Toronto: University of Toronto Press, 2006), p. 159, fn. 56.

[33] Brian Tamanaha, 'The Folly of the "Social Scientific" Concept of Legal Pluralism' (1993) 20 *Journal of Law & Society*, 192–217, 197; Franz von Benda-Beckmann, 'Who's Afraid of Legal Pluralism' (2002) 34 *Journal of Legal Pluralism & Unofficial Law*, 37–82, 53–55; Christoph Eberhard, 'Towards an Intercultural Legal Theory: The Dialogical Challenge' (2001) 10 *Social & Legal Studies*, 171–201, 176–81; Melissaris, *Ubiquitous Law: Legal Theory and the Space for Legal Pluralism* (n. 20), p. 30.

[34] Tamanaha, ibid., 197.

[35] Eberhard, 'Towards an Intercultural Legal Theory: The Dialogical Challenge' (n. 33), 176–84.

debate in the 1950s, critics questioned the appropriateness of using European legal categories – or even the label law at all – for cross-cultural study.[36] Definitions of law and acts of comparative analysis may themselves be ethnocentric, whether they assume a universal form, like rules or enforceable individual rights, or a function such as dispute resolution or centralised social control. Some see law's parochialism – always coming from particular histories and cultural locations – as a reason to eschew legal pluralism altogether because self-definitions of state law will inevitably haunt the conceptions of law that we use. They argue that it is better to recover suppressed or marginalised practices and discourses 'on their own terms'.[37] Furthermore, if measures of 'civilization' are passé, then so too should the need to make claims to having 'law' per se.[38]

Indigenist scholars voice similar concerns. For instance, Sákéj Henderson, Marjory Benson and Isobel Findlay argue that, given the embeddedness of law in language, culture and history, postcolonial justice in Canada rests on the possibility of being able to address Indigenous claims in Indigenous languages.[39] Taiaiake Alfred, a Haudenosaunee political theorist, challenges the use of English-language concepts like sovereignty, for so long a handmaiden in the attempted eradication of Indigenous peoples, preferring to orient his work through recovered Indigenous traditions, or at least to 'disconnect the notion of sovereignty from its Western, legal roots and transform it'.[40] Nevertheless, the insistent refrain about the existence of Indigenous law demands a

36 Bohannan favoured the use of vernacular or folk (emic) terms, which were not readily translatable, to represent local legal culture; Gluckman thought that using general (etic) categories was the only path to fruitful comparative analysis: see Sally Falk Moore, 'Comparative Studies: Introduction', in Laura Nader (ed.), *Law in Culture and Society* (Berkeley: University of California Press, 1997), pp. 340–42.

37 Simon Roberts, 'Against Legal Pluralism: Some Reflections on the Contemporary Enlargement of the Legal Domain' (1998) 30 *Journal of Legal Pluralism and Unofficial Law*, 95–106, 106.

38 Brian Tamanaha, *A General Jurisprudence of Law and Society* (Oxford: Oxford University Press, 2001), pp. 202–04. This debate about translatability and universality is of course a rehash of the Bohannen-Gluckman debate about the preferability of using emic or etic terms.

39 Sákéj Henderson, Marjory Benson and Isobel Findlay, *Aboriginal Tenure in the Constitution of Canada* (Scarborough, Ontario: Carswell, 2000), p. 401. See also Sákéj Henderson, 'Aboriginal Jurisprudence and Rights', in Kerry Wilkins (ed.), *Advancing Claims: Visions/Strategies/Directions* (Saskatoon: Purich Publishing, 2004), pp. 67–89, p. 73.

40 Taiaiake Alfred, 'Sovereignty', in Philip Deloria and Neal Salisbury (eds.), *A Companion to American Legal History* (Malden, Mass: Blackwell Publishers, 2002), pp. 460–74, p. 468.

response in the form of a pluralist jurisprudence that can meet the need for sensitive translation, and that aspires to transform legal thought and practice by engaging with Indigenous languages, cultures and histories.

Reclaiming alternative histories of legal relations. Of course, the lawless savage was not the only trope understood by Europeans in North America, and there are alternative histories to tell of the long and varied process of colonisation. Europeans engaging in the fur trade, and later, in military alliances with Indigenous groups, accepted them as self-governing polities, feared them as enemies, and valued them as allies. In the process, they adopted many of the protocols and idioms of treaty making from their Indigenous partners.[41] By the late seventeenth century, British officials had resolved (in theory if not always in practice) to treat the Indigenous peoples living in North America as owners of the land, which would have to be bought from them if it was desired for settlement.[42] This policy was formalised in the Royal Proclamation of 1763, which reserved to the 'Nations and Tribes of Indians' the hunting grounds of which they were in possession and required a formal surrender of land by representatives of that Nation to the Crown.

There was thus a cautious and self-interested respect by the British, Dutch and French for the autonomy of Indigenous groups in North America, and the pragmatic adoption, at various times, of modified Indigenous protocols and forms of law. Scholars point to the ways in which this led to various plural phenomena: at times to the careful carving up of jurisdiction, to negotiated co-existence, and to the generation of hybrid forms of normativity. For example, John Borrows and Leonard Rotman show how the Treaty of Albany from 1701 describes complimentary jurisdiction in which wrongs or injuries committed by the English or Dutch against Indians would be punished by the Governor at New York, and, conversely, wrongs committed by 'Indians belonging to the Sachims' against the English or Dutch would be punished by the Sachims.[43] Jeremy Webber traces the ways in which various ad hoc forms of criminal and civil justice appeared in the early years of contact in ways that represented a compromise between differing conceptions of crime

[41] Michael Pomedli, 'Eighteenth-Century Treaties: Amended Iroquois Condolence Rituals' (1995) 19 *American Indian Quarterly*, 319–39; H. R. Miller, *Compact, Contract, Covenant: Aboriginal Treaty-Making in Canada* (Toronto: University of Toronto Press, 2009), pp. 11–32.

[42] Banner, *How the Indians Lost Their Land: Law and Power on the Frontier* (n. 24), p. 1.

[43] John Borrows and Leonard Rotman, *Aboriginal Legal Issues: Cases, Materials and Commentary*, 4th ed. (Toronto: LexisNexis, 2012), pp. 14–16.

and punishment, and of land title.[44] James Tully's influential work *Strange Multiplicity* situates this negotiation of different legal orders as part of a longer European history of alternative constitutionalism, one that is a counterpoint to the dominant 'empire of uniformity' in which a uniform people unite to institute a singular constitution as an act of will. Instead, argues Tully, ancient or common constitutionalism is based on three conventions that have developed over time – namely, consent, recognition and cultural continuity.[45] These 'reclamation' studies adopt the lens of pluralist jurisprudence by looking for points of contact, interaction and responsiveness between distinct legal cultures and by seeing law in the spontaneous, emergent or negotiated norms that developed.

12.3 Thinking through Modern State Recognition

If these alternative histories are now being retold and used to inspire models of postcolonial law in the present, it is because there was a long intervening period, beginning at the close of the eighteenth century, in which there was a significant change in colonial attitudes towards the status of Indigenous nations in Canada. Following the end of the Seven Years' War between Britain and France in 1763, after which France withdrew from North America, Indigenous peoples lost their strategic importance for Britain. This and subsequent demographic and economic factors, such as the influx of settlers and the loss of traditional means of sustenance, completely changed the balance of power in North America.[46] That the embryonic colonial policy and practice of pluralism came to an end flowed from these changes but also from a cultural shift in colonial officials' understandings of law and sovereignty towards a unitary model based on the nation-state,[47] with dramatic consequences over the next two centuries. Treaties became perfunctory contracts

44 Jeremy Webber, 'Relations of Force and Relations of Justice: The Emergence of Normative Community Between Colonists and Aboriginal Peoples' (1995) 33 *Osgoode Hall Law Journal*, 623–60; Richard White, *The Middle Ground: Indians, Empires, and Republics in the Great Lakes Region, 1650–1815* (Cambridge: Cambridge University Press, 1991).

45 James Tully, *Strange Multiplicity: Constitutionalism in an Age of Diversity* (Cambridge: Cambridge University Press, 1995), pp. 99–129.

46 Miller, *Compact, Contract, Covenant: Aboriginal Treaty-Making in Canada* (n. 41), pp. 101–02.

47 Paul McHugh, *Aboriginal Societies and the Common Law: A History of Sovereignty, Status, and Self-Determination* (New York: Oxford University Press, 2004), p. 65.

for the sale of land rather than the negotiation of co-existence, the Canadian federal government assumed plenary legislative authority over 'Indians' as subjects of the Crown and subjected them to bureaucratic regimes of control and policies of assimilation, and courts denied any inherent Indigenous rights.

The modern character of legal pluralist claims emerged in the face of this history. The Haudenosaunee protested to the League of Nations and before domestic courts and officials that they were independent nations, allies and not subjects of the Crown.[48] In response to assertions by nations like the Nisga'a, Gitxsan and Wetsuet'en in British Columbia, and the Cree in James Bay, Quebec, to having legal entitlements to their territories under their own laws, ideas on Aboriginal title took shape.[49] Indigenous leaders resisted the proposal, in 1969, to repeal the racist distinctions of the Indian Act because becoming unmarked citizens would remove their treaty rights and their distinct status as 'Indians' under pre-confederation instruments, and then demanded a seat at the constitutional conferences in the 1970s along with the Federal and Provincial governments to insist on the 'recognition and affirmation' of their treaty and Aboriginal rights in the new constitution.[50]

Since the consolidation of the Canadian state on confederation in 1867, five typical strategies have been used to recognise claims of legal plurality:[51] translation, accommodation, delegation, deference and incorporation.[52] The first strategy, *translation*, involves courts according conventional legal status and effect to relationships or arrangements that are created 'informally' – such as through customary marriage or adoption – thus 'translating' them into state law terms and making

[48] Darlene Johnson, 'The Quest of the Six Nations Confederacy for Self-Determination' (1986) 44 *University of Toronto Faculty of Law Review*, 1–32, 17–24.

[49] Arthur Ray, *Aboriginal Rights Claims and the Making and Unmaking of History* (Montreal-Kingston: McGill-Queens University Press, 2016), ch. 3.

[50] Turner, *This is Not a Peace Pipe* (n. 32), pp. 19–36.

[51] The categories are similar to those used by the Australian Law Reform Commission, *The Recognition of Aboriginal Customary Laws*, ALRC Report no.31 (1986) at 199–208; and in Ralf Michaels, 'The Re-state-ment of Non-state Law: The State, Choice of Law, and the Challenge from Global Legal Pluralism' (2005) 51 *Wayne Law Review*, 1209–59, 1231–35.

[52] As always, this typology is not perfect, and the categories cross-cut one another: in a general sense, translation is always required in the intersection between normative orders, for instance; deference could also be understood as the accommodation of self-government and so on. Furthermore, because of their flexibility, these terms are used to denote different techniques of recognition by different authors.

certain benefits or liabilities under Canadian law applicable to the person(s) in question.[53] A second form is the *accommodation* of certain Indigenous practices or norms within the formal justice system. For instance, Cree/*Ininiew* belief in *wetigos* as dangerous spirits that are a threat to life might be accepted as part of the factual circumstances justifying a finding of reasonableness of a criminal defendant's actions in self-defence.[54] In tort compensation claims, the cost of hosting a feast – an obligation within some Indigenous polities in order to remove the shame of being the victim of an accident – has been accommodated in the calculation of damages.[55] *Delegation* involves permitting the self-regulating activities of groups, such as via contractual agreements, to be enforced via the mandate of the state. The regulatory and law-making powers of band councils under the Indian Act are sometimes conceived of as delegated powers from the Federal parliament.[56]

Deference refers to the zones of relative autonomy and non-interference that the state provides for the independent ordering of any individuals, families, professions and communities.[57] The strongest forms of deference to Indigenous self-determination and political autonomy may even create jurisdictional spaces where the general law does not

[53] See Douglas Sanders, 'Indian Women: A Brief History of their Roles and Rights' (1975) 21 *McGill Law Journal*, 657–72, 659–66. Another example is leadership selection. For bands who had not been subject to the Indian Act election provisions, the selection of leadership by customary means was, and continues to be, recognised as constituting the Indian Act band council and chief: Brian Crane, Robert Mainville and Martin Mason, *First Nations Governance Law* (Toronto: LexisNexis, 2006), p. 195.

[54] *R v. Jacko* [1998] 1 CNLR 164 (Ont. Gen. Div.); Hadley Friedland, *The Wetigo (Windigo) Legal Principles: Responding to Harmful People in Cree, Anishinabek and Salteaux Societies* (LLM thesis, University of Alberta, 2009). See generally Alison Dundes Renteln, *The Cultural Defense* (Oxford: Oxford University Press, 2005). The flexibility that judges have in ordering appropriate sentences can be used to permit community-based restorative justice practices with their origins in tradition (see Jarem Sawatsky, *The Ethic of Traditional Communities and the Spirit of Healing Justice: Studies From Hollow Water, the Iona Community, and Plum Village* (London: Jessica Kingsley Publishers, 2009)), or (as was common in the Northern Territory of Australia) take into account the fact that the defendant would receive a traditional punishment (see Heather Douglas, 'Customary Law, Sentencing and the Limits of the State' (2005) 20:1 *Canadian Journal of Law and Society*, 141–56).

[55] For eg *Williams v. Mould*, [1991] 3 CNLR 186 (BCSC).

[56] See Kiera Ladner, 'Visions of Neo-Colonialism: Renewing the Relationship with Aboriginal Peoples' (2001) 21 *Journal of Canadian Studies*, 104–35, 110; Frances Abele and Michael Prince, 'Four Pathways to Aboriginal Self-Government in Canada' (2006) 36 *American Review of Canadian Studies*, 568–95, 572.

[57] The ALRC Report on Customary Law refers to this form of recognition as 'exclusion'.

apply. Since 1986, with the formal adoption of a self-government policy, Indigenous nations have been able to negotiate an agreement for greater control over law-making in a larger range of subject matter than under the Indian Act, and spell out their relationships with federal and provincial governments. Based on the recognition of a 'limited form of self-government which remained ... after the [British] assertion of sovereignty'[58] these arrangements have been described as a distinct 'third order of government' that operates within the constitutional framework.[59] Finally, *incorporation* is a technique of formally embedding customary law into state law. This could happen through explicit codification, as in parts of India and Africa,[60] or via reference, such as the definition of an Inuit beneficiary of the James Bay and Northern Quebec Agreement as someone who is Inuk 'as determined in accordance with Inuit customs and traditions'.[61]

Aboriginal Rights: Limited Legal Pluralism. Although the use of some of these strategies dates to the confederation of Canada, the introduction of s.35 of the Constitution, in which the 'Aboriginal and treaty rights of the Aboriginal peoples of Canada are hereby recognized and confirmed' has, since 1982, provided the principal frame through which arguments about legal pluralism in Canada have been understood. At various times, judges have included legal pluralist language in their formulations of s.35 rights:

- 'the law of Aboriginal rights ... "is a form of intersocietal law that evolved from long standing practices linking the communities"';[62]
- 'the source of aboriginal title appears to be grounded both in the common law and in the aboriginal perspective on land; the latter includes, but is not limited to, their systems of law';[63]

[58] *Campbell v. British Columbia (Attorney General)* [2000] 189 DLR (4th) 333 (BCSC), [113], [181].

[59] Frances Abele and Michael Prince, 'Four Pathways to Aboriginal Self-Government in Canada' (n. 56); Patrick Macklem, *Indigenous Difference and the Constitution of Canada* (Toronto: Toronto University Press, 2000), p. 282, p. 284.

[60] T. W. Bennett and T. Vermeulen, 'Codification of Customary Law' (1980) *Journal of African Law*, 206–19; Neeladri Bhattacharya, 'Remaking Custom: The Discourse and Practice of Colonial Codification', in Romila Thapar, Radha Champakalakshmi, and Sarvepalli Gopal (eds.), *Tradition, Dissent and Ideology: Essays in Honour of Romila Thapar* (Oxford: Oxford University Press, 1996), pp. 20–51.

[61] Sebastien Grammond, 'L'Appartenance aux Communautés Inuit du Nunavik: Un Cas de Réception de l'Ordre Juridique Inuit?' (2008) 23 *Canadian Journal of Law & Society*, 93–119.

[62] *R v. Van Der Peet* [1996] 2 SCR 507 (SCC), per Lamer CJ, [42].

[63] *Delgamuukw v. BC* [1997] 3 SCR 1010 (SCC), per Lamer CJ, [147].

- 'Aboriginal interests and customary laws were presumed to survive the assertion of sovereignty, and were absorbed into the common law as rights''[64]
- '[t]reaties serve to reconcile pre-existing Aboriginal sovereignty with assumed Crown sovereignty';[65]
- 'what is required [in determining the existence of Aboriginal title] is a culturally sensitive approach to sufficiency of occupation based on the dual perspectives of the Aboriginal group in question – its laws, practices, size, technological ability and the character of the land claimed – and the common law notion of possession as a basis for title'.[66]

Commentators have seen in these statements the 'promise of legal pluralism':[67] rights are not dependent on exercises of legislative or judicial authority but have their origins partially in norms that pre-date the creation of the Canadian state. Henderson goes so far as to say that the Court's interpretation of s.35 provides a 'trans-systemic constitutional framework' which adopts Indigenous sovereignty as a *grundnorm* of the constitution.[68]

Nevertheless, as Patrick Macklem underscores, 'Canadian courts describing relations between Indigenous peoples and Canada as legally plural, as important as this development is, does not make them so.'[69] Almost without exception, broad statements about a role for Indigenous law in the elaboration of the *sui generis* nature of Aboriginal rights are not followed up with any substantive consideration of Indigenous law.[70]

64 *Mitchell v. MNR* [2001] 1 SCR 911, per McLachlin CJ, [10].

65 *Haida Nation v. BC (Minister of Forests)* [2004] 3 SCR 511 (SCC), per McLachlin CJ, [20].

66 *Tsilhqot'in Nation v. BC* [2014] 2 SCR 257 (SCC), per McLachlin CJ, [41].

67 Patrick Macklem, 'Indigenous Peoples and the Ethos of Pluralism in Canada', in Patrick Macklem and Douglas Sanderson (eds.), *From Recognition to Reconciliation: Essays on the Constitutional Entrenchment of Aboriginal and Treaty Rights* (Toronto: University of Toronto Press, 2016), p. 17.

68 James (Sákéj) Youngblood Henderson, 'Constitutional Vision and Judicial Commitment: Aboriginal and Treaty Rights in Canada' (2010) 14 *Australian Indigenous Law Review*, 24–48, 25, 29.

69 Macklem, 'Indigenous Peoples and the Ethos of Pluralism in Canada' (n. 67), p. 33.

70 Kent McNeil, 'The Meaning of Aboriginal Title', in Michael Asch (ed.), *Aboriginal and Treaty Rights in Canada: Essays on Law, Equality and Respect for Difference* (Vancouver: University of British Columbia Press, 1997), pp. 135–54, pp. 136–37; Minnawaaanagogiizhigook (Dawnis Kennedy), 'Reconciliation Without Respect? Section 35 and Indigenous Legal Orders', in Law Commission of Canada (ed.), *Indigenous Legal Traditions* (Vancouver: University of British Columbia Press, 2007), p. 86.

Despite the rhetoric, Indigenous law is treated not as a genuine source of rights, but merely as an evidentiary or interpretive aid in a 'culturally sensitive' application of the tests. It is treated as a social fact of existence rather than as living principles behind that practice.[71] For instance, in the only successful Aboriginal title claim to date, *Tsilhqot'in Nation v. BC* [2014], evidence from the Tsilhqot'in plaintiffs of the enforcement of trespass-like rules simply confirmed the European conception of exclusive occupation at the core of Aboriginal title, and were not used to establish their unique Tsilhqot'in understanding of title. As can be seen especially in cases that exclude contemporary commercial activities from the scope of Aboriginal rights unless the resource was traded in pre-contact times, Aboriginal rights are understood to be protecting culture as a temporally bounded collection of traits and not as a contextually contingent expression of collective self-determination.[72]

The weak regard for Indigenous law also shows up in issues of jurisdiction. Federal or provincial regulation of Aboriginal rights supposedly without 'inherent limitations' – such as fishing for commerce – is justified out of official concern for overuse. This ignores that there are also internal Indigenous legal regulations that very likely have conservation goals.[73] Provincial jurisdiction is said to apply to Aboriginal title lands because otherwise they would be 'wholly unregulated', for example.[74] Most significant, though, is a hierarchy between laws suggested by the fact that the '[Aboriginal] perspective must be framed in terms cognisable to the Canadian legal and constitutional structure',[75] that customary laws survived only to the extent that they were not 'incompatible with the Crown's assertion of sovereignty',[76] and

[71] Minnawaaanagogiizhigook (Dawnis Kennedy), Ibid., p. 85; Ghislain Otis, 'Constitutional Recognition of Aboriginal and Treaty Rights: A New Framework for Managing Legal Pluralism in Canada?' (2014) 46 *The Journal of Legal Pluralism and Unofficial Law*, 320–37, 325.

[72] Chilwin Cheng, 'Touring the Museum: A Comment on *R. v. Van Der Peet*' (1997) 55 *University of Toronto Law Review*, 419–34; John Borrows and Leonard Rotman, 'The Sui Generis Nature of Aboriginal Rights: Does it Make a Difference?' (1997) 36 *Albert Law Review*, 9–45; Ghislain Otis, 'Opposing Aboriginality to Modernity: The Doctrine of Aboriginal Rights in Canada' (1997) 12 *British Journal of Canadian Studies*, 182–94; Ronald Niezen, 'Culture and the Judiciary: The Meaning of the Culture Concept as a Source of Aboriginal Rights in Canada' (2003) 18 *Canadian Journal of Law & Society*, 1–26.

[73] Minnawaaanagogiizhigook (Dawnis Kennedy), 'Reconciliation Without Respect? Section 35 and Indigenous Legal Orders' (n. 70), p. 88.

[74] *Tsilhqot'in Nation v. BC* [2014] 2 SCR 257 (SCC), per McLachlin CJ, [115].

[75] *R v. Van Der Peet* [1996] 2 SCR 507 (SCC), per Lamer CJ, [49].

[76] *Mitchell v. MNR* [2001] 1 SCR 911, per McLachlin CJ, [10].

that Aboriginal rights may legitimately be restricted for a range of ordinary policy objectives in service of the broader community of which Aboriginal societies are a part, and over which the Crown is sovereign.[77]

There is thus a pervasive sense in which there is an 'unequal division of labour' between the respective roles that state law and Indigenous law play in the adjudication of s.35 rights.[78] In terms of the strategies listed previously, the role of Indigenous law in s.35 can be considered as *translated* into, for instance, title based on occupation, *deferred* to with respect to internal decisions about how collective treaty and Aboriginal rights and title will be exercised, or *incorporated* by reference in modern treaties.[79] In all this, however, Indigenous law only plays a subsidiary role, or an internal one, to rights that have been determined by state law. The inter-societal dimension, the work of reconciling Indigenous claims with state ones, is never done by non-state Indigenous orders.[80] Indigenous law has to fit with state law and the latter never has to reconcile itself with or to the former. Despite the pluralist or 'transsystemic' rhetoric, the courts struggle to displace ethnocentric bias embedded in their methods and assumptions about law.[81] But even were they capable of 'accurately representing' Indigenous law, argues Caroline Dick, they would still undermine its autonomy by assuming 'classificatory authority.'[82] The debate quickly turns to one of jurisdiction, and who gets to decide, rather than simply what the law *is*.[83]

These limitations are arguably intrinsic to state law. Writing on state recognition of non-state law more generally, Ralf Michaels contends that none of the forms of recognition mentioned constitute legal pluralism in the sense of an acceptance of multiple autonomous legal orders with independent sources of validity, because from the state's point of view the rules or norms of non-state communities 'acquire the status of law [only] from the very moment they are attached and subordinated to the state

77 *R v. Gladstone* [1996] 2 SCR 723, per Lamer CJ, [73].

78 Otis, 'Constitutional Recognition of Aboriginal and Treaty Rights' (n. 71), 328.

79 See, for example, the Tlicho Treaty which incorporated a Tlicho Constitution in which oral tradition was to be used as an interpretive aid; or the Labrador Inuit Agreement, under which a Constitution was authorised which recognised Inuit customary law.

80 Otis, 'Constitutional Recognition of Aboriginal and Treaty Rights' (n. 71), 328.

81 Henderson, 'Constitutional Vision and Judicial Commitment: Aboriginal and Treaty Rights in Canada' (n. 68), 28.

82 Caroline Dick, '"Culture and the Courts" Revisited: Group-Rights Scholarship and the Evolution of s. 35 (1)' (2009) 42 *Canadian Journal of Political Science*, 957–79, 974.

83 Shaunagh Dorsett and Shaun McVeigh, *Jurisdiction* (London: Routledge, 2012), p. 4.

and its law.'[84] This, of course, is the classic formulation of weak legal pluralism made by John Griffiths and against which a generation or two of socio-legal pluralist scholars have set their caps: that the empirical existence of legal plurality is not constituted by the extent of state recognition, and in fact, state recognition itself typically reflects the idea that law 'as law' must ultimately come from a single validating source.[85] Griffith's point was that the state's perspective should not be taken as reality, nor as the appropriate point of view for social scientists. However, Michaels' argument elaborated in this present volume is that, *contra* Griffiths, there is a real sense in which 'external' recognition of law by another legal order *is* constitutive of 'law as law' because 'effectively a legal system cannot operate vis-à-vis other legal systems unless it is recognized by those other legal systems'.[86] His point supports a 'relational concept of law' because external recognition is only important in the interaction between legal orders. Indeed, it means that the question to ask is 'law for whom and in what context?'

Consequently, the difference between strong and weak versions of legal pluralism may boil down to a distinction in disciplinary objectives – descriptive, analytical and comparative, in the case of social scientists, normative and pragmatic in the case of jurists. A dispassionate observer of social interaction will misunderstand people's behaviour if she is unable or unwilling to notice the interplay of different legal obligations and norms. But a judge who has to choose 'the' correct law, cannot be professionally committed to strong legal pluralism.[87] And yet, the post-colonial case for recognition is based on a conflation of the empirical and the normative, of the scholar and the judge: Indigenous law should be recognised in its own right because it exists and because Indigenous sovereignty has never been given up. With the characterisation of s.35 rights as the product of 'inter-societal law' and the reconciliation of perspectives required, state officials are being called on to step out of their juristic point of view and take Indigenous law as law for themselves. But there is a paradox in state recognition of strong or empirical legal pluralism in that it seems to be the very act of taking Indigenous law as

[84] Michaels, 'The Re-state-ment of Non-state Law: The State, Choice of Law, and the Challenge from Global Legal Pluralism' (n. 51), 1231–35.

[85] Griffiths, 'What is Legal Pluralism?' (n. 16), 8.

[86] Ralf Michaels, 'Law and Recognition – Towards a Relational Concept of Law', xx.

[87] Franz von Benda-Beckmann, 'Riding or Killing the Centaur: Reflections on the Identities of Legal Anthropology' (2008) 4 *International Journal of Law in Context*, 85–110, fn. 48.

fact that undercuts its autonomy as law for the state. It cannot be avoided in this case by simply pointing to the difference between juristic and sociological understandings of law. However, it might be explained once we appreciate the similarities between the positivist form of law and the empirical production of fact.

12.4 Law as Law; Law as Fact

Critiques of s.35 jurisprudence often suggest that the 'pluralist promise' would be served if the *sui generis* principle were taken at its word, such that Indigenous law would contribute as a normative source – as law – to defining the content of rights, in continuity with the historic inter-societal development of Aboriginal rights, in which dialogue, exchange and 'trans-systemic symbiosis'[88] produced hybrid norms. As LeBel J. writes in *R v. Marshall; R .v Bernard*: 'Aboriginal conceptions of territoriality, land-use and property should be used to modify and adapt the traditional common law concepts of property'.[89] But what is the difference, then, between the weak pluralism of incorporation in which, from the state's perspective, Indigenous laws can *only* be subordinate 'fact', and taking Indigenous law seriously as law?

One argument uses the private international 'choice of law' model: for a court to adopt strong legal pluralism in an s.35 case, it would have to rely on Indigenous law, as on the law of a foreign state, to resolve the issue and choose it as the governing law.[90] Michaels points out that 'choice of law' only operates between states because of political parity: states have a mutual interest in recognising each other as autonomous law-creating communities and are persuaded that the other has jurisdiction over the dispute.[91] Thus, and despite the rhetoric of 'nation-to-nation' relationships in current Canadian politics, substantial challenges arise due to the lack of political will to recognise the autonomy of Indigenous polities, and the degree to which the state can get by without recognition from Indigenous peoples. Michaels also argues that the

[88] Henderson, 'Constitutional Vision and Judicial Commitment: Aboriginal and Treaty Rights in Canada' (n. 68), 26.

[89] *R v Marshall; R v. Bernard* [2005] 2 SCR 220 (SCC), per LeBel J (Fish J concurring), [127].

[90] Otis, 'Constitutional Recognition of Aboriginal and Treaty Rights' (n. 71), 323.

[91] Michaels uses Paul Schiff Berman's term 'juripersuasion' to explain how states are convinced of this parity: Michaels, 'The Re-state-ment of Non-state Law: The State, Choice of Law, and the Challenge from Global Legal Pluralism' (n. 51), 1242–43.

constitutive function of external recognition is not a 'one-way street'.[92] The implications of this is that beyond the question of political will and self-interest, even state law, in a relational sense, is only law to the extent that it is recognised by other legal orders. There is much in Michaels' relational concept of law that resonates with literature on the politics of recognition generally, and, in particular, with Patchen Markell's powerful observation that the state is not simply the forum for identity claims but is itself a participant in exchanges of recognition.[93] The state and its law, like the rest of us, exist in conditions of interdependence,[94] a point to which I return below.

In addition to political parity, Michaels notes that choice of law works because there is structural parity between the laws of states: systems of legislation, enforcement and adjudication are relatively similar, and conflict of laws tests tend to require the bases of jurisdiction to be equivalent to those of the enforcing state.[95] The distinction between law and fact itself is an axiomatic characteristic shared by modern legal systems. State law institutional practices are organised around it, with rules of evidence governing the finding of fact, and protocols of legal argumentation governing the articulation of the law. Even though the distinction has been called a myth and situated as an artefact of our justice system,[96] it is a myth that most moderns buy into. In choice of law, for that matter, while foreign law is applied as the law governing the dispute, and is subject to appeal as a question of law, it is formally proved in evidence as a fact by expert testimony if a domestic judge cannot be assumed to know it.[97]

The question of what makes law 'law' as distinct from social fact has been a key preoccupation of positivist legal theory, even as law itself is

[92] Michaels, 'Law and Recognition – Towards a Relational Concept of Law' (n. 86), xx.

[93] Patchen Markell, *Bound By Recognition* (Princeton, NJ: Princeton University Press, 2009), pp. 25–32.

[94] For an elaboration of this argument, see Kirsten Anker, *Declarations of Interdependence: A Legal Pluralist Approach to Indigenous Rights* (Farnham, Surrey: Ashgate, 2014).

[95] Michaels, 'The Re-state-ment of Non-state Law: The State, Choice of Law, and the Challenge from Global Legal Pluralism' (n. 51), 1248.

[96] Ronald Allen and Michael Pardo, 'The Myth of the Law-Fact Distinction' (2002) 97 *Northwestern University Law Review*, 1769–807. It is also culturally specific: see Clifford Geertz, *Local Knowledge* (New York: Basic Books, 1983), ch. 8.

[97] Richard Fentiman, *Foreign Law in English Courts: Pleading, Proof and Choice of Law* (Oxford: Oxford University Press, 1998), pp. 3–4; Peter Hay, 'The Use and Determination of Foreign Law in Civil Litigation in the United States' (2014) 62 *American Journal of Comparative Law*, 213–40.

accepted as an artefact of human creation. While the ability to discern the legal depends on empirical criteria, such as a basic rule of recognition accepted in the practice of officials, getting at the legal dimension of brute observable facts requires attention to hermeneutics – interpretive practice – and attitude. H. L. A. Hart, notably, used the distinction between 'internal' and 'external' perspectives[98] to denote the difference between the attitude of participants in a legal system (who take it as law) and those practices that are observable to an uninvolved outsider. He claimed that law could not exist without a 'critical reflective' internal attitude to rules on the part of participants – that they considered themselves bound by the rule, that the rules were reasons for action and for the censure of their breach and so on – and that an observer would only be recording bare habits unless he or she inquired as to whether participants held this attitude.[99] To explain the normativity of law, Hart's internal perspective has been taken to have both a cognitive (or hermeneutic) and a volitional aspect.[100] According to one view, the descriptive theorist need only share the cognitive aspect to provide an accurate factual account of law.[101] By extension, the participant's internal perspective on law involves separately knowing or understanding the law and then accepting it as binding; it is a 'practical' perspective in the sense of using the law to decide what ought to be done.[102] From another view, however, it is not possible to separate the descriptive and the normative.[103] True 'understanding', even in the form of a theoretical description, requires one to participate in and endorse that

[98] To be clear, Hart's internal and external perspectives are those of the participant and observer of the legal system, respectively, whereas Michaels' internal and external recognition is a distinction between the secondary rule existing in the practice of officials that constitutes a legal order for *itself* and the recognition of that legal order by other legal orders as constituting law for *themselves*.

[99] H. L. A. Hart, *The Concept of Law*, 2nd ed. (Oxford: Oxford University Press, 1994), pp. 55–58, pp. 82–99.

[100] Melissaris notes the difference between the hermeneutic and volitional aspects of the internal point of view, where the former is able to be approximated by an outsider through a process of *verstehen* or empathetic understanding, but the latter is about adhering to the normative commitments of a participant in that legal order: *Ubiquitous Law: Legal Theory and the Space for Legal Pluralism* (n. 20), p. 8.

[101] Neil MacCormick, *HLA Hart* (Stanford, CA: Stanford University Press, 1981), pp. 33–39.

[102] Veronica Rodriguez-Blanco, 'Peter Winch and HLA Hart: Two Concepts of the Internal Point of View' (2007) 20 *Canadian Journal of Law & Jurisprudence*, 1–21.

[103] Lon Fuller, 'Positivism and Fidelity to Law: A Reply to Professor Hart' (1958) 71 *Harvard Law Review*, 630–72, 661–69.

legal order by evaluating its objectives,[104] a claim that has led to participant observation being a core methodology for ethnographers.

One reason why this debate does not matter much in private international law – and why foreign state law can so easily slip between fact and law procedurally – is that juridical techniques of recognition in the dominant positivist approach elicit a form of law that is of a piece with the propositional character of sociological statements of fact. Unlike law as practical knowledge, or stories, or ceremony, the articulation of positive law as explicit, propositional rules turns law *into* a reified fact taken out of its contextual flux, ambiguity and provisionality, and places it above and beyond potential disagreement about it and above any sense of what it should be.[105] In this sense, the practice of lawyers in producing statements of law, and of social theorists in producing statements of fact, are similar. Indeed it is the confluence between sociological and positivist approaches to law that has led rhetoric scholar Marianne Constable to use the label 'socio-legal positivism' to describe modern law.[106] Thus to the extent that Indigenous law would be treated as an object of recognition – a set of rules or principles to be identified, proven in evidence, and applied by a judge – it matters little whether this exercise is framed as the recognition of law or culture or simply values.[107]

In contrast, for Indigenous practices of governance, the question of structural parity raises the challenges of cogniseability, translation and incommensurability, and the dangers of reification and mistranslation. In the case of private international law, the reason judges are able to apply foreign law as law (even if procedurally it is proven through evidence as a fact) is that, despite the global differences in state law systems, judges across the world participate in a largely shared sense of legal order as state legal

[104] Ronald Dworkin, *Law's Empire* (Cambridge, MA: Harvard University Press, 1986), p. 420; H Hamner Hill, 'Hart's Hermeneutic Positivism: On Some Methodological Difficulties in *The Concept of Law*' (1990) 3 *Canadian Journal of Law & Jurisprudence*, 113–28; John Finnis, *Natural Law and Natural Rights* (Oxford: Clarendon Press, 1980), p. 3.

[105] See Jeremy Webber, 'Legal Pluralism and Human Agency' (2006) 44 *Osgoode Hall Law Journal*, 167–98, 174–76. As in Lon Fuller's classic critique of positivism, every attempt to describe simply what the law *is* is inflected at some level with the observer's sense of what it should be, however that *should* is decided: *supra* note 103, 664–66.

[106] Marianne Constable, *Just Silences: The Limits and Possibilities of Modern Law* (Princeton: Princeton University Press, 2005), pp. 9–10.

[107] See Kirsten Anker, 'Law, Culture and Fact in Indigenous Claims: Legal Pluralism as a Problem of Recognition', in Rene Provost, *Centaur Jurisprudence* (Cambridge: Cambridge University Press, 2016).

order, and law as positive, propositional rules. This is itself an effect of colonisation and neo-colonial globalisation. Beyond debates about the distinction between law and fact, which on most accounts are deeply entangled, modernity has led us to espouse both a scientific and a legal practice ostensibly preoccupied with what the world *is*, rather than the question of how to live in it.[108] Where law is claimed to be otherwise, where it is embedded in practice or in narrative or poetic language, *sui generis* law in Canada might then be calling us to eschew both the familiar, state-centric, juristic view and the sociological descriptive view. How then would those advocating Indigenous jurisprudence have us take law as law?

12.5 Indigenous Interventions in Pluralist Jurisprudence

Indigenist writers calling for Indigenous law to be taken seriously have addressed both the issue of political parity and the question of cogniseability (and its reverse, the incommensurability of concepts). Claims of parity are reflected in the prevalent call for 'space' for Indigenous legal traditions, which aims to establish the conditions for the exercise of autonomy through non-interference, as in Vine Deloria Jr's famous insistence on a 'cultural leave-us-alone agreement' between Indians and Whites.[109] This call resonates with the widely deployed Haudenosaunee *Kaswenta* model for inter-governmental relations embodied in the Two-Row Wampum, a beaded 'belt' used in agreements between the Iroquois Confederacy and various European groups in Eastern Canada and the United States. In this wampum, two rows of purple run parallel, representing the European ship and the Haudenosaunee canoe sailing separately but together in the shared river of life.[110] For some Haudenosaunee, this nation-to-nation relationship is one of strict separation of autonomous polities. Traditionalist Haudenosaunee do not vote in Canadian elections, do not consider themselves Canadian citizens, and travel on their own passports. They expect a similar degree of respect from others for their independence.[111]

[108] See Raymond Geuss, *Philosophy and Real Politics* (Princeton, NJ: Princeton University Press, 2008), pp. 40–41.

[109] Vine Deloria, Jr, *Custer Died for your Sins* (Norman: University of Oklahoma Press, 1988), p. 27.

[110] Taiaiake Alfred, *Peace, Power and Righteousness: An Indigenous Manifesto* (Ontario: Oxford University Press, 1999), p. 52.

[111] Audra Simpson, *Mahawk Interruptus: Political Life Across the Borders of Settler States* (Durham: Duke University Press, 2014); Johnson, 'The Quest of the Six Nations Confederacy for Self-Determination' (n. 48).

'Making space' can thus be a technical argument about exclusive and concurrent jurisdiction that is formally equivalent to state government counterparts,[112] or a strong form of deferral as a way to protect non-state Indigenous orders 'by ensuring that what is permitted, prescribed, granted or prohibited under indigenous law will not be prohibited, denied or prescribed by state law'.[113] The 'space' for Indigenous law may even resemble (state-like) territorial sovereignty.[114] But it can also be, in a less determinative fashion, about a capacity for self-definition which, according to Gordon Christie, includes the capacity for Indigenous peoples 'to project their own theories and particular forms of knowledge',[115] or, as Tracey Lindberg writes, 'to make decisions with an understanding of the content and fullness of our own Indigenous terminology and framework without impact of colonial mandate, intrusion or subjugation'.[116] For Audra Simpson, to occupy the space of sovereignty in her Kanienkeha/Mohawk community is to undertake a politics of 'refusal': both to be known ethnographically and be subject to the gaze of the politics of recognition, and to recognise colonial institutions in turn, a stance that raises the 'question of legitimacy of those who are usually doing the recognizing'.[117]

An emerging scholarly movement is directed to the revitalisation of Indigenous law so as to populate the space claimed for it; however, it also addresses the issue of structural parity and cognisability by working on articulating Indigenous lifeways in a legal vocabulary, and is often more interested in dialog than in being left alone, if this would mean a lack of engagement.[118] Spearheaded by Val Napoleon and Hadley Friedland at the *Accessing Justice and Reconciliation* project,[119] the movement has been inspired by the work of Anishnabeg legal scholar

[112] Macklem, 'Indigenous Peoples and the Ethos of Pluralism in Canada' (n. 67), 33.

[113] Otis, 'Constitutional Recognition of Aboriginal and Treaty Rights' (n. 71), 321.

[114] Bruce Duthu, *Shadow Nations: Tribal Sovereignty and the Limits of Legal Pluralism* (Oxford: Oxford University Press, 2013), p. 8.

[115] Gordon Christie, 'Law, Theory and Aboriginal Peoples' (2003) 2 *Indigenous Law Journal*, 67–116, 72.

[116] Lindberg, *Critical Indigenous Legal Theory* (n. 27), 16.

[117] Simpson, *Mahawk Interruptus* (n. 111), p. 11.

[118] Borrows, *Recovering Canada: The Resurgence of Indigenous Law* (n. 7); Sylvia McAdam (Saysewahum), *Nationhood Interrupted: Revitalizing nêhiyaw Legal Systems* (Saskatoon: Purich Publishing, 2015).

[119] Implemented in 2012 by the Indigenous Law Research Unit (Faculty of Law, University of Victoria), the Indigenous Bar Association, and the Truth and Reconciliation Commission of Canada.

John Borrows on the multi-jural nature of Canadian law, which both popularised the narratives and perspectives of his Anishnabe legal traditions and those of other Indigenous nations, and pioneered a case analysis method for working with stories as contemporary sources of law.[120] Echoing the 'trouble case' method of Hoebel and Llewellyn,[121] this approach uses classic law-school analytical categories – facts, issue, reason, decision – to render the (common) law-like quality of stories more obvious to a conventional legal audience.[122] Thus, while the movement aspires to strengthen and revitalise Indigenous legal orders so that they may first 'serve their nations'[123] by getting Indigenous people to articulate their law in new ways,[124] another goal of this method of translation is to allow Canadian judges 'suitable access' to these stories as legal texts so that they may be received into Canadian law.[125] Borrows has influentially made the case that Indigenous legal traditions should be considered a general intellectual resource for legal argument in Canada alongside the civil and common law traditions.[126]

While the use of Western legal methodologies and processes has been defended as appropriate if it allows Indigenous law to be useful as a contemporary legal resource or yields meaningful political advances,[127] others follow Audre Lorde in claiming that the tools of the master will never dismantle the master's house.[128] For instance, many Indigenist scholars

[120] Borrows, *Recovering Canada: The Resurgence of Indigenous Law* (n. 7); *Canada's Indigenous Constitution* (Toronto: University of Toronto Press, 2010); *Drawing Out Law: A Spirit's Guide* (Toronto: University of Toronto Press, 2010); *Freedom and Indigenous Constitutionalism* (Toronto: University of Toronto Press, 2016).

[121] E. Adamson Hoebel and Karl Llewellyn, *The Cheyenne Way: Conflict and Case Law in Primitive Jurisprudence* (Norman: University of Oklahoma Press, 1941).

[122] Napoleon and Friedland, 'Gathering the Threads: Developing a Methodology for Researching and Rebuilding Indigenous Legal Traditions' (n. 15).

[123] Alan Hanna, 'Making the Round: Aboriginal Title in the Common Law from a Tsilhqot'in Legal Perspective' (2013) 45 *Ottawa Law Review*, 365–402, 369.

[124] One aspect of the *Accessing Justice* project does this by partnering student researchers and Indigenous elders and community participants to work collaboratively on producing a synthesis of multiple story analyses.

[125] John Borrows, 'With or Without You' (1995–1996) 41 *McGill Law Journal*, 629–68, 653.

[126] See generally Borrows, *Recovering Canada: The Resurgence of Indigenous Law* (n. 7); Napoleon and Friedland, 'Gathering the Threads: Developing a Methodology for Researching and Rebuilding Indigenous Legal Traditions' (n. 15).

[127] John Borrows, 'Contemporary Traditional Equality: The Effect of the Charter on First Nation Politics' (1994) 43 *University of New Brunswick Law Journal*, 19–48, 20–21.

[128] Mary Ellen Turpel, 'Aboriginal Peoples and the Canadian *Charter*: Interpretive Monopolies, Cultural Differences' [1989–1990] *Canadian Human Rights Year Book*, 3–45, 6–7; Glen Coulthard, *Red Skin White Masks: Rejecting the Colonial Politics of Recognition*

argue that the whole liberal paradigm of autonomous individuals, social contract, and rights must be abandoned in favour of an alternative constitution growing out of Indigenous traditions; and I return to these arguments later in this chapter.[129] In addition, there are those for whom the incommensurability of Indigenous and non-Indigenous laws and their underlying cultural complexes requires not translation but a complete Indigenisation of legal theory. Sákéj Henderson has stated that in order for non-Indigenous jurists to take Indigenous legal systems into a *sui generis* definition of Aboriginal rights, 'non-Aboriginal scholars and judges will have to learn Aboriginal languages and jurisprudences.'[130] Calls are also made for alternative and 'culturally appropriate' forums for claims resolution in light of incommensurability, and of the misplaced authority of legal officials with respect to Indigenous law.[131]

The distinction between those who use the methodological tools of the common law to articulate Indigenous law, and those who say the two are incommensurable may be overdrawn. For Napoleon and Friedland, taking Indigenous law as law through their case method involves a non-reductive approach to legal principles as embedded in a larger system of thought, and treating them as a set of nuanced and complex responses to practical and philosophical questions that are then to be deliberated, and engaged with intellectually in a sustained way.[132] 'Law is not fruit', write Napoleon and Friedland, 'it is not something waiting to be plucked from branches, nor can it be 'preserved. All law, by its nature, is actually made and remade through people seriously applying themselves to deeply engage with it and struggling to make it their own.'[133] This is not the sociological picture of law as knowable fact, nor the

(Minneapolis: University of Minnesota Press, 2014); Taiaiake Alfred, *Peace, Power, Righteousness: An Indigenous Manifesto* (Toronto: Oxford University Press, 1999).

129 Christie, 'Law, Theory and Aboriginal Peoples' (n. 115), 108; Aaron Mills, 'What Is a Treaty? On Contract and Mutual Aid', in John Borrows and Michael Coyle (eds.), *The Right Relationship: Reimagining the Implementation of Historical Treaties* (Toronto: University of Toronto Press, 2017).

130 Henderson, 'Aboriginal Jurisprudence and Rights' (n. 39), 77.

131 Kirsten Manley-Casimir, 'Incommensurable Legal Cultures: Indigenous Legal Traditions and the Colonial Narrative' (2012) 30 *Windsor Yearbook of Access to Justice*, 137–61, 160.

132 Napoleon and Friedland, 'Indigenous Legal Traditions: Roots to Renaissance' (n. 28); Hadley Friedland, 'Reflective Frameworks: Methods for Accessing, Understanding and Applying Indigenous Laws' (2012) 11 *Indigenous Law Journal*, 1–40, 29.

133 Napoleon and Friedland, 'Gathering the Threads: Developing a Methodology for Researching and Rebuilding Indigenous Legal Traditions' (n. 15), 17.

positivist focus on propositional rules, but the rhetorical understanding of law as a culture of argument, an incomplete process embedded in ongoing relationships. And many incommensurabilists still advocate dialogue with the non-Indigenous legal order. When Henderson stresses that judicial use of Eurocentric analogies to 'master the knowledge gap' betrays a true transsystemic process, he nevertheless urges judges to attempt to understand Indigenous law at a deep level. In the end, unless we abandon all hope of communication, the issue is the adequacy of the translation, the degree to which translators struggle with what is unique to Indigenous law, and the degree to which the 'mark of the foreign' is allowed to impact the perceived naturalness of European categories and concepts.[134]

In my account so far, taking Indigenous law as law is presented as an intellectual engagement with Indigenous theories and philosophies. This resonates with Melissaris' argument for inter-perspectival, critical dialog as an appropriate methodology for legal pluralist theory.[135] In rejecting mainstream positivist approaches to legal theory as a false claim to the neutrality and generality of state law as *the* law (as a case in point Hart's pretention to describe the concept of law as an external observer was based on his participation in, and his internal perspective from within, his own specific legal order),[136] Melissaris asserts that while we can try to make sense of a cross-cultural understanding of law through our own conceptual categories, these should only be starting points that will shift as we engage with what other communities accept as law because we 'enter a process of self-reflection about [our] own preconceptions of legality.'[137] However, he agrees with Stephen Perry that our recognition of 'law *qua* law' can never be uncommitted: we cannot understand the concept of obligation from the external point of view, but only by participating in law's critical discourse and taking its concerns as our own.[138] Here, the insistence of Borrows, Napoleon and others on *engagement* with Indigenous law as an intellectual resource that should be argued with and subject to critique can be appreciated in light of this branch of legal theory. Robert Cover, on whom Melissaris draws heavily, observes that it is through personal acts of

[134] See Walter Benjamin, 'The Task of the Translator', in Hannah Arendt (ed.), *Illuminations: Essays and Reflections*, trans. by Harry Zohn (New York: Harcourt Brace, 1968), pp. 69–82; Kirsten Anker, 'Translating *Sui Generis* Aboriginal Rights in the Civilian Imagination', in Alexandra Popovici, Lionel Smith, and Régine Tremblay (eds.), *Les intraduisibles en droit civil* (Montreal: Thémis, 2014), pp. 6–8.

[135] Melissaris, *Ubiquitous Law: Legal Theory and the Space for Legal Pluralism*, pp. 71–77.

[136] Ibid., p. 10. [137] Ibid., p. 11. [138] Ibid., pp. 11–14.

commitment to a shared *nomos* or normative world that interpretation becomes 'legal' meaning.[139] The commitment that Melissaris argues makes legality possible is borne of a common experience 'of the possibility of transforming word into deed and vice versa in a real spatial and temporal context.'[140] Consequently, in Melissaris' account, inter-perspectival legal pluralism is 'dissociated from the external (and thus potentially unjust) point of view, but will also stop simply regurgitating arguments from well within the internal point of view and then trying to export them, lending them a false sense of universality.'[141]

Nevertheless, there are significant challenges in coming to terms with linguistic and conceptual differences – many of which relate to implicit underlying premises, and a whole background of lived practice or what Pierre Bourdieu called *habitus*,[142] of which we may not even be conscious.[143] Furthermore, as we have seen, to treat the exercise as simply an intellectual or descriptive one would not answer, even within positivist legal theory, the call to take Indigenous law as law. But while Hart included an element of acceptance so as to provide for the voluntary assumption of obligation by individuals (one that would distinguish his concept of law as rules from law as orders backed by threats),[144] Indigenist theorists point us elsewhere than the rational agent who assumes obligations. For example, Christie worries that the case law framework privileges the intellectual tradition at the expense of the spiritual, emotional and physical ones within which it is embedded.[145] Henderson warns that to take Indigenous law 'on our terms' means comprehending it through dreams and through ceremony.[146] In this light, Melissaris' emphasis on commitments as grounded in shared experiences 'of the possibility of transforming word into deed and vice versa' is important in shifting the emphasis away from simple

139 Robert Cover, 'The Supreme Court, 1982 Term – Foreword: Nomos and Narrative' (1983) 97 *Harvard Law Review*, 4–68, 45.
140 Melissaris, *Ubiquitous Law: Legal Theory and the Space for Legal Pluralism* (n. 20), p. 91.
141 Ibid., p. 77.
142 Pierre Bourdieu, *The Logic of Practice* (Stanford: Stanford University Press, 1990).
143 See discussion in Grace Li Xiu Woo, *Ghost Dancing with Colonialism* (Vancouver: University of British Columbia Press, 2011), pp. 31–40.
144 Rodriguez-Blanco, 'Peter Winch and HLA Hart: Two Concepts of the Internal Point of View' (n. 102), 12.
145 Gordon Christie, 'Law, Theory and Aboriginal Peoples' (n. 115), 108.
146 James (Sákéj) Henderson, 'Comprehending First Nations Jurisprudence' (Paper delivered at the Indigenous Law and Legal Systems Conference, University of Toronto Faculty of Law, 27–28 January 2007).

individual choice, as is his analysis of the ways in which state law is institutionalized around specific 'experienced presuppositions' that cannot be transported to other *nomoi*.[147] Nevertheless, he does not fully articulate the need to do more than engage in intellectual enquiry with respect to legal pluralism's meta-theory and meta-jurisprudence. I would argue that the shared experiences that figure so heavily in Melissaris' account of the legal within a community gives us reason to be open to other forms of law – ceremony, stories or land-based learning, for example – so as to build a store of shared experiences that can ground the taking of Indigenous law as law.

One powerful way of engaging with Indigenous law on its own terms turns on its head the question of 'making space': as non-Indigenous judge Lance Finch has said, the co-existence of the Canadian legal system with pre-existing legal orders depends, in part, on being able to 'find space for ourselves, as strangers and newcomers, within the Indigenous legal orders themselves'.[148] Indeed, Indigenous legal orders have a meta-jurisprudence about the relationship between legal orders; they provide their own 'rules of external recognition' that Michaels identifies as crucial to the relational existence of law. Looking to these, I argue, will shift us from the language of space and autonomy to other metaphors and principles. In what follows, I explore one such engagement that leads us to think of a form of plurality in terms of place and interdependence, and of normative commitments born out of ecological relations.

The model of the Two-Row Wampum as described earlier fits neatly into a version of postcolonial legal pluralism as matter of autonomy and political parity. However, the parallel purple rows can easily be taken out of context and become themselves a deceptive single story. Other readings emphasise that the vessels in parallel are also connected by three white rows of beads representing peace, friendship and respect,[149] and that their equal size denotes the equality of all life.[150] Furthermore, while the Two-Row Wampum is prominent in contemporary Haudenosaunee political discourse, an alternative metaphor for the

[147] Melissaris, *Ubiquitous Law: Legal Theory and the Space for Legal Pluralism* (n. 20), p. 78.

[148] The Honourable Justice Lance S. G. Finch, 'The Duty to Learn: Taking Account of Indigenous Legal Orders in Practice', paper presented at the 'Indigenous Legal Orders and the Common Law' British Columbia Continuing Legal Education Conference in Vancouver (November 2012), 20.

[149] Borrows, *Recovering Canada: The Resurgence of Indigenous Law* (n. 7), p. 149.

[150] Oren Lyons, 'Indian Self-Government in the Haudenosaunee Constitution' (1986) 55 *Nordic Journal of International Law*, 117–21, 119.

relationship between nations that has been historically important, and even jointly presented in belt form with the Two-Row,[151] is the Covenant Chain which, whether made of rope, iron or silver, connects two peoples or fastens the European ship to the land.[152] A similar linking image – this time with figures holding hands – was used in two belts at the Treaty of Niagara in 1764, in which the promises of the Royal Proclamation were presented to twenty-four Indigenous nations so as to extend the covenant chain to the Anishnabeg of the Great Lakes and their allies.[153] Wapshkaa Ma'iingan/Aaron Mills maintains, drawing on teachings from his *gete-anishnabeg*,[154] that the belts embody an organising logic of Anishnabeg constitutionalism – namely, mutual aid between interdependent but unique living entities – in contrast with the contractual model through which treaties are usually understood.[155]

While the characterisation of legal plurality as multiple and overlapping *spaces* has been a dominant imagery in the sociological approach,[156] the constitutionalism of interdependence speaks instead to a 'geography' of *place*. As Minnawaanagogiizhigook/Dawnis Kennedy argues, the issue is not simply the relations between the Canadian state and Indigenous peoples, but '[t]he development of the Canadian state and its legal orders

151 Timothy Winegard, *For King and Kanata: Canadian Indians and the First World War* (Winnipeg: University of Manitoba Press, 2012), p. 129; Genevieve Painter, 'A Letter from the Haudenosaunee Confederacy to King George V: Writing and Reading Jurisdictions in International Legal History' (unpublished).

152 Although the specific artefact of the Two-Row wampum is sometimes said to be of more recent origin (Darren Bonaparte, 'The Disputed Myth, Metaphor and Reality of Two Row Wampum' (8 September 2013) http://indiancountrytodaymedianetwork.com/2013/08/09/disputed-myth-metaphor-and-reality-two-row-wampum), perhaps emphasising a reaction by Haudenosaunee to undue interference by the British in the nineteenth century (see Kathryn Muller, 'The Two "Mystery" Belts of Grand River A Biography of the Two Row Wampum and the Friendship Belt' (2007) 31 *American Indian Quarterly*, 129–64), the language of chains connecting peoples or fastening the European ship to the lands of the Haudenosaunee (known as the Covenant Chain) date back at least to the seventeenth century: Jon Parmenter, 'The Meaning of *Kaswentha* and the Two Row Wampum Belt in Haudenosaunee (Iroquois) History: Can Indigenous Oral Tradition be Reconciled with the Documentary Record?' (2013) 3 *Journal of Early American History*, 82–109.

153 Mills, 'What Is a Treaty? On Contract and Mutual Aid' (n. 129).

154 'Old People': Aaron Mills, 'The Lifeworlds of Law: On Revitalizing Indigenous Legal Orders Today' (2016) *McGill Law Journal* [forthcoming].

155 Mills, 'What Is a Treaty? On Contract and Mutual Aid' (n. 129).

156 Desmond Manderson, 'Beyond the Provincial: Space, Aesthetics, and Modernist Legal Theory' (1995) *University of Melbourne Law Review*, 1048–71.

within Indigenous territories.'[157] This fact requires state law to 'demonstrate respect for Indigenous ways of *creating and maintaining relations between peoples and legal orders.*'[158] Mills puts it even more strongly: 'any settler constitutional order will have to reconcile itself to the confederal treaty superstructure that holds distinct Indigenous constitutionalisms together.'[159] As he explains it, for Anishnabe people, this meta-jurisprudence for relations between legal orders grows out of their concrete and lived experiences in a specific ecology. Among the principles animated by this *nomos* are that we are all 'interdependent but unique; aiding one another through [our] differences.'[160] To put it in terms of a familiar Canadian legal metaphor, unlike the 'living tree' of Canadian constitutionalism,[161] the Anishnabe constitutional tree is rooted in the real earth: a creation story 'of something [in] common: the earth beneath and all around us.'[162] Justice Finch's reversal of the 'making space' question giving a predominate role to Indigenous law is not just redressing a colonial hierarchy, but addressing a fundamental lack in the settler legal order that is founded on abstract ideals such as individualism and freedom, and that creates and reproduces an existential separation between humans and nature, mind and matter, subjects and objects.[163]

As a contribution to pluralist legal theory, this may seem odd. It may appear that, instead of the supremacy of state law, we are being asked to accept the temporal priority of treaty relations into which newcomers were welcomed, in continuity with Indigenous law, as the single superstructure for legal pluralism. As Mills points out, though, treaties are not law because we have bound or subjected ourselves – atomistic individuals or communities – through our promises to establish a particular relationship. They are law because they grow out of the primacy of ecological reality in which we are always and already in relation. They are based on respect for the uniqueness, and the particular contributions, of each treaty partner within that set of relations. Arising out of those grounded

157 Kennedy, 'Reconciliation Without Respect? Section 35 and Indigenous Legal Orders' (n. 70), 79, emphasis in original.

158 Ibid. 159 Mills, 'What Is a Treaty? On Contract and Mutual Aid' (n. 129).

160 Ibid.

161 *Edwards v. Canada (Attorney General)* [1929] J.C.J. No. 2, [1930] A.C. 124. (J.C.P.C.), 136.

162 Mills, 'The Lifeworlds of Law: On Revitalizing Indigenous Legal Orders Today' (n. 154).

163 See Cormack Cullinan, *Wild Law: A Manifesto For Earth Justice* 2nd ed (White River Junction, VT: Chelsea Green Publishing, 2011).

relations, they are – therefore – singular, but not single and universal. The claim to treaty is 'an ontological claim, not a normative one',[164] but this is not a return to sociological pluralism as empirical fact. It is embodied knowledge and embodied law born out of and sustained through the experience of living in and with places. The interconnection between legal orders alluded to in Michaels' relational concept of law is then a small part of a larger tapestry of interdependence.

12.6 Conclusion

There is a natural fit between theories of legal pluralism and a postcolonial critique of law imbued with Indigenous perspectives. Both seek to challenge the monologue of colonial state law, to tell other stories of law and sovereignty, and to name and critique the legal and political concepts and presuppositions that blind us to them. However, to the extent that legal pluralism has been associated with limited and flawed forms of state recognition, in which Indigenous law is merely culture, custom or fact, it has had bad press in Indigenous circles, leading to critiques that echo those of 'weak' forms of legal pluralism in which the state maintains its hegemonic position as the sole source of 'real law' in a given territory. And yet a shift to the language of strong legal pluralism, the sociological claim that the plurality of law is a fact, does not work for the normative claims of postcolonial jurisprudence. For those invested in state acknowledgement, there is already too much fact and too little law. For others, both law and social sciences have a disciplinary gaze that is problematic because it turns Indigenous peoples and their law into objects. To accept that Indigenous law being law should rest in any way on state recognition grates against the instincts of legal pluralists and postcolonial scholars alike, even as recognition remains to a large extent politically and pragmatically necessary.

In his critique of the politics of recognition, Dene scholar Glen Coulthard writes that while Indigenous anti-colonialism is a struggle primarily around the question of land, the struggle is 'not only for land in the material sense, but also deeply informed by what the land as a system of reciprocal relations and obligations can teach us about living our lives in relation to one another and the natural world in non-dominating and non-exploitative terms.'[165] The contribution of this

[164] Mills, 'What Is a Treaty? On Contract and Mutual Aid' (n. 129).

[165] Coulthard, *Red Skin White Masks: Rejecting the Colonial Politics of Recognition* (n. 128), p. 13.

'grounded normativity' to pluralist jurisprudence is not just that it occupies a space in the pantheon of legalities, jostling for attention and recognition. Neither is it simply a postcolonial struggle against oppression, seeing law through a critical lens and attempting to challenge the monopoly of the state, the ethnocentrism of law, and the single story of colonial relations, although it does do that. Law from place affirms our uniqueness as collective and individual selves, as well as our inherent relatedness. As Mills puts it, it is a way for all of us to be invited to a political community on, and of, this earth.[166]

[166] Mills, 'What Is a Treaty? On Contract and Mutual Aid' (n. 129).

13

Legal Pluralism and the Value of the Rule of Law

MARTIN KRYGIER

13.1 Preliminaries

The rule of law, needless to say, is an old jurisprudential *topos*, a lawyers' commonplace. Jurists have extolled it and specified what they take its elements to be, philosophers have sought to clarify the concept and debated the virtues of the phenomenon, and more recently a large industry of rule of law promoters has attempted to generate it ('build' is the unfortunate metaphor of the trade), where it is judged absent or weak or challenged (which is a mighty lot of places). Again needless to say, there are controversies about all these matters.

Less controversial, however, indeed part of the shared understandings presupposed in such debates, is the social-institutional *location* of both the rule of law and the diseases for which it is the remedy of choice. The standard, rarely reflected-upon assumption in both cases is: in the practices and law-producing-and-administering institutions of states. The practices of state institutions are the primary *targets* of the rule of law, and insofar as these practices are deemed to have certain rule of law attributes, or are supervised by institutions that do, they and societies so blessed have the rule of law. To the extent state practices and institutions lack such practices and attributes, then correspondingly they lack it.

Thus Dicey locates the rule of law primarily in three allegedly distinctive elements of the British institutional order. Some critics argue about the parochialism involved in this selection and the specific institutions and practices he chooses,[1] but not about their official institutional location. More recently, Gianluigi Palombella has also drawn on English practice,

[1] See Judith Shklar on 'Dicey's unfortunate outburst of Anglo-Saxon parochialism. . . . The Rule of Law was thus both trivialized as the peculiar patrimony of one and only one national order, and formalized, by the insistence that only one set of inherited procedures and court practices could sustain it.' See Judith Shklar, 'Political Theory and the Rule of Law' in *Political Theory and Political Thinkers* (Chicago: University of Chicago Press, 1998), pp. 21–37 at p. 26.

though for richer and more cosmopolitan purposes.[2] He has intriguingly revived the medieval English conception of a balance *within the law itself* between the sovereign's power to govern (*gubernaculum*) and the subject's protected sphere of right (*jurisdictio*). Such a balance between both elements is necessary for the rule of law which, in Palombella's understanding, is 'an institutional idea concerning law.' Its *telos* is to prevent the possibility of legal domination by sovereign power, and its means of doing so is this particular legal-architectural equipoise. Unlike Dicey, Palombella does not limit the ways this might be achieved to a parochial or particular set of institutions. But whichever way it works, the answer is to be found within the legal order. It has nothing to do, either in end or means, with extra-legal social, political or indeed moral practices or arrangements.[3]

And then there are the listers. Lon Fuller famously/notoriously stipulates eight formal features of legal rules that make up what he calls 'the internal morality of law.' These have been widely endorsed in Anglo accounts as a catalogue of the elements of the rule of law, even among legal positivists, though they typically don't rate them so high. Thus, in a very influential article, Joseph Raz expands the list, as have others,[4] but details apart, these are lists of precisely the same sort, their elements to be found in or emanating from the same places. And though Raz finds virtue in the rule of law, he is less charmed by it than is Fuller. It is, he argues, 'a purely negative value ... merely designed to minimize the harms to freedom and dignity *which the law might cause* in its pursuit of its goals however laudable these might be'.[5]

Recently, Jeremy Waldron has criticised such accounts on several grounds. First, he makes the important point that:

> [w]e want the Rule of Law for new societies – for newly emerging democracies, for example – and old societies alike; for national political communities and regional and international governance; and we want it to extend into all aspects of governments' dealings with those subject to them ... getting to the Rule of Law does not just mean paying lip service

[2] Gianluigi Palombella, *È possibile una legalità globale?* (Florence: Il Mulino, 2012).

[3] See ibid., and Martin Krygier, 'Inside the Rule of Law' (2014) 3 1 *Rivista di filosofia del diritto*, 77–98.

[4] Joseph Raz, 'The Rule of Law and Its Virtue', in *The Authority of Law* (Oxford: Clarendon Press, 1979), pp. 210–29. See also Friedrich von Hayek, *The Constitution of Liberty* (Chicago: University of Chicago Press, 1960), pp. 149–50; and Geoffrey de Q Walker, *The Rule of Law: Foundations of Constitutional Democracy* (Melbourne: University of Melbourne Press, 1988).

[5] Raz, *The Authority of Law*, p. 228. My italics.

> to it in the ordinary security of a prosperous modern democracy: it means extending it into societies that are not necessarily familiar with the ideal; and in those societies that are familiar with it, it means extending it into these darker corners of governance as well.[6]

This insistence that we should think of the ideal of the rule of law in ways that might stretch to countries outside the First World, is to be applauded. Its implications, however, have rarely been reflected upon in the writings of contemporary legal philosophers. Yet it would need real argument, which has not so far been forthcoming, to justify the conception of an arguably general political ideal that turns out so closely to track the congenial and familiar (in the main inherited) state legal (best) practices and traditions of a relatively few prosperous countries.

We may not be particularly good at extending the rule of law very far, and because 'ought' implies 'can', that is a practical problem worth taking seriously for normative, not merely descriptive, purposes. But cosmopolitan invocations of the ideals of the rule of law are not oxymoronic, even if specific institutional embodiments might need to be rethought, again and again. For such invocations and such rethinkings, a specification of the term such as Dicey's, which doesn't even reach France let alone points further east or south, can be of little use.

Moreover, there is another reason for reflecting on applicability of the rule of law in legal and political settings different from our own. Only by comparisons with societies which lack some of what we take for granted, and/or have what we do not, and/or do what we do but in guises we do not recognise,[7] are we likely to discern what such differences might reveal. One can always ask, and it is commonly worth asking: why here and not there, or there and not here, and what follows from these differences? These naive questions can help us to question the apparent naturalness of causal stories that seem obvious to us because all their elements are in place and familiar, as well as open our imaginations to what, though unfamiliar, may yet be compatible with – even necessary for – the pursuit of valuable ideals.

With this cosmopolitan agenda in mind, Waldron also notes that

> [w]hen I pay attention to the calls that are made for the Rule of Law around the world, I am struck by the fact that the features that people call

[6] Jeremy Waldron, 'The Rule of Law and the Importance of Procedure', in James Fleming (ed.), *Getting to the Rule of Law* (New York: New York University Press, 2011), pp. 3–31 at pp. 3–4.

[7] I owe this last possibility to Miranda Forsyth.

> attention to are not necessarily the features that legal philosophers have emphasized in their academic conceptions of this ideal ... this formal conception is not what ordinary people have in the forefront of their minds when they clamor for the extension of the Rule of Law into settings or modes of governance where it has not been present before.[8]

Waldron purports to capture such features, what 'ordinary people are urging', by supplementing Fuller-style *formal* features with 'elements of legal *procedure* and the institutions like courts that embody them'.[9] He commends a list of ten such features, mainly to do with the fair, impartial, open and appealable conduct of legal hearings before 'a legally trained judicial officer' and with a 'right to representation by counsel'. The point is to ensure that 'no one should have any penalty, stigma, or serious loss imposed upon him by government'[10] in the absence of such legal procedures. This is an important supplement, with a morally well-motivated core – respect for human dignity – that has no geographical, ethnic, or religious boundaries. It might be noticed, however, that it all happens (or, to the detriment of the Rule of Law, fails to happen) in the procedures adopted by the central legal institutions of state, and ones familiar – to us – at that. The big shift in institutional focus between Fuller and Waldron is from official legislatures to official courts. That is not an enormous distance to travel, even from the point of view of a domestic lawyer who doesn't get out much. In comparative or sociological perspective, such procedures move barely an inch from the formalities they supplement.

What of keeping faith with 'what ordinary people are urging'? Again, this is a welcome recommendation. The rule of law is not an arcane and hermetic coinage of Western jurists. It is a common English term, with analogies (though rarely exact equivalents) in a variety of languages.[11] Rule of law values are called in aid in many parts of the world. Lawyers might seek to explain its workings and philosophers might elucidate some of the term's presuppositions, but it is not obvious why their stipulations should override common understandings of a term in common use, and values in common demand. Indeed, elsewhere Waldron makes precisely this point: 'For this ideal is not the property

[8] Waldron, 'The Rule of Law and the Importance of Procedure', p. 4.

[9] Ibid., 5. My italics. [10] Ibid., 6.

[11] See Martin Krygier, 'Rule of Law (and *Rechtsstaat*)', in James Wright (ed.), *Encyclopedia of the Social and Behavioral Sciences*, 2nd edition, volume 20 (Oxford: Elsevier, 2015), pp.780–87.

of the analytic philosophers and it is certainly not our job to go round reproaching laymen for not using the term in the way that (for example) Joseph Raz uses it.'[12]

Yet it is not clear that Waldron's salutary supplement to traditional understandings goes anywhere near far enough. As he would doubtless agree, the vulnerabilities, aspirations, and values that lead people to clamour for the rule of law are not primarily to be judged by what it does for lawyers, still less legal philosophers. If the rule of law is a good, it is a social good, and it is challenged, inter alia, by social bads. Not all of these have much to do with what goes on before judicial tribunals. If Afghan citizens, for example, or Syrians or others, lament the absence of the rule of law in their societies, is it obvious that they are talking only about receiving unclear legal messages from the government (Fuller), or having a hard day in court (Waldron)? Perhaps the irrelevance of the law or any other institutional constraints, to the ways power is experienced in their everyday lives, might matter to them more immediately, and even more, than their (likely rare) appearances before judicial tribunals (where they exist).

In pursuing Waldron's agenda, then, we should be open to expanding the social and institutional range of our 'conceptual geography',[13] to use a phrase from another context. We need at least to consider whether the values that animate concern with the rule of law might need and draw support from other than the usual suspects, as well as whether there might be other conditions for, and alternatives to, effective state-law contributions to that putatively charmed state of affairs. In seeing these contributions and conditions and challenges more clearly we might have to reconsider the role and contributions of state law to the rule of law, more than anyone I have mentioned hitherto appears to have done, or even thought to do.

There is a third and overriding concern, not merely descriptive or analytical, but normative. It is already implicit here and is also explicit in Waldron's argument, indeed drives it. Partisans advocate the rule of law and analyze it, not merely as cartographers of some piece of landscape interesting for itself. They do it for reasons; typically they see *value* in the rule of law. The procedural elements Waldron chooses are, after all, connected to what he takes to be the specific normative contribution of

[12] *The Rule of Law and the Measure of Property*, The Hamlyn Lectures, Cambridge University Press, 2012, (Kindle Edition) 16.

[13] Tony Judt, 'The Rediscovery of Central Europe' (1990) 119 *Daedalus*, 23–54, at 25.

the rule of law – respect for the person who confronts the law. So too, implicit or explicit reasons ground the components of Fuller's list, Hayek's stipulations and so on, even when they are presented as deriving *from*, rather than leading *to*, the elements taken to characterise the rule of law. The values proposed might differ, and the importance they are thought to have, but the rule of law is a concept pervaded by what Putnam calls, 'the entanglement of fact and value'.[14]

Invocations of the rule of law link purported description with evaluation. Whether the link is at bottom thought of as conceptual or causal, it is commonly assumed that the rule of law has a normative component or at least value-relevant results. If it is strong in a society, its partisans assume, something good has been achieved. If we say, for example, that there were lots of laws under Stalin and a lot of rule, but there was not much rule of law, we are not employing a distinction that is inherently controversial, either as a description or – at least these days – as an evaluation. So, at least among the legally and philosophically unwashed, the rule of law means something more than the mere existence of law, or indeed any particular formal or even procedural attributes of laws. Even critics acknowledge such value-laden assumptions, if only in seeking to debunk them.

This is often obscured by the apparently descriptive character of conventional accounts of the rule of law, among them the several lists and catalogues I have referred to previously, and more generally those that I have elsewhere described as anatomical or morphological rather than teleological in character.[15] These *begin* their accounts of the rule of law by characterising features of laws – clear, prospective, non-contradictory, and so on – but they routinely end with endorsements of some achievements or other attributable to such features, and their authors don't seem to think the links are coincidental. Though that is not the order in which things are usually presented, one might be forgiven for thinking the evaluation has spurred the lists rather than merely followed from them. After all, laws have many features. What guides the selection of just some of them, particularly those that are then

[14] Hilary Putnam, 'The Entanglement of Fact and Value', in *The Collapse of the Fact/Value Dichotomy and Other Essays* (Cambridge, MA: Harvard University Press, 2002), pp. 28–45.

[15] See Martin Krygier, 'The Rule of Law. Legality, Teleology, Sociology', in Gianluigi Palombella and Neil Walker (eds.), *Relocating the Rule of Law* (Oxford: Hart Publishing, 2009), pp. 45–69.

argued to support predictability, freedom, security, dignity, and so forth? Why those features? Why those effects?

I have long contended that the conceptual priority of *telos* over anatomy, function over form, ends over means, should be made explicit.[16] To start otherwise, as is typical, with legal institutional checklists, constrains thought and blocks imagination. Familiar features of legal rules or institutions, so often those that just happen to be taken to embody the rule of law in our own time and place, come to be thought of as default settings for its achievement, even as necessary settings. That can tie us simply to what we happen to know, rather than allow us to explore whether there are other ways of getting where we want to go. It makes it hard to think either that the rule of law might be served in the absence of familiar hardware, or indeed of it being disserved even where the hardware is present. And it often leads to what organisation theorists call 'goal displacement' (commonly found, and complained about, among bureaucrats), where ostensible guardians of the rule of law become expert at explaining what rules or procedures must be followed but not why.

We do better to start by asking what value(s) we hope the rule of law can serve, and only then and from there move to explore what might be needed to achieve or approach those values, than operate the other way round. All the more because, with the animating value(s) clear in mind, we might find that what we need to accomplish it/them is different from what we have been taught. We should begin with teleology, then, not with anatomy. And so I do, shortly.

This chapter explores what it might mean to think about the rule of law in the light of these preliminary reflections: in a way that at once is ready to travel, heedful of what 'ordinary people' might hope for from the rule of law, and begins with the value(s) for which the rule of law might matter. It turns out that acknowledgment of legal pluralism (whatever one calls it) is key to such a way of thinking.

Two more pieces of throat-clearing. First, thinkers have cashed out the values they attribute to the rule of law in many ways. I do it in a particular way that I would wish to defend. However, for the purposes of this essay, though not others, not too much hangs on the specific value I propose. It is not bizarre to suggest that the rule of law has something to do with what I choose: reduction of arbitrariness in the exercise of power.

[16] Ibid.

Indeed it would be highly unusual to reject the suggestion outright. Some people, however, would consider it does not go far enough. Such criticisms are worth arguing about, but I don't think they affect the significance of legal pluralism for attempts to redeem the value of the rule of law. If my claims are plausible in relation to the modest but precious value I propose, they should not be less so in relation to more ambitious proposals.

Second, though I speak of legal pluralism in what follows, I could as well have settled with a term such as normative, maybe even just social pluralism, or coined some other term, such as those favoured by two authors from whom I draw heavily later: Sally Moore in Section 3 below ('reglementation', 'semi-autonomous social field'[17]) and Marc Galanter in Section 4 ('indigenous ordering').[18] Conceptual questions about whether 'law' is a term that should be limited to acts and institutions of state, a matter of considerable jurisprudential controversy, make no difference to the argument here. All the points I make go through (or not) whether or not that conceptual issue is settled.

13.2 Value

No one can dictate a uniquely correct meaning for the rule of law, or any uncontestable stipulation of the values it serves. It is too late for that. The concept has become altogether too protean, not to say (and who would want to say?!) chameleonic; the purposes for which it is invoked are too many and varied; the freight carried by this short phrase too distant from anything that could be derived from dictionary definitions of its component words. At best we offer a proposal which we seek to justify as connected to common understandings or to particular traditions of reflection and discussion that we endorse or seek to refine or repair, and that we proffer as in some way helping to clarify our subject: for example, by illuminating both what is characteristic but also distinctive of the phenomenon, without tautologous overlap with concepts already adequate to their tasks, and so on.

[17] See Sally Falk Moore, 'Introduction' and 'Law and Social Change: The Semi-Autonomous Field as an Appropriate Subject of Study', in *Law as Process. An Anthropological Approach*, 2nd edition (London: James Currey, 2001), pp. 1–31, 54–81.

[18] Marc Galanter, 'Justice in Many Rooms. Courts, Private Ordering, and Indigenous Law' (1981) 9 *Journal of Legal Pluralism*, 1–47.

My proposal is this: the rule of law has a specific domain – that is, the way *power* is exercised, and it responds to a specific antipathy – that is, the arbitrary exercise of power. The proposal is not original (which in this case I take to be a virtue), though not unanimously endorsed. It distinguishes the rule of law from other substantive values connected with law: those one might want to animate the *content* of laws, for example, such as social justice, or a particular tax regime, or whatever. And though its implications are not small it is also modest, in at least two senses. First, it has to do not with social values at large but rather with a specific issue: how power is exercised. Second, it has a specific enemy – arbitrariness in the exercise of power – rather than power itself. We need power to be available and effective for good uses; emasculation is not the aim.[19]

My proposal, though again quite familiar, has an element different from much that seems to animate contemporary debates. There has, for example, been much discussion of whether we should prefer a 'thin', 'formal', institution-focused conception of the rule of law or a 'thick', 'substantive' one. The former settles for some institutional set-up that conforms, say, with Fuller's or Raz's lists or some such, while the latter requires substantive elements from a larger vision of a good society and polity – democratic, free-market, human rights respecting or some such – to be present before the rule of law can be said to exist.[20] Elsewhere I have criticised both ends of this alleged dichotomy as misconceived,[21] but here I simply want to claim that the plane on which they contend should not be thought to exhaust our concerns. In particular, it should not obscure the particular bearing of the rule of law, which occurs on another plane – not that of social value at large, but the value of a particular achievement in a particular domain: tempering the exercise of power.

There are many other domains of value and anti-value besides the ways power is exercised, and many accounts of goodness and justice concerned with them. My claim is merely that the *distinctive* domain of the rule of law is the exercise of power. That domain is not more important than others, but it has a specific importance not reducible to

[19] Cf. my 'Tempering Power', forthcoming in Maurice Adams et al. (eds.), *Constitutionalism and the Rule of Law: Bridging Idealism and Realism*, (Cambridge: Cambridge University Press, 2016).

[20] See Randall Peerenboom, 'Varieties of Rule of Law: An Introduction and Provisional Conclusion', *Asian Discourses of Rule of Law* (London: RoutledgeCurzon, 2004), pp. 1–55.

[21] Krygier, 'Rule of Law (and *Rechtsstaat*)'.

other things, and often not separately considered. There are many ways to exercise power, and arbitrary ways should be shunned. That is so even independently of the ends for which power is exercised, though I share Lon Fuller's belief that some of the worst ends are more difficult to pursue in accordance with the rule of law than not.[22]

There is a lot to be said, and a lot has been said over millennia, about why arbitrary exercise of power is so odious, but again I do not go into that much here.[23] I just want to stake the fairly uncontroversial position that the arbitrary exercise of power is typically obnoxious, whatever else is, and that we have good reasons to value ways of avoiding it. On this view, a special anti-value, to which power-wielders are prone and against which some forms of legal institutionalisation are thought able to help us avoid, is the propensity of power untempered to be exercised in arbitrary ways.

Arbitrariness is, then, a specific vice when added to power. The ends for which power is exercised have their own significance but they are the concerns of political morality more broadly conceived, not – on this account – specifically the rule of law. Otherwise we too easily fall foul of Raz's caution that to equate the rule of law with the rule of 'good' law, or with whatever we take the good to be, robs the concept of any separate significance. Loading wide-ranging substantive ideals into the concept threatens to melt it into everything else we might like, and renders a separate and distinct concept otiose. As Raz expresses the point, 'if the rule of law is the rule of good law then to explain its nature is to propound a complete social philosophy. But if so the term lacks any useful function. We have no need to be converted to the rule of law just in order to discover that to believe in it is to believe that good should triumph.'[24]

The specific ambition of partisans of the rule of law is to *temper* the exercise of power, so that it might more readily be exercised in non-arbitrary than in arbitrary ways and directions.[25] Not only is anti-arbitrariness a pre-eminent rule of law value; I would distinguish it, as

[22] Martin Krygier, 'Hart, Fuller and Law in Transitional Societies', in Peter Cane (ed.), *The Hart-Fuller Debate in the Twenty-First Century* (Oxford: Hart Publisher, 2010), pp. 107–34; and Kristen Rundle, 'The Impossibility of an Exterminatory Legality: Law and the Holocaust' (2009) 59 *University of Toronto Law Journal* at 65.

[23] See Martin Krygier, 'Four Puzzles about the Rule of Law: Why, What, Where, And Who Cares?', in James Fleming (ed.), *Getting to the Rule of Law* (New York: New York University Press, 2011), pp. 64–104, and Krygier, 'The Rule of Law: Pasts, Presents, and Two Possible Futures' (2016) 12 *Annual Review of Law and Social Science*, 199–229.

[24] Raz, *The Authority of Law*, p. 211.

[25] Krygier, 'Tempering Power'.

an *immanent* value, the specific vocation or *telos* of the rule of law, from other values with which the rule of law is often and perhaps rightly connected.

It is common today to claim all sorts of goods as flowing from the rule of law – economic development, human rights, democracy, and so on. Indeed these claims are the lifeblood of the international rule of law promotion industry: if they didn't think these results flowed from the rule of law, they would not be interested in it. But I'm not talking about those external, purported, blessings allegedly bestowed by the rule of law. Perhaps it is good for all these things, though the claims so popular in international circles today can be debated.[26] But if it is, that is because of the extent to which it approaches its immanent, often latent, *telos*, reducing arbitrariness in the exercise of power.[27]

Law is specifically and characteristically – at its core – a vehicle for the exercise of power; that is what it does. In certain configurations and circumstances, or so is the rule of law hope, it is also a potent means by which power – state *and* non-state – might be channelled, directed, constrained, tempered. One question, perhaps the central one for the rule of law, is what difference law can make to the ways power is exercised. Ways of exercising power, including non-arbitrary and non-dominating ways are, in other words, tied to the concept of the rule of law in ways that other goods, say, economic development or even democracy are simply not, though they might flow from it. The former are not external but immanent values of the rule of law, their *telos*. The latter are external benefits said to flow from it.

13.3 Social Causality

Having identified whatever value we find central to the rule of law – and this goes for *any* value we might prefer, not merely the one I propose – it makes sense to ask how it might be furthered. And that in turn

[26] See for example, Stephan Haggard and Lydia Tiede, 'The Rule of Law and Economic Growth: Where are We?' (2010) 39 *World Development*, 673–85; Bojan Bugaric, 'Law and Development in Central and Eastern Europe: The Neo-liberal Development State and Its Problems', in Randall Peerenboom and Tom Ginsburg (eds.), *Law and Development of Middle-Income Countries: Avoiding the Middle-Income Trap* (Cambridge: Cambridge University Press, 2014), pp. 131–56 at p. 136.

[27] This is also Philip Selznick's understanding. I don't think he is my source, and I had other reasons for adopting this conception, but because I've borrowed so much else from him, the possibility cannot be discounted.

necessarily raises questions of 'social causality', a phrase I take from the legal anthropologist, Sally Falk Moore. Moore points out that 'legislation is based on folk notions of social causality, on ideas of how to make things happen through the use of the power of government'.[28] What she says of legislation is no less true of jurisprudes' accounts of the rule of law. And though jurists typically leave the systematic analysis of social causality to others, among them social scientists, they do not avoid the notion. Indeed much that they say about what the law is and does, and what it should be and do, depends and must depend on notions of social causality, notwithstanding that like most folk notions these are typically implicit and not deeply considered. Moreover, the folk notions of both legislators and jurists are not those of folk-in-general, but of legal folk. No surprise that when they think of law and social causality, state law is assumed to stand front and centre.

To complicate that assumption, I draw on three of what – once articulated – seem to me elementary sociological truisms. I find it hard to think how anyone could dispute any of them, though the history of legal thought makes plain that they are easily ignored. I identify each with a source of articulation, though one could have got to the point in many other ways. The first source is Lon Fuller; the second Sally Falk Moore; the third Marc Galanter.

13.3.1 'And' or 'In'

The trade association of U.S. socio-legal studies is the 'law and society association.' This language mirrors or is mirrored in 'law and society' (and numerous other 'law and . . .' programs, e.g. literature, politics, etc.) associations, programs, journals, throughout the country and in many other parts of the world. The phrase is revealing in two ways, one that has to do with the copula that links the two nouns, the other with their order.

First, 'law and': Lon Fuller disapproved of this formulation. He insisted that law was a *part* of social life, not merely a partner of it. So, 'law *in* society', not 'law and'.[29] This is a very general point, of course, and in

[28] Moore, 'Introduction', p. 6

[29] 'Jurisprudence and Social Policy: Aspirations and Perspectives' (1980) 68 *California Law Review*, 206–20 at 216. Cf. Lon L. Fuller, 'Some Unexplored Social Dimensions of the Law' in Arthur E. Sutherland, *Path of the Law from 1967* (Cambridge, MA: Harvard University Press, 1968), pp. 57–69 at p. 57: 'The intensified interest in the sociology of law that has developed in recent years has come to assume the proportions of something like an intellectual movement. In the United States this movement has found a kind of

truth Fuller adorned it with little detail and not everything he wrote – including the famous enumeration of the features of law's internal morality – was drenched in its implications.

These are pursued more vigorously, and for non-accidental reasons, in strands of socio-legal writings that emanated from Russian and east European multi-national empires before World War I, and then colonial ones after it, where what the imperial code might have said, and the normative frames within which locals of varying languages and ethnicities and religions lived, typically diverged. The key names are Leon Petrażycki (who distinguished and gave priority to 'intuitive law' over official law), Bronisław Malinowski (who, by focusing a central European tradition, made famous the 'discovery' in Papua New Guinea of law without 'central authority, codes, courts and constables') and Eugen Ehrlich (explorer of the 'living law' to be found within the 'inner order' of human 'associations'). Ehrlich considered living law to be both chronologically prior to and sociologically more fundamental than rules for official decision developed by lawyers and legal officials. In all his work, Ehrlich sought to redeem the dictum anathema to Kelsen, that 'the center of gravity of legal development lies not in legislation, nor in juristic science, nor in judicial decision, but in society itself.'[30]

Secondly, the order: Why should law come to mind *before* society. Chronologically, and particularly if we are thinking of state law, the order was certainly otherwise. Synchronically and sociologically, it is arguably so as well; or perhaps it makes no sense to assign priority. At least the mix(es) deserve close attention.

13.3.2 Social Fields

Let us start at the conventional end-point with 'society', rather than begin with 'law', as lawyers typically do. Moore's writings are particularly illuminating in this connection. They have had great influence on the growth of interest in legal pluralism, even though she prefers not to use

sloganized expression in the title, *Law and Society*. . . . It would be captious indeed to pick any serious quarrel with this innocent renaming of the familiar. . . . At the same time there are, I believe, some dangers in this new title and in the allocation of intellectual energies it seems to imply. By speaking of law *and* society we may forget that law is itself a part of society, that its basic processes are *social* processes, that it contains within its own internal workings social dimensions worthy of the best attentions of the sociologist.'

30 Eugen Ehrlich, *Fundamental Principles of the Sociology of Law* (Cambridge, MA: Harvard University Press, 1936), at xv.

the term. She favours 'reglementation' as an overarching concept for 'all those attempts to organise and control behavior through the use of explicit rules',[31] reserving 'law' specifically for state reglementation in complex societies. She thinks this accords with common usage, preserves significant distinctions, and is less confusing.

But if she chooses not to call all non-state reglementations law, she more than almost anyone has reminded us of how significant such often very law-like, but not state-produced, kinds of reglementation are for the normative regulation of societies – *all* societies – and in particular of the variable complexity of the inter-relations between various sorts of non-state reglementation, and between that (or better, those) and state law.

Folk notions of 'society' in modern societies often take one of two forms, both of which can mislead.[32] Often, the term is just a collective shorthand for 'all of us', understood as a mass of individuals. To speak of society in this way is just to refer in a word to all the individual persons living in some bounded space. When Margaret Thatcher denied there was any such thing as 'society', she was actually saying there was nothing more than individuals (though she added their families). Less polemical individualists might be less fastidious about use of the word, but say it adds nothing but economy of expression.

Alternatively, society can be conceived holistically, as a kind of collective entity. On some interpretations, that is how Durkheim understood it. And this is often how the word is used when media editorial writers and Bar Association after-dinner speakers expatiate on the need for law to 'keep up with social change', 'serve the needs of society', 'reflect social values', and so on.

However, to live in a society is not merely to have a lot of neighbours, but nor to be part of some sort of vast undifferentiated blob. On the one hand, individuals are profoundly affected by their social relations that mould and connect them, and these are not just general but particular. On the other hand, society is not a *thing*, and certainly not an undifferentiated unit. Instead, its individual members typically inhabit what Moore has influentially described as 'semi- autonomous social fields',[33] usually

[31] Moore, 'Introduction' pp. 2–3.

[32] This section is drawn from, and extends, a section of my 'Why the Rule of Law is too important to leave to Rule of Law Promoters', forthcoming in Raimond Gaita and Gerry Simpson (eds.), *Who's Afraid of International Law?* (Monash University Publishing, 2016).

[33] Moore, 'Law and Social Change'.

several simultaneously. Such fields, or perhaps in today's language networks, are affected, more or less, in one way and another, by official norms (and so, 'semi-'), but not without interpretation, reconfiguration, and competition from norms generated outside the official sphere. Such norms emanate from within our core fields of operation (and so are, to that extent, 'autonomous') and from other overlapping fields as well (and so again, in relation to them, 'semi'). Not only do they have direct significance of their own, but they mediate other norms, and so contribute to whatever significance those latter are liable to have.

Semi-autonomous fields include the organisations in which we work and with which we deal, families, localities, people we trust, perhaps ethnic and religious communities – particularly when they are what Avishai Margalit calls 'encompassing groups': 'a group whose culture stands out, encompasses many aspects of life, and covers important and varied areas of its members' lives, especially those significant for the well-being of the people belonging to the culture.'[34] All of these generate normative imperatives and social connections, some strong some weak, sometimes loose sometimes tight, sometimes open sometimes closed, sometimes egalitarian sometimes clientelistic, sometimes honest sometimes corrupt.

To the degree that these fields have salience for those within their sway – whether because they are members of a particular field or interact with members of other fields – semi-autonomous fields are likely to generate distinctive ways of viewing and handling affairs including internal disputes and those with people in other fields. Also, distinctive ways of hearing, interpreting, valuing, attending to, official law. Even in the most law-observant societies, these informal norms have sources other than state laws, and they will affect much that happens in the fields, sometimes without more, sometimes in interaction with external norms, including official ones; sometimes by redirecting the interpretation and effects of those norms in unpredictable ways, sometimes in ways that block or frustrate their legislative or curial formulators. Sometimes such blocking and frustration is intentional, or would be if their targets knew what lawmakers were asking (or commanding) in their laws, but often they don't. Often it is merely a product of unavoidable interactions between different, sometimes inconsistent, norms, of different and variable salience. Much to which official laws might in theory

[34] Avishai Margalit, *The Decent Society* (Cambridge, MA: Harvard University Press, 1996), p. 138

relate but that never comes within the purview of state institutions will be handled on the ground, often without reference to state laws at all, sometimes 'in the shadow of the law',[35] other times under various other shadows. Such dealings may at times be inconsistent with state law or reflect idiosyncratic interpretations of that law, or ignore it. They have other concerns, other questions and other answers. Whether consistent or cognisant or whatever, they will have effects that mediate, refract, and often redirect and refashion the significance and consequences of state law, whatever lawmakers intended it to accomplish.

These, it should be stressed, are general truths, not just what happens in countries with defective legal systems or little or no rule of law; though in many such countries, where the rule of law industry is hard at work, the balance between 'semi' and 'autonomy' frequently favours the latter, often dramatically, and the disjunction between official and not is often extreme. Networks are often more autonomous and powerful in such countries, and lead to greater and more dramatic deviations from official aspirations. The state, and state law, are often correspondingly weaker.

However, it is a common mistake to compare a society thought to be awash with 'informal practices', as legal pathologies in benighted countries are often characterised,[36] with some idealised model of an impersonal and sovereign western legal order, with nothing in between the state's laws and its individual subjects. As we all know, except when we play at legal philosophy, sociologically there is no such order. These subjects, or today citizens, have many other things to do than wait to interpret the law in the ways its creators had in mind, or to evade or subvert it. It may just not be on their minds. The character, impact and salience of informal practices in relation to official law are almost infinitely variable. These differences can matter greatly, but their existence is universal. And apart from them, there are the *actors* in these variously choreographed scenes: '[s]ocial transactions usually take place in the service of objectives to which legal rules are merely ancillary shapers, enablers, or impediments. Conformity to the rule is seldom in itself the central objective.'[37]

[35] See Robert H. Mnookin and Lewis Kornhauser, 'Bargaining in the Shadow of the Law: The Case of Divorce' (1979) 88 *Yale Law Journal*, 950–97.

[36] See for example Vladimir Gel'man, 'The Unrule of Law in the Making: the Politics of Informal Institution Building in Russia' (2004) 56 *Europe-Asia Studies*, 1021–40.

[37] Moore, 'Introduction', p. 4.

In the light of these truisms, let us move back to state law, that is, to where rule of lawyers start and often end.

13.3.2.1 Legislation

Against this background Moore makes the very obvious point, the implications of which are so often overlooked, that '[l]egislation is intrusive. It is a tinkering with an ongoing social field that has areas of relatively autonomous activity and self-regulation.'[38] A nice metaphor of Gunther Teubner's can help here. Teubner argues that so-called legal transplants are better understood as 'irritants'[39], sometimes in some places more able and likely to irritate, at other times and in other places less, sometimes with predictable effects, often not; for reasons as much dependent on qualities of the irritated as of the irritator, the chemistry between them, and then what populates and what happens in the spaces between. This is most obviously true of the specific subject of Teubner's essay, deliberately introduced laws from other jurisdictions (transplants), but the metaphor can apply more widely. To be sure, in some societies, much state law has been around long enough and accepted well enough that it forms part of the generally accepted, often unconsciously assumed, normative background of everyday life. It no longer irritates everyone painfully, though its unguent character is unlikely to soothe everyone equally. Even in such societies, however, new laws can open new wounds,[40] or reopen old ones, and in modern societies the continuous introduction of new law frequently irritates and unsettles existing practices. In societies which have, or have come to have, great plurality within, it will encounter and generate many social antibodies. And this is all the more so in societies where even the source of the law is alien.

An upshot is that again unless it is brutally enough administered to pulverise anything in its path – a rare event, even in totalitarian countries, and hard to sustain – the effectiveness of state laws will be heavily dependent on their degree of synchronisation with the 'indigenous' orderings generated from within, and that generate, social fields. Indeed in totalitarian and authoritarian polities, the very *lack* of synchronisation between exercise of state power and social realities and possibilities often

[38] 'Introduction', p. 7.

[39] Gunther Teubner, 'Legal Irritants: Good Faith in British Law or How Unifying Law Ends up in New Divergences' (1998) 61 *Modern Law Review*, 11–32.

[40] For a classic reflection on the interaction of novel legal irritants with just such a legal background, see E. P. Thompson, *Whigs and Hunters* (Harmondsworth: Penguin, 1977).

generates informal practices in the society which at the same time subvert the official order and try to make up for its inadequacies.[41] Both in these situations of chronic lack of sync and ones where the mesh is smoother, one can talk as much of 'the law in the shadow of indigenous ordering'[42] as of the more familiar 'bargaining in the shadow of the law.'

Finally, while these points are generally true, their weight and salience also vary greatly in significance and implication. Whenever law stakes a claim to rule, the upshot of the many potential sources of normative, structural, cultural and institutional overlaps, collaborations and competitions in every society will differ markedly between (and often within) societies. Whether and how people will interpret the state's law and respond to it, how highly it will rate for them in comparison with other influences – these things depend only partly on what it says, how it says it, and what the law is intended by its makers to do. In complex and variable ways, people's responses to state law depend on how, in what form and with what salience and force and communicated residue of initial purpose, that law survives to be able to penetrate all these intervening media, how attuned to it putative recipients are, and how dense, competitive, resistant or hostile to its messages they might turn out to be. So much writing on 'the state' and 'law' ignores, however, how various are the phenomena and relationships clumped under these apparently simple and single concepts, and what happens in between.

Moreover, lest one think this is only significant in pre-modern or developing societies where social connections are strong, and state law is alien and weak, there is a sense in which the complexity of the roles of semi-autonomous fields is even greater in developed societies with overarching states, than elsewhere. Thus Moore again:

> It seems incontrovertible that the more complex a society, and the greater the appearance of rational control, the more delegation there will be in government and administration and the more areas of discretion and semi-autonomous activity there will be in the subparts of the society, formal and 'informal'. . . .
>
> This view of complex society, or of any society, leads one to a paradox. Formal reglementation can control certain behavior, but not the aggregate of behavior in a society. The more 'rational' a society seems in its parts,

[41] See Alena V. Ledeneva, *Russia's Economy of Favours* (Cambridge: Cambridge University Press, 1998) and Ledeneva, *How Russia Really Works. The Informal Practices that Shaped Post-Soviet Politics and Business* (Ithaca: Cornell University Press, 2006).

[42] See Galanter, 'Justice in Many Rooms' at 17.

> and its rules, and its rules about rules, the thicker the layer of formalism and ideological self-representation to be penetrated to find out what is really going on. . . . [O]ver time, reglementary control can be only temporary, incomplete, and its consequences not fully predictable. The study of reglementation is therefore the study of the way partial orders and partial controls operate in social contexts.[43]

To work out the implications of these sociological realities requires evidence and reflection on matters of social theory. But how many lawyers and legal philosophers think that is their business? International rule of law promoters have started to think so after repeated disappointments in the field. Since the industry is relatively new, that has only happened recently (though with some, at least intellectually, disruptive force),[44] even though sociological reflections on social causality are actually quite old and have not been far to seek. Much of the disappointment found in rule of law promotion in fallow fields abroad could well have been predicted ahead of time, as indeed it was, by thinkers to whom promoters didn't listen. And neither sociology of law nor the experiences of rule-of-law promoters has had much resonance among legal philosophers who concern themselves with the rule of law. And yet, to quote Moore one last time, from her 1978 collection of essays published even earlier:

> Ordinary experience indicates that law and legal institutions can only effect a degree of intentional control of society, greater at some times and less at others, or more with regard to some matters than others. That limited degree of control and predictability is daily inflated in the folk models of lawyers and politicians all over the world.[45]

[43] Moore, 'Introduction', pp. 29–30.

[44] See Gillian K. Hadfield and Barry Weingast, 'Microfoundations of the Rule of Law' (2014) 17 *Annual Review of Political Science* 21–42; Lant Pritchett and Michael Woolcock, 'Solutions when the Solution is the Problem: Arraying the Disarray in Development', Centre for Global Development Working Paper No. 10, September 2002, 17, at http://papers.ssrn.com/sol3/papers.cfm?abstract_id=1106236; more generally, for disruptions that I favour, see particularly the publications of the Justice for the Poor group in the World Bank, among them by Deborah Isser, Michael Woolcock and their associates; and see http://blogs.worldbank.org/governance/towards-justice-in-development.

[45] Moore, 'Introduction', p. 2. See similarly Galanter, 'Justice in Many Rooms' at 20: '[t]he mainstream of legal scholarship has tended to look out from within the official legal order, abetting the pretensions of the official law to stand in a relationship of hierarchic control to other normative orderings in society. Social research on law has been characterised by a repeated rediscovery of the other hemisphere of the legal world. This has entailed recurrent rediscovery that law in modern society is plural rather than monolithic, that it is private as well as public in character and that the national (public, official) legal system is often a secondary rather than a primary locus of regulation.'

13.3.2.2 Litigation

What about courts, and their procedures, on which Waldron sets such store? Doubtless they are important for those who find themselves there, as well as for those many more who anticipate such a possibility at some time in their lives, whether or not it eventuates. However, much that has already been said about society and legislation applies, virtually without remainder, to the significance of what happens in courts as well. Here, too, what in socio-legal studies might be counted as truisms are relevant and often ignored. I will present them in all their truistic banality, again drawing on a classic in the field, Marc Galanter's 'Justice in Many Rooms.'

In briefest summary, the significance of courts, like that of legislation, must be understood against the background of Galanter's epigrammatic observation that '[j]ust as health is not found primarily in hospitals or knowledge in schools, so justice is not primarily to be found in official justice-dispensing institutions. People experience justice (and injustice) not only (or usually) in forums sponsored by the state but at the primary institutional locations of their activity – home, neighbourhood, workplace, business deal and so on.'[46] Law is 'in' society, here too.

Given the significance of the fields and orderings to which we have referred in every society, an enormous amount of social activity to which state law might relate will never find its way to state institutions, but will be dealt with, if at all, elsewhere and without the intervention of officials. This is common knowledge, but acknowledgment of the implications of this fact requires a rearrangement of the conceptual maps many of us rely on to understand the positions and roles of official agencies in society. American socio-legal scholars speak of the 'disputing pyramid',[47] at the broad base of which is a hurt of some kind, and at its peak is the highest court. Many layers of social processes intervene between suffering a law-related harm, then choosing to engage in the three analytically separate, and often practically far apart or never pursued, activities of

[46] 'Justice in Many Rooms,' 17. Compare Philip Selznick, 'Sociology and Natural Law' (1961) 6 *Natural Law Forum*, 84–108 at 84: 'education, politics, religion, and other social activities are found outside of the specialized institutions established to deal with them. Sociology has located these phenomena "in society," that is, in more informal and spontaneous groupings and processes.' Selznick thought the same was true of law.

[47] William Felstiner, Richard Abel, and Austin Sarat, 'The Emergence and Transformation of Disputes: Naming, Blaming, Claiming . . .' (1981) 15 *Law and Society Review*, 631–54. For more extensive discussion of the (varying) characters of such pyramids, see my 'Why Rule of Law Promotion Is Too Important to Be Left to Lawyers', in Raimond Gaita and Gerry Simpson (eds.), *Who's Afraid of International Law?* (2016), pp. 133–68.

'naming, blaming, claiming', and only then reaching *any* official channel, least of all those that issue judgments that jurists most like to read. Few of us climb very high at all up that pyramid, even indeed come in contact with its lowest officially constructed levels. Those who do will certainly and rightly value the presence of the procedural features Waldron enumerates. But while court procedures indeed matter greatly to the skewed sample of litigants who endure them, and they might be of legal importance disproportionate to their numbers, socially the situation is more complicated.

What follows from this? Certainly not that dispute settlement by courts is unimportant. The fact that 'health is not found primarily in hospitals' is not an argument for the unimportance of what happens in hospitals. Even if I have plenty of stubbed toes but only one heart attack in my long life, it's enough. And so it is with courts. Treated for the moment just in terms of what they do for those who reach them, this will include serving many who found nowhere else to go, no other independent institution capable of doing justice to their claims. There is an incalculable difference between societies where this possibility is available to citizens, and ones where it is not, or is available only to certain categories, or deals so badly with them that they have no use for courts, or costs so much that they can't afford to use them. All of this has to do with the ways power is exercised, and so all of it has to do with the rule of law.

Moreover, this is so, whether or not one ever has occasion actually to use the institutions. In the previous paragraph, I spoke only of individuals with disputes or grievances that actually do make their way to official institutions. But the absence of a real, even if distant, possibility of enforceable intervention by a third party independent of the parties to disputes can have tragic social consequences. In such circumstances, people do not merely, as we often do, fend for themselves in the first instance, but are liable to do so without curb or limit, if they lack even the in-principle anticipation that they might call on official agencies if all else fails. So nothing I say in what follows is intended to detract from the strategic, ultimate and salutary significance of state institutions – where they exist and operate effectively and well – to hear and do justice to the parties who make their way to them, and of procedures to vindicate the dignity of those who appear before them.

And yet, this acknowledgment of the fundamental significance of an effective state legal system (where it exists) must remain consistent with two other truisms that I would stress: first, a crucial part of the social importance of state legal institutions stretches well beyond what it does to any specific litigants in legal proceedings; second, that significance can only be assessed in the light of other sources of social influence than the law itself. These may support, refract, re-channel, transform or totally block that influence.

Legislation, of course, is always directed outwards,[48] but court proceedings too have fundamentally important effects that radiate well beyond their direct participants. For apart from citizens' (generally rare) direct invocations of official channels, there is the extent to which they are able and willing to use and to rely upon legal resources as cues, standards, models, authorisations, immunities, what the socio-legal literature identifies as 'bargaining chips', 'regulatory endowments', in relations with each other and with the state. In this respect, as Galanter has emphasised, courts act less as magnets than beacons. If they were to be judged simply by the numbers of social disputes they suck in for official treatment, they might well be accounted failures everywhere, given the very small proportion of disputes that reach them. Rather, apart from and at the same time in the very process of dealing with those disputes, they send signals about law, rights, costs, delays, advantages, disadvantages, aggravation, anguish and other possibilities, into the community. This is what gives meaning to 'bargaining in the shadow of the law.'

It matters to at least two constituencies (apart from those – lawyers – who make their living from them) how legal institutions settle disputes. The smaller and frequently atypical constituency is the litigants themselves, whose days in court are nevertheless often of extremely highly charged significance to them and therefore significant in themselves, and who also are part of the second, much larger, constituency affected by law: all those who, often subconsciously, act and react, in their relations with other citizens and with the state itself, on the basis of their interpretations of signals that emanate from those institutions, or their attitudes towards those signals and to their sources.

However, even when official signals are bright and visible, they do not necessarily signal or beckon engagement of the sort the signallers intend. Not everything depends on the message or the messenger. And here we have come full circle: once we get to message sending, everything said earlier about fields, orderings, and legislation applies equally to messages

[48] Though not always to citizens, and increasingly to administrative agencies. This, as Edward Rubin argues brilliantly, much complicates the Fullerian and similar understandings of the rule of law. See Rubin, 'Law and Legislation in the Administrative State' (1989) 89 *Columbia Law Review*, 369–426.

that emanate from courts. The officials' job is over when the messages are sent; the interpreters', evaders', ignorers', has just begun. And there are many other messages, from many other sources, that fill the airwaves. People listen to different ones, in different ways, and don't listen to some because they listen to others. And there are plenty of others, for all the reasons Moore has explained.

Overarching all the official activity, then, is the fact that official agencies are only some of the reglementary sources in play in *any* society, whether religiously or ethnically plural or not. Who can know *in general*, when, where and how, one centre should be picked as the key from all this mix?

None of this is to say that state law is unimportant. Nor that we should simply upend legal centralism and put some vaguely characterised, bulbous and undifferentiated 'society' in its place. In modern circumstances, and virtually the whole of the developed and undeveloped world is affected by those circumstances, the state is a potentially crucial institutional factor in the fate of the whole of society, and its laws are often crucially important. But how important, and even if important, in what ways acts of state work out in the world, are questions whose answers are necessarily and heavily dependent on the plural and complex social, economic and political contexts in which they occur and into which they intervene.

Again, these are general truths, and so those interested in the rule of law need to come to terms with them. Where state law fits, and what it does, in relation to them depends on how effective it is in affecting chains of social causation, many links of which precede it, outlast it, and at any particular moment are more powerful than it is. How all this is likely to pan out will differ from place to place and time to time. It cannot be decided a priori, but only by social investigation and theorisation. Jurisprudes attracted to the rule of law have not, however, been prominent in either. That has never appeared, however, to lessen their confidence in linking attributes of 'law' with the achievement they called the rule of law.

13.4 Social Powers and the Rule of Law

Where does all this take us in relation to the rule of law? Briefly: beyond state law. The state-law-centredness of conventional discussions of the rule of law stems from at least one, and often both, of two assumptions. The first is that the arbitrary power of *governments*, or state agencies more generally, are the proper subjects, the primary targets, of the rule of law. The second is that fundamental to tempering arbitrary power is the character and effectiveness of state laws and legal arrangements.

Many who make the second assumption imagine it is a corollary of the first: because states are the prime sources of arbitrary power, moulding their legal implements and vehicles in non-arbitrary shapes is the best way in which to temper their power. However, that is not necessarily so. State power might be the most dangerous animal on the planet, but state laws might not be the best way to cope with it. A free press or active civil society might be more significant. Conversely, one might concede that there can be non-state sources of arbitrary threat, but still believe state laws are the best ways to cope with them. Or one can countenance that there are other ways, and what works depends.

However, if any of what I have been arguing is the case, or even part of the case, that is, if the arbitrary exercise of power is a foe worth fighting, social causality is so multifactorial and complex, and all societies are full of plural sources of normativity, some implications follow for anyone interested in the ideal of the rule of law. These implications would follow, moreover, whether or not you agree with my specification of the point of the rule of law, just so long as you think it makes sense to begin by thinking about what that point is, and exploring its social implications, rather than by assuming you know them without looking. I will, however, use my specification of the value of the rule of law to make the argument. Changing that value would not change the direction of that argument.

The general implication is that the *ideal* of the rule of law should be understood as extending – both as target and as weapon – not merely to official laws and other acts of state but to *exercises of substantial power* writ large, whether that be by the state or other actors. Recall, by contrast, Raz's claim that the rule of law is 'a purely negative value ... merely designed to minimize the harms to freedom and dignity which the law might cause'. This is false. The rule of law is not simply an attempt to minimise the harms done by *law*. It is about harms done by *arbitrary power*. Unless it affects the ways power is exercised, whether within or outwith law, and within or outwith the state, I see little reason to be interested in it. Even if we restrict ourselves to states, there are many ways they can do harm without law; shooting is just one, fining, harassing, and so on, the list is not hard to extend. Extra-legal exercise of state power can be a terrible thing. If states are constrained by the rule of law, even on Raz's version, there have been two accomplishments not one: their power has been constrained to operate within law, *and* this law has the characteristics Raz stipulates. Raz ignores the first, key, step: limiting the range of power-wielding options available to the state. And though non-state actors do not typically produce law, they can exert power, and preventing that from being arbitrary is a significant and positive achievement.

But tempering power, not the formal character of laws, is the achievement to be sought. Even if we have laws of particular kinds, why should anyone care about the prospectivity or publicity of laws, say, if no one who throws their weight around is listening or needs to? Or if those who listen are not those with power? Wild power is a terrible thing, whether that is despotic power or anarchic, or many points in between. Arbitrary power is liable to be wild, but even when not it is odious enough. And the road from arbitrary to wild is an unhappy place to travel. Arbitrary is bad, and more is worse. As Montesquieu taught, the *moderation* of power (not just law) is a great achievement. Societies that value the rule of law seek ways to tame and moderate its exercise, among them – though their contribution is an empirical question with varying answers – legal ways.

So, if arbitrariness in the exercise of significant power is a threat to be combated, governmental power should not be the only target, in many circumstances not even the primary target. Sources of arbitrariness and of power are many in many societies. There are numerous societies in which arbitrariness flows as much or more from extra-state exercises of power, sometimes aided by suborned official agencies, sometimes opposed to them. To the extent that non-state organisations, or all sorts of inhabitants of semi-autonomous fields, are in a position to exercise significant power in ways that offend the values of the rule of law, they diminish its sway, whatever the state of official legal rules or institutions. Once, but far from always in human history, one might have been confident that states were uniquely more powerful than all other forces, and that is why they were rightly the centre of attention for anyone concerned with the values of the rule of law. But it is an empirical and variable matter whether threats to those values are going to come from the state or somewhere else or both. And today things are more complicated, even in nation-states. If non-state power is arbitrarily exercised by oligarchs, Mafiosi, warlords, tribal elders, Al Qaeda, NGOs, business executives, currency speculators, international ratings agencies, financial institutions or indeed university administrators, it too has the potential to bring with it the vices of arbitrariness mentioned earlier. Banks can do a lot of damage too, and in recent relatively unregulated years and countries, they have. We have an interest in tempering power that has significant public consequence, whoever or whatever wields it.

This is the gist of Robin West's forceful response to Waldron's focus only on threats to the rule of law that emanate from governments:

> Law does a lot of things, but one of its core functions is to protect individuals against what would otherwise be undeterred privations against them – not by overreaching state officials, but rather by undeterred private individuals, corporations, or entities. In my view, a society that claims to regulate conduct under the ideal of the "Rule of Law" – as opposed to the rule of the stronger, or the rule of the more mendacious, or the rule of the more richly endowed, or the rule of the more vindictive, or the more manipulative, or the more fraudulent, or the more violent and so forth – should, seemingly, require that law do as much. Rule of Law scholarship, then, one would think, should reflect these ideals.[49]

West's point is true of every society, including my own (and yours) where the state is relatively effective. All the more so of many conflictual, post-conflict, transitional and failed states, where the miseries from which the rule of law would be a deliverance are closer to those imagined by Hobbes than to those understood by Locke.

Conversely, taking the value of the rule of law seriously requires recognition that many of its most significant potential sources of support are likely to be found, indeed will need to be found, in institutions, practices and traditions in the wider society, not merely in or even near the obvious institutional centres of official law. So, the salience of features of legal institutions, formal and procedural characteristics or whatever, nominated to constitute the rule of law and recommended to countries in need of it, depends on how successfully they can support the attainment of this value. That has to be the test.

To the extent they can temper power, they are properly called upon to support the rule of law – at least in *that* society. To the extent that they cannot, however – and this extent will vary between societies, times and circumstances – it is not at all clear why we fix on them so, still less try to extend them to places where they might merely have parodic roles. The challenge for anyone seeking the rule of law anywhere is not primarily to emulate or parody practices that might have worked somewhere, but to find ways of reducing the possibility of arbitrary exercise of power, whatever that takes, what-or-whoever has it, wherever one happens to be.

If barriers to arbitrary power might come from non-state sources as well, in other words, there is no reason a priori to limit one's attention

[49] Robin West, 'The Limits of Process', in James Fleming (ed.), *Getting to the Rule of Law* (New York: New York University Press, 2011), pp. 32–51 at p. 47.

either to state power or to state-based laws as constraints on arbitrariness of the exercise of such power. To the extent that extra-state institutions, practices and so on, contribute to diminishing the opportunities for arbitrary exercise of power, they serve the *ideal* of the rule of law, perhaps more than can the law itself.

State law should be viewed, then, not as the always-necessary centre-piece of power-tempering craftsmanship to which other measures are inferior or supplementary addenda, but as one implement among several, in some respects and particular circumstances of potentially distinctive importance, but dependent for its success on many other things, and often arguably not more important for the achievement of its own goal than they. That, again, does not make state law unimportant, but it might enable us to see its importance in perspective and as variable with time and circumstance. The state/non-state designation cannot be the pivot for people who value the rule of law, because the state is not the only power-wielding institution with significant public consequence, either as source of threat or of promise.

To say that the rule of law is strongly or weakly in evidence is to appraise a social *state of affairs*, with complex, multi-layered elements of various provenances, rather than simply to characterise any particular set of legal institutions. You have it insofar as, to the extent that, power is routinely exercised in ways consistent with the ideal, and certain other ways of exercising power – capriciously, willfully, arbitrarily, wildly, say – are rare. Because many of the major threats to the ideal of the rule of law come from outside the state, and many means of achieving that ideal are also to be found in the wider society, the rule of law must be sought there too.

13.5 Conclusion: Time to Try a 'Social Science That Does Not Quite Yet Exist'[50]

In much of what has gone before, I have contrasted jurisprudential blind spots with socio-legal insights. But that is because I was trying to signal to jurisprudes the importance of sociological issues they seem to me to neglect, not because I think sociology has all the answers. Indeed in relation to the rule of law it has few answers. The sociology of the rule of law is not a well-populated field. Almost fifty years ago, Philip Selznick

[50] Karol Edward Soltan, 'Selznick and Civics', in Robert A. Kagan, Martin Krygier, and Kenneth Winston (eds.), *Legality and Community. On the Intellectual Legacy of Philip Selznick* (Maryland: Rowman and Littlefield, 2002), pp. 357–72 at p. 357.

argued that, given its centrality among legal values, the rule of law 'must be a chief preoccupation of legal sociology',[51] and he pointed to a good deal of research that spoke to that theme. Though they might have spoken *to* it, however, in the sense of bearing on it, most sociologists did not speak *of* the rule of law or analyze it particularly closely.[52] The rule of law is not a mainstream sociological concern.

In recent years, some social scientists, particularly economists and political scientists, have become interested in what they understand as the rule of law. However, they rarely engage with philosophical issues of either a conceptual or normative sort. Their conceptual investigations typically have to do with identification of things to measure, rather than niceties of meaning, and their normative concerns are strictly utilitarian. They are generally uneasy with values, perhaps because it remains largely true, as Selznick long ago lamented, that '[t]o put it bluntly, our keenest minds in the social sciences didn't know what to do with an ideal except handle it gingerly and view it with alarm.'[53]

Moreover, the conceptual space within which social scientists who do discuss the rule of law situate it is not far from those I have already discussed. As Hadfield and Weingast put it, in a survey of this sort of work, 'Despite its centrality to many literatures, the concept of the rule of law is woefully undertheorized. ... Indeed, the great majority of academic and policy work takes the concept for granted, generally equating it with the institutions and practices in those (relatively few) parts of the world where the rule of law has been largely achieved.'[54]

If there were ever a subject that could benefit from interdisciplinary connection between jurisprudence and social studies, however, it is the

[51] Phillip Selznick, 'The Sociology of Law', in *The International Encyclopedia of the Social Sciences*, volume 9 (New York: Macmillan, 1968), pp. 50–59 at p. 52.

[52] Although Selznick certainly did. See my *Philip Selznick: Ideals in the World* (Stanford: Stanford University Press, 2012), ch. 6–9. And for some others see Franz L. Neumann, *The Rule of Law* (Leamington Spa, UK: Berg, 1986); and other works from associates of the Frankfurt School, particularly Otto Kirchheimer. See also Vilhelm Aubert, *In Search of Law* (Totowa, NJ: Barnes & Noble, 1984).

[53] 'The Dialectic of Fact and Value: Foundations of a Humanist Social Science', unpublished Bernard Moses Lecture, University of California, Berkeley, 1973, on file with me. And see the exchange: Marc Hertogh, 'A Sociology of the Rule of Law: Why, What, Where? And Who Cares?' (2013) *34 Recht der Werkelijkheid: Tijdschrift voor de sociaalwetenschappelijke bestudering van het rech*, 42–46 and Martin Krygier, 'Still a Rule of Law Guy' (2013) 34 *Recht der Werkelijkheid*, 42–55.

[54] Gillian K. Hadfield and Barry Weingast, 'Microfoundations of the Rule of Law' at p. 22.

rule of law.[55] This might begin with a normative range of questions, among them: what are the reasons for which people have 'clamoured' and we might still clamour for the rule of law? Are they good reasons? This would involve examining existing answers, perhaps revision of them, perhaps devising of new ones. If persuaded that the reasons justify the quest, one might *then* seek to think about how this clamour might be satisfied.

It would then need to be asked where the dangers to whatever values were settled on were likely to come from, where effective responses might be found, and what those might be. Because many of the key dangers are likely to be socially generated, many of the major goods that flow from tempering arbitrary power (or whatever other value is chosen) will be delivered in the wider society, and many of the major sources of defence against arbitrariness need to be found there too, the normative quest would lead us to make observations and theorisations about things other than law. And, yes, because law is *in* society, to understand how it does what it does, and why it doesn't always do what we might like it to do, among other things effectively temper the exercise of power, we need to understand the workings of law in society and of society in law. Therefore, accounts of the rule of law, billions of dollars spent on rule of law promotion, anatomical dissection of the 'essential elements' of the rule of law, which focus their energies almost exclusively on central, state, legal institutions are misconceived.

These are exceedingly complicated matters, where lawyers', or anyone's, intuitions are unlikely to be helpful. Therefore, we would necessarily be led beyond intuitions, however intelligent, to facts about the social world, and in particular about causality in that world. We would have to consider, and maybe even do some empirical research and social theory, asking how those values have been secured – where and if they have – how they might be where not, and how much of what we have discovered to work somewhere is likely to work elsewhere. There is, or that is an implication of this argument, no single all-encompassing recipe to be found, and it is a waste of time to look for one. But there might be fruitful possibilities, law is likely often to be among them, and intelligent, self-consciously modest, extrapolations from one place to another might be available.

[55] I expand on the argument of the next three paragraphs, and the theme of this section, in 'The Rule of Law: Pasts, Presents, and Two Possible Futures', pp. 222–23.

I know of only one author, Philip Selznick, who seeks to make any such systematic connections between jurisprudence, social science and the rule of law in a deep way. The ambition imbued half a long life of thought, and found its clearest expression in two books, *Law and Society in Transition. Toward Responsive Law*,[56] and *Law, Society and Industrial Justice*.[57]

Law and Society in Transition was very short, but it did many things, was remarkably rich and had deceptively large ambitions, among them 'to recast jurisprudential issues in a social-science perspective'.[58] What does that involve? Above all, grasping the significance of *variation*, and, associated with that in classical pragmatist fashion, variation in *contexts*. That is what he thought social science was distinctively good at. Philosophical accounts of the concept of law, by contrast, tend not to do this. Staples of legal philosophy are built around universal answers to single questions: What *is* law? What *is* the relationship between law and morality, between law and coercion, law and politics, law and reason? What is the rule of law? (and so on). Typically such questions are posed as though a single universal answer is appropriate to each of them: for John Austin, law is the command of a sovereign, for H. L. A. Hart it is a system of two types of rules. For natural lawyers there is a necessary connection between law and morals, for legal positivists, not.

Selznick, by contrast, believes it is a characteristic and fundamental sociological insight that law and the relationships between it and other phenomena, like all social phenomena, vary in characteristics, form, presence and salience. Moreover, these variations are often not merely random or contingent but systematic and susceptible of explanation. Thus one turns to 'a social science strategy [which] can more readily and explicitly recognize the plurality of legal experience'.[59] Which I believe is where we came in.

That is a useful general agenda for the social science that doesn't (yet) exist, but of more concrete relevance to our subject is *Law, Society and Industrial Justice*, published nine years earlier. This book doesn't do all I ask, as its primary focus is on one social sphere – industrial relations – and one country – the United States. But in many ways the venture is exemplary.

[56] Philippe Nonet and Philip Selznick, *Law and Society in Transition. Toward Responsive Law* (New Jersey, Transaction Publishers, 2001 (first published 1978)).

[57] Phillip Selznick, *Law, Society, and Industrial Justice* (New Jersey: Transaction Press, 1969).

[58] Selznick, *Law and Society in Transition*, p. 3.

[59] Ibid., p. 18.

Selznick starts with the rule of law, noting that it 'refers to aspirations that distinguish a developed legal order from a system of subjection to naked power'.[60] Taking those aspirations seriously must involve 'the refinement of basic principles, their application in depth, and their extension to new social settings'.[61] This in turn requires a perspective that 'helps to bridge the gap between a normative theory of law, which centers on latent values, and the more stringent perspective of sociological realism.'[62]

Selznick recognises that there are many, particularly corporate and organisational sources of power in modern societies (his particular subject, and more particularly still the United States) that rival in their social significance the powers of government, and that have led to new reorientations of old concerns:

> In recent years we have seen a transition from preoccupation with freedom *of* association to a concern for freedom *in* associations. This renewed awareness stems from a realization that the private organization can be more oppressive than the state. The loss of a job, or the right to pursue a profession, or the opportunity to continue one's education, may be far more hurtful than a term in jail. When these deprivations are inflicted arbitrarily and there is no recourse, a gap in the legal order exists. We become more sensitive to that gap when the decisions are made by organizations that seem large, powerful, and impersonal, and by men who have the look of an officialdom.[63]

But preaching is never enough. Receptiveness to institutional prescription, in the domains we are trying to affect, cannot be assumed, and without such receptiveness little effective can be done: 'We cannot argue from an abstract ideal to an institutional prescription. The whole point is that the conditions for governance must be found in the life of the institution itself. On that basis, the law of governance may be invoked. Without that basis the law is irrelevant, its application self-defeating.'[64] This is no counsel for despair but a prompt to look for 'incipient', 'inchoate', 'emerging' forces, complaints, demands, social and ideological shifts, that could generate, or support generation of, a 'receptive institutional setting' that might support, and be supported by, sensitive invocation and institutionalisation of the values of the rule of law, and might ultimately allow its advance, even in contexts quite far from where it was originally conceived. The aim is 'the institutional embodiment of

[60] Selznick, *Law, Society, and Industrial Justice*, p. 11. [61] Ibid., p. 28. [62] Ibid., p. 32.
[63] Ibid., p. 38. [64] Ibid., p. 273.

values', not an easy task, not possible to do everywhere in the same way, but not impossible either.

The book involves, from start to finish, a rich interweaving of philosophical reflection, sociological insight and evidence, legal knowledge and institutional assessment. This is not just a matter of taste but of conviction, general as to the nature of social science,[65] and particular in relation to the rule of law:

> To extend the rule of law is to build it firmly into the life of society, to make the master ideal of legality a true governor of official conduct. If this is to come about, political and legal theory must lend a hand. It can do so by fashioning concepts and doctrines to bridge the gap between the new social realities and the received legal tradition.[66]

Though not without limitations and a highly specific social and geographical focus, *Law, Society and Industrial Justice* is a remarkable pioneering work. If the rule of law is to be 'buil[t] firmly into the life of society', it will need to extend far beyond official conduct, and it might take a lot beside law for that to happen. Though his is scarcely the last word on the subject, explorations of Selznick's kind help us think about what that might involve. It is not clear that conventional jurisprudential accounts of the rule of law, and the programs for rule of law implementation that ride alongside them, do so. On the argument of this chapter, it is in particular unclear how seriously they can be taken while they fail to address the pluralist settings that so crucially affect the characteristic achievements they set for law, and the characteristic values they anticipate from those achievements.

[65] See Phillip Selznick, *A Humanist Science* (Stanford: Stanford University Press, 2008).
[66] Selznick, *Law, Society and Industrial Justice*, p. 35.

14

The Promises and Pursuits of Pluralist Jurisprudence

NICOLE ROUGHAN AND ANDREW HALPIN

14.1 Preliminary Expectations

The expectations we entertained for a pluralist jurisprudence in Chapter 1 were threefold: to be given an explanation of the relationship between pluralist jurisprudence and its monist predecessor; to be provided with clarification of the precise role of pluralism within a pluralist jurisprudence; and, to be offered understanding of the part played by normative or aspirational agendas within a pluralist jurisprudence. We are now in a position to reconsider these expectations, having benefited from the detailed acquaintance with Chapters 2–13.

An obvious point to make is that the different authors do not each meet all of these expectations in their contributions, nor engage with them in quite the same way. To take the relationship between pluralist jurisprudence and monist jurisprudence first, some authors show little interest in examining this relationship. There are those who take the state of legal pluralism to be a self-evident fact and their interest lies in exploring that condition, at the most noticing in passing that a monist perspective on law is no longer adequate (Del Mar, Mac Amhlaigh, Taekema, von Daniels, Walker, Davies and Anker). Others specifically address the inadequacies of certain approaches to monist jurisprudence within a pluralist setting. Both Cotterrell and Krygier remark on the inadequacies of analytical or philosophical approaches, on the one hand, and social-science or sociological approaches on the other hand, within monist jurisprudence, and encourage a fusion between these often opposed intellectual preferences in order to deal effectively with the challenges of a legal plurality. By contrast, Sciaraffa employs the pluralist setting to re-run a contest between positivist and non-positivist approaches from monist jurisprudence, using that setting to at least enhance the credentials of a non-positivist approach. Michaels suggests the need for a particular addition to the standard (Hartian) monist jurisprudence in order to cope with pluralist law. More radically, Taekema uses pluralist phenomena to encourage embracing an interactionist understanding of law across any monist-pluralist divide. Raz, while acknowledging the need for some revision to take account of pluralist legal phenomena, nevertheless, maintains the conventional framework of monist jurisprudence in considering the credentials of global law.

As for the precise role of pluralism and the degree of accommodation of diversity associated with it, we can again detect quite different approaches. For some authors, pluralism is not given a precise role within a fully theorised jurisprudence but is accorded recognition for its direct involvement with the accommodation of diversity. Davies and Del Mar are found expressing this viewpoint. Other authors are motivated to examine how an endorsement of pluralism can be theoretically linked to the interaction between the members of a recognised plurality, dealing with the abstract accommodation of different normative orders (notably, Michaels and Sciaraffa) or the practical accommodation at the point of the legal disposition of concrete cases. Cotterrell, Taekema and Anker engage with this concern. Mac Amhlaigh and von Daniels redirect pluralism away from the simple recognition of a plurality of normative orders, to envisage a theoretical pluralism.

Finally, on normative or aspirational agendas for pluralist jurisprudence, some authors directly address a clear normative agenda. Walker's concern with global justice, or Krygier's commitment to advancing a definite understanding of the rule of law, both display such an approach. For other authors, a normative agenda fits into other theoretical concerns regarding the outworking of a legal plurality. The invocation of legal values by both Cotterrell and Taekema falls under this description. Yet another approach can be discerned where a normative or aspirational agenda is linked to the promotion of pluralism, such as found in the contributions of Davies, Del Mar and Anker – as well as von Daniels, if we include a notion of theoretical pluralism. More obliquely, it would also be possible to trace the active part played by social values in theoretical understandings of legality that employ some form of social commitment to broach the challenge of pluralism, as seen in different ways within the contributions of Raz, Sciaraffa, Anker and Cotterrell.

One way of responding to the quite different engagements that we have observed with our preliminary expectations is to question their value as possible ways into a pluralist jurisprudence; even to abandon them and seek an alternative route. However, the above observations do disclose some meaningful engagements from our contributors with what were taken to be core concerns for a pluralist jurisprudence. The varied and piecemeal connections to these concerns within the different chapters of this book suggest two things. First, we should acknowledge that the issues underlying our expectations do not readily lead to a uniform template for a pluralist jurisprudence. That is not to say that our preliminary expectations are unimportant, but rather to treat them as possibly incidental to a wider variety of theoretical concerns that can be pursued within pluralist jurisprudence. Secondly, it follows that the greater diversity found within contributions to pluralist jurisprudence can be better approached by a more refined understanding of the variety of theoretical pursuits it provokes, springing from quite distinct motivations.

We shall undertake a more refined profiling of the pursuits of pluralist jurisprudence in Section 14.2.1, again drawing on the rich illustrative material found in Chapters 2–13. Prior to that, we shall explore more fully each of the preliminary expectations in the present section, in order to draw out any lessons that might provide for a fuller portrayal of pluralist jurisprudence.

It is important to note a broader consequence of this strategic development in our approach to pluralist jurisprudence. Recognising that the field of pluralist jurisprudence is open to a disparate variety of pursuits raises a basic question about the standing of pluralist jurisprudence. Can we treat it as a distinctive intellectual discipline, or should we rather concede that there is not an intellectual coherence to be found in addressing a set of disorganised and unrelated phenomena, capable of lending themselves in support of any theoretical speculation that takes the theorist's fancy? If that is the sole direction of travel between the raw data and the theory, then we may reasonably doubt the credentials of a pluralist jurisprudence. Our own position, however, is that, given the messiness of the pluralist reality, it is even more important for legal theorists (whether philosophers, sociologists, historians, or indeed jurists) to contribute in some way to understanding the phenomena, however disparate or disorganised they may appear. And if we take seriously the suggestions made by a number of our authors (notably Anker, Cotterrell, Davies, Del Mar, Krygier and Michaels) over the importance of pluralist jurisprudence for the challenges posed by legal practice, we should expect that theoretical illumination to shed light on the practical legal character of these phenomena.

There is, accordingly, a secondary refinement required, if we are to achieve a credible pluralist jurisprudence. Having moved from theoretical engagement with pluralist phenomena to the opportunity for multiple theoretical pursuits, we then need to consider what demands to make of these pursuits in order to secure effective illumination of the subject matter within a coherent pluralist jurisprudence. Clarifying these demands is the critical moment in ensuring that a pluralist jurisprudence has the promise to deliver a specific understanding of plurality and pluralism in the practice of law. The magnitude of this task lies not simply in portraying a pluralist environment in which law can be seen to be operating, but also in identifying what it is that provides a distinctively pluralist character to those legal operations. We commence this task in Section 14.2.2 by placing the types of pursuits within a coordinated framework and showing the sort of way they need to be combined so as to deliver a pluralist jurisprudence.

In Section 14.3, we propose our own candidate pluralist theory of law. This amounts to a tentative filling out of the framework identified in Section 14.2.2, to demonstrate how it can generate a theory that can be characterised as both legal and distinctively pluralist. The crucial attribute we need to claim for our candidate theory is that it is capable of revealing the conditions under which the potential of pluralist law can be realised, in ways that are not discernible from a conventional monist jurisprudence. Capturing this potential within a pluralist jurisprudence delivers on a technical promise, in providing a coherent disciplinary account of pluralist jurisprudence. Beyond that technical achievement of delivering an understanding of plurality and pluralism in the practice of law, the fuller promise of a pluralist jurisprudence extends to an appreciation of the wider social significance of plurality and pluralism in the practice of law, or, the idealist promise of legal pluralism itself.

With some brief concluding remarks in Section 14.3.6, we subject our candidate theory to further scrutiny and reflect more widely on the promises of a pluralist jurisprudence. Alongside the technical and idealist promises just mentioned, which relate to an appreciation of the internal character of legal pluralism, we point to an instrumental promise that can be associated with pluralist jurisprudence: showing how the greater resources it reveals for legal pluralism can be harnessed to an external normative or aspirational objective.

14.1.1 The Disciplinary Challenge: Pluralist Jurisprudence and Monist Jurisprudence

One advance represented by the preceding chapters, in combination and in conversation with one another, is a de-escalation of an old contest for the territory of jurisprudence as a discipline. There are few remnants of the view of jurisprudence in which 'sociological' questions about law were sharply distinguished (and disconnected) from 'philosophical' ones. For instance, even within Raz's monist-derived and referential framework for considering global law, there is an ultimately sociological grounding of the quality and character of pluralism (on which more to follow in Section 14.2.1).[1] Formerly deep rifts between self-proclaimed philosophical approaches to jurisprudence, and the work of theorists of legal pluralism who identified more strongly with social-scientific approaches, appear to have narrowed.[2] This in turn suggests a more interesting space for confronting ideas that are central to understanding law and laws – however one may then design or delimit a theory so as to emphasise its pluralist or monist qualities.

While former turf wars may have diminished, theoretical differences still leave open a range of options for the relationship between monist and pluralist jurisprudence. One option is for theories to attempt an integration of pluralist and monist concerns via the confrontation of substantive questions in jurisprudence (about institutions, systems, authority, normativity, legal reasoning, legitimacy, and values), with an eye on the interaction of both pluralist-conceived and monist-conceived phenomena, rather than being stymied by debates over their respective demarcation as state-legal or pluralist objects. Another option is to assimilate theories of monist jurisprudence into theories of pluralist jurisprudence, or vice versa, creating a single dominant perspective which overcomes any troublesome distinctions. A third option chooses to concentrate on what is perceived to be important about either monist or pluralist objects in jurisprudence, notwithstanding the presence of the other.

With no way to adjudicate between these different ways of relating monist and pluralist jurisprudence, the narrowing of the gap between those interested in pluralism and those favouring a monist standpoint seems to reveal and perhaps reignite an important tension over the

[1] Commented upon in the contributions from Cotterrell and von Daniels.

[2] Compare this to the earlier work of some of our contributors, who sought to expressly challenge the divide. Margaret Davies, 'Pluralism and Legal Philosophy' (2006) *Northern Ireland Legal Quarterly* 577; and Roger Cotterrell, 'Why Jurisprudence is not Legal Philosophy' 5 *Jurisprudence* (2014) 1;. Also see the integrative work offered in Brian Z. Tamanha, *A General Jurisprudence of Law and Society* (Oxford University Press, 2001); W. L. Twining, *General Jurisprudence* (Cambridge University Press, 2009). To the extent that pluralist disciplinary developments have been driven by taking those challenges seriously, they represent a major (and perhaps rare) jurisprudential success.

standards for what counts as a successful theory. That tension is made all the more complicated by the elusive character of the pluralist subject matter, which causes us to worry that, not knowing exactly what we are pursuing, we cannot know whether a theory counts as a successful pursuit. While there is some reason to be hopeful that the work offered here and elsewhere may enrich understandings of pluralist phenomena such as customary law, indigenous law, transnational and international law, the contributions here also reveal, and in some cases perpetuate or even embrace, a particular kind of vagueness that may yet push apart pluralist and monist positions in jurisprudence.

The worry is that pluralist jurisprudence can seem unpromisingly vague, and perhaps antithetical to the manner in which monist jurisprudence has typically been conducted. Monist jurisprudence is avowedly fond of conceptual clarity, finely articulated distinctions, classifications, justifications and conclusions that proceed with the armour of logic and/or the authority of work that has gone before. It is not only that monist jurisprudence embraces theoretical values of cogency, precision, simplicity and logic, but something about law itself is often thought to invite a certain degree of clarity. After all, monist/state law as it is practiced deals in (and values) classifications, dividing lines in the application of rules and concepts, finality and hierarchy of decisions, and clarity of arguments. The monistic jurisprudent, as philosopher of law at least, has been primed to marry both philosophical and distinctively legal technical expertise, argumentative skill, and preferred styles of scholarship, with an object of study seemingly well-suited to that approach.

To pursue pluralist jurisprudence is to take away that apparent match. The pursuit unsettles the object of study by introducing matters of degree, multiplicity and heterarchy. Everything – subject matter, methods and theories – gets pluralised. Instead of law we have laws, instead of methodology we have methodologies, and even plurality itself is observed and analyzed pluralistically, noting that plurality is not susceptible to analysis or evaluation from a single general framework, but from within multiple contingent frameworks. The fields of legal-theoretical analysis with relevant contributions are also multiplied, so that there are important contributions to pluralist jurisprudence to be found within the voluminous literature on constitutional pluralism, global law, transnational law, indigenous laws, religious laws, international law, customary law, as well as on state-centred responses to the realities of plural legal phenomena.

While there is a need for creative and sometimes novel ways to think about what happens to the central ideas of jurisprudence when confronted with such a plural reality, there are ever-present risks of giving away too much of the precision that jurisprudence itself has to offer, The basic concern, reflected, evident, and discussed in many of the chapters presented here, is that such opening up of the object of jurisprudential interest renders ideas about law – including its authority, validity, institutionalisation and justification – less sharply articulated, more contingent, and less absolute than they appear to be in monist jurisprudence. Accounts of law in this pluralised sense become rich in nuanced matters of degree, subtle non-distinctions and spectrums along which particular phenomena may be situated. For instance, instead of institutions organised into comprehensive and bordered legal systems, there are institutions of diverse forms, whose connections with each other are thought to include non-systemic, sometimes even non rule-governed interactions. In place of jurisdictional borders that match the effective boundaries of political and/or de facto sovereignty, there are norms that defy jurisdictional limits or which creep or seep into those limits. Rather than a legal system making claims to independent, supreme authority, there are plural legal systems making claims to relative authority. The very idea of law that is under the microscope of pluralist jurisprudence is, we are told, fuzzy.[3]

While this feature of fuzziness may draw some support from complex normative interactions of the sort discussed below, it remains problematic for exploring relationships between monist and pluralist jurisprudence. Are ideas and theoretical standards that have been honed and tested within monist or state-centric jurisprudence simply to be left out or left behind? And most importantly, would a mismatch in the standards for successful theories, between monist and pluralist pursuits, strengthen the adoption of one or another extreme (either the strong separation of the two, or the assimilation of one under the dominant framework of the other)? Our concern is that, if there is to be any kind of engagement in the middle, then pluralist and monist approaches need somehow to bite upon shared jurisprudential concerns in ways that force

[3] Oren Perez, 'Fuzzy Law: A Theory of Quasi-Legal Systems' 28 *Canadian Journal of Law and Jurisprudence* (2015), pp. 343–70; on the prevalence of fuzziness, also see Haris Psarras, 'Law's Authority and Overlapping Jurisdictions' in Cotterrell and Del Mar (eds.) *Transnational Authority: Theorising across Disciplines* (Edward Elgar, 2016) and Davies, in this volume.

their re-examination, either to reveal strengths and weaknesses in existing approaches or to generate new ones. Fuzziness will not generate that engagement. It is one thing to represent a reality that is indeed fuzzy, unfocused and somewhat hazy, but the theorist's role is to help find, map and follow pathways through an unclear subject matter with some form of precision. At the same time, debates over ways to sharpen the focus will have to be conducted in a way that does not commit the opposite sin of dogmatism, where the desire for rigour is used to close off any destabilising factors introduced by recognising matters of degree, contingency and contextuality. The middle road, as always, is a tricky path to find.

14.1.2 *Plurality and Pluralism: Conceptual and Practical Challenges*

The conceptual and practical challenge for pluralist jurisprudence is to explain what (if anything), pluralism amounts to, and calibrate its associated degree of accommodation of diversity among legal phenomena. In addressing this challenge, contributors to this volume reveal both explicit and underlying preferences for either openness or closure of their theoretical objects, and in particular, openness or closure around the idea or practice of law, and the status that legality confers. Within their various positions on legality, the contributors offer a range of positions on the issue of vagueness or flexibility surrounding legal categories. One path opts to temporarily accept or excuse vagueness. Raz, for instance, suggests that temporary vagueness, which avoids premature conclusions or conceptualisations about law-like systems and features, may help to re-open jurisprudential lines of inquiry that had been shut down. If we are not quite ready to say that these alternatives or additions to state law are indeed law, or are at least apt for jurisprudential attention of the sort devoted to state law, then we are also not ready to say that they are not. Such an approach treats vagueness as a useful interim measure, but it is also suggestive of a substantive opening in a former fortress of canonical monist jurisprudence.

An alternative path embraces vagueness about legality for different reasons – offering it as a weapon against monistic jurisprudence itself, a potential kryptonite reinforced by the broader insights of critical theory. In Davies's chapter generally, and in Del Mar's extended discussion of Glenn, pluralist jurisprudence embraces the power of loosened categories and non-binary approaches to thinking about and doing law. Yet other contributions would suggest that the time for vagueness is past, and that vagueness, far from being a weapon, may end up being a driver for exclusion rather than inclusion, despite the best intentions of its handlers. The chapter from Anker, for instance, as well as a body of work from Cotterrell, suggests that vagueness may be partly to blame for allowing a bifurcation between 'state-legal' and 'other-legal' (or 'law-like') to be theorised and practiced as a distinction between 'state-legal' and 'non-legal'. Instead, vagueness should be met head-on with one or more direct strategies.

One such strategy, expressly offered by Cotterrell, notes the messiness and fragmentation of normative realities, and indeed the presence of vagueness, but confronts them not in the abstract, but from the particular perspective of the jurist. That standpoint then gives a reason to prefer a set of normative arguments that are appropriate for the legal purpose, and a long way from embracing vagueness. Yet if this is to offer either a conceptual or practical account of plurality and pluralism, a juristic perspective on pluralist jurisprudence then needs tools for the task it sets itself. The tools offered by Michaels' external recognition rule, Del Mar's legal imagination processes, Mac Amhlaigh's roles of legal officials, Taekema's interactional law, or Sciaraffa's approach to customary law, begin from familiar technical foundations then work through vagueness by tweaking the uses we can make of old tools in legal theory. Alternatively, a juristic approach may reject orthodox legal analyses and conventional jurisdictional spaces in favour of a juristic perspective that reimagines pluralist space without a frame in which a dominant legal enterprise is the starting point from which to theorise, as Anker suggests. In all these approaches, the emphasis on a juristic, practiced, and concrete focal point, from which to theorise pluralism. may invite major contests over whether the particular perspective chosen is plausible or defensible, but they attempt degrees of precision in dealing with the challenges of plurality and ways in which theorists and jurists might respond to them.

Aside from the adoption of a particular perspective (such as that of the jurist), a second type of approach locates particular histories and traditions of thinking about legal pluralism in order to identify the objectives that any further engagement with normative plurality must keep in sight. The weight of these traditions, and the authority of their proponents, give any residual vagueness and flexibility of legal categories their own kind of pedigree. From MacCormick's heuristic pluralism, Glenn's cosmopolitanism, or Cover's inter-subjective normativities; to the greats of philosophy of international law and the precise contributions of empirical analysts of particular pluralist phenomena; these approaches suggest that even if normative plurality throws up imprecisions that may be hard to work with, they have in fact been worked with to produce insights which reveal that vagueness itself cannot be used as an excuse for lack of progress.

Such traditions and their insights can also be used in an evaluative way to deal with the challenges of a pluralist legality. Krygier's extension of a rule of law tradition to the valuation of pluralist legality, for instance, would confront vagueness with the value of the rule of law, with the aim of being clear about what is at risk, and what is lost, when pluralist power is not 'tempered' by the rule of law. Just as vagueness might be offered as a weapon against dogmatic exclusionary legality, it may also be embraced by a power-holder in order to avoid triggering the demands of legality itself. Krygier's work here reveals that alongside the concerns over legality, there must be attention not only to categories of legality and non-legality, but also to the values that each can carry.

Finally, it is important to reflect upon the extent to which attempts to propose a theoretical solution to vagueness using conceptual organisation and analytical categorisations might either stick to the usual business of jurisprudence, or attempt a distinct offering in a pluralist setting. Walker's work on Global Law is exemplary of a strategy which acknowledges that the sheer diversity of legal phenomena, and the range of commitments to diversity embodied in different articulations of pluralism, present too great a challenge to a single precise concept of law. Yet rather than water down or avoid such conceptual working out of legality, Walker multiplies the concepts, multiplies the options for thinking about kinds of legal phenomena and the relations between them, and multiples the available abstractions to be drawn in order to avoid giving up on the task of making sense of them all.

In all of these theoretical approaches, both the characterisations of legality, and the range of strategies for addressing vagueness about whether or where there are demarcations of legality, might seem like a purely conceptual exercise. Viewing this challenge of pluralist jurisprudence in this way has the effect of rekindling attention to the old jurisprudential question, 'What is law?', and the associated debate over law's inclusivity or exclusivity vis-à-vis morality. Yet whatever else it entails, the debate over the reach of legality across a normative plurality offers precisely the point of practical bite that engages pluralist and monist theories, as well as rendering them juristically and not simply academically important. The challenge here is a shared conceptual and practical challenge, not a matter for either alone.

For jurists and legal officials, the facts of plurality require a normative response that relies more or less explicitly upon either the attribution or denial of legality. In both political and legal institutions, conflicts between pluralist phenomena and monist state law generate moments of decision where plurality is either validated or ruled out. While some have argued that, by conceptual necessity or by definition, judges and other officials can only recognise the supremacy and exclusivity of their own system, the actual practice of judges and other officials reveals instances in which inclusive toleration, accommodation or promotion of other legal statuses has been preferred. The potential reimagining of both legal reasoning and the role of jurists, in pluralist directions, squarely challenges the notion of practical and epistemic closure that monist jurisprudence had easily assumed. On the other hand, while those who operate with pluralist conceptions of law tend to make do, sometimes expertly, with nuanced distinctions, normative ambiguities, revisable or partial solutions, and indeed vagueness, they must still deal in decisions, settlements and other binary resolutions. The jurist, or other practitioner or official, cannot ultimately get away with fuzziness, and the results they produce are decidedly 'unfuzzy'.[4]

The mostly monist responses of jurists reflect that the problems inherent in the exclusive and inclusive legality debates are much more complex than agents at the coal-face of plurality may have time to resolve. Not only are the phenomena of plurality unclear and diverse, but they may present themselves unevenly or as being laden with normative contestability whose resolution requires political rather than legal or even juristic argument. While jurists (and theorists) are accustomed to using legal status to demarcate legal versus moral norms, or law versus fact, or legal versus political claims, they are less used to dealing with clashes between purported legal orders.

Aside from dividing theorists and jurists, the range of responses to plurality may also divide subjects of laws, though aside from those with the sorts of normative commitments and agendas discussed in the following subsection, these may be pragmatically delegated to the responses of jurists. This raises all sorts of empirical possibilities. If jurists and officials engage in exclusively monist legal practices, will law-subjects, as law-users, tend towards similarly exclusive views of law shaped by what

[4] For further discussion, see Andrew Halpin, 'The Applications of Bivalent Logic, and the Misapplication of Multivalent Logic to Law' in H Patrick Glenn and Lionel Smith (eds.), *Law and the New Logics* (Cambridge: Cambridge University Press, 2017).

they see of the officials' work? Subjects may never even contemplate that legality could be something other than what a state's legal officials practice it to be – so closely is law identified with its officials, and those officials with the state. Many subjects, furthermore, may never think of themselves as potential subjects of plural laws, unless of course they are the ones posing the pluralist challenge.

Alternatively, if officials embrace more inclusive pluralist practices, will these be accepted and utilised by law-subjects? In cases where an ethnic, religious, or indigenous minority has claimed a legal right on grounds other than state law, for instance, subjects are confronted with (or instigators of) a squarely pluralist challenge to an exclusively state notion of legality. Resulting debates over the actual and/or justified inclusivity or exclusivity of legality then tend to spiral outside of legal fora into public, political and social debates. Thus the range of normative responses to plurality are not simply (and indeed not primarily) the responses of theorists to theory; rather they are responses of law-users and indeed law-subjects, to facts that have ramifications beyond abstract characterisations of jurisprudence, and which are connected to ideals and agendas that, on both sides, people think are worth fighting for.

14.1.3 Normative and Aspirational Agendas

The diverse agendas found within legal pluralism present some familiar features. Among the most prominent arise in situations where more or less distinct polities assert claims to use 'their own' law (as law) in order to self-govern or govern interactively with a competitor (such as the state). This may be characterised as 'polity-driven pluralism'. Other advocates of pluralism are driven by pragmatic or technical/expertise-based arguments for the value of pluralistic 'problem-solving', favouring alternatives to state regulation of issues which individual states are not thought to be (as) good at regulating, or are unable/unwilling to regulate or govern together. Call this more pragmatic version 'problem-solving pluralism'.

None of these pluralisms support plurality for its own sake, but for what it entails (including status and symbolic value) and what it allows law-subjects or law-users to achieve. Legal pluralism is not committed to legal diversity as such, rather it advocates the ways in which a plurality of laws either solves problems that monist approaches cannot, or supports values that monist approaches would ignore or deny. In cases of polity-driven pluralism, legal status (and its application) is sought because of the instrumental and/or inherent value of that status for the community whose law is being invoked. In cases of pragmatic problem-solving pluralism, legal status (and its application) is valued for its potential to generate and/or sustain public settlements of common concerns. Pluralist jurisprudence's thematic concern for inclusive concepts and practices of legality are thus grounded upon substantive theories defending the institutionalisation of practices representing political or value pluralism; cosmopolitanism or self-determination. The normative preferences behind inclusive and exclusive responses to plurality are themselves positions in debates in political theory and moral philosophy, and not technical or analytical constructs of a more narrowly conceived jurisprudence.

Yet although the contributions in this collection are mostly sympathetic to pluralism, or at least open to its potential values, it is important that pluralism is not (and should not be) romanticised nor oversimplified. This is all fairly obvious, but it bears repeating in order to avoid missing the nuanced connections between the three topics under discussion here. Importantly, claims for pluralism do not always insist upon watertight demarcations of legality and non-legality. Pluralism's normative agendas sometimes include a critical bent which denies the very value of legal status, and/or which avoids seeking that status which, even if inclusive of a particular pluralist challenger to state law, remains exclusionary of others. The persistence of an exclusively monist model of legality in juristic theory and practice may encourage pluralist critics of exclusivity to pursue their normative agendas through more promising means (such as the rejection of analytical categories of legality in favour of social-scientific concepts of law; or the articulation/demonstration of softer or looser practices of authority, obligation, regulation and governance).[5] Thus the normative advocacy of pluralism is sometimes used to skirt or trump the question of how inclusive or tolerant legality can or should be; that question is deemed less important than the substantive agendas which pluralism is claimed to advance.

One does not have to be a critic of pluralism, however, to see that its potential should not be overstated. For every proponent of pluralist arrangements there will be opposing claims for some special value of state-centred, monist alternatives which reject plurality. The response to

[5] See, e.g., Nico Krisch, 'Authority: Solid and Liquid, in Transnational Governance' in Roger Cotterrell and Makysmilian Del Mar (eds.), *Transnational Authority: Theorising across Disciplines* (Cheltenham: Edward Elgar, 2016).

the polity-pluralists who advocate for space and recognition for that polity's law, for instance, may be grounded on majoritarian or liberal-democratic preferences. Why should a liberal democracy defer to one part of its polity, or a distinct sub-polity or overlapping polity, especially if the law being claimed is itself non-democratic or contains non-liberal values? The responses to the problem-solving pluralists, in turn, divide into scepticism about the pluralist alternatives' problem-solving capacities, or sovereigntist rejections of their procedural or substantive value. For instance, responses to those who favour transnational private or hybrid regulation may be sceptical of technical expertise, and may feature outright, even 'post-truth', denial of the expertise itself. (If there is doubt or disagreement over the right answer, then shouldn't a society take its own chances rather than follow supposed experts?) This may then be married to a more foundational defence of sovereignty that rejects the public or collective agendas of problem-solving pluralists, in favour of the supposed value of serving more local and parochial interests.

Normative and aspirational ideals or agendas, then, appear on both sides of pluralist v monist debates, as well as within different pluralist positions (as notably explored in Walker's chapter). The exploration of these ideals must therefore take care to account for nuances in the claims that are made. Pluralist and monist agendas do not consistently or neatly track claims for more inclusive or exclusive state legality, nor are they consistently defended in opposition to one another. For instance, an advocate of tolerance, inclusivity or deference towards an ethnic, religious or other minority's legal order might simultaneously wish to retain state institutions and state law for certain purposes (e.g. protection of individual rights within that order, or protection of state-secured social or political rights or statuses that benefit the group in isolation or in interaction with the wider polity). The pluralist challenge may also recognise or rely upon state institutions for the very pursuit of plurality itself. In particular, the strength of state institutions might be used to combat potential or actual popular rejection of normative plurality, as in cases of judicial or executive insistence on the place of an alternative legal system, in the face of public or even legislative opposition.

Looking beyond single polities to the international sphere reveals similarly complicated combinations of ideals and commitments. An advocate of international legal authority or global constitutionalism, for instance, might yet reject the coercive enforcement of such authority as being unjustifiable on the grounds of there being too much distance between those enforcing the rules and those subject to them, or the lack of a legitimate enforcement body. Meanwhile, a sovereigntist defence of the primacy of state law might carve out very significant space for supra-state law in some domains of activity where that is seen to be in the interests of the state itself – as in the example of international investment rules and dispute resolution. Despite the polarity of their extremities, neither pluralist nor monist agendas in jurisprudence operate in silos from each other or removed from the possibility of borrowing from each other's good ideas or worthwhile practices.

What becomes most interesting, for a pluralist jurisprudence, is the difference it makes to think about these normative preferences as matters for legal theory and not simply political or moral theory. Pluralist jurisprudence needs to fill in the details of the difference it might make (if any) to have general pluralist values applied in legal pluralist forms. What difference is made, in other words, by features such as law's institutionalisation, normativity, comprehensiveness, or coercive enforcement? What is the further significance of the reality check in which legal institutions and officials, and their processes such as legal reasoning, adjudication, and drafting, shape the ways in which abstract pluralist ideas can be operated through legal forms? The enticing further challenge for jurisprudence, in general, is to revisit the possibility that these very forms and processes are marked and altered by pluralist challenges, with potential implications for shifting pluralism's justification from political or moral debate into legal theories and practices.

14.1.4 Greater Expectations

Our reassessment of the preliminary expectations canvassed in Chapter 1 has led us to a more realistic view of the role those expectations might fulfil, but with that comes a more exacting set of demands to be made of pluralist jurisprudence. The lessons we take from this exercise can be summarised as follows:

1. From further reflection on the relationship between pluralist and monist jurisprudence and the disciplinary challenge it presents, we take it to be desirable for a pluralist jurisprudence to be identified with some shared jurisprudential concerns found within monist jurisprudence, yet crucial for it to offer a distinctive theoretical perspective that illuminates the subject matter of a legal plurality.
2. From the variety of roles encountered for pluralism within examples of pluralist jurisprudence, and the conceptual and practical challenges

that it raises, it is apparent that a pluralist jurisprudence must confront problems of vagueness in the characterisation of legality and follow this through to the point of practical impact.

3. From consideration of the diversity of normative or aspirational agendas that can be detected both within the subject matter and the theorising of pluralist jurisprudence, it becomes essential to account for this diversity and also to explain the ways it may have particularly legal significance within a pluralist jurisprudence.

If our preliminary expectations, and the more exacting demands that they give rise to, are not met individually by our contributors, it is time to follow the alternative route: to commence with the variety of theoretical concerns that can be pursued within pluralist jurisprudence, and then to work through those concerns towards the realisation of an effective pluralist jurisprudence, that is capable of meeting the demands which have been placed upon it. We take the first steps along that route in the next section by profiling the types of pursuits of pluralist jurisprudence that can be found within the previous chapters.

14.2 The Pursuits of Pluralist Jurisprudence

14.2.1 Profiling the Pursuits

It is important to preface the exercise we undertake in this section with some preliminary remarks on the pursuits profiled here, and how they relate to the contributions to this volume. We are not suggesting that each contribution should necessarily be identified with a single exclusive pursuit. In some cases this may be so, but the differentiation between the pursuits we profile here is not based on attribution to individual authorship but rather on their presence within the literature, and their standing as a type of pursuit that lends itself to discrete engagement – whether or not a particular pursuit happens to feature alongside one or more other pursuits within a particular piece, and even though there may at times be an overlap between one pursuit and another. Another point to make is that we have been guided in selecting the following profiles by the objective of coming up with pursuits that could be regarded as typical pursuits, not simply in terms of being representative of the pursuits found within the contributions to this volume, but also as those commonly found within the wider literature. A final comment on our selection is that we consider the four pursuits profiled in this section as being collectively required to portray an effective pluralist jurisprudence.

To put that last point another way, our contention is that work within pluralist jurisprudence may valuably contribute to only one of the following pursuits, but in so doing cannot pass off such work as capable of capturing pluralist jurisprudence as a whole. In much the same way that work in any theoretical field may narrow its objectives and focus on a very specific issue in that field, but cannot then take that limited contribution as exhaustively covering the field and rendering other insights redundant.[6] The four pursuits we have selected involve the recognition of pluralism, a practical outworking of pluralism, a normative or aspirational agenda for pluralism, and a theoretical account of pluralism.

(a) *Pursuing the recognition of pluralism.* For some authors, pursuing the recognition of pluralism is regarded as valuable in broadening the perspectives and expanding the resources available for investigating the subject matter of law. This enthusiasm can be justified in terms of analytical rigour: pluralism provides the missing parts of a picture that monism overlooked, and accordingly provides the material to take corrective measures to deal with the distortions that a monistic approach imposed. Often, it runs into normative or ideological concerns when the non-pluralist approach is taken to disadvantage or suppress interests and values that become evident with the more accommodating recognition of pluralism. Nevertheless, the recognition of pluralism in itself does not necessitate a particular analytical standpoint or a definite normative outlook. Anker pointedly reminds us that pluralism has been used historically to serve both colonial and postcolonial outlooks.

Where the pursuit of pluralism is accompanied by an open, expansive embrace of a number of normative possibilities, it appears that it is accommodating them on an equal footing. This would make pluralism both an accommodating and authenticating theoretical perspective on plurality. Certainly, as 'strong' pluralism it seeks to confer valence on each member of the normative plurality on its own terms. Yet, as has been noted in Chapter 1, 'weak' forms of pluralism have also been suggested. This indicates that the recognition of pluralism is one thing

[6] On this, see the comments from von Daniels and Davies, as picked up in the commentary in ch. 1, on spurious pretentions to theoretical comprehensiveness. Broader discussion of such a tendency is found in Andrew Halpin, 'Austin's Methodology? His Bequest to Jurisprudence' (2011) 70 *Cambridge Law Journal* 175; 'The Creation and Use of Concepts of Law when Confronting Legal and Normative Plurality' in Seán Patrick Donlan and Lukas Heckendorn-Ursheler (eds.), *Concepts of Law: Comparative, Jurisprudential, and Social Science Perspectives* (Farnham: Ashgate, 2014).

and the extent of its authenticating aspect another. Strong pluralism then comes across as pluralism plus: pluralism with a full normative accommodation.

It is worth pausing to emphasise the point that the normative accommodation afforded by pluralism to a plurality of normative orders is the crucial feature of a pluralist perspective. Other arrangements between a plurality of normative orders, such as hierarchical authorisation or division into discrete realms of influence, make no call upon pluralism. Yet there is an ambiguity in this idea of pluralist accommodation, which straddles both the initial pluralist recognition of the normative plurality and the subsequent interaction between the recognised members of that plurality.[7]

At the point of initial recognition it is easy to proclaim the strong position that each normative order is fully authenticated on its own terms, but once the recognition of a plurality of normative orders has been made, there is nothing that follows by way of exploring the interaction between members of the plurality. Indeed, nothing can obviously follow from the strong pluralist premise that each normative order is authenticated on its own terms. It would be contingent, even accidental, if it happened that the different normative orders, accommodated on their own terms, also happened to be accommodating of each other.[8] As we shall see below, in order to overcome this contingency attached to

[7] Neil Walker, in his illuminating 'Constitutionalism and Pluralism: A Conflicted Relationship?' in Anthony Lang & Antje Wiener (eds.), *Handbook on Global Constitutionalism* (forthcoming, Edward Elgar), commences by citing Victor Muniz-Fraticelli, *The Structure of Pluralism: On the Authority of Associations* (Oxford: Oxford University Press, 2014) 11, for the general proposition that all forms of pluralism recognise a variety of normative sources and 'the need to accommodate that multiplicity and diversity in terms that are not reducible to a set ranking or any other general ordering formula' ('they are incapable of being categorically ranked', as Muniz-Fraticelli puts it). Here accommodation is used by Walker to refer more specifically to the point of interaction between normative orders. Accordingly, Walker proceeds to consider different attempts at constitutional pluralism and distinguishes them on 'a gradation between "thin" and "thicker" – between provisional and ad hoc forms of accommodation on the one hand and relatively stable and generalised rules or guidelines on the other.' He places 'radical' (or 'strong') pluralism at the 'thin' end of this spectrum in that the accommodation (in the sense of interaction) is sketchy and loosely defined. Yet Muniz-Fraticelli in stressing the lack of a categorical ranking is arguably more concerned with the pluralist recognition of the normative sources as 'foundationally independent' with a '[normative] basis … incommensurable with that of the state' (at 4), rather than with their subsequent interaction on which his remark on the possibility of 'tragic conflict' is more germane.

[8] Hence the possibility of 'tragic conflict' for Muniz-Fraticelli (previous note).

the initial strong premise an additional premise is required, to ensure such mutual accommodation or mode of interaction.

This might suggest that strong pluralism should be limited to the point of initial recognition and weak pluralism associated with the subsequent stage of practical interaction. However, this simple move would betray the subtlety and nuance to be found in the arguments over different (weak and strong) forms of pluralism, at both stages of recognition and interaction. A crude demarcation between strong recognition and weak interaction would also imperil the distinctive credentials of pluralism, if that weak interaction simply dissolved into an alternative arrangement between normative orders, such as hierarchical authorisation. Something has to be retained of the initial pluralist recognition at the point of interaction. On the other hand, mere pluralist recognition cannot of itself produce a mode of interaction.

Here we face a conundrum, particularly for legal pluralism which has a peculiar need for a practical outworking of pluralism. Our own attempt to work through this conundrum is provided in Section 3. What we suggest more generally, for the moment, is that distinguishing (though not ultimately separating) the pursuits of recognition and interaction provides important assistance in taking theoretical bearings in the face of this intimidating conundrum.

Self-evidently, some kind of recognition of pluralism is a threshold pursuit for a pluralist jurisprudence, and even if it leads on to other pursuits, as our prefatory comments have suggested, there may well be value in treating it as a dedicated pursuit, to compensate for the distortions of monism. In the present volume, Davies offers the most single-minded example of this pursuit. Del Mar's contribution displays similar qualities in the more restricted context of legal reasoning; and, at times, the recognition of pluralism is treated as a valuable pursuit in itself by Taekema and Anker.

(b) *Pursuing a practical outworking of pluralism in the legal setting.* Other authors, taking it as a given that pluralism has been recognised, are concerned to pursue a broader understanding which will account for the interaction between the members of the recognised normative plurality. There may be a tendency here towards a form of 'weak' pluralism, diluting a strong pluralist premise that each normative order is authenticated on its own terms by the additional premise that the status of each member is subordinated to an external mechanism or ulterior values that makes interaction possible. A hierarchical ordering around state law, mentioned in Anker's recollection of colonial pluralism, provides a simple example of an additional mechanism; deference to juristic values, encouraged by Cotterrell as a means of negotiating regulatory plurality (and hinted at by Taekema as a possible resource for achieving harmony), illustrates a recourse to ulterior values.

On the other hand, pursuit of a practical outworking might be attempted while seeking to maintain a strong pluralism; that is, keeping intact the authentication of each member of the normative plurality on its own terms even to the point of its practical outworking with other normative orders, by finding within each of those sets of terms a mechanism that fosters mutual recognition between members. Michaels' device of an external rule of recognition, which serves just such a role, is representative of other devices to be found in the literature;[9] and again we can find a parallel strategy in the narrower context of legal reasoning in Del Mar's 'relational pluralism'.

The interesting question to be asked of Michaels' external rule of recognition is whether it should be treated as a descriptive, analytical claim about the existence of pluralist normative orders or as an additional premise which provides a normative theory of how pluralist normative orders can best function together. As we mentioned in Chapter 1, within Michaels' own chapter there is to be found empirical material relating to the relations between EU and municipal legal orders suggestive of a lack of mutual recognition. As a purely empirical matter, this then reiterates the contingency or accidental character of the interaction between members of a normative plurality, which we noted in our comments at (a) previously, even after the more sophisticated device of an external rule of recognition is introduced. In order to overcome the contingent impact of the device, an additional premise would be required to ensure such mutual accommodation or mode of interaction. Advancing that as a normative or aspirational premise, we take to involve another pursuit.

(c) *Pursuing a specific normative or aspirational agenda.* We have just mentioned the possibility that a normative or aspirational premise may be imposed upon a contingent interaction identified from a strong pluralist perspective, so as to ensure that members of the normative plurality are required to interact in a mutually supportive way. This is one way in which the pursuit of a pluralist jurisprudence may turn to advancing a specific normative or aspirational agenda. In this kind of

[9] As we noted in Chapter 1, Michaels refers in particular to von Daniels' linkage rules among other similar devices.

case the agenda can be regarded as internal to the understanding of pluralism itself, which is taken to constitute pluralism that is both strong and interactive. The agenda, whether described as normative or aspirational, is to ensure that pluralism (and a pluralist jurisprudence) serves a non-discriminatory, liberal accommodation of different legal (or, more loosely, normative) orders on their own terms, even to the point of considering the practical outworking of those normative orders.

Earlier we raised the prospect that a set of ulterior values (such as juristic values) may be adopted to dilute strong pluralism, in order to achieve a practical outworking of pluralism. Although this can also be regarded as pursuing a specific normative or aspirational agenda, the difference here is that the values are extrinsic to the understanding of pluralism; they are brought in to deal with the aftermath of recognising a regulatory plurality. Even though these values are regarded as juristic or legal values, as they are (at least in part) by Cotterrell and Taekema, and as such might be thought of as in some way internal to law, it is important to see that they are not internal to the understanding of pluralism being proffered. Unlike Michaels' pluralism which is strong and interactive due to the interactive mechanism being constitutive within each of the members of the normative plurality,[10] in this case we have a weak form of pluralism where the normative reach of each member cannot be treated simply on its own terms but is subjected to a set of external values.

What is common to both of these cases is that the normative or aspirational agenda being pursued tackles the problem of interaction between members of the normative plurality. There is a third type of case, where the richer resources provided by a plurality of normative phenomena are used as an opportunity to promote an extrinsic normative or aspirational agenda. Such an agenda is not primarily concerned with the interaction between the members, although some degree of interaction may be an incidental beneficiary of pursuing the agenda. The broader normative landscape created by a normative plurality makes it easier to facilitate that normative or aspirational agenda. Walker's pursuit of global justice and Krygier's pursuit of the rule of law fall under this third type of case. If each normative order within the normative plurality were to comply with common standards of global justice or a common notion of the rule of law, then to that extent there would be no interaction problems between members of the normative plurality.

[10] We noted in Chapter 1 that Michaels sees this as an effective response to Griffiths' rejection of weak pluralism.

However, since there will be other normative measures undertaken by members that fall outside of the particular concerns of global justice or rule of law, potential interaction problems here will not be covered, even incidentally.

(d) *Pursuing a theoretical basis to account for legal pluralism.* Other authors adopt a more removed interest in the theoretical puzzles that pluralism throws up, concentrating more on metatheoretical questions or the investigation of aspects of a theoretical groundwork from which other pursuits of pluralist jurisprudence could proceed. This pursuit is intimately connected with establishing (or questioning) the disciplinary integrity of pluralist jurisprudence. We might expect this pursuit to be elevated from the precise concerns of the previous pursuits, but we find here a variety of theoretical endeavours whose progress is affected by factors arising in the other pursuits. Perhaps the purest instance within this category is von Daniel's pursuit of theoretical pluralism. Yet, as we noted in Chapter 1, his theoretical complementarity leaves open a number of issues, and the 'context' of his theoretical inquiry will be established from factors related to the extent to which a pluralistic recognition of normative phenomena is embraced (as in (a)), a practical legal outworking is confronted (as in (b)), and any normative agenda is selected (as in (c)).

The connectedness latent in von Daniel's approach is more evident in Mac Amhlaigh's treatment of theoretical pluralism. He is content to point out from an empirical encounter with instances of legal (constitutional) pluralism how any theoretical account will itself have to assume a pluralistic character. Mac Amhlaigh's study centres on a practical legal outworking by the judiciary, and so draws from pursuit (b) to demonstrate a variable rather than a theoretically discoverable constant affecting interaction. Implicitly, we can also read into his account a connected restriction on the pursuit of pluralism in (a); and, more obviously, see the recognition of a variable approach to a normative agenda in pursuit (c).

Two other contributions obviously fall within pursuit (d), which it is illuminating to compare. First, Raz's close questioning of the relationship between a pluralist jurisprudence and conventional monist jurisprudence effectively suggests a stop on the open embrace of pluralism in pursuit (a) until a criterion of legality linked to social legitimacy can be met. For him, this criterion is linked to the institutional character of law, so equally related to the practical aspect found in pursuit (b). A wholly extrinsic normative agenda for pursuit (c) is ruled out by Raz consistent with his positivist outlook, although there remains a place for any values that might undergird social legitimacy. The second contribution from Sciaraffa expounds an avowedly non-positivist approach, but, as we pointed out in Chapter 1, his use of socio-political commitment overlaps interestingly with Raz's emphasis on social legitimacy.

Socio-political commitment is used by Sciaraffa as the basis for working through potential conflicts within a plurality of normative orders, and so curtails a strong embrace of pluralism in pursuit (a). It favours a practical legal outworking of pluralism in pursuit (b), suitably informed by the socio-political agenda in pursuit (c). Although Sciaraffa is considering a non-positivist outlook, it is clear that he does not allow for an extrinsic normative agenda beyond those politico-moral values that are incorporated within his expanded understanding of legal reasoning. In this respect, his 'content-independent' approach to legality draws him towards the positivist side of the fence with regard to pursuit (c). These brief observations in comparing Raz and Sciaraffa are hardly sufficient as the basis for any grand pronouncement, but they do at least stimulate further thought on the possibility that within pluralist jurisprudence there may be de-escalation of another old contest from monist jurisprudence.

A final contribution which includes material falling within pursuit (d) comes from Anker, in her suggestion that an indigenous ontology can provide a theoretical foundation for legal pluralism. She adopts pursuit (a) in the strongest possible terms, and when it comes to pursuit (b) concedes that the approach is not judicially tenable. Anker effectively relies on an ontological disposition rather than a judicial determination to keep the interaction among a plurality of normative orders one that is strongly pluralist. Although this may be regarded as pursuing an aspirational agenda for strong pluralism, any pursuit (c) found in Anker's contribution is hard to characterise as a normative one. She takes an ontological turn to avoid the normative impasse encountered within a plurality of normative orders. This raises the question whether an ontological commitment can be insulated from the contestability associated with normative commitments.[11]

[11] The recourse to an indigenous ontology found in Anker's chapter is also adopted and defended at length by other scholars of indigenous legal theory such as Christine Black, John Borrows, or Gordon Christie. It raises the matter of choosing between different ontologies that may be deployed for confronting pluralism. For instance, our colleague, Alec Stone Sweet has been undertaking a project which explores the possibility of a Kantian framework to account for the resolution of a European legal pluralism involving different state legal orders and the European Convention of Human Rights. In this case,

14.2.2 *Coordinating the Pursuits*

The questions to consider now are how far a satisfactory pluralist jurisprudence needs to address all four of the pursuits identified in Section 14.2.1, and how this might be attainable. We stressed at the beginning of Section 14.2.1 that particular projects within pluralist jurisprudence may make valuable contributions to the field without covering the whole field. However, for these individual contributions to be regarded as valuable there must be some appreciation of the standing and worth of the field itself. An effective pluralist jurisprudence must be capable of rendering that standing and worth to itself as an academic discipline, in ways that we amplified in our extended reflection on the preliminary expectations and the more exacting demands that process disclosed in Section 14.1.4. Our response to the current questions amounts to an attempt to deliver that status, and to meet those more exacting demands, through showing the collective importance of the four pursuits we have introduced here. We commence here with some general discussion of the way that coordinating these pursuits is necessary for an effective pluralist jurisprudence, and then continue in Section 14.3 with our own attempt at meeting these requirements.

The discussion of pursuit (d) at the close of Section 14.2.1 illustrated in some detail the connectedness between that pursuit and the previous three pursuits. We amplify that connectedness here by considering some other key connections between the pursuits and then addressing their collective importance in producing a theory of the pluralist legal environment, and so providing a credible status to pluralist jurisprudence.

We took it to be self-evident that the recognition of pluralism in pursuit (a) is a threshold pursuit for a pluralist jurisprudence, but that in itself does not engage with the deeper problems of what kind of pluralism (weak or strong) and what extent of pluralism (which legal or normative orders are accepted into the plurality[12]) is envisaged. Our

the ontological underpinning is Western, liberal and individualistic, rather than indigenous, involving ecological interrelationships. The significance of a choice of ontology is likely to rekindle, rather than avoid, contestable normative commitments. See further, Gordon Christie, 'Indigenous Legal Theory: Some Initial Considerations' in Richardson, Inai and McNeil (eds.), *Indigenous Peoples and the Law* (Oxford: Hart Publishing, 2009); Christine Black, *The Land is the Source of the Law: A Dialogic Encounter with Indigenous Jurisprudence* (Abingdon: Routledge, 2011); Alec Stone Sweet and Clare Ryan, *A Cosmopolitan Legal Order: Kant, Constitutional Justice, and the ECHR* (forthcoming, Oxford University Press).

12 There are two ways in which this second problem has been addressed. The first is through conceptual analysis in order to establish a theoretical boundary between law and non-law

further discussion of pursuit (a) spilled over into pursuit (b) and made it clear that for pluralist jurisprudence, with its particular burden to illuminate legal practice, the recognition of pluralism had to be connected to the practical outworking of pluralism in pursuit (b). That in turn led us to the different ways in which the pursuit of a normative or aspirational agenda in pursuit (c) would be implicated in how the practical outworking (or interaction between normative orders) is perceived in (b).

So we can establish a fairly straightforward, connected progression from pursuit (a) to pursuit (c). The onward connection to pursuit (d) is called for as an exercise in tidying up theoretical loose ends emerging in the previous pursuits, and, in particular, establishing the disciplinary integrity of any proposed pluralist jurisprudence. Taking into account our earlier review of how efforts under pursuit (d) could be related back to the previous pursuits, we complete a picture of the four pursuits as having a collective importance in delivering an effective pluralist jurisprudence. If this picture is accepted, then the failure to integrate any one of these pursuits into a pluralist jurisprudence would suggest severe limitations to the theoretical endeavour; and in the absence of remedial work on those limitations, would challenge the standing and worth of pluralist jurisprudence.

That leaves one part of the earlier discussion unaccounted for in the picture just presented. In pursuit (c) we noted three types of aspirational or normative pursuits, only two of which were directly connected to the problem of interaction. The third type of case was described as promoting an extrinsic normative or aspirational agenda: global justice or the rule of law. We should be careful to point out that the agenda in these cases was considered extrinsic to the issues of pluralism, but that is not to say it therefore has an inferior part to play in a pluralist jurisprudence.

If the pluralist legal environment, once effectively surveyed, yields richer normative resources which make the pursuit of these agendas

normative orders. The second is by assuming empirical data regarding interconnections between different orders will vindicate a theoretical postulate that those orders that are legal will mutually reinforce their legal status through interconnection. Neither approach can be regarded as successful in dealing with all the issues that arise from this problem of the extent of recognition. (For discussion of some of the issues, see Andrew Halpin, 'Conceptual Collisions' (2011) 2 *Jurisprudence* 507; 'The Creation and Use of Concepts of Law' (n. 3).) What can be confidently maintained is that any recognised plurality which is brought into a pluralism characterised as legal will have to be confronted with the interaction problem.

plausible in a way that could not be contemplated in a leaner normative environment, then it is appropriate to extend the ambit of a pluralist jurisprudence to include such concerns. To claim that the pursuit of global justice, or the tempering of arbitrary power, takes on a distinctive character within a pluralist legal environment, nevertheless, requires a plausible account of that environment. The recognition of these pursuits as part of a pluralist jurisprudence is, accordingly, still dependent on the collective importance of the four pursuits, integrated in the way our basic picture presents. The basic picture is put forward as a condition for pluralist jurisprudence, but not as a limitation on how a pluralist jurisprudence might develop.

14.3 A Candidate Pluralist Theory of Law

14.3.1 An Overview

In this section we offer our own candidate for a pluralist jurisprudence. In its own way it meets (and so illustrates) the basic picture reached in Section 2 of the four integrated pursuits: (a) the recognition of pluralism, (b) a practical outworking of pluralism, (c) a normative or aspirational agenda for pluralism, and (d) a theoretical account of pluralism. Our approach gains its particular connectedness between these four pursuits by offering a distinctive account of the working of law in a pluralist legal environment – meeting (b), which at the same time involves an authoritative recognition of pluralism – meeting (a), and incorporates a dual mode of normativity for law encompassing both formal jurisdiction and legitimate authority – meeting (c); and then, in order to reinforce the pluralist credentials of the proposed jurisprudence – so meeting (d) – draws out a distinctive interplay between legal interventions and social responses within the pluralist institutional and normative social context adumbrated in the previous pursuits. Nevertheless, what we offer here is only a preliminary sketch of a fully integrated theory. It is offered in an ambitious spirit, but one which is conscious of both optimism and scepticism, constraint and creativity, idealism and realism, about the promises and pursuits of a pluralist theory of law.

These dispositions play out amidst each of four components found in our candidate theory. The first two of these are: (1) the openness and (2) the decisiveness of law; features which, whilst present in monist practices and theories of law, are modified and take on particular significance in a pluralist context. Law's characteristic openness and decisiveness not only mark law (and laws) as distinctive kinds of normative social practices, but can also double as virtues, notwithstanding some degree of tension between them. A candidate pluralist theory of law must somehow account for these two features to explore their operation in the juristic encounters with pluralism, or even to bring them together by exploiting the tension between them for its pluralist promise. That search for accommodation or engagement means avoiding both a tendency of pluralist theories to assume or favour openness over decisiveness, and a tendency of monistic theories to assume or favour decisiveness over openness. Pluralist theories typically entail openness towards normative alternatives if not parallel normative universes, which legal theory can recognise through ascribing the quality of legality to diverse kinds of law. In that narrative, decisiveness is sometimes treated pejoratively, as a kind of closure that excludes these normative alternatives. In contrast, monistic jurisprudence has tended to champion law's ability to make and impose decisions, to resolve or dissolve disputes, and manifest some kind of decisive authority. In those narratives, law's openness is carefully and formally contained by the idea of jurisdiction, in which only rules or practices of legal validity can confer the force of decision upon norms, whatever their origin.

The third component explores this idea of formal jurisdiction as a constraint upon or a containment of law's openness, and a delimitation of law's decisiveness. It considers (3) the relationship between openness and decisiveness, and conceives that relationship to operate in one of two modes of normativity: formal jurisdiction and legitimate authority. It explores whether these are strictly distinct or separable modes of normativity, as well as the possibility that in pluralist contexts, there may be greater reason to integrate or at least re-engage the two, mindful of both the constraints of law's formal jurisdiction and the potential scope for evaluating law's legitimate authority

The fourth component is (4) a direct account of this pluralist institutional and normative social context itself, made distinct by plurality both in the form of diffuse legal interventions in social practices (institutionalisations) and the social responses to those interventions which dictate their ultimate acceptability and effectiveness. Within a pluralist institutional context, then, we find diffuse institutions, whose interactions and entanglements with one another involve both the work of officials (as those who design and operate institutions) and wider subject communities (as those who use and accept or reject institutional offerings). The interplay between the work of those charged with institutionalised roles, and those who are subject to and responsive to the institutions, generates the normative social practices which, reflexively, shape the institutions themselves as well as the extent to which their pluralist status will be acceptable and effective.

14.3.2 Law's Openness and Jurisdictional Constraints

Law's openness is its search for reasons for a decision, or more precisely, the search for reasons that will validate and/or justify a particular legal decision. This is not a new idea. The canon of jurisprudence is well-versed in the notion that law (and legal systems) are open, and/or that legal reasoning is in some sense an open process in which external norms or principles can be incorporated or integrated into a system. It is common for theories of legal reasoning to embrace degrees of openness amidst practices of norm-interpretation and norm-generation, as well as practices of norm-guided degrees of discretion.

In more detail, an orthodox juristic approach comfortably admits the openness that arises from treating law's normativity as continuous in some way with social and/or moral normativity. An orthodox monistic theory of law (typically of state law) analyses how legal systems control their borders with these other norms, thus constituting a formal jurisdiction. That does not, at first sight, look very open. Yet having constructed some idea of jurisdiction, law and legal reasoning can then entail a more open search for norm-content from these other normative domains. In its search for or receptivity to external norms, law and legal reasoning may also be open to norms that can be incorporated from other legal systems using a system's jurisdictionally valid channels, or norms whose content might be copied from other legal systems without being directly incorporated. Law might also be considered to be, more generally, diachronically open, so that at any point in time there will be potential legal norms which include candidate norms from other systems, which can be activated, as legal norms, through subsequent processes and practices of jurisgenerative activity.

A monistic account might use these forms of openness to downplay the significance of any pluralist challenge. For instance, doctrinal tools for containing openness are available in the form of rules dealing with the application of public international law, or the conflict of laws, and these may be turned, with a little modification, upon pluralist instances of laws other than the laws of international law or the law of foreign states. Thus, although the content of legal norms may be open to outside influence (sometimes confusingly termed 'persuasive authority'), both synchronically and diachronically, those norms' authority is always determined intra-systemically. Either a system has its own valid norm which dictates the conditions under which an external legal norm might be incorporated, or the terms on which an external legal system is to attract deference or even a deferral of jurisdiction; or it has norms of systemic closure. The importation of an external norm's content, or its formal incorporation into a host system, does not amount to treating that norm as authoritative in its own right. Monist jurisprudence may insist that in these practices of responding to plurality, a norm's provenance is still essential to its authority (or lack thereof), and that authority is still conferred by a monistic jurisdictional approach, contained by the 'host' norms and their formal jurisdiction. Thus, while law may be open to influence from another law's content, its authority is thought to remain systemically closed. Rather than combatting jurisdictional containment, these approaches multiply the sites of jurisdictional containment, which then operate in parallel or sometimes in conflict. In those circumstances, legality's effectiveness is not determined juridically at all, or not merely juridically, but by matters of social fact such as the strength of one system's de facto authority or the extent to which it is accepted.

Yet the full pluralist challenge is broader than that. It recognises forms of openness that are not so consistent with a formal jurisdictional approach. On the most robust pluralist interpretation of practices responding to plurality, these forms of openness do not simply alter the content of what is contained within formal jurisdiction, they do not simply open jurisdiction up to infiltration by plural legal norms and institutions, only to close it off again by reference back to the monist moment of decision. Instead, they may be regarded as challenges to the very operation of jurisdictional containment, so that jurisdiction becomes a matter of constraining legal norms, systems and agents, rather than containing them within formal boundaries. The interaction of norms, systems and authorities in these expanded forms of openness are treated as defeating the normative closure that formal jurisdiction seeks to impose.

It is instructive to consider three different forms of this kind of openness in turn. The first makes use of law's institutionality not to explore the ways in which one legal system can be open to another while ultimately protective of itself, but to de-link institutional forms from single legal systems. On offer are conceptions of inter-institutional norms, linkage norms, or other rules that are institutional but not monistically institutional. The inter-institutional approach sets out a juridical account of law's openness, but must still acknowledge that, as juridical tools, even inter-institutional norms need to be operated within an institution by its agents. This raises key questions over how those operations occur and how they should be interpreted. Are they still contained by formal institutional domains of jurisdiction? To what extent are such inter-institutional norms actively used by institutions; do their applications attract sufficient acceptance as to make them effective? These questions are raised not to discount the existence or peculiar potential of inter-institutional legality but to suggest the need for further exploration of the ways in which such inter-institutional practices amount to challenges to orthodox juridical concerns, and/or may be examined in light of socio-political as well as juridical concerns.

The second form of pluralistic openness that is arguably constrained but not contained by jurisdiction appears in practices of interaction between legal systems interpreted as revealing law's openness to other systems' authority, not just their content. These point to practices in which particular non-state laws have direct effect or similar status within the state legal system, and which are understood to involve a 'host' system giving space to an outsider's authority. Examples include legislative (or even constitutional) provisions that not only recognise the content but also uphold the authority of some other normative system (often regional law or public international law, or the law of a particular religious or ethnic group, or indigenous law). More controversial examples appear in some adjudicatory practices (such as reliance on customary international law or even unincorporated treaty norms; or courts treating indigenous law as law, not simply as fact) that reveal more openness to extra-jurisdictional authority than a conventional monist may expect or accept.

The third kind of openness is still more diffuse, and involves practices of open interaction of systems in which the matter of authority is not settled by one system accepting or deferring to another's authority, nor by each system claiming exclusive authority for itself. Instead, each system's claims to authority can be understood as claims to some kind of interdependent authority, which entails the existence of the other's authority without amounting to deference to that other system. Thus despite claiming authority, the systems do not render themselves juridically closed; they blur jurisdiction through practices of interaction which entail the sharing of juridical space, rather than its management through doctrines of jurisdiction or deference. This is the kind of openness often analyzed by accounts of constitutional pluralism such as those examined in Mac Amhlaigh's chapter, but also in practices of interaction between state and indigenous or other polities' laws. It cannot be analyzed or addressed through jurisdictional containment of openness, because there are multiple jurisdictions in play such that their interaction defeats or pre-empts each other's claims to closure. This is not an abstract problem. Rather, overlap and contestation of normative systems, and their authority, arise from the overlap and interaction of the subjects of those systems. This much is recognised, for instance, in Raz's suggestion in this volume that the relations between rules that generate the identification of 'law-like systems', include the relation between rules and people, so that the identification of systems includes 'identifying the people who are relevant by reference to the rules that apply to them.' If this is right, and if Raz is right that rules can be part of more than one system, it highlights the fundamental scale and scope of the pluralist challenge, in which norm-subjects can be subjects of multiple norms and systems, and rules can belong to different systems each claiming authority. In that full pluralist challenge, both the subjection to authority and the claim to authority may be better interpreted without the monistic notion of exclusivity, so that instead the matter of laws' authority is open for negotiation or contestation between those who act to represent and serve the overlapping or interacting subjects. This form of openness plays out as a fundamental challenge not only from a pluralist starting point, but also as a central problem for jurisprudential accounts of the authority of law.[13]

In order to make sense of each of these forms of openness, it is crucial to situate openness, and its interpretation and responses, within the pluralist institutional context in which it is operated. This context may involve diffuse institutional forms and complex sets of subjects, which differ in their management of and responses to plurality. Thus in some plural institutional contexts, pluralist legal reasoning may still be reined in by jurisdiction, simply a jurisdiction that is shaped by norms other than those of a host system, e.g., norms which generate concurrent or competing jurisdictions, or which entail deference to another system. In those cases a host system's jurisdiction is not self-contained; unlike a pre-pluralist setting, in which the constraints of jurisdiction are closely controlled by the local norms of the legal order associated with that

[13] See Nicole Roughan, *Authorities: Conflict, Cooperation, and Transnational Legal Theory* (Oxford: Oxford University Press, 2013).

jurisdiction, in a pluralist setting the jurisdictional feature itself constrains in ways that are not simply contained in a set of local norms but are informed by an interaction with norms of other legal orders. In other contexts, however, an institutional response may still give effect to a locally determined jurisdiction. This would capture, for instance, a pluralist account which appears 'weak' in that it concedes that the orthodox toolkit for managing pluralism seeks to contain it through explicit rules of incorporation, or other jurisdiction-affirming rules, which empower judges to engage in such open critical inquiry while still structuring an interaction in which a 'host' system determines the space it creates for another. Even that weak, pluralist account emphasises that the juristic enterprise is, at that point, already pluralist to some degree. It suggests that those who make such rules of association between systems, whether they are made as legislative enactments, constitutional amendments, or common law rules of substance or procedure, have already embraced plurality and wish to assert some control over its operation. In Section 14.3.5, we return to the significance of the work of these agents who handle plurality, to see how they work through these distinctly pluralist forms of openness in order to arrive at decisions.

14.3.3 Decisiveness: Against Accommodation?

For all its openness, law remains decisive. Law's decisiveness is its characteristic of stopping and settling, at least in a static and sometimes partial sense, both legal and political disputes. From a synchronic perspective, law is decisive in its enactment or application of particular rules, or in simply reaching a particular momentary decision; while in a diachronic sense, law retains a claim to decisiveness at any particular moment, even if it holds off deciding at a given time or decides 'for now', leaving open the prospect of later revision.

Law, in this sense, is not conciliatory or accommodating. For all the appeal of theories that emphasise law's features beyond its creation of binaries – winners and losers, appeals upheld or dismissed, rights awarded and duties imposed – these binaries remain the business of the decisive part of legal reasoning. This does not deny that legal institutions can utilise conciliatory tools and mechanisms where these are thought useful and suitable, but they will, ultimately, be either backed up by or at the mercy of divisive and binary resolutions. In this light, decisiveness is a troubling virtue. It upsets more relational or conciliatory intuitions (including those of some pluralists), and there is a lot to criticise in its form and substance. Decisiveness is nevertheless a virtue for those who use the law, in both private and public capacities, to seek enforceable determinations of their status, their rights, and obligations vis-a-vis one other, both individually and collectively.

Legal reasoning leads to decisions that effect this virtue, but legal reasoning does not cease once a decision is made, just as decisiveness itself does not entail ultimate finality. In a dispute resolution setting, a decision will eventually be final for its subjects once appeals are exhausted, but legal reasoning both precedes that decision, and continues in the work of jurists who work to challenge or improve that decision for the next time around. The structures for appeal of judicial decisions, and the opportunity for political challenges leading to reform of law's content, mean that law's decisiveness is itself open to evaluation and resistance. Decisiveness is in this way tempered by openness, and in the space provided by a diachronic perspective of legal reasoning, as well as in the physical and normative space provided by institutional structures of appeals, law's decisiveness finds a kind of humility.

Where, if anywhere, does a pluralist jurisprudence find an inroad amidst all this decisiveness? From a diachronic perspective, there is obvious potential for pluralist infiltration of a system of law through the work of its decision-makers. Legal reasoning leads to decisions that can be informed by plurality even as plurality is subsumed and thus eroded by the decider's jurisdiction. Again, however, there is more to it than that. Plurality of laws also multiplies the normative and physical spaces in which law's decisive virtues can be given effect. With such diffusion of law's decisiveness comes the possibility that decisions made in one legal system may be challenged in another. It adds the prospect of both forum-shifting and system-switching, and thus the creation of decisions that might sit in contrast and even conflict with one another. A decision made within state law might be at odds with one made in a transnational, international, religious or indigenous legal system. Importantly, however, it also adds the prospect of influence or interplay between decision-making locations. Decisions in one system may be made either in the light or in the shadow of decisions made elsewhere. Yet we only get to see this interplay of decisions, and recognise it for what it is (rather than mere learning from others or copying or matching what they do) if we first recognise plurality of legal orders and their own decisive virtues.

The concern here may be that such plurality of decision-making could undermine the value of decisiveness itself, in so far as a decision, once made, may be reopened elsewhere, sometimes including a direct challenge to the original decision. This vulnerability of decision-making in a pluralist context, however, may also add value. Decisiveness is more demanding but potentially richer, for having to take into account a plurality of resources as well as for taking note of the interaction of one's own decisions with those of others. Pluralism thus features among the factors that may affect those who make legal decisions, not in every case, but in cases where the processes of open legal reasoning we have described put pressure on the very achievement of decisiveness, as well as enhancing its virtue.

14.3.4 Re-Engaging Jurisdiction with Legitimate Authority

The pressures generated by pluralistic openness, and the ways in which it is met with decisiveness can then be explored through the third component of our candidate pluralist theory, which reassesses the role of jurisdiction in pluralist challenges to monist jurisprudence, as well as its relationship to law's legitimate authority. One way of exploring the pressures generated by pluralistic openness, and the ways in which it is met with decisiveness, is to relate these features to two different, and arguably distinct, modes of normativity in which law's openness operates and is constrained; and law's decisiveness is valued or achieved. One mode is the domain of legitimate authority; the other is the mode of formal jurisdiction. There is often slippage between the two modes, to the extent that in some accounts a domain of legitimate authority is determined by or simply synonymous with formal jurisdiction. Yet the two are importantly distinct in ways that may be of significance for a pluralist jurisprudence.

Formal jurisdiction is constituted and governed by legal rules and is manifested in their operation over a range of subjects and activities, while a domain of legitimate authority is constituted and governed by both social facts (which determine de facto authority as a precondition of legitimate authority) and reasons, or in some accounts, values (which determine the matters on which authority is legitimate, and over whom). While a domain of authority can be conceived pluralistically as open to contestation and perhaps subject to relativity, it is both more difficult, and more pressing from a juristic perspective to reconcile the formal jurisdictional mode with pluralistic openness. As a matter of legitimate authority, plurality presses jurisprudence to offer a justification and ratification of jurisdictional borders, or to explore their relaxation or even disintegration. Yet even if, as a matter of legitimate authority, there is justification for openness beyond the constraint of formal jurisdiction, the juristic worry remains. How, if it all, could legal reasoning engage in such a practice of pluralist openness? This is a problem about both the potential and constraints of legal reasoning, the role of rules, and the nexus between rules, systems and a buttressing idea of jurisdiction.

The pluralist challenge is to monistic approaches to legal theory and legal reasoning that treat jurisdiction as a kind of fortress, within which legal reasoning, and law's openness, is both protected and contained. In the most profound of the pluralist challenges, the question for the practical juristic problem of plurality asks what legal reasoning permits or requires when there are rules belonging to different systems (and thus featuring different institutional protections), which, when triggered by a legal dispute or other inter-systemic legal engagement between subjects, directly challenge each other's protective layer of jurisdiction. In these challenges, the modes of normativity (authority and jurisdiction) become entangled because of the relationship between the twin factors of institutionalisation of norms and individuals' subjection to multiple systems of institutionalised norms. Adding these factors together creates a problem. For we can view the institutionalisation of a legal system operating to alter the relation between rules and the social practices that give rise to them (as Raz's chapter suggests), such that there is an intervening layer of validity (or other protective notion such as jurisdiction). This implies that such jurisdiction/validity is then supposed to be operable without needing to revisit questions of legitimate authority, because such institutionalisation is designed to operate as a proxy for legitimate authority. Yet it does not replace the domain of legitimate authority itself, which remains in the background and may be applied in order to evaluate the protective doctrines themselves. If there is reason to doubt the manner in which jurisdiction is being applied, or to question the location of its limits, its content, or its substantive doctrine, then jurisdiction itself can be subjected to an evaluation against the standards of legitimate authority. Perhaps the strongest (and most salient) instances in which such evaluations of jurisdiction are warranted, are conditions of multiple jurisdictions offering their own parallel modes of normativity with no means of either integrating or ordering those domains.

Consider, for instance, what happens when the traditional account of the institutionalisation of rules that is typical of law, and the role of institutions in altering the relationship between rules and the social practices that give rise to them, is placed in a pluralist context of both institutions and subjects, as well as both institutionalisations and their constitutive social practices. Now add the prospect that these constitutive social practices might divide polities either internally or among each other, with nothing to determine the ordering among the different institutionalisations (except the order that each claims for itself, or the order resulting from de facto power differentials). The social practices that support institutionalisation may well claim some hierarchy or supremacy over other similar practices, but even if they do so, their claim is just that; and it raises rather than answers the matter of its own relation with others. In a situation of conflict, it seems appropriate then to turn back to ideas of legitimate authority to attempt an evaluation of the competing jurisdictional claims. It is appropriate for either of two reasons. First, if the point of jurisdiction is to carve out and separate a domain of legal authority, then from an external perspective, at least, the point at which a jurisdictional protection runs into another is the point at which the case for its protected mode of authority runs out. Alternatively, if the reasons to value jurisdictional authority, and the reasons to institutionalise and protect a normative domain of law, lie in the difficulty of working out what would be legitimate, or the incommensurability/equality of multiple legitimate options, then in the (perhaps rare) circumstances in which there actually is an available answer to that question, it should, arguably be followed.

When there is no ready answer, for instance where notions of legitimate authority are manifested differently and/or contested among the plurality of formal authorities, two related prospects remain. One looks to an idealised version of legitimate authority, to be used to assess the pluralistic claimants of authority. This need not subject plurality to a single ulterior value, rather it may be a standard of legitimate authority that embodies multiple values and commits their advocates to seek their accommodation. The second, either with or without the first, looks for a further venue of openness, either formal or informal, authoritative or guiding, where the particular view of legitimate authority from one formal jurisdiction can be decisively challenged by or made answerable to that from another.

While the first prospect might satisfy some external perspective on the implications of plurality, what would it mean for (and from) an internal perspective, for those tasked with its management? While an abstract account of legitimate authority might be able to offer an ideal response to such plurality, the institutionalisation of norms requires that these concerns also be met with some form of the second prospect. We need to offer an institutionalised theory – legal theory – that responds to conflicts by reference to the institutional layers set up precisely for that purpose, and, arguably, with attention to those who are tasked with treating law as authoritative. This includes the layer of empowered and authorised legal reasoners – those officials whose role it is to effect law's institutionalisation, and operate both its open and decisive features.

14.3.5 Pluralist Legal Practices among Officials and Subjects

A pluralist jurisprudence offers itself as a point at which some kind of resolution between openness and decisiveness, and between jurisdiction and legitimate authority, might be found. The resolution offered in this section, tentatively for now, emphasises the role of open and decisive yet pluralist legal reasoning in the hands of legal officials, who work with an account of jurisdiction that can re-engage with (but does not collapse into) legitimate authority. In the hands of officials, that is, there is a potential for pluralist openness in pursuit of legitimate authority that might be obscured if we looked only at the content of institutions and their formal jurisdictions.

At this point the pluralist intervention challenges the simpler, conventional relationship outlined earlier between formal jurisdiction and legitimate authority. It asks whether jurisdiction itself can bend in the direction of legitimate authority, to the extent we might say that in circumstances in which more than one system of legal norms is implicated in a legal dispute, or where more than one set of legal institutions is needed to resolve a particular legal problem facing subjects, then as a matter of legitimate authority, there may be no justification for one system/set ignoring or excluding the other under the rubric of jurisdiction. To render jurisdiction responsive to legitimate authority is itself also undoubtedly an ideal, but the bending of jurisdiction to authority may be evident in small steps of pluralist legal reasoning by officials, so that, rather than containing the operation of legal reasoning or the tools or content with which such reasoning is concerned, jurisdiction still harbours an openness to legitimate authority for its own modification or displacement.

The institutional layer of law thus contains both barriers and opportunities for pluralist jurisprudence. The key barrier is the one already described in the formal notion of jurisdiction. Yet, jurisdiction neither constitutes nor controls itself; rather it is operated by the official agents who, though institutionally constrained, retain capacities to act which, in a pluralist setting, include the capacity to render law more or less pluralist. While law's institutional agents can be specifically directed (by linkage norms or inter-institutional norms) to reason inter-systemically and/or pluralistically, those agents may also, without further direction, engage in pluralistic legal reasoning. Pluralistic legal reasoning makes the first part of the legal reasoning process one of systemically open inquiry, which canvasses, contemplates and critically evaluates legal norms that do not necessarily fall within the host legal system but which are made pertinent to the resolution of a dispute or a legal problem either because of the identities of the parties or its substantive issues which render the subject matter of the dispute interactive or overlapping. This does not simply entail a free-for-all; rather, at the moment of decision, there is a choice to embrace plurality of norms either by adopting their content, by deferring to their authority, or more subtly, by claiming something other than exclusive authority. That choice is unresolved by a theory of legal reasoning, and indeed by a theory of law in the narrowly institutional sense. Rather, its analysis and evaluation falls to an understanding of the roles of those who are tasked with deciding: those officials who make, apply and enforce the law.

This is not the place to defend a full account of the roles of legal officials,[14] but rather to outline any potential of those roles for thinking about pluralist jurisprudence. In even a non-pluralist setting, the agents of law who engage in legal reasoning retain the capacity, because of their agency, to reflect upon and potentially challenge jurisdictional solutions. They may even come under some pressure to do so when there are strong reasons (perhaps counting in the direction of legitimate authority) for adopting less rigid jurisdictional constraints, even if this interferes with formal jurisdiction. If they hold themselves out as having authority over subjects, then they ought to pursue its legitimacy for those subjects. This may, in a pluralist setting, lead to pluralist engagement rather than monistic isolation; especially, if subjects themselves are conceived pluralistically, or as overlapping or interacting. A robust pluralist account of legal official roles may go further, to explore the potential for officials to operate in dual or multiple institutional roles (e.g. as state officials and international officials), which may require them, at times, to choose between respective jurisdictional constraints. Or it might conceive of officials' roles as being in the service of subjects, conceived pluralistically, rather than bare institutions themselves. The element of choice here is important – it emphasises that legal reasoners are not automatons, and

[14] A fuller account is currently being undertaken by Nicole Roughan as a book to be published by Oxford.

also that legal reasoners may be assessed not only by the quality of what they do measured against standards of formal competence and their contribution to furthering their institution(s), but also the reflective ability and, indeed, judgment that they bring to their judgments. It positions officials as being institutionally created, but it maintains that, as agents, they are constrained but not contained by their institutional character.

Yet the emphasis on the roles of officials, as bearers of promise for pluralist jurisprudence, then opens up a further and foundational element bearing on the manner in which openness and decisiveness in legal reasoning, the engagement of jurisdiction with legitimate authority, and any pluralist practices of officials, may operate. The foundations of all of these components of pluralist jurisprudence lie in the social practices which ultimately determine their degree of acceptance and effectiveness. The roles of officials, for instance, may be best understood as being generated socially, not only by the officials themselves, but also by those subject to their powers, and what they accept or require of the official role. There is thus a de facto constraint on pluralist legal practices (their success depends on the extent to which they are effective), as well as a sociological vulnerability (their effectiveness may depend on the extent to which they are accepted or at least tolerated by subjects). Importantly, plurality itself may be politicised, so that a subject community may actively embrace or reject attempts by officials to reason pluralistically; just as officials may embrace or reject the pluralistic claims and practices of subjects. In so far as roles are shaped by normative social practices, as well as shaping those practices, pluralism itself stands or falls upon a critical degree of normative acceptance.

Evidently, pluralism is often perceived as a threat to the positions of those who embrace or at least assume the primacy of monist legal forms and content; it may be seen to threaten the security of institutions and practices that subjects familiar with monism have simply assumed. This perceived threat, moreover, is amplified wherever plurality is not just a matter of managing the interaction of formal jurisdictions, but a matter of different polities contending for spaces or places for their law, involving conflicts over territory, authority, or power.

A complete analysis of 'pluralist legal practices', then, both reveals and must account for the contingency of the promise of pluralist jurisprudence, a dependence upon how prepared legal reasoners are to reason pluralistically, and the extent to which law's subjects welcome the results of those processes. It suggests that the work of officials and subjects in dealing with plurality and their responses to pluralist claims, rather than bare institutional arrangements or even inter-institutional tools, ultimately holds out or holds back the full promise of a pluralist jurisprudence.

14.3.6 Concluding Remarks

The candidate pluralist jurisprudence sketched out in this chapter was introduced at the beginning of this chapter as needing to reveal something of the potential of pluralist law beyond what a conventional monist jurisprudence could deliver. This was linked to a technical promise for pluralist jurisprudence, in attaining a credible disciplinary status. The achievement of this status was subsequently amplified (in Section 14.2) in terms of a basic picture of four integrated pursuits of pluralist jurisprudence: (a) the recognition of pluralism, (b) a practical outworking of pluralism, (c) a normative or aspirational agenda for pluralism, and (d) a theoretical account of pluralism.

Four components were identified in our candidate theory: (1) the openness of law; (2) the decisiveness of law; (3) the relationship between openness and decisiveness operating within the dual modes of normativity associated with formal jurisdiction and legitimate authority; and (4) the pluralist institutional and normative social context with its distinctive interplay between legal interventions and social responses. In Section 14.3.1 we indicated how these components could be viewed together as satisfying the basic picture of the four integrated pursuits of pluralist jurisprudence we had previously introduced. The plausibility of our candidate theory is not, however, simply a matter of demonstrating it might meet these technical requirements. It is to be found in the detail of the argument and illustration through which these components are integrated together to portray a distinctively pluralist jurisprudence. So, for example, the three forms of pluralistic openness portrayed in Section 14.3.2, or the peculiar impact of a pluralist setting on the institutionalisation of rules and the role of institutions in altering the relationship between rules and social practices that was discussed in Section 14.3.4, need to be examined carefully for the plausibility of their individual accounts before any judgment is made of the credibility of the candidate theory as a whole.

The candidate theory is put forward as a theory to which detailed critical responses of this sort should be made, but in advancing it we hope to make a more general point. It illustrates the way that any secure future for pluralist jurisprudence is to be found in a legal theory that is technically competent according to criteria appropriate to its subject matter, and can withstand detailed critical scrutiny of its specific elements.

The future of pluralist jurisprudence, as we have discussed it and as it is frequently approached, is often tied up with a normative or aspirational ambition, which can be associated with pluralism itself. Our own candidate theory has an idealist edge in looking to unlock what might be regarded as the promise of pluralism itself through the outworkings of pluralist law, and in that respect acknowledges the possibility of an idealist promise for pluralist jurisprudence. That should be regarded as distinct from an idealism which is not associated with the technical outworkings of pluralist law but with the subjection of those legal practices and the theory that informs them, instrumentally, to some extrinsic vision of what those practices might achieve, if aligned with an appropriate conception of global justice, or a cosmopolitan enlightenment, or even the proper appreciation of the values informing the rule of law.

In our own candidate pluralist theory of law we tempered idealism with realism in stressing that any fulfilment of the full promise of pluralism could not be secured by theoretical appreciation of institutional arrangements and inter-institutional tools, but was dependent upon the responses of officials and subjects to plurality and pluralist claims. This may serve as a second general point made by way of illustration, regarding the idealist promises (whether inherent or instrumental) of a pluralist jurisprudence.

INDEX

For EU product safety concerns, contact us at Calle de José Abascal, 56–1°, 28003 Madrid, Spain or eugpsr@cambridge.org.

www.ingramcontent.com/pod-product-compliance
Lightning Source LLC
Chambersburg PA
CBHW060339210525
27036CB00004B/284

* 9 7 8 1 1 0 7 1 8 3 9 6 4 *